CONFIDENTIAL INFORMANT

Law Enforcement's Most Valuable Tool

John Madinger

CRC Press

Boca Raton   London   New York   Washington, D.C.

Library of Congress Cataloging-in-Publication Data

Madinger, John.
    Confidential informant : law enforcement's most valuable tool /
by John Madinger
       p. cm.
    Includes bibliographical references and index.
    ISBN 0-8493-0709-0 (alk. paper)
    1. Informers—United States. 2. Informers—United States case
studies. 3. Criminal investigation—United States. 4. Law
enforcement—United States. I. Title.
    HV8138.M33 1999
    363.25′2—dc21   99-39503
                                                                                     CIP

© 2000 by CRC Press LLC

No claim to original U.S. Government works
International Standard Book Number 0-8493-0709-0
Library of Congress Card Number 99-39503
Printed in the United States of America 1 2 3 4 5 6 7 8 9 0
Printed on acid-free paper

Preface

"Now this foreknowledge cannot be elicited from spirits; it cannot be obtained inductively from experience, nor by any deductive calculation. Knowledge of the enemy's dispositions can only be obtained from other men." —Sun Tzu, The Art of War

Our story begins 2000 years ago with the words of Sun Tzu, a Chinese general and a man who valued information and those who brought it to him. The informant is an institution as old as history. Controversial for nearly as long, the informant's role in law enforcement is as important today as it was in Sun Tzu's day. One might suppose that, at a time when science has given the police more tools than ever before to use in the war on crime, we would not need to rely so much on the informant. Unfortunately, Sun Tzu was right in saying that knowledge of the enemy's dispositions can only be obtained from other people.

Law enforcement's challenge is to make effective use of this valuable resource and to do so in an ethical way. This book is written primarily for criminal justice professionals to assist them in meeting this challenge. Although I believe it offers some relatively new perspectives on a very old subject, much of what is contained in these pages is also found in the collective wisdom of a hundred generations of law enforcement officers.

Transported to the present day, the officers who paid Judas Iscariot his 30 pieces of silver and escorted him to the garden of betrayal would find the techniques of informant management little changed in the intervening 20 centuries. Certainly the outcome — a swift resolution, conviction, and sentence — is still the common result of an informant's cooperation, even in cases that otherwise defy solution for years.

We will be visiting with Sun Tzu throughout the book. Because he possessed significant insight into the secret world of informants and spies, the Chinese philosopher-warrior is quoted extensively. In *The Art of War,* he outlines principles a general can use to conquer his foes. Many of these principles are still valid today, and none more so than those which focus on the importance of the spies who collect the intelligence for the general who runs the war. Much of what Sun Tzu says is common sense, plainly understood by a thoughtful and interested student. He does, however, propose a fairly complex system with respect to acquiring information for use in the war. Within this system are several types of informants who perform different functions and act for different reasons. As we shall see, the characteristics of the spies of Sun Tzu's ancient system are as likely to be found in the informants of the 21st century.

But understanding, rather than mere acceptance of, Sun Tzu's principles is required for our success. In order to realize the full potential of the confidential informant, it is necessary to understand the individual — how and why he behaves the way he does. This understanding transcends tactics. Therefore, the objective of this book is not to teach technique, although some techniques are discussed to provide insight.

If we can understand why trust is so important in human relationships, we may understand why the betrayal of trust carries such a heavy burden. If we know the barriers to betrayal, we can understand some of the motivations which cause people to pass those barriers. And, if we know what motivates people to inform, we can learn how to control the entire process, realizing the full potential of each informant.

This is a very challenging set of ifs, but the rewards are substantial. To illustrate how these rewards might be reached, the text refers to scores of criminal cases, all of which involve an informant in some way. Each chapter also includes a case study that illustrates the principles discussed in that chapter. The cases outlined in the studies are well known to most in law enforcement. As such, they provide us with the opportunity to look at familiar facts from a new perspective. In our study of the informant, we should be analyzing these examples, not as a faultfinder, hoping to detect the mistakes or failings of another, but as a student who can learn from the experience of others.

The text and the case studies are designed to provide the reader with insight into the informant's life. The strains of this existence and the emotional pressures of informing are reflected in the actions of the characters of these short stories. It is my hope that by viewing these actions in light of the additional information and perspective of this book, we may better understand the informant. This understanding, more than a flat knowledge of procedures or techniques, will make law enforcement officers better able to develop and manage informants.

This ability is important, because informants solve cases in amazing numbers, not only in drug enforcement, where informants are indispensable, but also in crimes such as murder, terrorism, gambling, kidnapping, bank robbery, perjury, obstruction of justice, bootlegging, and assassination. These are some of the crimes that are described in the case studies. The law enforcement officer, regardless of his or her assignment or duties, can almost always benefit from the assistance of a good informant.

One of the themes of this book is that good informants are not born, but made, and the law enforcement officer is the maker. Whether we succeed or fail in this construction will depend upon the insight we have into the character of the person giving the information. Do you understand why he is here? Do you have all the information he possesses? Can you use the informant in an effective and ethical way to exploit the information he provides? If we are going to succeed in making the best use of informants, we are going to have to find the answers to these questions.

Informants work so well that, although they play a critical role in the American system of criminal justice, the use of informants is often attacked. Defense attorneys, civil libertarians, and the victims of informant betrayals all decry law enforcement's use of this investigative technique. Informants are criticized as intrusive, in violation of civil rights, abusive of due process, and just plain unfair. The pacts that are made to secure the cooperation of informants are routinely denounced as "deals with the devil." The worst of this condemnation is reserved for "paid" or "bought" informants who sell their information (and some would say, their souls) for mere money or those who seek a chance at a lighter sentence.

We must accept that there is more than just a grain of truth to these complaints. Informants *are* terribly intrusive. Some informants do lie, cheat, and violate the rights of the people we are supposed to be investigating. Some corrupt the officers with whom they work. Worst of all, the act of betrayal is often so catastrophic as to destroy relationships built up over decades. The effects of the informant's breach of faith are felt long after the judge's gavel falls.

Therefore, it behooves us to listen to the people who make these denunciations. Abuse of this investigative resource could result in official or judicial disapproval of informants, something that could, in turn, deprive society of law enforcement's most valuable tool. But, those who scorn the informant should stop for a moment to consider the fact that it was an informant — a paid one, in fact — who reported plots to bomb bridges, tunnels, and other public places in New York City to the FBI. Had it not been for the actions of this informant in coming forward, thousands of Americans could have been killed.

That information was priceless and so was the informant who brought it to the attention of the FBI. As law enforcement professionals, we have a responsibility to protect that resource. We also have the obligation to employ this invaluable weapon in a way that preserves its usefulness for future cases. In this regard, we must find ways to employ informants in the most effective and ethical way possible. The purpose of this book is to provide some ideas about achieving this very worthy goal.

The Author

John Madinger is a Senior Special Agent with the Criminal Investigation Division of the Internal Revenue Service. In his 25-year law enforcement career, he has also served as a narcotics agent, supervisor, and administrator. He earned a Bachelor's degree in Criminal Justice from Indiana University and has extensive experience in the investigation of drug trafficking, organized crime, money laundering, and financial crimes. He is also the author of an earlier book on money laundering.

Contents

Chapters 1 through 12

The Divine Manipulation of the Threads

"Thus, what enables the wise sovereign and the good general to strike and conquer, and achieve things beyond the reach of ordinary men, is foreknowledge." —Sun Tzu, *The Art of War*

"Good informant, good case. Bad informant, bad case. No informant, no case." —drug enforcement adage

Sun Tzu was a man who understood the value of information and knew a thing or two about how to get it. Simply put, he used spies, an ancient technique even in his time, 2000 years ago. History has shown over and over that such a person can provide the key to a city or unlock the door concealing a criminal conspiracy.

Whether the informant's tip prevents an act of international terrorism or leads to the arrest of a serial killer depends not so much on the informant himself, for many people may possess the information; rather, the potential of an informant is only realized through the effectiveness of the officer who works with and controls the flow of the information. By developing the skills needed to recruit and manage informants, the law enforcement officer can "strike, conquer, and achieve things beyond the reach of ordinary men."

This process is part art and part science — a blend that is as old as law, crime, and human weakness. Surprisingly, given the important role that informants have played in many criminal investigations, relatively little has been written about their employment. They are rarely featured in mystery novels or in film screenplays. There are a couple of reasons why this might be so. First, this may be due to the public's desire for their hero or heroine to triumph over overwhelming odds and solve crimes by sheer force of mind and will. Having someone come in and spoil the climax by telling us "whodunit" (and how and why) can diminish our champion. Second, there is a fundamental distrust in our culture and, indeed, in others around the world, of the informant.

Listen to the popular names for informants: "snitch," "rat," "stool-pigeon," "fink," "squealer." These are not terms of endearment or affection because people associate informants with treachery and betrayal. Even the very young are cautioned against "tattling" by their parents. Being told as a child that "nobody likes a tattletale" provided each of us with some early conditioning against the betrayal of confidences.

This well-entrenched animus makes informants unsympathetic characters, not only in fiction but in real life. Intelligence officers who work with the spies who are betraying their countries and police officers who work with the informants who betray their comrades in crime often describe very mixed feelings in their relationships with such persons. Although we will explore these conflicts in more depth later, they must be acknowledged as products of the early values instilled in people which condemn disloyalty and breach of trust.

These negative attitudes are in direct conflict with the obligation of law enforcement officers to uphold the law by all of the legal means available to us. Employment of informants as one of these means has, in spite of our personal reservations, been a part of our legal system for hundreds, if not thousands of years. J. Edgar Hoover noted in the FBI's *Law Enforcement Bulletin*:

> *Experience demonstrates that the cooperation of individuals who can readily furnish accurate information is essential if law enforcement is to discharge its obligations. The objective of the investigator must be to ferret out the truth. It is fundamental that the search include the most logical source of information — those persons with immediate access to necessary facts who are willing to cooperate in the interest of the common good. Their services contribute greatly to the ultimate goal of justice — convicting the guilty and clearing the innocent. Necessarily unheralded in their daily efforts, they not only uncover crimes but also furnish the intelligence data so vital in preventing serious violations of law and national security.*
>
> *There can be no doubt that the use of informants in law enforcement is justified. The public interest and the personal safety of these helpful citizens demand the zealous protection of their confidence. Unlike the totalitarian practice, the informant in America serves of his own free will, fulfilling one of the citizenship obligations of our democratic form of government.*

Mr. Hoover, who, despite his long service at the FBI, never personally worked an informant in his life, nevertheless clearly understood the importance of informants to law enforcement.

Everything about informants is a study in conflict: Our parents' warning that "nobody likes a tattletale" directly contradicts Mr. Hoover's assertion that "the cooperation of individuals who can readily furnish accurate information is essential if law enforcement is to discharge its obligations." These two statements, both of which are completely true, graphically illustrate this basic dissonance. We, as a society, may not "like" the idea that a person is betraying a trust or telling someone else's secret, but we still need to have those people who do have inside information about crimes to come forward. We reluctantly accept the betrayal in favor of what most agree is the common good. The act of betrayal always exacts some sort of fee, however, and not just against the person betrayed. The very act of informing — the transfer of loyalties and the rejection of the convention against "tattling" — entails serious social and psychological conflict, fraught with all sorts of peril for the person informing, the officer who receives the information, and our society of laws.

There is obviously peril, also, for the person whose trust is betrayed. It is unlikely that the Unabomber, a man who eluded the police for over 17 years, would have been identified had not an informant — in this case, his brother — come forward with information. John Dillinger was caught as a result of an informant's cooperation with the FBI. An informant provided the critical information which led to the impeachment of President Bill Clinton. Informants have given advance word of presidential assassination plots, contract killings, robberies, and other terrible crimes. An informant told the Romans where to find Jesus Christ. Each of these actions represented a betrayal of someone's confidence, a breaking of someone's faith. This is the price we pay for information that can be of inestimable value.

A Study in Conflict

Sun Tzu, the Chinese philosopher-warrior enjoyed tremendous success on the battlefield but achieved his lasting fame as the author of the oldest known treatise on military science, *The Art of War.* One chapter of this essay is devoted to the means by which a general can obtain information, summarized as "The Use of Spies." In this chapter, Sun Tzu outlines a system for the employment of spies which he describes as "The Divine Manipulation of the Threads." This ancient system is eerily familiar to those who work with informants in our present day war on crime. This should remind us yet again that the value of secret information has been understood and appreciated probably for as long as people have been in conflict.

This wily old soldier unquestionably knew the effect a spy's information could have on the outcome of a battle:

> *Hostile armies may face each other for years, striving for the victory which is decided in a single day. This being so, to remain in ignorance of the enemy's condition simply because one begrudges the outlay of a hundred ounces of silver in honors and emoluments [for spies] is the height of inhumanity.*

Is this not exactly the situation faced in the hunt for the Unabomber? A 17-year search costing millions of dollars came to an end with one name spoken by an informant. If crime, in general, or one person's crime spree is allowed to go unchecked, or if the criminal could be stopped through the use of a recognized investigative technique and is not, those in law enforcement would be failing in their duty to act. As Judge Learned Hand noted in *United States v. Dennis* (183 F.2d 201, 1950): "Courts have countenanced the use of informers from time immemorial." They have done so because an informant may be the *only* means by which a crime can be solved. To turn away from an informant who could have solved a case such as the Unabomber's before other innocents were killed would indeed be "the height of inhumanity."

The tradition of the American justice system calls for citizen involvement in crime prevention and control. As "peers" of the accused, citizens serve as jurors in criminal trials. Even before a case reaches trial, the citizen is expected, even required, in some cases, to bear witness against wrongdoers. Federal law (Title 18, U.S. Code, Sec. 4) describes the offense of misprision of felony as follows:

> *Whoever, having knowledge of the actual commission of a felony cognizable by a court of the United States, conceals and does not as soon as possible make known the same to some judge or other person in civil or military authority under the United States, shall be fined under this title or imprisoned not more than three years, or both.*

Although some states have similar statutes, others do not. Recently, in one of the latter states, a young man who witnessed at least part of a terrible rape-murder of a young girl could not be prosecuted because state law did not require that knowledge of such crimes be reported. Public outrage was directed at the witness, even to the extent that people protested against his presence on his university campus. Anger was also focused on the state, which found itself without the legal means to punish the witness for failing to do what was perceived as at least a moral duty, to turn in the perpetrator, a school chum.

As a result of this case, efforts are now underway to mandate the reporting of this type of crime, effectively forcing people, under pain of imprisonment, to become informants. There is precedent aside from the misprision of felony law. Doctors must report gunshot wounds encountered in the course of their practices. Teachers may be required to notify authorities of signs of physical or sexual abuse against their minor students. Government employees are obligated to report fraud, waste, or other malfeasance. Statutes such as these, sometimes referred to as "snitch laws," have proliferated as people seem to grow more remote from one another within society and less likely to "get involved" in the solving of crimes.

The statute books are laced with other, more positive incentives for citizen cooperation in the war on crime. In federal law, numerous provisions allow for the payment of rewards for information on a wide variety of crimes. There was a $1 million reward for the Unabomber suspect, and there is currently a $5 million reward for Osama bin Laden, the suspected mastermind behind terrorist bombings at American embassies overseas. The payment of rewards is, of course, not a new means of promoting citizen involvement in the resolution of crime. Reward posters from the age of piracy or the Wild West demonstrate an understanding by the authorities that, as Sun Tzu said, "to remain in ignorance of the enemy's condition simply because one begrudges the outlay of a hundred ounces of silver" really is penny wise and pound foolish.

The need to offer rewards for information points out the beginning of a contradiction in attitudes, one which will persist throughout our discussion of informants. An observer completely ignorant of human nature might ask why, if assistance to law enforcement is one of the obligations of citizenship, is it necessary to offer money to those who provide the assistance? The answer is that there are numerous disincentives for that cooperation, all of which militate against giving something valuable for nothing.

And information about crime is extremely valuable — in some cases more precious than gold — and apparently far more valuable than the warm, fuzzy feeling which accompanies doing one's civic duty. Two thousand years ago, Sun Tzu described the measure of these riches, and exactly where they could be found:

> *Thus, what enables the wise sovereign and the good general to strike and conquer, and achieve things beyond the reach of ordinary men, is foreknowledge. Now this foreknowledge cannot be elicited from spirits; it cannot be obtained inductively from experience. Knowledge of the enemy's dispositions can only be obtained from other men.*

Information — the "foreknowledge" of which Sun Tzu speaks, has always been critical to effective law enforcement, of course. The entire investigative process is a search for facts, which come to us from a wide assortment of sources. As we occupy the "Information Age" and approach the 21st century, not only is the sheer volume of information greater than ever before, but so, too, is the variety of sources.

Despite the many advances in forensic science and technology, there is still only a limited number of ways to skin the criminal cat. One author, Richard Nossen, a former IRS Special Agent and administrator, identifies seven basic investigative techniques which can be used in the resolution of criminal cases. According to Nossen, these are

1. Surveillance
2. Acquisition and analysis of physical evidence
3. Interviewing and interrogation
4. Wiretapping and electronic surveillance
5. Undercover operations
6. Informants
7. Financial investigation

Some of these techniques are as old as Sun Tzu himself, while others would scarcely be recognized by law enforcement officers of even a generation ago. All have their places in the unending battle against crime, but, as cases old and new illustrate, none is as valuable as a well-placed informant.

Definitions

What exactly is an informant, other than a person who fits all of the pejorative descriptions we heard earlier? An informant is the person who can provide the "knowledge of the enemy's dispositions," but how does he come by this knowledge and why does he tell us about it?

Law enforcement agencies have come up with a number of less colorful (but less disparaging) descriptions of what constitutes an informant. The terms *cooperating individual, cooperating witness, cooperating defendant, cooperating source, source of information, confidential source, restricted source,* and *confidential informant* all describe "a person who provides information about a crime to law enforcement."

This definition is much too broad, however, for it includes casual observers who phone in anonymous tips to Crimestoppers or *America's Most Wanted.* The definition also encompasses witnesses to crimes, such as the tellers at a bank being robbed or the victims of a telemarketing scam. For that matter, it includes other law enforcement officers who share information with a colleague. None of these people would be considered "informants" in the popular definition.

A better definition of the informant includes a description of three qualifications that such a person must possess. Informants are people with access to information about crime. They become informants when they are somehow motivated to bring this to the attention of the police. These factors plus the control of the informant and his information by the investigator are what make informants so essential to effective law enforcement, though not without considerable cost.

Motivation + Access + Control

These three attributes determine whether a person is or is not an informant. Without one or more, you've got something, but it is not an informant. Only someone who possesses all three characteristics will be effective as an informant. Our ability to develop and manage these individuals will provide us with the foreknowledge Sun Tzu cherished:

> *Hence the use of spies, of whom there are five classes: (1) local spies; (2) inward spies; (3) converted spies; (4) doomed spies; (5) surviving spies. When these five kinds of spy are all at work, none can discover the secret system. This is called "divine manipulation of the threads." It is the sovereign's most precious faculty.*

The Threads

As each of us proceeds on our respective paths through life, we weave around us a fabric of ties or bonds to others in our society. The threads in this fabric link us through association to friends, family, employers, co-workers … to everyone our lives touch, directly or indirectly.

Some of the filaments are thin and weak; perhaps they represent a passing acquaintance or a half-forgotten school classmate. Other ties bind strong and tight: the bonds of blood, love, marriage, kinship, and long, intimate association. New threads are woven constantly, while others weaken or break, though none ever completely disappears. The result is a very large and very intricate tapestry, so complex that no one, not even the individual himself, can fully appreciate the pattern that surrounds him.

These threads form our connections to society, but in them are found the three elements of the informant, as well. One end of each thread obviously links to another person or group, providing the access that is required of anyone who would report the knowledge of a crime. And each strand is comprised not of wire or fiber, but of memories, emotions, values, and needs. Love, respect, honor, and pride compete with greed, ego, fear, longing, repentance, and the desire for revenge to weaken or strengthen the ties. The latter form the motivation for betrayal. Finally, those emotions, values, and needs afford the ability to control the informant and his information. This is the system that Sun Tzu called "the divine manipulation of the threads."

Every informant is unique in his or her access to information. Although more than one person might have similar knowledge of a crime, no two people could ever be completely alike in this regard. The motivations of these individuals will vary as well. Because all of us perceive our needs differently, our behavior in response to those needs will also differ. The individual response to discipline or control is also variable. An understanding of the need to learn what others know and the process of finding out is Sun Tzu's system:

> *Having* local *spies means employing the services of the inhabitants of a district. Having* inward *spies, making use of officials of the enemy. Having* converted *spies, getting hold of the enemy's spies and using them for our own purposes. Having* doomed *spies, doing certain things openly for purposes of deception, and allowing our spies to know of them and report them to the enemy.* Surviving *spies, finally, are those who bring back news from the enemy's camp.*

Sun Tzu's "divine manipulation of the threads" involves the use of five classes of individuals, each of whom has dissimilar access and a different motivation and is controlled by the general for disparate purposes. Together, these diverse types of spies provide the leader with the foreknowledge needed to triumph in battle. Each category of Sun Tzu's spies has a modern equivalent, although only four of the five are really used much in today's war on crime. (The ominously labeled "doomed spy" has fallen out of common usage, to the undoubted relief of the ones who might be selected to fill that role.)

The modern counterparts of "local spies" are the good citizens of our society. These people provide information to law enforcement because of a sense of obligation or because they disapprove of criminal activity. These are the folks who call police with the location of a fugitive whose wanted poster hangs in the local post office or who record the license numbers of cars visiting a neighborhood crack house. The information possessed by these citizens may not be extensive; because they are not criminals themselves, it is probably fairly limited. Nevertheless, this source of information can be significant. For example, the informant who solved the Unabomber case described in this chapter fits into this category.

"Inward spies," those "officials of the enemy" whose loyalty has been subverted, are more similar to the modern confidential informant. Such individuals have access to much information by virtue of their positions in the criminal organization. If they can somehow be motivated to provide this information to law enforcement, the result can be an important victory for justice. One of the best examples of this type of informant is Sammy "The Bull" Gravano, long-time lieutenant of Mafia boss John Gotti.

Tu Mu, a contemporary of Sun Tzu, wrote of the type of person most likely to serve in this capacity (see *The Art of War*):

> *Worthy men who have been degraded from office, criminals who have undergone punishment; also, favorite concubines who are greedy for gold, men who are aggrieved at being in subordinate positions, or who have been passed over in the distribution of posts,*

others who are anxious about the distribution of posts, others who are anxious that their side should be defeated in order that they may have a chance of displaying their ability and talents, fickle turncoats who always want to have a foot in each boat. Officials of these several kinds, should be secretly approached and bound to one's interests by means of rich presents. In this way you will be able to find out the state of affairs in the enemy's country, ascertain the plans that are being formed against you, and moreover disturb the harmony and create a breach between the sovereign and his ministers.

We will be examining the principal motivations for informing in more depth in a later chapter, but Tu Mu has summarized most of them — greed, fear, ego, revenge, perversity — quite nicely in one short paragraph.

"Converted spies" are something like those double agents we read about in spy fiction. Sun Tzu values this category above all the others because the converted spy can provide the insight to allow the others to be effective. The true worth of the converted spy or double agent comes from two critical factors: the trust reposed in him by his original master and the access this trust provides. Because a spy knows so much more of the "big picture" than an ordinary foot soldier, this type of spy is more prized by the opponent who can convert him. This is exactly why the officers from the CIA, FBI, British Secret Service, and KGB spent decades trying to recruit each other (and are still trying), in addition to file clerks and diplomats. The list of such spies on both sides who have been caught or exposed is lengthy enough so that we can conclude this sort of treachery is not all that uncommon.

In one sense, law enforcement does not use this type of informant much. For the most part, criminals do not employ people whose job it is to spy on the police, although that has happened before. In a broader sense though, all those who participate in criminal activity and agree to become informants qualify as converted spies. The participant informant has access to much more information than would an outsider. He has been motivated to change his loyalty, and, under the control of law enforcement, he passes along information which will allow the police to act and possibly destroy the informant's organization or arrest his associates.

Certainly the admonishments Sun Tzu makes about the handling of a converted spy reflect the importance of this type of informant and are still highly relevant today:

The enemy's spies who have come to spy on us must be sought out, tempted with bribes, led away and comfortably housed. Thus they will become converted spies and available for our service. ...The end and aim of spying in all its five varieties is knowledge of the enemy; and this knowledge can only be derived, in the first instance, from the converted spy. Hence it is essential that the converted spy be treated with the utmost liberality.

Under our criminal justice system, the converted informant is "treated with the utmost liberality." Most often, this type of informant is one who is providing substantial assistance to the government in hopes of obtaining a reduction in his sentence or the charges against him. Thanks to the inside information provided by the converted spy, the general can more effectively employ the other types of spies in the entire subtle "manipulation of the threads." This process includes the grimly captioned "doomed" and "surviving" spies. Sun Tzu writes:

It is through the information brought by the converted spy that we are able to acquire and employ local and inward spies. It is owing to his information, again, that we can cause the doomed spy to carry false tidings to the enemy. Lastly, it is by his information that the surviving spy can be used on appointed occasions.

The doomed spy is given false or misleading information to take back to his master in hopes of deceiving him into some hasty or perilous decision. Expecting his trusted agent to return with valuable knowledge of the enemy's plans or dispositions, the master does not know of the shift in his subordinate's loyalty. The information he receives is that which his enemy wants him to have. If he survives the unpleasant discovery that his trust has been misplaced, it is expected that the annoyed master will demonstrate to the disloyal operative exactly why they are called "doomed spies."

This practice might still have some validity in wartime espionage, although getting volunteers to serve in this capacity might be a problem. (In one case as recently as 1904, a doomed Japanese diplomat spread false information to the Russians, enabling the Japanese to surprise the Russians in the Russo-Japanese war of 1904–1905.) Law enforcement has no use for informants in this category. Dooming people, in addition to being unethical and inhumane, is rightly considered bad for business. The number of people willing to offer themselves to become informants would drop precipitously if word got out that they were expected to fall on someone's sword.

Finally, the "surviving spy" described by Sun Tzu is more properly characterized as a "scout" sent to reconnoiter the enemy's camp or movements and return with the information. Because these people commonly wore the enemy's uniform, they were, and still are, considered spies, to be treated to the same penalty as one of their "doomed" cousins if caught. Law enforcement officers may take on this role for themselves, operating undercover or doing plainclothes surveillance to obtain information. On occasion, however, an informant is used for this purpose. One such instance would be sending an informant who was a resident of a building, housing project, or neighborhood to a location in that area where illegal activity was taking place. The informant, who might not be a participant in the illegal activity, would still have better access than a police officer from outside and could report back on who was present, when the activity was taking place, and other useful facts.

The Divine Manipulation

When these five kinds of spy are all at work, none can discover the secret system. This is called "divine manipulation of the threads." It is the sovereign's most precious faculty.

It is never enough to simply have the informant; some constructive use must be made of his or her services. The management of these valuable resources is the responsibility of the law enforcement officer, who must *always* be in control of the informant and his information. Sun Tzu offers some advice on this subject as well:

Hence it is that which none in the whole army are more intimate relations to be maintained than with spies. None should be more liberally rewarded. In no other business should greater secrecy be preserved.

Three important aspects of the officer-informant relationship are touched upon in this passage. First, an "intimate relationship" between the general and his spy is required, or at least a relationship more intimate than that with others in the army. A measure of trust is necessary — certainly the informant must have trust in the officer. The relationship also requires frequent contact in which information is conveyed by the informant and instructions given by the officer, often in covert or secret circumstances.

Second, spies are to be "liberally rewarded." This reflects Sun Tzu's estimation of the spy's value, but it also demonstrates a means of controlling the informant. In *The Art of War*, Chang Yu, another of his contemporaries, echoed the old general's thoughts: "When you have attracted them by substantial offers, you must treat them with absolute sincerity; then they will work for you with all their might."

Finally, Sun Tzu stresses the all-important need for secrecy. Even the disclosure that the informant is meeting with law enforcement could cause problems for all concerned. That the informant's confidentiality must be preserved is so fundamental it almost goes without saying. After all, it's why they are often called "confidential informants."

Implementation of all three of these aspects is the province of the officer, who sets the conditions of the informant's cooperation. It is the officer's responsibility to manage the informant. Another general, Henri de la d'Auvergne de Turenne, who knew and used spies extensively in 17th-century France, offered similar advice:

> *Spies are attached to those who give them most; he who pays them ill is never served. They should never be known to anybody, nor should they know one another. When they propose anything very material, secure their persons, or have in your possession their wives and children as hostages for their fidelity. Never communicate anything to them but what is absolutely necessary that they should know.*

Law enforcement insists upon, and has the right to expect, fidelity from informants but is obviously not prepared to take families hostage to achieve this end. We often do "secure [the] persons" of the informants, themselves, however. Turenne echoes Sun Tzu on the need for secrecy and sets forth the "need to know" rule that should be followed in all dealings concerning informants. We are going to discuss the management of informants in much greater detail, but it is interesting to note that Sun Tzu, whose writings have recently found their way onto the bookshelves of business executives, had some very modern ideas about motivation, leadership, and personnel management. One of his management principles has special meaning for the law enforcement officer dealing with informants:

> *Spies cannot be usefully employed without a certain intuitive sagacity. They cannot be properly managed without benevolence and straightforwardness.*

"Straightforwardness" is one of the most important qualities an officer can bring to a relationship with an informant. In fact, one of the premises of this book is that, without this attribute, the relationship will fail. Being straightforward with an informant is the first step toward obtaining the informant's trust in the officer. Absent that trust, most potential informants will refuse to cooperate with law enforcement, will withhold information, or will simply take their business elsewhere. This is an association between two people that begins because one of those people has or is about to betray some third party. Those who betray are fully aware of the ramifications of that choice and need the assurance that someone will play straight with them even as they are breaking faith with someone else.

Sun Tzu's last word of advice in the management of informants relates to the bottom line for criminal investigators:

> *Without subtle ingenuity of mind, one cannot make certain of the truth of their reports. Be subtle! be subtle! and use your spies for every kind of business.*

No informant's word should ever be taken for any material fact. No informant's statement should ever go uncorroborated if the means are available to verify it. Does this mean more work for the investigator? Of course, but that is the commitment the investigator must make in agreeing to work with informants in the first place. In making "certain of the truth of their reports" we reaffirm our control over the investigation, fortify our confidence in the information, and protect ourselves from the destruction that can result from misplacement of *our* trust.

The result of all this manipulation is the steady flow of secret information into the hands of law enforcement, who, it is hoped, will put it to good use. Sun Tzu's *The Art of War* describes the expected outcome when information is properly used:

> *Hence it is only the enlightened ruler and the wise general who will use the highest intelligence of the army for purposes of spying and thereby they achieve great results.*

Note carefully, though, that enlightenment and wisdom on the part of the informant manager are required, for the dangers associated with informants can be as great as the results one hopes to achieve.

In addition to the ever-present danger that valuable information may be overlooked or ignored, other perils lurk in the shadows with the informant. The wise and enlightened officer is well-advised to use extreme caution in dealing with those who are already in the midst of one betrayal. In *The Art of War*, Sun Tzu's contemporary, Tu Mu, cautions:

> *Just as water, which carries a boat from bank to bank, may also be the means of sinking it, so reliance on spies, while productive of great results, is oft-times the cause of utter destruction.*

As we will see later in this book, informants have caused great personal destruction, often to the officers charged with their management. Because we can see the "great results" which can sometimes be wrought by a good informant, we must continue to make effective use of this valuable resource. We must not lose sight of the attendant risks, however, and we must learn how to manipulate the threads in such a way as to achieve the former while avoiding the latter.

Summing Up

Informants are essential components of the criminal justice system. In many cases, an informant may represent the best, even the only, chance to solve a major crime, but the use of informants is laden with conflict and is the subject of public discomfort, even scorn. If informants are to be employed successfully, law enforcement officers must understand the process by which people become informants and how they function.

Informants are more than mere witnesses to crimes and are less than law enforcement officers. They have clearly determined roles in the process of investigating and apprehending criminals. We define informants as persons who have the motivation to provide information, who have access to that information, and who are willing to accept the control of a law enforcement officer. Those individuals who possess these attributes and cooperate in an investigation can achieve the "great results" of which Sun Tzu spoke — a worthy objective.

Case Study: Am I My Brother's Keeper?

The first bomb went off on May 26, 1978, injuring a campus police officer at Northwestern University in Evanston, IL. The last exploded on April 24, 1995, and killed Gilbert Murray, President of the California Forestry Association in Sacramento, CA. In the 17 years between those two blasts, the mystery man who called himself "FC" punctuated the greatest manhunt in American history with occasional flashes of terror, destruction, and death.

His bombs claimed the lives or limbs of scientists, businessmen, a computer store owner, and executives. When he threatened to blow up an airliner, air traffic and mail service were disrupted for a week. Better safe than sorry — after all, he had bombed a plane before. Although he "signed" his meticulously crafted bombs with the "FC" initials, the man who emulated a character from a Joseph Conrad novel was completely anonymous. To the frustrated law enforcement officers who chased him, even his very existence must have seemed questionable — except when the bombs went off.

The hunt for the serial killer who became known as the Unabomber took 17 years and cost the federal government over $60 million. Officers from three federal and a host of local and state law enforcement agencies tracked the elusive suspect over two decades and an entire continent without ever having a clue as to his real identity. A sketch, made from an eyewitness description in 1987, was the best lead to the 25- to 30-year-old male Caucasian, depicted wearing aviator sunglasses and a hooded sweatshirt. A billion-byte computer database used by the FBI in the Unabomber investigation held over 50,000 names, but FC's true name was not among them.

Although the investigators had labored for years in relative silence, initially refusing even to publicly acknowledge a connection between the explosions that went off periodically around the nation, this was to change dramatically in 1995. The public had become aware, through the well-publicized sketch and news stories about the explosions, that a domestic terrorist was at work. There was a $1 million reward on the man's head, and scientists, airline executives, and university professors around the country were taking extreme precautions with their mail. And it was the mail that was to be the beginning of the end for Unabomber.

In April and May of 1995, the bomber began writing letters to news media outlets, shopping a 35,000-word manuscript on the evils of modern technology. Before, all of the clues to this mysterious existence had resided in secret within the federal Unabomber task force, but the best clue of all was about to be placed on public view by the killer himself.

The bomber's manifesto was published on September 19, 1995, in the *New York Times* and *Washington Post*. Excerpts appeared in other newspapers around the country, and a California publisher printed it in book form, selling 3000 copies. The FBI had encouraged publication, hoping that someone would read the manifesto and recognize the author. In Schenectady, NY, someone did.

David Kaczynski, assistant director of a youth shelter, needed some prodding from his wife to look at FC's manifesto; he was skeptical of her suggestion that his "screwy brother" Ted might be the guy. Expecting to be able to dismiss his wife's concern, he was distressed when, after reading the essay, he could not rule Ted out. In fact, some of the facts known to David fit all too neatly. Not only was the writing very similar, down to certain expressions and phrases Ted had used in letters or earlier writings, but at least two of the bombings appeared to coincide with loans that David had made to Ted. Had David's money been used by the bomber to kill other people for 17 years? This thought tormented as much as the grief he felt at losing his brother to what David saw as mental illness. Nothing less, he thought, could explain the deterioration in Ted's condition. Certainly some other person, not the boy David loved and grew up with, had to be the serial bomber with the $1 million price on his head.

But the writing haunted David. He found an old essay his brother had written in 1971. There were similarities. Letters written over the years contained more thoughts David recognized from the manifesto, as well as spelling or grammatical characteristics that were identical. Ted, a Harvard graduate and former mathematics professor at the University of California in Berkeley, used "wilfully" for "willfully," "analyse" for "analyze," and "instalment" for "installment." So did FC.

After agonizing over his decision for weeks, David sought the assistance of others, including a private investigator friend of his wife, an investigation firm, and a Washington attorney. These roads inevitably led David and his assistants to the Unabomber task force. David knew that if his brother did turn out to be the elusive bomber, his action would be seen by Ted as nothing less than total betrayal, and the fragile bond between them would probably be irrevocably severed. This was a high price to pay, and the torment was made worse by the knowledge that FC was wanted for multiple murders. This was a capital case; David could be sending his brother to the death chamber.

Through his attorney, David made contact with the FBI on Valentine's Day, 1996. The process of walking in and becoming a government informant had taken 4 months. David provided the government with all the information he had about the brother he had not seen in person for 10 years. He did know that Ted had moved to a cabin outside Lincoln, MT, in June of 1971; David had co-signed the note for the $2100 purchase of the property. He knew of jobs Ted had held in Salt Lake City in 1972, as well as in the Chicago area in 1978.

This information was of interest to the task force. They had long suspected that their quarry had resided in the Salt Lake area, where one of the explosions had killed a computer store owner. They also recalled that the very first of the explosions had occurred in a Chicago suburb — in 1978.

As David described his brother, he painted a picture of deep contrasts. Theodore Kaczynski was a National Merit Finalist who graduated from high school at 16 and Harvard at 20. He had a Ph.D. from the University of Michigan, where he was regarded as a brilliant mathematician. He taught mathematics for 2 years at the University of California at Berkeley, something else that interested the agents, who had long theorized a connection between the Unabomber and the Bay Area.

Yet, the man David described had almost completely rejected society. He lived in a cabin he built with his own hands, grew his own vegetables, hunted for his own meat. The cabin, only 10′ × 12′, had no running water, electricity, or any provision for waste disposal. It certainly did not have the machine tools the agents believed the bomber possessed to build the complicated pipe bombs he sent to his victims. As he spoke, David must have wondered whether the man known to his neighbors as "The Hermit" was really the elusive FC as well as his brother Ted.

Investigation of David's information confirmed his worst fears. The FBI quickly gathered the evidence needed to arrest and convict the man who had been hidden for so long. In a search of the cabin, agents recovered 20,000 pages of Ted's writings, including detailed descriptions of the bombings, and his preparations for, and reactions to, these attacks. They also recovered bomb parts and one live package bomb, ready for mailing.

Ted Kaczynski eventually changed his initial plea of "not guilty" and was sentenced to spend the rest of his life in a federal prison, escaping the death penalty David feared. He did not acknowledge David or other family members who attended the court proceedings. Prior to his arrest, Ted had written to his brother, setting forth his feelings about future contact with the family he rejected as he had the rest of the world. "I get just choked with frustration at my inability to get our stinking family off my back once and for all, and 'stinking family' emphatically includes you. So get this straight … I don't ever want to see you or hear from you, or any other member of our family again." Fortunately for the intended recipient of that live bomb found in the cabin, Theodore Kaczynski cut his brother's access off too late.

Analysis

David Kaczynski is an unusual informant in many respects. By all accounts, he is a decent, caring man who wanted to prevent more harm and loved the man he betrayed. He was not an accomplice to his brother's deeds and knew nothing of bombs, crime, or even why his brother acted in the way he did. He had no current access to his brother; in fact, he had not seen him personally since 1986 and could not be sure his brother had even left Montana after 1979.

David had none of the traditional motivations for an informant that we will examine in subsequent chapters. He did not want to keep the $1 million the government offered for the Unabomber's identity and offered to give the money to his brother's victims. Yet, in many ways, the story of this unlikely informant can be very helpful in understanding others who inform. We can understand the price of betrayal and its impact on both betrayer and betrayed. Most of all, David Kaczynski shows us the value of a person who has the necessary attributes of an informant: motivation, access, and control. Once the FBI had this one person, their futile 17-year pursuit was over.

Motivation

David's motivations were powerful and as pure as any informant's will ever get. Although he was guilt-ridden at the thought that his money might have financed the bombing campaign and the deaths of other people, he could in no way be considered a willing accomplice to his brother's crimes. David took a long time finally getting his information to the FBI, but fortunately no bombs exploded in this period, something which undoubtedly would have increased the burden of his guilt.

A good citizen, David Kaczynski reported his suspicions about his brother to the proper authorities, as good citizens are supposed to do. He said he planned to give the reward to the victims of his brother's attacks, although the tax consequences of such a gift seem to have made this something of a problem. There were also legal fees incurred in the period between October 1995 and February 1996, during which the negotiations were underway with the FBI. Some of the reward money will be used for these expenses.

In interviews with the news media after his brother's arrest, David described his motivation: "Our interest from the beginning was to protect life." He also said, "Clearly part of my whole involvement in coming forward in this whole thing was a respect for life, that human life is really valuable, that certainly Ted did not in my mind have adequate justification. If he did attack and kill people, that was wrong." David's desire to prevent his brother from killing again paid off. The live bomb, packaged and ready for mailing, that was found in the bomber's cabin after his arrest would never be sent.

Access

This case that took so long and cost so much was finally solved by one informant who walked in with the bomber's identity. That was the full extent of David Kaczynski's access. He knew nothing of the bombings, nothing of bombs or explosives. He knew none of the victims and had not even seen Ted for over 10 years. In periodic correspondence, Ted made it abundantly clear that he did not want to have any contact with his "stinking family," which included the brother who had loaned Ted the money he needed to travel and plant his bombs.

Informants' access comes in an amazing array of shapes and sizes. Some will have years worth of detailed experiences, a veritable treasure-trove of criminal knowledge. Others will walk or call in with nothing more than the address of a wanted person they obtained through a passing association. As David Kaczynski proved, even those with the most tenuous of ties can resolve major crimes. It therefore behooves the officer to pay attention to would-be or potential informants, especially those who sound like they know what they are talking about.

David may not have known much about the crimes, but he knew his brother, probably better than anyone else in the world — at least until 1979, when Ted effectively dropped out of that world. David had accumulated scores of letters from his brother, along with other writings from earlier times. His access to these letters made him the only person (with his mother, who supported David's decision to stop Ted) who was able to recognize the style, grammar, and thoughts expressed in the Unabomber manifesto. This access antedated Ted's rejection of his family. There was literally no way Ted could call back the words he had written to his brother years before. In any event, what David had was not much, but it proved to be enough.

Control

David Kaczynski took over 4 months to come to the agonizing conclusion that he should go to the FBI. In that time, he researched the Unabomber case himself and worked with a private investigator friend, an investigative firm, and an attorney. The conclusion he initially reached in October was only strengthened in the following months and finally led to his approach to the FBI.

David was a walk-in, an informant who comes forward on his own initiative to report information about a crime. The actual approach was unusual, in that it was made through an attorney who had himself gone through intermediaries to get to law enforcement's door. Once there, David's attorney asked for and received a set of assurances from the FBI. The attorney's agreement to cooperate read:

> Our client is fully prepared to cooperate with the Bureau … conditioned upon receipt of certain written assurances by the Bureau and set forth below.
>
> First, the Bureau agrees that our client's identity, his cooperation and his role as a source of information shall remain confidential and shall not be revealed to persons other than the authorized Department of Justice employees with a need to know. Our client will be given the status and entitled to Bureau procedures applicable to confidential informants. This confidential treatment shall continue indefinitely, unless and until our client indicates otherwise in writing.
>
> Second, the Bureau agrees that its investigation of the subject will be conducted in accord with all applicable laws, regulations and guidelines.
>
> Third, the Bureau agrees that its investigation of the subject, if any, will be conducted in phases beginning with the most discreet and least intrusive measures to minimize any publication of the fact that the Bureau is investigating the subject.

On its face, this agreement cedes a good deal of control of an investigation over to an informant, something which law enforcement can *never* allow to happen. In fact, the lawyer's words are more in the way of reassurance for the informant; the terms describe how the FBI would have conducted its investigation anyway. The FBI needed one thing from David Kaczynski — the name of his brother, but they got lots more.

Under the FBI's direction and control, David provided his brother's previous writings — 86 letters and a 1971 essay — which could be compared with the bomber's manifesto. He outlined what he knew of his brother's background and psychological state of mind. He described the money he had given his brother, which he feared had been used to finance the bomber's travel and other expenses. David Kaczynski lived up to his end of the agreement.

He questions whether the FBI lived up to theirs, however. After his brother's arrest, news leaks from law enforcement resulted in the disclosure of the informant's identity — a violation of the agreement. The media camped out in front of the Kaczynski house, jokes were made on late-night television, and a brother's private agony became public spectacle. Feeling betrayed, David stopped cooperating with the FBI, but too late; Ted Kaczynski was already in custody.

Summing Up

Ted Kaczynski could still be out there, killing. He left few clues to his real identity behind. He struck so infrequently, in such seemingly random fashion and over such a wide area, that his chances of being caught in the act were minimal. "Minimal" also describes his contacts with the rest of the world. He knew so few people, or rather so few people knew him, that the risk that he would be betrayed by someone in whom he confided was almost nil.

One person knew Ted Kaczynski well enough and had enough access to the workings of this brilliant and twisted mind to recognize the connection between the hermit and the bomber. This was the one man who could, and did, betray Ted Kaczynski.

There are so many ironies in this case. The betrayal — one brother informing on another in a capital case — is enormous, almost unimaginable, yet public sympathy is solidly with the person perceived as the betrayer. This is something which, as we will see, is unusual. The motivation for the betrayal is also ironic. A $1 million reward was offered and paid in this case, but the informant did not do it for the money. Another irony lies in the incredible lack of access anyone had to this criminal. So deep was this secret that no one, not even David, was entrusted with the knowledge that Ted was the bomber. Yet, when FC showed the world one small piece of the puzzle, he also gave it to the only person who had enough access to the bomber to know what the puzzle piece meant.

This case was unusual for many reasons, but in the end, it concluded, as so many criminal investigations do, with the perpetrator saying the wrong thing to the right person. Informants are people who have access to information about criminal activity and the motivation to go to law enforcement with that information and are under law enforcement control as the information is exploited. This was exactly David Kaczynski's role in the Unabomber investigation. After an investigation that lasted 17 years and cost over $60 million, the case was resolved by the only person in the world who had all three of the attributes required of a Unabomber informant.

There are some who criticize law enforcement's use of informants out of hand, who reject "snitches" and their betrayal in all forms. Perhaps this condemnation can be tempered with one final thought about David Kaczynski. Agents who worked for years on the Unabomber task force will admit that, until Ted Kaczynski was identified, they had no idea who he was or where he would strike next. The tens of thousands of interviews, millions of hours of time spent in the field or the laboratory, and the tens of millions of dollars spent brought them no closer to the bomber than they were in 1978. The cold fact is that dozens, perhaps hundreds, of Americans may owe their lives to David Kaczynski, for, if not for a confidential informant, FC could still be out there, killing.

The Informant in
Law Enforcement

2

"And they watched him, and sent forth spies, which should feign themselves just men, that they might take hold of his words, that so they might deliver him unto the power and authority of the governor." —Luke 20:20

"Courts have countenanced the use of informers from time immemorial; in cases of conspiracy, or in other cases when the crime consists of preparing for another crime, it is usually necessary to rely on them or upon accomplices because the criminals will almost certainly proceed covertly." —Judge Learned Hand, United States v. Dennis

THE FAR SIDE by Gary Larson

"A few cattle are going to stray off in the morning, and tomorrow night a stampede is planned around midnight. Look, I gotta get back. ...Remember, when we reach Santa Fe, I ain't slaughtered." (The Far Side Farworks, Inc. Used by permission of Universal Press Syndicate. All rights reserved.)

Gary Larsen's cartoon perfectly captures the essence of the informant in law enforcement; a strange (and in this instance, possibly smelly) individual is surrounded by skeptical men with guns. The informant, whose access to his cow buddies is unquestionable, is busy selling out those buddies' plans for a very clear (and obviously very important) motivation. Motivation, access, and control — all of the elements — are neatly packaged in a very descriptive image of the informant system.

Cows probably do not do much informing except in the cartoonist's world. In our world, though, people inform a lot. In fact, although it may be a practice dating from time immemorial, the informant business has never been better. The list of cases in which an informant participated in the solution is impressively long. Indeed, it is rare to find a case in which more than one perpetrator was involved where an informant did *not* emerge as a factor in the solution. This is especially true of crimes such as drug trafficking, which ordinarily have no complainants. Very few of these cases are solved without an informant. Sometimes, as we will see in the case study for this chapter, an informant can be involved even when the perpetrator acts alone, confiding in no one.

From Then to Now: A Short History of the Informant

Providing information to law enforcement is one way a citizen can become involved in the process of preventing and resolving crime. It sometimes seems like everybody is getting involved. On television shows such as *America's Most Wanted* or *Unsolved Mysteries*, viewers are urged to call toll-free numbers, where officers are "standing by" to take the caller's information about the criminal's whereabouts. Hundreds of law enforcement agencies maintain special hotlines by which crimes can be reported, even anonymously.

There are more substantial rewards for "information leading to the arrest and conviction" of criminals than ever before. Not only are the monetary rewards higher — as high as $5 million in one case — but other benefits, such as reductions in charges or sentences, are also offered to criminals who provide "substantial assistance" to the government.

But none of this is new. The *Bible* makes a number of references to spies or others who would today be known as informants. In Judges 1:24–25, we read of one betrayal:

> *And the spies saw a man come forth out of the city, and they said unto him, Shew us, we pray thee, the entrance into the city, and we will shew thee mercy.*
> *And when he shewed them the entrance into the city, they smote the city with the edge of the sword; but they let go the man and all his family.*

The man who "shewed" them the city had access to information and a strong motivation to disclose it (coincidentally, the same motivation as Gary Larsen's cow). As a result of this informant's cooperation, the opposing army triumphed and the informant was rewarded with his life and the lives of his family. A more prominent Biblical informant was Judas Iscariot, one of the twelve disciples of Christ. Using his access, Judas, who, on paper at least, was motivated by greed, delivered Jesus "unto the power and authority of the governor," earning himself a not terribly coveted place in history.

Although the informant has been a part of the machinery of criminal justice for thousands of years, the role has changed along with that of the police over time. In the beginning, there was very little distinction between informants and the civil police. In fact, in most places, there *was* no civil police — the army was responsible for maintaining public order. The army was effectively the "edge of the sword" used to smite crime, but the citizen who reported those crimes was the means by which the sword was aimed.

Over time, the process of law enforcement changed with the society it protected. As people congregated more closely in cities, and as the rule of law began to replace the "might makes right" approach of earlier times, the police service changed as well. One of the first changes took the military out of its law enforcement role. Armies were becoming more professional and generals were more reluctant to allocate troops — especially in time of war, which was most of the time — to duties that made those soldiers unavailable for combat.

Rulers also found that having large numbers of armed troops standing about in major cities was not only wasteful but could be unsettling or irritating to the populace. Another problem was that those idle soldiers were also available for coups, something which unsettled the rulers. Withdrawal of the military created something of a vacuum in law enforcement which was filled by several innovations, all of which substituted citizen involvement for military power. Civil authority replaced the military presence, but the problem of effective enforcement of the law remained.

One institution created very early in the English common law was that of the grand jury. Dating from around the year 1166, the grand jury was originally a group of freemen who were drawn from the neighborhood in which they lived. These people met periodically, perhaps once every year or two, when a representative of the government, such as the sheriff, came to hold a session. At this time, all of the evidence of crimes committed since the last session would be presented.

In the grand jury session, the jurors themselves served as the witnesses. The law obligated them to report evidence of any crime within their knowledge, and "evidence" included hearsay, gossip, and rumor, along with the juror's personal observations. If, after reviewing the information, the grand jury felt there was sufficient basis for a trial, the suspect would be indicted by way of a *billa vera*, or true bill.

If the juror failed to report a crime he could be punished for misprision of felony, but this was just a taste of what awaited someone who was indicted by the grand jury. In medieval times, trial was conducted by ordeal, an unpleasant and often fatal experience, even for the innocent. The names of the various trials — *trial by cold water, trial by hot water, trial by hot iron,* and *ordeal of the morsel* — are suggestive of some of the tribulations faced by the accused. The intent of the trial was to let God sort out the innocent from the guilty. While the outcome of such trials might have been in God's hands, the information putting the accused in those hands came from the mouths of what we would today call informants.

Another institution, known as the "hue and cry," also existed to apprehend criminals. It, too, involved citizen participation. If someone observed a felony in progress, he was obligated by law to "raise the hue and cry," a general alarm to his neighbors, who, upon hearing the cry "Out! Out!" were legally required to arm themselves and assist in capturing the offender. Failing to raise the hue and cry or respond to it was a criminal offense, punishable by imprisonment and a fine.

The relatively modern equivalent of the hue and cry is the sheriff's posse of the American west. The western sheriff had the legal authority to call on people from the community to assist in a specific case, deputizing those individuals to serve until no longer needed. The federal government and many states still have statutes requiring citizens to respond to a request for help by a law enforcement officer. One such law (19 U.S. Code, Sec. 507) reads:

(a) Every customs officer shall—

>*(1) upon being questioned at the time of executing any of the powers conferred upon him, make known his character as an officer of the Federal Government; and*

>*(2) have the authority to demand the assistance of any person in making any arrest, search, or seizure authorized by any law enforced or administered by customs officers, if such assistance may be necessary.*

If a person, without reasonable excuse, neglects or refuses to assist a customs officer upon proper demand under paragraph (2), such person is guilty of a misdemeanor and subject to a fine of not more than $1000.

All of these institutions were best suited for relatively sparsely populated rural areas, but the demographics of Europe and, later, America were changing. Cities were growing in size, with a general trend in society of migration from the countryside to new and larger cities. Raising a hue and cry might work well in an open rural district or small village, but it was impractical in the crowded streets of a major city.

Crime flourished in cities such as London and Paris, where the ability of government to prevent criminal activity or apprehend the perpetrators was very limited. One innovation that emerged was the creation of watches, in which watchmen either guarded property or patrolled certain defined areas, usually at night. The watchmen were initially citizen volunteers and were sometimes armed and equipped with a whistle, bell, or rattle to attract attention if a crime was observed. Upon hearing the alarm, others in the community were expected to go to the watchman's aid. Over time, the volunteer watch was replaced by one with hired watchmen, a development that foretold the beginning of the modern police department.

Two other aspects of the criminal justice system of this period also relate to our study of informants. First, the law was extremely harsh. Perhaps compensating for the fact that they were so ineffective in actually capturing criminals, lawmakers passed draconian laws that penalized even minor crimes such as petty theft with prison, torture, transportation, or death. Criminals could expect severe punishment if apprehended, something that had a bonding effect on the perpetrators, who were "all in this together." A criminal underworld began to develop in the larger cities, in which criminals associated with and trusted only other criminals. In this segregated society, those who would inform about crime were the same ones who had access to the activity. Unlike the grand juror or the watchman with his rattle, the informant was almost certainly a criminal, just like the one he or she was betraying.

The second factor was that under English common law, felony prosecutions were private in nature, like lawsuits of today. There was a hodgepodge of courts and no district attorney or prosecutor. If a homeowner apprehended a burglar, the homeowner, not the government, was required to "bring charges" before the court. Further, the homeowner was required to pay the costs of the prosecution himself, something that no doubt inspired some "street justice" at the time of apprehension. It also placed a much heavier importance on the recovery of the stolen goods. The entire criminal justice system operated on very much of a "catch as catch can" basis, with people, including "common informers," often making false charges. At one point, a law was passed banning the common informer from the courts, so poor was their reputation.

In cases where the criminal was at the scene or escaping from it, a constable or watchman could be called upon to chase down and assist in the capture of the criminal. However, there was no one in the system who would do the investigation necessary to identify an unknown perpetrator. Once the lawbreaker left the scene of the crime, he or she was pretty much home free unless someone informed against the criminal to the authorities. But, the authorities, consisting of appointed constables, marshals, and sheriffs, were, as often as not, criminals themselves, crooks or incompetents who had purchased their positions. In large cities such as London, various officials had some official role in crime control, each of whom had his own small organization that competed with those of other officials. It was not a very efficient system, if it could even be called a "system" at all.

All of these factors — a disjointed legal process, ineffectual police, lack of any capability to conduct criminal investigations — led to a predictable result: massive growth in crime. By

1720, crime was overwhelming London. Highwaymen stalked the roads around the city, robbing travelers in broad daylight. Muggers known as "footpads" were common sights on the streets. In gangs of as many as 20, they outnumbered the intimidated constables. Pickpockets worked every crowd (they were especially active at the public hangings, where criminals, including other pickpockets, were executed) and the number of professional thieves was estimated at between 10,000 and 12,000.

The response, raising the number of capital offenses to more than 350, was completely inappropriate. The problem was not laxity in punishment; rather, it was in laying hands on someone to punish. The police, a dozen or so independent organizations, were uncoordinated, antagonistic toward each other, outnumbered by the criminals, and hopelessly ineffective.

In dealing with the crime problem, each citizen was essentially on his or her own. The wealthy kept their wealth by surrounding themselves with armed retainers and traveling about in what amounted to war-parties. The poor and the middle class were essentially left to fend for themselves. Into this gloomy picture stepped perhaps the most outrageous informant of all time, Jonathan Wild, Britain's "Thief-Taker General."

Thief-takers were the forerunners of the modern private detective. For a fee, these individuals would locate thieves and perhaps recover the stolen property. Acting without any sort of official sanction, those who took up this calling needed nerves of skill, muscles of iron, skill with weapons, and, above all, information from inside the underworld.

For the latter, thief-takers relied on networks of informants who were paid for their information. All of these informants were criminals. Some were receivers of stolen property and others were the ones who stole the property in the first place. Wild's network was by far the most extensive. He maintained agents in London and in other cities, particularly ports, where fugitives or other criminals might be found. He also had the ability to pursue criminals to other areas of the country, something none of the police of the time could do.

Wild was almost astoundingly successful. He completely destroyed the four large gangs that had controlled most of the crime in London, reducing the numbers of active criminals by transportation and hanging. Certain crimes almost disappeared. Highway robbery cases fell to nil for almost three years (there was a £140 reward for highwaymen, whom Wild hunted enthusiastically). Fugitives, especially those on whom rewards were offered, lived in fear that someone would "peach" on their whereabouts to Wild. ("Peach," a popular term for informing at the time, is derived from the word "impeach," to accuse.)

The heart of Wild's operation and the source of his wide public acclaim was his recovery of stolen property. Through contacts with receivers, fences, and pawnbrokers, Wild was able to quickly locate many stolen items. The owners were only too happy to pay a percentage of the value as a reward to Wild for his services. As for the thieves, they were quickly convicted on Wild's information and then transported to Virginia or just hanged.

Crime was down, property was being recovered, and criminals were being caught in large numbers. The whole rosy picture looked almost too good to be true. In fact, it was. Jonathan Wild was a crook who manipulated the system to his advantage at every turn. He organized the thieves of London into gangs under his control, assigning each a territory. He used the justice system against the competition, ruthlessly hunting down any who failed to follow the new order.

Wild arranged thefts, then sold the property back to the victim for the reward. Often, innocent people were accused in these thefts in order to cover the real thief — one of Wild's associates. Many were transported to the colonies or executed. Wild even double-dipped on the transportees. If they returned before their 7-year term was up or without authorization afterward, they faced a 14-year term or hanging. A £40 reward was offered for each such person, most of whom foolishly tried to hide in the London underworld where Wild's agents watched. He collected many rewards.

Wild's career came to an end in 1725 when he was convicted of taking a £10 reward for returning some stolen lace to its owner. Wild had arranged for the theft in the first place. After a trial in the same courts where he had held near-absolute power for so long, Wild was convicted, sentenced, and hanged. Street crime rates took off again.

During the time that Wild reigned, he set a couple of important precedents others would follow down to the present day. Wild's activities emphasized that if a crime was going to be solved *after the fact*, the investigator would need information. Some of this information could be obtained from the victim or witnesses at the scene, but a perfectly viable alternative was to acquire it from the criminal's associates. These people, who increasingly lived, worked, and schemed together in a criminal subculture or underworld, could be convinced to cooperate for promises of reward or possibly a break at sentencing. Wild affirmed the value of the informant in criminal investigation.

His career also demonstrated the darker side of this valuable coin. On one side, the crimes would not be solved without an informant. On the other side, the potential for great harm was ever present. Because his operations were completely uncontrolled by law enforcement, Wild was able to use the law for his own purposes. Innocent people suffered and died as a result. Hundreds, perhaps thousands, of real criminals were caught and punished by this man, but many innocents also fell into the traps laid by the thief-taker. No modern informant would or should have that kind of control over any investigation.

Still, Wild's contribution, the beginning of criminal investigation, was emulated in the three centuries to come. The crucial role of the informant in these investigations would continue as well. In France, a man who began his career as an informant but who is today regarded as the first modern detective, would create the distinction between officer and informant and introduce some techniques still used in law enforcement today.

The remarkable career of Francois Eugène Vidocq spanned 60 years and carried the dapper Parisian from the notorious prison galleys of Brest to the top of the *Brigade de la Sûreté*, the world's first detective bureau. He claimed to have been responsible for the arrest of over 20,000 criminals and no one scoffed at the claim. Vidocq experimented with the use of scientific techniques in crime detection, including handwriting analysis and fingerprinting. The filing system of the *Sûreté* was the first to document comprehensively the identities and activities of thousands of criminals, many of whom could be identified by their description or their *modus operandi* (method of operation).

Although his contributions are well documented, Vidocq's life is an enigma. He cherished the limelight but lived much of his life in the shadows, operating undercover in the Paris underworld. It is known that he served as an officer in the French army with a distinguished combat record. He was arrested for forgery and imprisoned, escaped, received a longer sentence, escaped again, and became an informant to avoid a return to prison for life.

Vidocq was a remarkably good informant. He was intimately familiar with the underworld, having spent time in prison and on the run. He was also courageous, intelligent, and resourceful, good qualities in anyone, informants included. His first job as an informant was to go back to prison and report on the activities of his fellow inmates. Vidocq's information cleared up a number of murders, thefts, and robberies and resulted in the recovery of a great deal of stolen property. After an arranged "escape," Vidocq continued to operate in the criminal society outside the prison, trusted by all of the criminals he encountered. This experience convinced Vidocq that only someone intimately familiar with the ways of the criminal world could obtain information from that world.

Vidocq's successes caused police officials to consider his suggestion that a special detective unit be formed to investigate crimes the regular police could not handle. These special agents would operate in plainclothes and be able to penetrate the secrecy which surrounded criminal activity. The only people who could do this, Vidocq believed, were ex-convicts like himself.

The concept that "it takes a thief to catch a thief" was popular at the time. Certainly the agents of the *Sûreté* were far more effective than the regular police officers of Paris. Vidocq and his carefully selected agents had extensive underworld contacts of their own, and they developed a large networks of informants. Some of these informants were given rewards or paid based upon the recovery of stolen property, but Vidocq also pioneered the "hammer" — using the threat of imprisonment as a means of motivating cooperation.

Vidocq obtained informants in a way which is familiar to law enforcement officers today. He put out the word that those with information would be rewarded and that confidentiality would be guaranteed. Whether the reward took the form of a lighter sentence or a substantial cash payment, Vidocq followed Sun Tzu's advice that the converted spy be "treated with utmost liberality." His own reward was an astonishing record of success in the war on crime. Within 5 years of its creation, the detectives of the *Sûreté* were making more arrests than any other police agency in France.

This success did not sit well with the regular police, who deeply resented the criminal backgrounds of Vidocq and his detectives and the fact that they were paid fees based upon arrests and property recoveries. Accusations were frequently made that the ex-convicts of the *Sûreté* were involved in theft or other corruption. Vidocq himself was arrested in a swindling case involving stolen property. These charges all appear to have been based more upon jealousy than fact, but they reinforce the need for professional police officers to control the criminal investigation process.

One of the accusations against Vidocq was that he acted as an *agent provocateur* — one who incites others to commit an illegal act so that they can be prosecuted. In 1999, this would be called entrapment, just another potential problem lurking in any officer-informant relationship. It is the officer's responsibility, both legally and morally, to prevent entrapment by the informant, but in Vidocq's time, the detective whose fee depended on an arrest had a motive for entrapment, and he *was* the officer in control of the case. Many of the ex-convicts whom Vidocq employed were involved in all sorts of graft and corruption, blurring the distinction between officer, informant, and criminal.

In later years, Vidocq wrote to Victor Hugo that, "It was my belief that to keep the criminals down one had to use men who knew them and had lived among them. Deprived of such tools I felt reduced to impotence. I refused to sacrifice them, so I resigned and left the police." His ideas foreshadowed modern criminal investigation and he developed techniques in use today, but Vidocq's "it takes a thief to catch a thief" philosophy was to become outmoded.

Beginning in 1829, law enforcement underwent a great metamorphosis, taking its first steps toward professionalism. In great cities such as London, Paris, Boston, Philadelphia, and New York, police departments were organized, many along the lines of the London Metropolitan Police as structured by Sir Robert Peel. Institutions such as formal rank and uniforms served to clearly distinguish police officers from both civilians and criminals in the public eye.

For the first time since the military got out of the police business, law enforcement was not in the hands of citizen volunteers or criminals. Now, people who were hired and paid to serve the public filled this role. This did not mean that all of the problems had instantly been solved; many of those who took jobs as police officers were drunks, incompetents, sadists, cowards, or just plain criminals. Nevertheless, an important distinction was becoming more reality than illusion.

Criminal investigation — the detective business — was also developing in this same period. Agencies such as the Pinkerton National Detective Agency and specialized investigative units such as the *Sûreté*, the Secret Service, postal inspectors, or city detective bureaus created an image of the detective as a detached professional with a clearly defined role and function. Fictional detectives in the mold of Sherlock Holmes and his police counterpart, Inspector

Lestrade, reinforced this perception. Crime was a hot item in the newspapers and magazines of the day, and the public learned through the media to expect these detectives to solve even the most notorious crimes or perplexing mysteries.

Although the officer-informant distinction became more defined, the very close relationship between the two continued. The number of ways in which an investigation could be conducted were limited. Of Nossen's Seven Basic Investigative Techniques (surveillance, acquisition and analysis of physical evidence, interviewing and interrogation, wiretapping and electronic surveillance, undercover operations, informants, and financial investigation; see Chapter 1), only three were widely employed before the 20th century. Law enforcement had always relied most heavily on two techniques, interviewing or interrogation and the informant.

For centuries, the criminal investigation process consisted of a fairly standard formula: (1) discover that a crime has been committed; (2) interview the victim and witnesses to the crime to identify the perpetrators (beating on them if necessary); (3) if no witnesses can be immediately found, use informants to locate witnesses or the perpetrator, then repeat step two; (4) obtain a confession from the suspects (beating on them if necessary).

This simple but effective system worked for thousands of years, but it obviously has some drawbacks, and both the rule of law and modern technology have thankfully made it obsolete. But in the 1800s, information was just as critical to a criminal investigation as it is today. Most detectives were not like Sherlock Holmes, able to solve a mystery by deductive reasoning; instead, they relied more heavily on informants to gain access to underworld secrets.

Officers cultivated networks of informants, and their reputations and potential for advancement were based upon the number and quality of their informants. This condition of mutual dependence promoted extremely close relationships between officers and informants. Because each had very strong incentives for preserving the association, both were much more likely to bend the few rules that existed to prevent abuses. To keep an informant "on the street," an officer might overlook crimes committed by the informant. It would not have taken long for the informant to recognize the potential benefits of that arrangement, but even worse temptations were out there.

The coziness of this relationship did not go unnoticed by police administrators. Those who were interested in making their departments more professional were in a predicament. On the one hand, they were uncomfortable about the close proximity of their officers to known, active criminals. On the other hand, every administrator who wanted to clear crimes (and keep his job) knew the absolute need for informants.

Corruption permeated many American police departments in the period before 1940. Salaries were low, opportunities for graft were great, and the quality of police personnel was not uniformly good. Informants, who were already corrupt by virtue of their criminal status, placed officers in potentially compromising situations on a daily basis. These situations grew even worse during the period known as Prohibition, which propelled police corruption to stratospheric levels. The Volstead Act, widely ignored by the public, joined several other laws which were soon generating a large portion of law enforcement's workload. Statutes relating to drug trafficking, gambling, commercial vice, and bootlegging were relatively new to the criminal code. They contained the seeds for more corruption, as well as problems with informants.

Unlike crimes such as burglary or highway robbery, these offenses were generally not accompanied by a complainant. Without a victim or a complaining witness, these statutes were (and still are) virtually unenforceable absent the assistance of an informant. They were also crimes of conspiracy, requiring multiple participants in various roles (e.g., buyer, seller, manufacturer, etc.). Investigating such activity kept the officer in direct contact with an informant who was invariably still involved in a profitable and very corruptive illegal activity.

At the same time these developments were taking place, technological advances were literally bringing law enforcement into a new age. Now investigators had access to innovations such as fingerprint identification, electronic surveillance, the scientific analysis of physical evidence, and analysis of financial data. This made possible the solution of crimes by means other than informants or interviewing.

As these modern methods were incorporated into law enforcement's arsenal, a couple of the old tools were taken away by the courts. Two reliable tactics that had worked for centuries were suddenly gone. No longer could the police coerce a confession from a suspect. Such statements would now be inadmissible for use against the defendant. Also, the courts were going to exclude evidence obtained as a result of an illegal search or seizure. As a society, we are better off for these changes, but they definitely affected the way the police did business.

Law enforcement's response to this good news/bad news situation was to attempt to find a balance with informants, an effort that continues to this day. We recognize the tremendous usefulness of informants in resolving crimes, but we also understand the equally significant hazards that always accompany our association with these people. The solution has been to create a new foundation for the officer-informant relationship. Several structures have been put in place to formalize this new paradigm:

1. Establish a detached, professional relationship between the officer and the informant.
2. Institute a set of rules, essentially a code of conduct for both the officer and the informant.
3. Whenever possible, employ other investigative techniques, either in conjunction with an informant's information or as a substitute.

In this way, abuses connected with informants can be reduced, if not completely eliminated, while still preserving the benefits to law enforcement and society of receiving information from this source. Like most compromises, the solution has never been completely successful. Sometimes important information is lost and sometimes those bad things still happen.

Generally speaking, though, the compromise works pretty well. Most law enforcement officers cherish the distance that exists between themselves and the informant. Our occupation has become more professional, with higher minimum qualifications, rigorous training, and strong ethical standards. Certainly no one is advocating a return to the days when the officer was indistinguishable from an informant, who in turn was interchangeable with a common criminal. Those days, though they lasted a very long time, are gone forever.

A Field Guide to Informants

Informants come in all sizes and shapes. While there may be a temptation on the part of some people (usually criminal defense attorneys and civil libertarians) to lump all informants into the same class, this is mistake. As we will see, the motivations of informants vary, as does their access to information about crime. Some, like Sammy "The Bull" Gravano, have 19 or so murders under their belts before they "flip" on their crime boss. Others are employed in civil services positions at the Pentagon and testify in cases involving the President of the United States.

It is difficult to categorize all informants into neat little pigeonholes (pardon the pun). Still, if the officer is going to assert the control necessary to make the informant a success, he or she must have some understanding of where the informant fits into the overall picture. Perhaps the best way of doing this is to classify the informant based upon what exactly he is going to do for us.

This was the approach used by Sun Tzu in his book, *The Art of War*. As we saw, he classed his spies into five types: local, inward, converted, doomed, and surviving. Each type had a different role or function and was used by the general for a specific purpose. This classification system has some validity in the contemporary setting. A look at modern-day spies reveals similar classifications, also based upon what the spy will be doing for the intelligence agency. Some types found in espionage are the defector, the agent-in-place, the agent-of-influence, the double agent, and the sleeper.

For the most part, neither motivation nor access is a decisive factor in classifying any of these types of informants; a converted spy and a defector might have exactly the same motivation and similar access. What sets all of these informants apart from each other is what role they will be playing *after* they make the decision to cooperate with the government.

Witness/Informant

Cooperative witness is the term used by the FBI to describe just about everybody we are calling informants. For our purposes, however, "witness/informant" applies to a specific category of individual whose primary function is to testify about historical events. The witness/informant is someone whose access may have been cut off by way of an arrest, or, as in the case of Mafia informant Joseph Valachi, a threat by one of his associates.

The witness/informant's role is to provide investigators with information about events that transpired in the past, or perhaps current activity if the informant knows about it. Most often, the witness/informant agrees to cooperate after an arrest or some other defining event, after which there is not only no going back, but there is also no continuing with the criminal side of his or her existence. Everybody, or at least the important people, know this person is cooperating. This was the case with Monica Lewinsky after she was approached by the Special Prosecutor and she refused to talk. By the time she eventually got around to agreeing to testify, everybody in America knew what she was doing.

Notable informants from this category, some of whom are described in detail in this book, include Valachi, Sammy Gravano, Vincent Teresa, Monica Lewinsky, David Kaczynski, John Dean, and Nelson Cantellops. Some of these people went into the Witness Security Program following their agreement to cooperate.

Active Informant

The informant who can provide information while remaining in position in the criminal setting is most prized by law enforcement. Having someone in this position allows the officer to corroborate the informant's information through other investigative techniques and to address crimes as they happen or even before they occur. If the informant's identity can be kept secret, he may continue to provide inside information for extended periods, allowing the officer tremendous flexibility in conducting the investigations which arise. The active informant is not unlike Sun Tzu's converted spy, whose information can be used to develop and use the other types of spies.

Agents-in-place are the espionage community's equivalent. When confronted with a would-be defector, intelligence officers may attempt to send the walk-in back for a while, just to exploit the incredible advantage of having someone on the inside. These informants are invaluable in drug enforcement, for they can introduce undercover agents, purchase evidence, and enter places where drugs are stored or sold. This situation is much preferable to that where a witness/informant merely describes some historical event.

The problems associated with this type of informant are significant. For one thing, in order to maintain their criminal status, they may have to do criminal things. This has led to big trouble for the DEA, FBI, and other agencies who are placed in the position, essentially, of having to authorize criminal activity by someone operating under their control. At least one recent case, involving two Boston-area FBI informants, has led to a review of Justice Department informant policies and potential changes in the guidelines relating to this type of informant.

Still, the active informant is the "brass ring." It is difficult to imagine a single witness/informant who could not have produced more or better cases had he or she been actively working before surfacing. Some informants who fit this bill include Judas, Anna Sage, Francois Vidocq, Linda Tripp, Eddie O'Hare, Emad Salem, Sarah Jane Moore, and John Condon

Source of Information

These folks may not qualify as informants at all, mostly because they are lacking one of the three required attributes (usually control). Included in this number are good citizens, people who call in tips, business people who can provide information about criminal customers or clients, people who work in occupations that come into contact with criminal activity through their employment, and neighbors in areas where criminal activity is taking place.

Cultivating these sources can be a very worthwhile enterprise for the officer. Narcotic agents who work at airports may find that airline employees make good sources of information about suspicious travelers. Parcel service employees can provide good information about questionable shippers or shipments. Pawnbrokers may have access to people attempting to sell stolen property. In all of these cases, the source may have valuable information, needing only the motivation to convey it and an officer who will listen. This is exactly why wanted posters are printed with a reward offered and the name and phone number of a law enforcement agency listed.

Special Categories

Jailhouse Informants

A very controversial type of informant, the "jailhouse snitch" is one who may be either a witness or actively involved. They are obviously incarcerated as they provide information usually, but not always, about other inmates. Informants from this category can be very productive — many unsolved murders and other major cases have been resolved with information provided by these individuals. Unfortunately, a good number of problems have also arisen in connection with the use of these people.

Jailhouse informants are highly motivated. They want out, or at least out sooner. It is probably not surprising that quite a few will lie, cheat, and steal to get what they want; after all, this may be how they wound up in jail in the first place. In some cases, they will provide information about a past crime that one of their fellow inmates might have admitted. For example, in the movie *The Shawshank Redemption*, one inmate goes to the warden to tell of another inmate's confession to a double murder. In this instance, as in so many others involving the jailhouse informant, the only evidence of his allegation is that provided by the informant himself.

In other cases, the inmate might actively assist in the investigation of ongoing criminal activity inside the prison, either by other inmates or by correctional staff. These are extremely difficult investigations to conduct, but at least the officer has the benefit of a very motivated informant (you also know exactly where that person is and what he is doing).

Jailhouse informants are deeply mistrusted by other inmates, their attorneys, and anyone else who has dealt with the breed. Because their motivation to lie is so great and because they come carrying a lot of "baggage" in the form of their criminal histories, prosecutors may be extremely reluctant to use a jailhouse informant on the witness stand. Law enforcement should be equally wary of these people and the stories they tell.

Unwitting Informant

Relatively rare in law enforcement, but more common in espionage, this person does not know that he or she is providing information to law enforcement. Undercover agents sometimes benefit from this type of informant, who does not know the officer's true occupation or assignment. Believing himself to be talking to another criminal, the individual provides information to the agent.

A variation in the intelligence community is the "false-flag" recruitment, in which the spy thinks he is spying for one country but is really working for another. An Arab diplomat who would not consider spying for Israel, but might be willing to work for the Americans, could be recruited by the Israelis if they could convince the diplomat they were from the CIA.

Law enforcement has no control over the unwitting informant. This lack of control represents a hazard to the officer, who may not be able to predict the informant's reaction if he were to discover that his "friend" is really an agent. The police should not be using false-flag recruitment tactics. Unlike the intelligence business, where a good spy can continue to report for decades without ever being exposed, the information provided by police informants is supposed to be used for criminal investigations and prosecutions. Disclosure of the fact that we tricked someone into talking to us by pretending to be someone such as a reporter is eventually going to cause major public relations problems. Like so many actions an officer can take with respect to an informant, it may work but only at a very high price.

Agent Provocateur

This class of informant is not often seen. Like Francois Vidocq, the prototype for this category, these informants provoke or incite crimes, often involving otherwise innocent people. The *agent provocateur* was especially useful in domestic security investigations, where he could induce his associates to riot or take some other action that would enable the police to move in, arresting (or shooting) the lot. Javert, Victor Hugo's relentless police officer in *Les Miserables*, plays something like this role on the barricades in Paris.

Law enforcement officers should not be deliberately using this type of informant, but there is the danger that someone may act as an *agent provocateur* without the officer's knowledge. In order to avoid this very nasty surprise, precautions should be taken to avoid entrapment, especially by having the officer, not the informant, maintain control of the investigations.

Special Employees

Prior to 1967, this term was used by the Federal Bureau of Narcotics and other agencies to describe active informants who were used to buy drugs and testify in court. Special employees could be either criminal informants or citizens who filled a special need (e.g., "we need someone who is Chinese and speaks Cantonese for a heroin case").

The term is no longer used for a couple of reasons. First, informants are not employees and should not think of themselves in those terms. At least one did, filing a suit claiming civil service benefits based upon his years of service as a "special employee." Second, law enforcement wants to preserve the now-clear distinction between officers and informants. Calling someone a "special employee," even if you are paying him or her, blurs the distinction.

Summing Up

The history of law enforcement is also a history of informants. In deciding how to conduct a criminal investigation today, we have many more options than did our ancestors of a thousand or even a hundred years ago. Where those law enforcement officers had to rely heavily on criminal informants for the information that is the lifeblood of any investigation, officers now have more alternatives. Where officers once had to maintain close relationships with active criminals, they can now maintain a more professional detachment.

Melvin Purvis, the FBI agent who tracked down John Dillinger, "Pretty Boy" Floyd, and other notorious criminals in the 1930s, says of informants in his book *American Agent*:

> *There has always been one untidy phase of police work, a distasteful but vitally important ingredient in the chemistry of man-hunting. I refer, of course, to the employment of informers, those people of the underworld and the underworld's fringe who spy upon the activities of their fellow criminals and betray them to the law.*

Informant assistance to law enforcement is still vitally important; in many cases, this information would be unavailable except through the mouth of an informant. None of the risk associated with informants has gone away, but law enforcement has found better ways of controlling this valuable but "untidy" resource and managing those risks. The result should be an improved criminal justice system.

Case Study: We Could Have Shot the Well-Meaning Old Meddler

The kidnapping of the first son of aviator Charles Lindbergh was widely billed in 1932 as "The Crime of the Century." Ultimately, the case was solved 2 years later by means of a lot of hard work and dogged persistence by investigators from several different law enforcement agencies. The kidnapper, Bruno Richard Hauptmann, a Bronx carpenter, was identified through his spending of some of the $50,000 ransom. Quite a bit of the money was also found concealed in a garage behind Hauptmann's home. All of the evidence collected by the New Jersey State Police, New York Police Department, FBI, and the Treasury Department was enough to put Hauptmann in the electric chair, a process which took over 4 years from the date the baby was stolen.

The evidence that pointed to Hauptmann also indicated that he acted alone. He tried to create the impression that he was part of a gang, but there was little evidence that he was part of some larger conspiracy. Moreover, Hauptmann was not exactly the talkative sort, and no one ever came forward to relate some foolish admission or confession Hauptmann made in their presence. In short, this case was not the type in which an informant would ordinarily have been of much use. Unfortunately, an informant was deeply and disastrously involved.

Charles A. Lindbergh was America's hero. In 1927, the "Lone Eagle" made his non-stop solo flight from Long Island to Paris, instantly becoming one of the most famous people in America. His luster had not dimmed 5 years later as an adoring public followed Lindbergh's courtship, marriage, and the birth of his first son, Charles A. Lindbergh, Jr. On March 1, 1932, little Charles was kidnapped from the family's Hopewell, NJ, home. A handwritten ransom note left at the scene demanded $50,000 and warned against "making anyding public or for notify the police." The note wasn't found until after the police had been notified, and keeping *this* kidnapping a secret was an absurdly impossible request.

Word of the crime flashed around the world in a matter of hours with the type of urgency usually reserved for declarations of war and presidential assassinations. Across America, people were united in a common desire to see the child returned to his parents, and those people followed every word of the case in the nation's newspapers and on radio. For the vast majority, merely watching and perhaps keeping an eye open for a small blonde boy in strange company was enough. For dozens, even hundreds of others, waiting passively was not enough.

High-profile crimes often generate would-be informants who have a variety of motivations for becoming involved in the case. Some may be well intentioned, passing on information they truly believe has value. Others may be seeking to cash in on a reward or earn some credit with law enforcement. Some people just want to play detective, but another type may have a perverse motivation. They may be seeking personal publicity, tormenting a distraught family, or possibly trying to throw blame onto an innocent person. All of these invariably have two things in common — they have utterly no real access, and because they cannot be dismissed out of hand, they consume valuable law enforcement resources in proving they have no access.

The publicity surrounding this case was by far more intense than for any other case in recent memory. It brought out the fakes and charlatans by the hundred. Gaston B. Means, a con man and former FBI agent, used the kidnapping to con a well-meaning millionaire out of a substantial sum she thought was being paid for the return of the baby. Al Capone, recently imprisoned on tax charges, claimed from his Atlanta prison cell that he could find the baby. He wanted his freedom in exchange for the information. There were people who advocated releasing Capone, and others who thought he might have orchestrated the kidnapping for just that purpose.

It was very clear to the investigators assigned to the case that neither Capone nor Means had any more information about the kidnappers than any other American who was reading the newspaper, but this was not the case for a retired school teacher and do-gooder from the Bronx, John Francis Condon, who would come to be known to the world as "Jafsie."

Shortly after the kidnapping, the Lindberghs made a public appeal which was reproduced in virtually every newspaper in the country. In their letter, they said, "We urge those who have the child to select any representatives of ours who will be suitable to them at any time and at any place that they may designate. If this is accepted, we promise that we will keep whatever arrangements that may be made by their representatives and ours strictly confidential and we further pledge ourselves that we will not try to injure in any way those connected with the return of the child." Thousands of letters poured in to the Lindbergh household, many of the authors volunteering to be a suitable "representative" of the family.

On the theory that the kidnapper was part of an underworld gang, Lindbergh initially selected a couple of characters from the criminal element to represent him in negotiations with the kidnapper. These two, like everyone else in the country, had utterly no idea where the baby was or who had taken him. Furthermore, the person who *had* taken the child had no intention of dealing with these people. Instead, he chose the 74-year-old retired school teacher who had offered in a letter to the *Bronx Home News* to add $1000 of his own money to the $50,000 ransom and to act as a go-between as well.

Two days after his missive appeared in the small daily paper, Condon received a letter that read, "If you are willing to act as go-between in Lindbergh case pleace follow stricly instruction. Handel incloced letter personaly to Mr. Lindbergh. It will explain everything." One of the most unlikely informants in American history now had his foot in the door of the Lindbergh kidnap case.

Condon telephoned the Lindbergh residence and actually managed to speak directly with the skeptical colonel himself. Skepticism vanished, however, when Condon described the signature on the "inclosed letter," a special design that had appeared on the ransom note but had not been made public. Condon was immediately invited to bring the letter to the house, heralding his new role as a key part of the effort to recover the baby.

This effort already included several different police agencies. Although the President had ordered all federal law enforcement agencies to provide every assistance, kidnapping was not a federal crime, so control of the case nominally rested with the New Jersey State Police. In fact, Lindbergh was making the key decisions along with a couple of close associates. Reservations were expressed by the professional law enforcement officers about the wisdom of placing a 74-year-old retired school teacher in a position of direct contact with the kidnapper, but any objections were quickly overruled by Lindbergh's urgent need to recover his child.

Condon, we will remember, had no real access to the kidnapper. By handing over the letter to Lindbergh, he had furnished all of the information in his possession. With the decision made to use Condon as a go-between, Lindbergh essentially allowed Condon to expand his access. This was a major error, not because more access was not needed, but simply because Condon was the wrong man for the job. At this point in the investigation, Condon's motivations for becoming involved were, as far as we can tell, completely pure. He sincerely wanted to see Colonel and Mrs. Lindbergh reunited with their son. He was prepared to take some personal risks, even to spend some of his own life's savings to achieve this end. Altruistic motives are all too uncommon among informants, but Condon was a very unusual informant.

Condon was a man completely confident in his own wisdom, courage, and ability to instruct others. In his 46-year teaching career he had not missed a single scheduled class. He still lectured on teaching at Fordham University, quoted Hamlet or the *Bible* for hours, was knowledgeable about a universe of subjects, and, like the law enforcement officers advising Lindbergh, had lots of ideas about how to resolve this case. Unfortunately, the people who were making the decisions listened to Condon.

One of Condon's first suggestions involved his name. To maintain secrecy, he proposed that he use the name "Jafsie" in the published correspondence with the kidnapper. This nickname was a play on Condon's initials, J.F.C. Because the kidnapper wanted to use personal-type ads in New York newspapers, it was important to keep Condon's identity from the public. Although his idea had merit, it established a troubling precedent — the kidnapper and a retired schoolteacher were calling the shots.

Condon also asked for access to the baby's things and to information about the kidnapping itself. He wanted to be sure, he said, that he would be dealing with the real kidnapper and not some impostor. Lindbergh gave Condon the information, revealing much more than had previously been released to the public and far more than Condon needed to do his job. Indeed, in one breathtaking evening, Condon had been transformed from a retired pedagogue into a member of the most exclusive inner circle in the country. Predictably, this heady treatment went straight to his head.

All of this was extremely frustrating for the law enforcement officers who were trying to do their jobs. The first priority was the baby's return, of course, but the kidnapper needed to be caught, too. At times it seemed that this objective was being completely ignored — and so were the law enforcement officers pursuing it. Colonel H. Norman Schwartzkopf, Superintendent of the New Jersey State Police (and father of Desert Storm commander "Stormin' Norman" Schwartzkopf) tried repeatedly to gain control of the case from Lindbergh, with only partial success. The Treasury Department's Elmer Irey, who originally came into the investigation as a result of the Capone offer, stayed but shared Schwartzkopf's frustration. In an environment in which the professionals had no say and the amateurs had no experience, a void was created for the likes of Condon. He stepped right in.

Condon began communicating with the kidnapper via a convoluted process. He placed ads in the personal section of designated newspapers, then received mailed letters from the kidnapper at his residence. The kidnapper relayed instructions and assurances about the baby's health and Condon accepted conditions and asked for more assurance. Meanwhile, the ransom demand was upped to $70,000 because of all the publicity, and Lindbergh began making arrangements for its payment. It was understood by everyone that the person paying the money was going to be the one signing the newspaper ads "Jafsie."

On March 8, 1932, Condon received instructions to go to a Bronx cemetery at a designated time. He followed the directions and was rewarded with a lengthy meeting with a man who identified himself only as "John." Condon detected that this person was in his thirties, 5'9" tall, and 165 pounds and spoke with a distinct German accent. This turned out to be a fair description of Hauptmann. Condon spent over an hour trying to convince "John" to abandon the criminal colleagues John described as having orchestrated the kidnapping. He also wanted to be allowed to see the baby. John refused. Although these efforts failed, Condon received a promise that John would send the baby's sleeping suit as proof that he had the child.

Based on Condon's description of the meeting, Lindbergh authorized a newspaper ad reading, "Money is ready," as the kidnapper had requested. Payment required another three weeks of back and forth communication, but on April 2 the ransom package was prepared by Irey and other law enforcement officers. Irey insisted that the ransom contain a large number of gold certificates, which were more noticeable than the more common Federal Reserve notes. He believed that this would make detection of the ransom much easier, a belief which was subsequently proved accurate.

Lindbergh, who had promised the kidnapper that the 5150 bills would not be marked and the serial numbers not recorded declared that he intended to honor this promise. Fortunately, the law enforcement officers, including Schwartzkopf and Irey, refused to go forward if the serial numbers were not recorded and Lindbergh backed down.

Following the kidnapper's instructions, Condon took the ransom to another cemetery. This time John appeared with his face uncovered, the first time Condon had been able to get a good look at the man he would ultimately identify in court. In a brief conversation, Condon, on his own initiative, talked John out of $20,000, then turned over $50,000 for an envelope which was supposed to tell where the baby was hidden. Condon turned away, his access to the Lindbergh kidnapper gone forever. It would not be discovered for another month, but the baby was gone, as well, killed on the same night he was taken from the nursery. Now the hunt turned to finding the most despised man in America, someone only Condon had seen up close.

For the law enforcement officers who had been planning to trace the kidnapper through his spending of those gold certificates, Condon's involvement had been a disaster. His initiative in saving Colonel Lindbergh had cost this effort dearly; all of the most distinctive $50 gold certificates had been in the $20,000 packet Condon had withheld. As one said, "We could have shot the well-meaning old meddler." Now the pursuit would take another 2 years.

Condon was, thankfully, out of the picture for the most part. He received enormous publicity for his efforts and was the subject of much public scorn and some police scrutiny after the baby was found dead. Condon would come back into the case with the arrest of Bruno Richard Hauptmann, a German immigrant and Bronx resident, who was identified through his spending of the gold certificates from the ransom.

Called to the police station for a lineup that included Hauptmann, Condon, who later said he "immediately recognized John," hemmed, hawed, and refused to make a positive identification. He asked to be allowed to question Hauptmann and, incredibly, was allowed to do so, apparently in a vain attempt on his part to elicit a confession. Condon also recited poetry to the suspect in German and generally mucked up the entire identification process. To the amazement and fury of the police, Condon then publicly announced that he was "withholding my identification," whatever that meant. The law's best eyewitness link to Hauptmann was completely out of control.

At the trial, Condon did identify Hauptmann, although he took a pounding from the defense for his earlier failure to do so. He also admitted having done some investigating of the case on his own, interviewing witnesses and developing theories which were contrary to those of the police. Hauptmann was convicted despite Condon's eccentricities, though one wonders what would have happened had the trial occurred 60 years later.

Analysis

Motivation

Condon's initial motivation for becoming involved was altruistic, placing him in the "good citizen" category. He sincerely wanted to see mother and child reunited. He also wanted to be the one to bring off this wonderful accomplishment. His letter to the editor propelled Condon into a world far different and much more interesting than the one he had just left. Once in, the school teacher did and said whatever was necessary to stay in that new world.

This motivation could easily have been used to establish much stronger control over Condon's actions. Once it was understood that he wanted Lindbergh's approval, that approval could have been arranged in a public ceremony as a reward for something law enforcement *wanted* Condon to do. This would have had the dual effect of reinforcing Condon's motivation and priming him to follow directions for his next assignment. In actuality, almost all of Condon's negative attributes were reinforced, creating only more problems for all concerned — including Condon himself.

As the case developed, Condon's motivation broadened. He loved the publicity, loved being in the public eye and having the chance to expound on various subjects. By all reckoning he was a bit player in this great drama, but he constantly sought more attention and recognition. Until Hauptmann went to the chair, the government needed the testimony of the man who had physically handed over the ransom money. This galled those in law enforcement who had actually solved the case.

Ironically, Condon had a powerful and positive motive for getting involved in the case. This motivation could have been used to much better effect, except for the fact that Condon had no access and not much control. This combination made Condon an ineffective and dangerous informant.

Access

After the case was concluded and Condon's fleeting notoriety had vanished, he authored a book, *Jafsie Tells All.* Unfortunately, Jafsie did not really have very much of import to say, mostly because he never had any access to begin with. Although he was the only person to see Hauptmann up close after the kidnapping — he spent over an hour on one occasion before the ransom was delivered trying to convince Hauptmann to "come to Jesus" — he actually had almost no information of value to anyone. He did not know who Hauptmann was, where he lived, or anything about the man that would enable law enforcement to catch him. He did not know the big secret — where the baby was — or the *really* big secret — that the baby was already dead and the ransom was being paid for naught.

Once the ransom was paid, Jafsie had no access at all, something which even the desperate Lindbergh eventually began to appreciate. This made Condon's continued attempts to remain important even more pathetic. Sadly, the one thing he needed to really *be* important — access — was one thing he never really had.

Control

Little or none existed. Condon's sincere desire for the return of the baby coupled with his craving for the approval of Charles Lindbergh were sufficient to keep him with the program until the ransom was delivered — though always on his own terms. Afterward, Condon tried to maintain his formerly high standing with Lindbergh, even though his access was completely gone and he was valueless as an informant. He compensated by becoming even more difficult to deal with. His performance at Hauptmann's lineup disgusted the law enforcement officers present, as well it should have. Even his pedantic and grandstanding testimony at Hauptmann's trial could have had the effect of "turning off" the jury. I imagine that having Condon as a teacher was probably a trying experience. Having him as an informant was undoubtedly a major pain in the neck.

Law enforcement could have obtained better control over this individual by taking the following steps:

1. Operate on a "need-to-know" basis with Condon, providing him with the minimum amount of information necessary to accomplish his limited task and nothing more.
2. Provide Condon with *one* law enforcement handler to relay instructions and take his information. This person should have been someone of significant authority, such as a school principal, as Condon came from the educational establishment. He needed a boss, but at bare minimum he needed one person to be his link to the investigation.
3. Familiarize Condon with the rules governing criminal investigations, then use compliance/influence principles to commit Condon to following these rules. This man was a teacher; teachers understand rules, even if they are usually the ones making them. Condon should have had the rules explained for him, then been made to commit to following them. For example, Condon received several letters from the kidnapper. There was absolutely no reason why he should have been allowed to do any more than put on a pair of gloves and pass the unopened letter to his control in some rigidly defined transaction. The "official procedures" governing such contacts should have been explained to Condon in a way that would allow him to commit to following them.

None of this was possible, because the law enforcement agencies themselves were unable to wrest control of their investigation away from Lindbergh until after the baby was found murdered. The frustrated comments of people such as Schwartzkopf and Irey show that they clearly understood the need to control the case. Circumstances prevented this from happening. John Condon never should have been allowed close to this investigation. He contributed next to nothing to its solution and almost prevented it from being solved. These are the potential consequences when control of an informant is lost.

Interestingly, in the aftermath of the Lindbergh kidnapping, Congress passed legislation which gave the FBI jurisdiction over kidnappings in which the victim was transported across state lines. One of the first things the FBI did in preparing to enforce this legislation was to promulgate some rules and procedures for their investigations. One of these rules was that outsiders were to be kept out of the investigation, no matter how well-meaning they were. One cannot but suppose that they had Condon in mind.

The Weight of Betrayal

3

> "In this world of dismal deeds, people keep their secrets. The secret is the thing above all others. The secret, in the eyes of these wretches is unity which serves as a base of union. To betray a secret is to tear from each member of this fierce community something of his own personality." —Victor Hugo, *Les Miserables*

> "To betray, you must first belong. I never belonged." —H.A.R. "Kim" Philby, British traitor

Kim Philby, who betrayed the British Secret Service's deepest secrets to the Russians for years, was not only a traitor, but a liar as well. A communist who thoroughly despised the political system of his homeland, Philby, despite his protestations to the contrary, "belonged" to that society. He was born to it, raised in it, educated in it, joined its institutions, and was trusted by that society with its security. His claim that his political and emotional ties were *really* with Russia all that time ring hollow in the face of his monumental treachery.

Betrayal is one of those human actions that evokes a visceral, almost elemental response. It is shocking, yet not at all uncommon — relationships are betrayed every day. It is destructive, yet new relationships arise from the destruction; someone benefits from every betrayal. It is threatening because it lurks at the edges of all our relationships — we have all been there before. We know that bad faith exists elsewhere; its possibility alone can weaken even the strongest of human bonds, in love, marriage, friendship, or employment. When it becomes real, betrayal shatters those bonds, often beyond any hope of repair. Betrayal is our heart of darkness. It is also the essence of the informant.

Trust

In the beginning of all human relationships there is trust. From the time we are infants, totally dependent upon our mothers for survival, we have a presumption of good faith, not just in our one-on-one interaction with each other but also in larger society. We presume that someone is telling the truth and "playing it straight" because we (usually) are ourselves. We are correct in this presumption often enough to validate the basic premise that others (usually) act in good faith, too.

Consider for a moment a world in which everyone always acted in deceit or bad faith, a world in which lies, cheating, and nefarious ulterior motives were the rule rather than the exception. Our entire existence would be immensely more complicated. Even an activity as simple as grocery shopping would be a trial. Is the pull date on the milk correct? Are the ingredients on the label accurate? Is that *really* an all-beef hot dog? If this uncertainty were to be carried over into the rest of our lives, pure chaos would ensue. Is the money there to cover that check? Are you going to have my daughter back by midnight? Is that law you just passed *really* going to end welfare as we know it?

Social harmony — the ability of everyone in a group to get along — depends upon trust. Because we all recognize this fact, both on a conscious and a subconscious level, and because everybody would be at each other's throats all day if we behaved otherwise, we start off trusting. Not completely or implicitly, however. I will not sign my paycheck over to the first person who comes through my door, and most of us are at least a little skeptical of the all-beef hot dog. Every day, all of us are compelled to make dozens, even hundreds of decisions. Some are trivial, perhaps even unnoticed ("I've got time to make that yellow light"); some are monumental ("Honey, I think we should get married"). We base these decisions on a variety of factors, the evidence of our senses, our education and experience, and often, when we are dealing with others, a sense of trust or distrust.

A host of conditions determines whether and how much we trust someone. Some basic social beliefs have evolved to describe these factors, which may not, as we shall learn, have much to do with the wisdom of our choices. For example, "blood is thicker than water" describes the close and presumably trusting relationship between people who are related by blood.

In general, time and personal experiences will have the most significant impact on how far our basic trust will take us. If I have extensive shared personal experiences with a person over a long period of time, I am far more likely to trust that person than I would a perfect stranger. Stating that "he's never let me down" implies a lot of confidence in that person's future conduct.

In circumstances such as these, the individual is admitted to a group. This group may be small — as few as two. The bonds of trust in this group may be extremely tight. The bond of shared personal experiences is also strong in larger groups — witness an organization such as the U.S. Marine Corps. "Trust your fellow Marine" is a concept taught from day one of basic training. Indeed, the Marine Corps' motto, *Semper Fidelis* ("Always Faithful") speaks clearly of this trust. But we simply cannot experience everything (or everyone). We cannot determine through trial and error whether every person we meet or every proposition we receive merits our trust. What are we to do when confronted with the claim that, yes, this is, in fact, an all-beef hot dog? We obviously were not present when the hot dog was manufactured. We do not even know anyone we trust who *was* there and can vouch for it. We probably are not even personally acquainted with the person who is selling the product, yet we still have some confidence in the claim.

In instances such as these we are forced to rely on a more complex set of factors that will determine our attitude. Here is where things get interesting and decision making gets much more chancy. Much of our trust at this level is derivative — it is received or obtained from another, trusted source. Our faith in the hot-dog label might be derived from our knowledge that hot dogs are regulated by the Food and Drug Administration (FDA), a government agency that we trust would never allow a manufacturer to lie about its product. Is our basis for believing this well founded? Maybe not, considering the number of hot dogs and the number of FDA hot-dog inspectors, but when it is coupled with our understanding and experience that people generally act in good faith, it is usually enough to allow us to make the purchase.

In my younger days I bought a lot of drugs from a lot of people. One of the questions I was often asked in my undercover dealings with these folks was, "Are you a nark?" Well, the correct answer, of course, was "yes," but these individuals, who were already making the mistake of selling drugs to a stranger, were always prepared to accept my "no." Taking this particular "no" for an answer was one of those monumental decisions of which we spoke earlier, one with serious consequences, such as a prison term.

Why would someone do something so contrary to their own interests and something which their instincts were obviously warning them against? They did it because they trusted me enough to risk their freedom, yet they had utterly no basis for this totally misplaced confidence. In most cases, they did it because an informant told them that "John's okay." They trusted the informant who introduced me, and I derived my trustworthiness in their eyes from his. I attempted to validate the seller's decision by my appearance, demeanor, and language, but the presumption of the informant's good faith was the key. (Greed being what it is, having cash also helped.)

"She's got a good reputation." "He's a stand-up guy." When offered by someone you trust, phrases such as these extend the concept of presumed good faith throughout our relationship set. Even the contrary comment, "I don't trust that guy," would have a powerful impact on the decision-making process if spoken by someone you *did* trust; I would not have bought nearly as much dope if the informants had started every introduction off with *that* line.

Some rather subtle psychological factors are at work here, too, influencing the way we think and the decisions we make. We will be talking more about these later, but we need to understand that people can be influenced in their decision to trust or mistrust by a number of psychological principles over which we largely have no control and of which we may not even be aware. For example, research has shown that people "like" or trust other people who have an appearance similar to their own. They are more inclined to believe, trust, or buy something from someone from their own racial or ethnic background, age group, or economic class.

Does the idea of trusting someone just because both of you are black or German or because you are both from Chicago make logical sense? Certainly, statistics and anecdotal evidence, even perhaps our own experiences with others "just like us," should tell us that not all such people are worthy of our trust. As we will see, logic may not always play a major role in decisions involving trust and betrayal.

What ordinarily happens in our relationships is that people start off with an initial measure of trust, if only because they do not have the time to check everything out personally for themselves. They proceed on this assumption of good faith, which will continue to grow as the relationship progresses or until something happens to cause the assumption to be challenged. One such something is betrayal.

Betrayal

Betrayal is a very big deal in a relationship. First of all, if betrayed, the trust one has carefully built up in another does not retreat a little or merely go back to the original presumption of good faith. Depending on the scope of the betrayal, the reservoir of trust takes a big hit and may be completely emptied. Consider your personal experience. Assume that you catch your teenager in a lie about something fairly important — say, what he was doing with the family car. You have trusted him to be truthful, and that trust was betrayed. Would you once again automatically assume that he was telling the truth the next time he came to you for the car keys? Probably not. This mistrust now affects every aspect of your relationship. All of your decisions involving this person are going to require more time as well as more input from sources in which you still have some confidence. The bond between two people has been weakened.

In a more global sense, betrayal challenges not only an interpersonal relationship, but the basic "good faith" presumption as well. In this regard, even the smallest of betrayals by one person has a wider effect on everyone's ability to function in society. This contention is born out by the frequently heard expression, "Gee, if you can't trust _____, who (or what) can you trust?" In the case of those all-beef hot dogs, our confidence in every frankfurter might be shaken by the revelation that one manufacturer was cheating on the ingredients. Our faith in the word of all politicians may be challenged if one gets caught in a lie (though not necessarily, as recent events seem to indicate).

Because betrayal is such a threat to both the individual and to social harmony, there are numerous incentives, both internal and external, to "keep the faith." Together, these incentives form a powerful barrier to betrayal. We *know* intuitively that this is an act with severe consequences. Internally, we understand that deception complicates things, making our own life difficult. As the French essayist Michel de Montaigne (1533–1592) said, "Unless a man feels he has a good enough memory, he should never venture to lie." And because we know how *we* would respond if we were betrayed, we also understand how our betrayal will affect the ties we have built to others.

Another of the responses that form the internal barrier against betrayal is guilt, the "avenging fiend that follows behind us with whips and stings" (Nicholas Rowe). Guilt — the feeling of responsibility or remorse for some wrong, real or imagined — often accompanies betrayal. Judas Iscariot, once he realized the enormity of his deed, tried to return the 30 pieces of silver he had received for betraying Jesus Christ. Rejected, he hanged himself. David Kaczynski, who helped identify his brother in the Unabomber case, was wracked by guilt, before and after he called the FBI.

The pressures from outside can be even greater. The *Bible* (Ecclesiastics 21:28) speaks of these pressures: "A talebearer defileth his own soul, and is hated wheresoever he dwelleth." Putting it bluntly, nobody likes a squealer. This message is brought home to us from the time we are old enough to tattle on our siblings. In Mark Twain's *The Adventures of Tom Sawyer*, Tom's brother Sid informs Aunt Polly about Tom's absence from school that day, time profitably spent at the swimming hole. Aunt Polly sews Tom's collar closed every morning so he cannot remove his shirt (possibly indicating a previous loss of trust in the boy). Tom has covered that base this day — but with the wrong color thread. "She'd never noticed if it hadn't been for Sid. Confound it! sometimes she sews it with white, and sometimes she sews it with black. I wish to geeminy she'd stick to one or t'other — I can't keep the run of 'em. But I bet you I'll lam Sid for that. I'll learn him!"

Tom's intention to "learn" his brother about the consequences of betrayal is echoed in the public's generally negative attitude toward those who play false. From those invariably harsh popular terms for informants — *stool pigeon, rat, squealer, spy, fink, stooge, stoolie, telltale, turn-coat, snitch* —we get a definite sense that such people and their activity are not exactly held high in the public esteem. The people who would wear those names know this as well and clearly risk all of the accompanying opprobrium if they become what others despise.

On an interpersonal level, the sanctions against informing can be quite severe. Tom was planning to "lam" Sid for his perfidy and did so later with some handy dirt clods. Physical violence is only one (though perhaps the most important to the recipient) response an informant can expect. In a major prison riot some years back, the first thing the rioters did was get access to the files that documented the "rats" in the facility. The second thing they did was exterminate the "rats."

People have a long memory for betrayal, which might confuse an observer who was not familiar with the bigger picture. For instance, the informant who shot outlaw Jesse James in 1882 is still remembered in song as "the dirty little coward who shot Mr. Howard." James, a noted bank and train robber and murderer, was hiding under the name "Howard" at the time.

His assailant, Bob Ford, had contacted the government and with his brother Charlie was planning to give James up in exchange for amnesty and a reward. Fearing that his plan had been discovered, Ford decided to take preemptive action and shot James in the back while he was straightening a picture. Ford, the informant is reviled as a coward and a traitor, while James, who killed several lawmen, not to mention numerous bank and railroad employees and assorted civilians, is remembered in the same song: "Jesse was a man, a friend to the poor. He'd never see a man suffer pain."

The ends of these two would-be government informants form a neat parable about the weight of betrayal, and illustrate both the internal and external pressures on an informant. Charlie Ford, always fearing the gang's retribution, got drunk one night and shot himself in the head. Bob was killed 10 years later by a relative of one of the members of Jesse's gang.

Institutionally, the penalty for treachery can be high. Legislatures have had to pass whistleblower protection acts to protect the people who report fraud, waste, and corruption. Among the things addressed by these laws are harassment and ostracism of the whistleblower, both common reactions by the betrayed, but also by others in the environment who feel threatened by the actions of the one who upset the apple cart.

Even the government shows its disapproval of betrayal, although it has a somewhat schizophrenic approach to the subject. On one hand, the government has made embezzlement — the theft of something from an employer who entrusted it to the employee — a criminal offense. Treason, the betrayal of one's country, is a capital crime. Spies and traitors are still routinely shot in parts of the world where the victimized government is fortunate enough to lay its hands on them. On the other hand, governments routinely encourage people to provide information about crimes and betray criminals, including embezzlers. And, of course, some governments employed those spies that were shot by the other government.

Nowhere is the public's attitude toward betrayal more evident than in the endless saga of Bill Clinton and Monica Lewinsky. In fact, if we created a "betrayal scale" in which we relate the public opinion ratings of all the participants to whether they are perceived as betrayer or betrayed, the result might explain some otherwise puzzling poll numbers.

In this case, government agents and prosecutors investigating potential wrongdoing by the President employed the services of one informant, Linda Tripp, and made a wholehearted effort to develop Lewinsky as a second informant. Ultimately, Lewinsky, though she initially "stood up" for the President, was given immunity in exchange for her information. Her standing in the public's opinion is not high and is nowhere near that of the party who was "betrayed" by Tripp and Lewinsky — Bill Clinton. And *his* popularity is lower than that of the person *he* betrayed, his wife Hillary. Kenneth Starr, the man who encouraged all of this betrayal or who at least brought it all out into public view, has approval numbers even lower than Lewinsky, who, after all, is seen as having been "betrayed" by Tripp. Fair or not, given what we know about attitudes toward betrayal, it is hardly surprising that the public approval ratings for Linda Tripp, who "wore a wire" against her friend, Monica, are only slightly above Judas Iscariot's.

Clinton-Lewinsky Betrayal Scale

Player	Poll Ranking	Betrayed by	Betrayed
Hillary Clinton	1	Everybody	Nobody
Bill Clinton	2	Lewinsky, Starr, Tripp	Hillary Clinton
Monica Lewinsky	3	Starr, Tripp	Bill and Hillary Clinton
Kenneth Starr	4	Nobody	Bill and Hillary Clinton
Linda Tripp	5	Nobody	Everybody but Starr

Law enforcement officers and investigators should probably be somewhat concerned with Starr's ranking. After all, he was only doing the job he was being paid to do — our job. His approval ratings probably reflect the public's perception that he connived in Tripp's betrayal of Lewinsky and Lewinsky's betrayal of the President.

In his first inaugural address, another President, Franklin Delano Roosevelt, spoke of confidence and its importance to society: "Small wonder that confidence languishes, for it thrives only on honesty, on honor, on the sacredness of obligations, on faithful protection, on unselfish performance. Without them it cannot live." Informants are not widely viewed as having the positive characteristics of which Roosevelt spoke, and society responds to them accordingly.

So, we come to the $64,000 question. Why, in the face of all of the negative ramifications, do people still become informants? We can be sure that, given the social pressures, the stigma, and the moral and even physical hazards, the motivation to inform against another must be very strong indeed. In fact, the motives for cooperation are many and varied and are (at least temporarily) powerful enough to overcome the massive social and emotional incentives against betrayal. Because these motivations are the key to developing, managing, and controlling informants, we must have an absolutely clear understanding of what they are and how they work.

Case Study: The Weight of Betrayal, a Clash of Loyalties

Sally Moore was in the middle of a real identity crisis. The San Francisco woman had flipped back and forth so many times in her life that she did not know who she was anymore. No one else did, either, so she decided to kill the President. Gerald Ford had been having a bad month himself. On a previous trip to California less than 3 weeks before, a petite vegetarian follower of multiple murderer Charles Manson had leveled a .45 automatic at Ford from less than 2 feet away. Secret Service agents wrestled Lynette "Squeaky" Fromme to the ground before she could get off a shot, but the President's California troubles were only just beginning.

Sarah Jane Moore, who preferred to be called Sally, was a middle-aged, middle-class mother of four. She had been married five times and divorced four, given three of her children up for adoption, and been fired from her job as an accountant. Disenchanted with her sedate suburban lifestyle, Sally abandoned it, her accounting career, and her latest marriage to join the radical political scene in 1974 San Francisco.

This was an interesting, exciting time in radical San Francisco. Heiress Patricia Hearst had recently been kidnapped by the shadowy Symbionese Liberation Army (SLA). One of the ransom demands on Hearst's father was that he donate $2 million in food to the poor. Moore worked on this project as something of a liaison between Randolph Hearst and the radicals, and she watched with the rest of America as Patty Hearst took the revolutionary name "Tania," converted to the radical cause, and became a bank robber with the SLA.

If Tania Hearst made an unlikely radical, Sally, the pudgy 44-year-old product of the middle-American establishment, made an even more improbable one, but she was accepted into a world that contrasted sharply with the one she had just left. One of her contacts, an ex-convict known in the movement as "Popeye" Jackson, introduced Sally to, as she later described it, "a murky world of drugs, of wholesale screwing, of filthy language." She moved steadily deeper into this world and gradually gained the acceptance of the other inhabitants, building an element of trust among people who were on the fringes of such groups as the Communist Labor Party and the SLA. Just as she came to belong to this new world, another called and Sally answered.

In April 1974, Sally began providing information to the FBI. She was approached by agents of the Bureau who had observed her radical connections when she was working on the distribution of Randolph Hearst's $2 million. The agents asked her to infiltrate and report on the radicals with whom she now associated. Sally was flattered and intrigued by the FBI's approach. She was also attracted to the cloak and dagger excitement of her double life; she identified with the FBI's mission and her role in it. She later talked about her recruitment: "The picture they [the FBI] painted was the very thing designed to make a nice, middle-class lady go off and save the country."

Presumably, Sally passed along valuable data on the drugs, wholesale screwing, and filthy language she encountered. She does not seem to have had access to any of the movement's deep secrets and certainly did not know the whereabouts of Patty Hearst, the fugitive in whom the FBI was most interested at the time. Her primary assignment from the FBI was to make contact with an individual whom the FBI believed did have SLA connections, a man Sally later identified as "Tom." Sally did establish a relationship with Tom and reported regularly back to the FBI.

Her informant career did not last long. After only 3 months, she began to identify more closely with her targets. Guilty about her betrayal of the people who had accepted her before the FBI did, she confessed to Tom about her double life. This news was not received well by her radical acquaintances. Word traveled quickly as Moore was efficiently cut off from any further access to the movement. This was something Moore had not anticipated when she went to Tom with her confession. She also (with charming naiveté) had not carefully thought about the possibility that these people who were promoting "armed protest" and advocating the violent overthrow of the U.S. government might retaliate against someone as potentially threatening as an FBI informant. As she became more isolated she became more fearful of her former friends.

She reported all of this to her FBI case agent, who told her that as her cover had been blown she was no longer of use to the FBI. She was also advised that, for her own safety, she should completely sever all ties with the radical movement and even leave the Bay Area. Recognizing that she had made a number of mistakes in her various betrayals, Sally, deeply confused, managed to make things worse. She went back to the radicals to try to reestablish those ties and regain their acceptance. This effort was only partially satisfactory, so she also returned to the FBI, this time with the intent of becoming a "double agent." As she described it (in *American Assassins,* by J.W. Clarke):

Nobody knew I was doubling. There were not two but three Sally Moore's operating at that point: one, the Sally Moore moving toward armed protest and starting to work with people dedicated to violence, telling no one — not the FBI, not friends on the left; two, the Sally Moore, converted informant, struggling to find acceptance among the theoreticians and "respectable" Communists; and, three, Sally Moore, FBI informant, reporting on who was asking me what about my "past," as well as on the new groups I was meeting.

It appears that Sally carried on in this extremely stressful situation for a time, but matters came to a head in June 1975, when her friend "Popeye" Jackson and his girlfriend were shot to death in their car a short distance from Sally apartment. Sally received an anonymous threat that "you're next." She believed the caller suspected she had somehow betrayed Jackson. In response, she began looking for some way to convince her revolutionary friends that she was one of them, fully committed to the cause. Whatever it was, it would have to be something pretty spectacular. Right about this time Squeaky Fromme drew down on President Ford in nearby Sacramento.

By coincidence, on September 18, the FBI caught up with Patty Hearst, who turned out to be living in an apartment in San Francisco. Moore, believing that she would somehow be blamed, became increasingly desperate, and the plan to shoot the President moved forward.

This plan, like everything else in her life, was a study in contrast. First, she bought a .44 caliber revolver. Then, she called the San Francisco police to tell them she had a gun and was planning to "test" the President's security on his upcoming visit to the city. She gave her name and address, so the San Francisco police department came by and took her gun, then sent the Secret Service over for a chat.

Deemed not sufficiently threatening to warrant surveillance, Moore went and got another gun, this one a .38 Smith and Wesson revolver, then drove recklessly, loading the gun in plain sight, hoping to be stopped and arrested. In a phrase that could sum up Sally's rather bleak existence, no one was paying any attention. In the crowd that awaited the President, Sally tried at least once to leave but could not move through the crush of people. Trapped in a life that must not have made much sense and a crowd full of strangers, she finally saw someone she knew and took her shot at him.

Analysis

Sally Moore's unhappy experience as an FBI informant is included to show the extreme pressures which informing can generate. It also demonstrates the extreme, even irrational responses which an admittedly unstable individual such as Sally Moore might have to those pressures. These are the pressures associated with betrayal. Sally was deeply conflicted in her loyalties. If we look at her actions, we can see the emotional effects of the internal and exterior barriers to betrayal. On a personal level, she is obviously torn by guilt at her betrayal of her radical friends, while on an external level she fears those same friends may be trying to kill her because of her betrayal.

Yet, Moore still broke faith with the Movement, informing against them to the FBI. At some point, at least, her motivation to take this step carried her over the barriers. In the time she was cooperating with the government, Moore's own loyalties were divided. It is true that the FBI did not retain sufficient control over her to keep those loyalties from shifting back to her radical associates. I believe that given her background and emotional state it would have been virtually impossible for the FBI to keep that control. An examination of Sally's motivation may show why this is so.

Motivation

Informants generally act in what they perceive to be their best interest, fulfilling the needs most important to them at the time. Sarah Jane Moore's problem was in trying to establish in her own mind exactly what this best interest was. As she described it, she went through two periods or phases as an informant, and her motivations for each period were distinctly different. We know that as she went off to serve her life sentence for shooting at the president she viewed herself as an individual who was completely committed to "armed protest." Her action validated that commitment for all her radical friends to see. What is less clear is why she earlier agreed to cooperate with the FBI against those same people.

Sally's primary motivation for originally becoming an FBI informant was what we are referring to here as ego or vanity. She liked the adventure of the thing, the excitement of a double life, and as she said, "The picture the FBI painted was the very thing designed to make a nice, middle-class lady go off and save the country." She was escaping from a bad marriage, a boring suburban existence, and a job as a department store accountant. Infiltrating a group of dangerous radicals and reporting on their activity to the FBI was the ultimate abandonment of her humdrum former existence.

Other common motivations for informing were not present in Moore's case. She was not paid, was not under any threat of prosecution, was not seeking revenge against some slight by the radicals. She certainly had no desire to repent or reform, as she had committed no wrong for which some atonement was called for. Sally Moore became an informant because she liked playing spy, but also because she craved the acceptance of her fellow humans. Being an informant gave her the opportunity to be accepted by two groups of people who were now very important in her life — the people in the groups she was infiltrating and the FBI. This motivation was strong enough to allow Moore to function as an informant for almost exactly three months.

In the second period of Moore's double life, she clearly had a perverse motivation for informing. She saw herself as a double agent, justifying her continued communication with the FBI on the grounds that she was now keeping the radicals informed about the questions the FBI was asking, who they were interested in, and even details about her FBI agent contacts. Because Sally had revealed her affiliation with the Bureau to her radical friends, they made sure she no longer had anything of importance to give to the FBI, which in turn told her to sever her ties with the groups. This lack of access meant she probably was not a very good informant to either side, neither of which would have trusted her. She had betrayed the radicals by informing to the FBI, and she had betrayed the FBI by telling the radicals about her activity as an informant.

Access

Sally had somewhat more access to the radicals than did the FBI, which is why she was approached in the first place. She came to the government's attention through her work on the People in Need (PIN) program, which was set up to distribute $2 million of Patricia Hearst's ransom money to the poor. She also knew "Popeye" Jackson, the ex-convict who headed the United Prisoners Union (UPU), one of the less viable labor organizations in the Bay Area. Neither Jackson nor the UPU was apparently taken very seriously by the FBI.

Interestingly, Sally had no initial access to the target that did interest the FBI, the mysterious Tom. Moore claimed later that she had been assigned by her Bureau handler to "establish contact with and observe" Tom, which essentially means that she was required to expand her access *after* becoming an informant. She did gain Tom's confidence, and within three months was telling him about her FBI assignment, effectively ending her access to her principal target.

When word got around about the FBI informant in their midst, Sally's friends cut off her access to them as well. Thereafter, she had little ability to collect the type of information which would have made her valuable to any law enforcement agency. The FBI knew this, as she told them about her confession to Tom and the radicals' reaction, at which time they took steps to end her association with them, advising her to drop her ties to the radicals.

In her comeback as a "double agent," Moore probably had little access to either the FBI or the radicals. It is highly unlikely that, given her obviously confused loyalties, anyone would have trusted her with any information of value. The FBI appears to have clearly recognized the peril and merely tolerated Moore. The same is probably true of the radicals.

Control

The FBI was obviously unable to control their informant. Sally burned herself to the targets, intended to double-cross the FBI by informing on their activity to those same targets, and finally tried to shoot the President. She was not the best informant in FBI history. Motivation is the best means of control, and her motivation was suspect from the beginning. She really had no reason for being an informant in the first place, but then she really had no reason to leave the department store for the street, either. She was an emotionally unstable individual with an even more conflicted personality than most other informants. When the flattering attention of the FBI and the excitement of her undercover life wore thin, which took three months, the "nice, middle-class lady" changed allegiance yet again.

An officer who is required to work with someone like Sally must secure better control, and this requires establishing a stronger motivation than the one she had at the time. One technique used by the intelligence community is to make regular payments to the informant, even in relatively small amounts. As the payments are received, the informant adjusts his lifestyle accordingly and becomes dependent on them. This has the effect of refocusing the informant's motivation, providing another, perhaps stronger reason for remaining with the program. This alternative might not have been practical in this case, given the meager value of Sally's information.

It would also have been possible to employ some of the various compliance/influence techniques we will discuss to secure a more lasting commitment from her. Careful handling might have strengthened the commitment she had made to cooperating with the government.

Sarah Jane Moore was an active informant with limited access and shaky motivation. She appears to have been seeking acceptance and wanted to be taken seriously by someone. She became an informant to save the country, was unsuccessful, became a revolutionary to change the country, failed here as well, and ultimately took decisive action to gain the attention she wanted. She did wind up being taken seriously, but she made a poor informant and fortunately she was a lousy shot as well.

Summing Up

The impact of betrayal is always felt beyond just the betrayer and the betrayed. The massive prejudice against treachery, both individual and in society, generally serves to discourage betrayal, preserving the customary trust and good faith that hold our social fabric together. Yet, people overcome the immense weight of this prejudice to betray every day. Some of these people cheat on their spouses, some steal from their employers, and others become informants. The impact of the latter's actions in cooperating with the government can extend far beyond the person whose trust they betray.

As Hugo said, "To betray a secret is to tear from each member of this fierce community something of his own personality." He was writing about the criminal underworld of Paris and he clearly understood the bonds formed there that are broken in the betrayal of an informant. The effect, he asserts, is felt not just by the betrayer, but by each member of the community, a heavy burden, indeed.

The question of motivation — what causes people to move beyond the barriers to inform against others — becomes of paramount importance. Because the psychological and social consequences are so intense, the motivation to accept these consequences must be equally strong or stronger. This issue will be examined more closely in the following chapter.

Motivation
and Behavior

4

"*It is a characteristic of the human being throughout his whole life that he is practically always desiring something.*" —Abraham Maslow, psychologist and author of *Motivation and Personality*

"*He'd give up his own mother if somebody gave him a reason to. Find a reason.*"

Motivation

Psychologists have been looking at the issues surrounding motivation, personality, and human behavior for some time, but the question of what moves people to work, learn, or achieve is of keen interest to others besides the clinician. We can easily see the direct application of such study to others in our lives. Bosses would like to stimulate people to produce more. Educators look for ways to interest students and impel them to learn better. Coaches seek the means to motivate their players to practice harder and achieve higher levels of performance. The answer lies in the human mind and how we view our needs in the world around us.

Abraham Maslow, a psychologist and professor at Brandeis University, examined the question in the 1940s and early 1950s, publishing his theory in a book, *Motivation and Personality*, in 1954. Maslow described motivation in terms of a "hierarchy of needs," a ranking of things that people valued or desired. He believed that people desire things all throughout their lives and only rarely achieve a sense of complete satisfaction. He based his research on observations of monkeys in the Bronx Zoo, which, because people fit the hierarchy he developed quite nicely, may not say much for us humans.

A fictional story about needs and how we view them might help to start the discussion. A small boy grew up in a household without ever speaking. Although he could obviously hear and understand the people around him, he never spoke a word, something his family eventually accepted. One day at breakfast, the boy suddenly said, "These pancakes suck." Everyone was amazed and his mother asked, "Why haven't you said anything before now?" His response was, "Up till now, everything's been fine." The boy's entire array of needs had always been taken care of, evidently to his complete satisfaction. Only when things were no longer completely "fine" was he motivated to fulfill a suddenly important need.

The rest of us are not so lucky. As we travel through life, Maslow thought, we address the needs in hierarchical order. We first take care of our physiological needs — the food we need to survive. Once that most immediate need has been addressed, we are free to move up to the next value on the list — security. This can be fulfilled with the roof over one's head, suitable clothing to wear, and the knowledge that there is a place for our things. We generally take care of the first two needs by working, earning the money needed to pay for food, shelter, and clothing.

If these problems are solved, then the need to be loved and to belong becomes urgent. This is often equated with a sexual need, but it also includes a desire for warmth, security, and belonging. Life is pretty good at this point, but a need for self-esteem, recognition, and the esteem of one's peers and neighbors emerges to complicate things. Maslow believed that, once all of these values have been realized, the individual becomes free to create, to seek understanding, to "self-actualize." He also recognized that some people, for various reasons, do not go past the fourth level. All in all, this theory explains quite a bit about human behavior, and especially why people do things which may not, at first glance, appear to be in their best interest.

It helps to view Maslow's hierarchy as a pyramid (see Figure 1). We spend a great deal of time, both in our lives as a whole and in our daily existence, dealing with the needs at the bottom of the pyramid. As the values in each level are fulfilled, we are able to climb to the next set of desires.

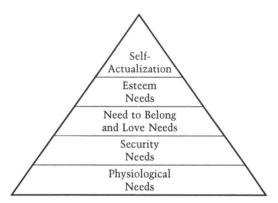

Figure 1. Maslow's hierarchy of needs.

Maslow's structure works equally well for cavemen and for high-powered attorneys. For example, a primitive hunter-gatherer would have spent a large portion of his life just dealing with the day-to-day problem of getting enough food to eat. When he was confident he was not going to starve, he could work on finding a new cave or tanning some hides for new clothes. Relatively little time could be devoted to sex, forming intimate relationships, and belonging to the group, although early societies were not very mobile and were structured in small groups, making belonging easier.

Even less time could be spent on enhancing personal esteem — only a few in the group might have that relative luxury. The fact that cave paintings and places like Stonehenge have been found suggest that some time was still found to create, to know and understand the universe around them, and to solve problems simply for the fun of it in the self-actualization phase of their lives.

For a high-powered attorney, a substantial income and advances in technology free much more time that can now be spent at or near the top of the pyramid. Our lawyer takes care of her survival and security needs with a few billable hours each day. The desire to belong and to be loved at the next level are also addressed in connection with the lawyer's lifestyle. She has many opportunities, through social contacts and the security obtained from having all of the other needs covered, to get access to a group, a sense of belonging, or to find love. Finally, our lawyer can focus on the esteem she acquires through her accomplishments. She is an associate or a partner or is being considered for a judgeship. She has the respect of her community. At this point, she is free to self-actualize, rock-climb, and write a novel, probably about some young attorney who outsmarts the police in some ingenious way.

Maslow believed that we have all of these needs within us all of the time; we just address them at different times and in the order dictated by circumstances. Each set of needs motivates us to behave in ways which allow us to reach those needs. Does this explain why one athlete works harder or succeeds more often? It can. Once his physiological and security needs are addressed (with a pro contract or a scholarship), he will be motivated to fit in with his teammates, to belong to the team. To be accepted, he will have to perform, which means hard work at practice and on the field.

Once the team's acceptance is won, an athlete with that "inner drive" coaches look for will seek the respect and esteem of peers and fans. "You've got to respect that guy's abilities" is a badge of pride worn by the best players on the field. He'll be motivated to keep that esteem, which is one reason why records are kept.

Maslow felt that our behavior was a reflection of our motivation. This proposition has been examined by other psychologists who tried to determine what factors in the workplace most inspired worker performance. Surprisingly, given all the talk about salary contracts, wages, raises, and the like, money was not a major factor in most people's thinking. Maslow would have said this was because the needs of those being questioned that could be best addressed by money — those in the physiological and security levels — had been addressed. People were now working on belonging to the group, which is why many responded that they valued the interpersonal relationships in the office above money. In other cases, they were seeking enhanced esteem, which is why they said they valued promotions, increased authority, an important-sounding title, and the ability to make decisions about the work itself.

Managers must understand this concept, because managers are motivators. An important management function is to ensure that the people have what they need to do the job, one of which is motivation. Supplying the wrong motivation will not boost productivity or make for a happier employee. (This reminds us of the sign in the slave galley that read, "The floggings will continue until morale improves.") Suppose a manager detects that an employee is unmotivated, something which can manifest itself in terms of poor performance, absenteeism, waste, or a host of other symptoms, all bad from the employer's perspective. Something must be done; the employee must be re-motivated, but how?

Flogging might do the trick, but probably not. Certainly Maslow would tell us that although flogging *will* change behavior — you will definitely row harder — it doesn't really address any of the needs in his hierarchy — you won't *want* to row harder, and you'll stop rowing just as soon as they stop hitting you. A better management response might be to address those needs, possibly by offering the employee a raise. Unfortunately, if those desires in the first two levels have already been fulfilled to the employee's satisfaction, this will be money wasted, for they are focused on fulfilling the now more urgent needs at the next level up.

Perhaps management could create work groups or product teams, in which the employees could acquire a greater sense of belonging and personal involvement in their jobs. Saturn, a division of General Motors, has taken this approach. They pay union scale, just as other auto manufacturers do, but their management-union-employee teams are an acknowledgment that people do not work only for the money.

All of this is critical to our study of informants because, as law enforcement officers we are expected to *manage* these individuals. Not only must we motivate them to take the initial step, to cross the line and become informants, we must also direct and control their efforts after the line is crossed. This entire process requires that we understand why informants do things — what motivates them.

Where does an informant fit into Maslow's pyramid? They are people like the rest of us, after all, so they will presumably follow the same pattern. At the bottom level, some people will be prepared to trade their access for the money they simply need to eat. Many police officers have provided individuals with small amounts of cash, sometimes even from their own pockets, to ensure that the informant will have a meal to eat. There are also those informants who will trade that same access for the money they require for the other staple of their existence, narcotics.

Dealing with an individual who is motivated solely by an urgent requirement to survive is relatively simple: provide for the need, usually with cash. Mercenary informants, even those who are making big money from their activity, will at least begin in these levels. Motivations change, however, as needs are fulfilled. As the managers or handlers of this informant, we must recognize that his motives for continuing to cooperate may not be the same or felt to the same extent as when he began. The law enforcement officer who fails to prepare for and recognize a change when it occurs has effectively lost control of that informant. As we will see, the potential consequences for loss of control can be serious, even fatal.

Informant Motivation

Several authors have described the motivations typically attributed to those who inform to law enforcement. Others have examined the motives of spies and what has impelled people to betray their countries. Because it is so critical that an informant's motivation be exactly understood, these descriptions are useful in outlining the motives of the vast number of informants. While I do not believe that *every* informant's motive for cooperating *always* fits neatly into one of these categories, they do describe most informants most of the time.

As we examine these lists we can use the case studies in this book and our personal experiences to confirm the validity of these categories. I believe such examination will show that (1) informants often have more than one motivation for their actions; (2) these motivations are flexible, and some will be stronger or less important, or even in competition with each other, at different points in the informant's career; and (3) knowing where we stand regarding the informant's motivation is the best means of exercising the control needed to ensure his success and our own.

The other thing to remember in reviewing these lists is that the most obvious motivation may not be the one the informant needs addressed most at that moment. For example, someone who is cooperating to avoid a long prison term has a readily apparent and very pressing motive for that cooperation. This is something that the investigator can address in the prescribed fashion, but that informant may also be concerned with another need — perhaps to belong to a group or merely to retain his sense of self-esteem or self-worth. An officer who is alert enough to understand this less obvious need may be able to motivate the informant to big things just by treating him with respect, listening, or perhaps speaking appreciatively of the value of a case the informant has assisted. This could be much more effective than simply threatening the individual with jail for the tenth or twelfth time.

In the 1950s, Malachi Harney and John Cross, two federal narcotic agents developed a series of lectures on informants for the Treasury Department's Law Enforcement Officer Training School. These lectures were eventually transformed into a book, *The Informer in Law*

Enforcement (Charles C Thomas, 1960). I have an old copy of one of Harney's lectures, given by him on July 26, 1961, in which he describes the motives which can be attributed to informants. As a new agent in the Treasury school some 27 years later, I attended the same training; comparing the handouts for both, I found they were substantially the same.

This is because, aside from the law, not much has changed in the world of informants and informing. People are still motivated to give information by the same things that motivated their fathers and grandfathers. As our case examples show, the lessons of criminal history are still valid today. Harney identified an informer as a "person who gives information to an investigator because of a definite personal motive." He then categorizes these motives as follows:

1. Fear
2. Revenge
3. Perverse
4. Egotistical
5. Mercenary
6. Repentance or desire to reform

Taking each of these in turn, we will try to relate these most common informant motives to Maslow's hierarchy of needs and begin to develop some ideas about how we can influence people to cooperate with an investigation and how we can stimulate them to perform successfully as informants.

Fear

Fear is a powerful emotion and an effective motivator. Self-preservation is often described as the first law of nature, so we should expect that a situation which threatens the safety or security of an individual will provoke a strong response. Confronted with a threatening or fearful situation, people (and other animals) resort to an instinctive fight-or-flight response. Though their approach may change, they will continue to respond to a threat for as long as it is perceived to exist. People who become informants out of fear generally do so because they are threatened by either the law or by other criminals.

Threat of Incarceration

This motivation more than any other is responsible for informants coming to law enforcement. Criminals who are in trouble with the law have a strong preference against going to prison for their crimes. They also have a powerful motivation to cooperate with law enforcement to reduce the chances of a long(er) sentence. Federal law and sentencing guidelines have been modified in recent years to provide that one of the few ways that a sentence can be reduced is if the defendant provides "substantial assistance to the government." The wording from the sentencing guidelines, which is included in the Appendices, makes it abundantly clear that the government wants people to cooperate with and assist law enforcement. People who are afraid of lengthy incarceration have a means to do something about that fear.

The discretion held by prosecuting attorneys in how cases are charged gives the government another means of encouraging cooperation. The plea-bargaining process provides another; a defendant can make his access to other criminal activity one of the chips on the bargaining table. This motivation is known in law enforcement as a *hammer* or a *twist*. These graphic terms emphasize the compelling nature of fear as a motive. Depending on the length of sentence the informant is facing, the hammer, which can be dropped at any time, could be very heavy. Federal drug laws, in particular, include mandatory minimum sentences with long terms and no parole, which makes that hammer fairly heavy. The prospect of a 20-year, 30-

year, or life sentence concentrates the mind most wonderfully. This is a strong stimulus to cooperate with law enforcement.

Many law enforcement officers believe that this motivation provides the best incentive for cooperation, as well as the best means for controlling someone once he has decided to cooperate. Because most law enforcement officers make arrests or develop evidence against people that can be used for an arrest, access to such people is relatively easy. Someone with a hammer over his head works cheap, too. There is no need for law enforcement to use funds from its limited budget to pay for the information — money is not the benefit the informant is seeking. The prosecuting attorney knows exactly what benefits have been promised to the informant, often because a written agreement was used to document the arrangement. All of these factors make the threat of incarceration a useful tool for obtaining someone's cooperation.

How does this fear of incarceration fit into Maslow's pyramid? It essentially threatens the individual's ability to fulfill his needs on every level. (One could argue that the food and security needs in a prison are certainly well provided for, but this would ignore the fact that almost no one is motivated to fulfill those needs under those conditions.) Individual responses to this fear will vary; not everyone will react with the same vigor or in the same way to the threat. You can be sure that people will do *something*, however; basic instinct requires some response.

Threat of Harm by Associates

People who get involved in crime also get involved with criminals. These relationships contain the seeds of all the problems that plague other interpersonal relationships, with the added stress of operating on the wrong side of the law. There really is not much honor among thieves, so not only do you have to worry about betrayal to the police, you also have to be concerned that one of your unscrupulous associates is going to rob you or retaliate for some perceived slight.

Informants who fear harm by their associates will respond with the same fight-or-flight reaction we noted earlier. Bob Ford, the man who shot Jesse James (see Chapter 3), feared that James had discovered Ford's treachery and was planning to kill him. A number of Mafia informants have been persuaded to cooperate as witnesses because they either knew or feared that a contract had been issued for their deaths. Famed mob informant Joseph Valachi received the "kiss of death" from Vito Genovese, who erroneously believed Valachi was already talking to the police. Valachi, whose numerous motives covered most of our list, took this threat seriously enough to kill the man he thought Genovese had sent to kill *him*. This turned out to be a case of mistaken identity on Valachi's part, but he responded by going to the law, which protected him from the very real fear of his associates for the rest of his life.

Law enforcement is the beneficiary of this dissension in the criminal ranks. For the most part, we just wait for the person fearing the harm to come to us. On occasion, we will receive information about a threat to someone, perhaps over a drug deal gone bad or a falling out within a group. In those cases, law enforcement has an ethical responsibility both to prevent harm to the intended victim and to give him the opportunity to provide information against those who planned the harm. The FBI notified John Gotti of a threat against his life which the Bureau had discovered in the course of one of their investigations of the crime boss. Gotti was not so grateful as to cease his criminal activity or become an informant, however.

One extremely unethical practice is *creating* the threat to the would-be informant to force his cooperation. Known as "hanging a snitch jacket" on someone, the officer either tells the potential informant's associates that he is informing or threatens to do so. Once the jacket is on, the potential informant has a real problem, one he can solve by becoming a real informant.

Although this approach is admittedly sometimes effective, it is beneath us as law enforcement officers, it does not engender the trust of the informant (or anyone else), and it could cause real harm to someone. Management should never allow this practice.

Prisons are good places to find informants who are motivated by fear of their associates. Prisoners can easily violate the complex inmate "code," then fear the resulting retribution. Their response is to seek the assistance of the prison authorities or law enforcement. Often a transfer to another facility or to protective custody is an easy solution to the prison informant's problem.

Revenge

In my earlier career as a narcotics agent, I encountered very few people who were interested in providing information as a means of obtaining revenge. This was always somewhat puzzling, considering the number of rip-offs, burn jobs, and general double-dealing that goes on in the drug world. Evidently the people who lived by the old phrase, "Don't get mad, get even," either did not get mad or had found some other means to even the score (probably a drive-by shooting).

When I began working at the Criminal Investigation Division of the Internal Revenue Service (IRS), I found out that the concept of "getting even" was alive and well. Like many law enforcement agencies, the IRS maintains a confidential hotline, in this case for people who want to report tax fraud. And plenty of people do want to report tax fraud, enough to keep the 1-800 number busy much of the day. One might suppose that many of the callers were civic-minded individuals who were appalled at the actions of those who cheat their government. Some were, but most of the ones I spoke with just wanted a little revenge.

Like fear, the desire for revenge is another very potent motivator. Hell may have no fury like a woman scorned, but folks other than scorned women can get pretty charged up for revenge, too. I classified most of these people as "ex-es:" ex-wives, ex-girlfriends (scorned women), ex-husbands, ex-boyfriends, ex-bosses, ex-employees, ex-tenants, ex-customers. All of these people had two things in common with every other informant; they knew something damaging about someone else and they were motivated to tell law enforcement about it. The motivation in this case, was vengeance.

Although we hear that "revenge is sweet," a desire to exact punishment for a perceived wrong is bitter fruit, indeed. It usually certifies the ending of a relationship in which one party now feels wronged or betrayed. The closer the relationship, the greater the sense of being wronged and more intense the desire for retribution. This desire can be translated into a telephone call to Crimestoppers, a fraud hotline, or a detective with whom the caller has dealt before.

The information provided by people with a revenge motive is often quite good. After all, they were closely, perhaps intimately, involved with the person who wronged them. They probably picked up quite a bit through this association. Depending on their position in the group or organization, the information they possess may be invaluable.

Get this valuable information *now*, however. Another old proverb says that, "Revenge is a dish that tastes better cold." It may taste better, but most people cannot wait for the temperature to drop. The desire for revenge is one of those emotions that burns very hot, but cannot sustain itself for long. We will talk some more about working with a revenge-motivated informant, but we need to appreciate the absolute need for speed in your initial contacts. Move quickly, because the first call is often the only one you will get. As emotions cool, the once-burning need for revenge will fade. People who were eager to bring the wrath of God (or at the very least, the IRS) on the head of the wrongdoer will wake up the next morning and discover they have much more pressing concerns.

A revenge-motivated individual may go through several stages in a usually short career as an informant. In the first phase, the informant is extremely emotional, angry, bitter, and anxious to convey every bit of damaging information. In the second stage, as emotions are tempered, the informant may be more calculating, but still cooperating, trying to weigh his previous actions against the physiological, security, belonging, and esteem needs which might have been ignored in the previous period. Finally, the informant may be trying to escape his "act in haste, repent at leisure" actions. These phases can be very brief. One call may be all you ever get; by the next day the informant is gone.

There are exceptions, of course, to this rule, one of whom was Joe Valachi, whose activities as an informant are described in Chapter 8. Valachi, who, asked in his testimony before the U.S. Senate about his motive, said, "Number one, it is to destroy them [his former organized crime bosses]." That's a desire for revenge talking.

With some informants, a hunger for revenge will be sufficient to propel them through the door, but they may stay on for other reasons The officer will have to identify some other motivator or some other need and fulfill it if that informant is to stay with the program for the long haul. With other informants, such as Valachi, revenge was not the initial reason for coming forward — fear of his associates was the prime mover — but his desire for revenge strengthened as time went by.

I believe that the transient nature of revenge as a motivator fits Maslow's theory quite well. While one might have an admittedly strong desire for revenge, probably to recover the respect or self-esteem one might feel was lost in the original wrong, other, more pressing needs will take precedence. This is especially true of any relationship which is ended. Our needs with respect to that relationship must inevitably fade as we progress into new relationships with more immediate and compelling demands.

An investigator who fails to recognize the fading of the desire for revenge is facing severe control problems with that informant. If we cannot motivate an informant to continue cooperating for some other reason, we are going to lose that person as a source.

Perverse

Harney included this category to describe all of those people who give information in hopes of receiving some unusual advantage. The informant is hiding the real reason for his "cooperation" because the benefit sought is ordinarily not one that law enforcement really wants to provide to such a person, which is why people with this motivation must be identified and dealt with carefully.

As is the case with all informants, they are providing information for *their* reasons, not *yours.* Someone with a perverse agenda is working especially hard for himself, trying to gain some advantage or benefit. Typical of these are

1. An informant who provides information about rivals in his own business, hoping that the police can be used to eliminate the competition
2. An informant who minimizes his own role or provides false or misleading information to deflect the attention of law enforcement from his own activities
3. An informant who maintains contact with law enforcement for the purpose of learning about investigative techniques, identifying officers (especially undercover agents), or discovering information about law enforcement operations.
4. An informant who uses the contacts to steal from law enforcement
5. An informant who wants to expose police "corruption" or misconduct

In all of these instances, the informant's true motive will be carefully concealed. If an officer cannot immediately identify a plausible motivation for the informant's coming forward, a perverse motivation must be suspected. This is *always* the case when the informant is a walk-in.

Perverse motivations can be identified and dealt with through extensive debriefing and corroboration of the informant's statements, something you should be doing anyway. Another useful device is asking, "*Cui bono?*" — a Latin expression asking, "Who benefits?" The information you receive from an informant always helps someone (preferably, law enforcement) and hurts someone else (preferably, the criminals). By asking *cui bono*, you can test the information against the result. Anna Sage, the informant who told the FBI where to find John Dillinger, was later accused of having a perverse motivation for doing so. As you read the case study that accompanies this chapter, periodically ask yourself the *cui bono* question about Sage's information and how her cooperation could have benefited Sage herself.

The personal, ethical, and legal hazards connected with perversely motivated informants are so substantial that they should be used only with the greatest care, if at all. In Chapter 7, we will examine some of these issues in greater detail.

Egotistical

Those informants who have egotistical motives are often small-timers who are trying to magnify their own sense of importance. One such individual was Louis Weichmann, a petty clerk in the War Department. Pudgy, bland, single, thoroughly trapped in a dead-end job, Weichmann had every reason to want to inflate his own sense of self-worth. As America's Civil War drew to its conclusion, Weichmann, who had an apparently deserved reputation for nosiness, carried tales of armed men plotting secretly in his Washington boarding house. Although Weichmann's information ultimately proved to have been timely and accurate, he was not taken seriously by his superiors, who viewed him as something of a busybody and self-promoter. Everybody took Weichmann seriously, though, after April 14, 1865, when the men he had been describing assassinated President Abraham Lincoln.

Egotistical informants are motivated by a desire to enhance their own self-esteem. They fall into two general categories: small-time criminals who are seeking to be well thought of by law enforcement and individuals who want to be a part of law enforcement but cannot qualify. Both seek to inflate their egos by providing information they hope law enforcement will see as valuable. As you might suspect by looking at Maslow's pyramid, informants in this category are usually satisfied in their physiological and security needs. They may be gainfully employed and otherwise settled in their lives.

People from both of these categories may exaggerate the importance of their information or the nature of their access, both of which could endanger an investigation. Another risk is that the informant may test the boundaries of the officer's control, acting independently or making decisions on his own.

A third category generally fits the egotistical/vanity criteria and includes people who betray because they feel superior to others. These people believe that they can prove their superiority by successfully "outwitting" those they see as inferiors. Informants from this group are more often found in the espionage game, which has certainly seen some supremely vain traitors. Because everything is a contest to see who is smarter, these informants can be difficult to deal with. They may also represent a serious control problem, as they also believe they are smarter than their controller and may try to prove it by outwitting him or her, too.

These informants are usually walk-ins, but not always. For example, a university instructor I arrested on narcotics charges agreed to cooperate from a fear motive — he was smart enough not to want to go to prison. This fear became less important to him as time went by and as he developed a strong self-esteem need to show us how intelligent he was. We were able to develop more significant cases because he was trying to win our respect and esteem for his efforts rather than just going through the motions to "work off the beef."

For the most part, their motivation is transitory, lasting as long as it takes for them to feel they have proved their point to themselves. When this moment arrives, the egotistical walk-in is likely to walk out, leaving the case in limbo. The same can be true for the informant who wants to be "bigger" through his connection with law enforcement, except that careful handling can keep this person motivated to continue to cooperate.

Mercenary

"Tell us where ye got all the money, Gypo. Ye had none this morning." Gypo Nolan, the title character in Liam O'Flaherty's novel, *The Informer*, got the money in time-honored fashion — by selling the whereabouts of bomber Frankie McPhillip to the police. There is a reason why wanted posters frequently include mention of a reward and why governments often see fit to pay "for information leading to the arrest and conviction of _____." The reason is that money talks, and so do the people who want it.

Relatively few informants do so solely for the money, although the federal government alone pays out tens of millions of dollars annually to informants. The FBI, in particular, has a higher proportion of informants who are paid for their information, but I suspect that even at the Bureau most informants' primary reason for informing is not mercenary. True mercenaries — people whose job description is "professional informant" — are rare.

Aside from these few individuals, most of those who receive payment for information have some other motivation. Anna Sage, whose case is studied at the end of this chapter, turned John Dillinger in for part of a $25,000 reward. She also had the pressing need for government help with her deportation case.

Money talks, and the government is prepared to pay to hear what it has to say. There is, as of this writing, a $5 million reward for the capture of terrorist suspect Osama bin Laden. There was a $1 million reward for the capture of the man who became known as The Unabomber. (Although this reward was ultimately paid, the good citizen who collected the money, David Kaczynski, had an altruistic motive for coming forward; see Chapter 1.)

People who provide information solely for the money are addressing needs at the bottom of Maslow's hierarchy. The clearest example is that of Gypo Nolan, the fictional informant who turned his friend in for the money. O'Flaherty writes:

> He stood looking at the ground with his hands deep in his trousers pockets. He seemed to be deep in thought, but he was not thinking. At least there was no concrete idea fixed in his mind. Two facts rumbled about in his brain, making that loud primeval noise, which is the beginning of thought and which tired people experience when the jaded brain has spun out the last threads of its energy. There were two facts in his brain. First, the fact of his meeting with McPhillip. Second, the fact of his having no money to buy a bed for the night.

Gypo Nolan had no money, something which emphasized an obvious physiological need (food), as well as a security need (shelter). He also had access to information which could be traded for immediate fulfillment of both needs. Nolan made the trade: " 'I have come to claim the twenty pounds reward offered by the Farmer's Union for information concerning Francis Joseph McPhillip,' he said in a deep low voice." His informant career was short, something which is typical of many mercenary informants. Anna Sage's career lasted as long as her access to John Dillinger did — almost exactly 24 hours. When the access is gone, so is the mercenary informant.

The disincentives for mercenary informants are even more profound than for other types of cooperators. "He did it for the money" seems a particularly base and sordid form of betrayal. This aversion dates at least to Judas, who is supposed to have "sold out" Jesus Christ for 30 pieces of silver.

You will find, however, that mercenary informants do not have nearly the same compunction about taking the money that others might. By the time they walk through the door, the mercenary informant has already made the decision to take the cash and will be fully committed to that decision. If, however, needs change, as Maslow predicts they will, the mercenary may not have the commitment to stay in the program. One agent commented, "They'll leave whenever the money isn't as important. Then what are you going to do?"

Researchers who have looked at informant practices at law enforcement agencies noted that mercenary informants are generally less trusted by the officers who work with them. One of the reasons for this distrust is the belief that the money is not sufficient to keep the informant reliably under control. There is also the general feeling that someone who will provide real information for money will also provide false information for the same reason. This attitude, by the way, carries over to other professions; the news media is frequently heard denying that they paid this source or that one, and even expert witnesses who are paid for their testimony in court come in for criticism on that score.

Nevertheless, the practice of paying for information continues. People still come in to collect outstanding rewards. Money can be an effective motivator, especially if it addresses an immediate need. In a mix of other motivations, money can be very useful means of obtaining control over an informant. The intelligence community uses this technique, apparently with success, as do some law enforcement officers.

In the approach referred to briefly in the last chapter, an informant or spy with some other motivation — say, revenge — is given relatively small regular cash payments. This money is to be used for incidental expenses, small luxuries, or special treats. The amount of money is not great, but the source is dependable and the informant comes to rely upon it, adjusting his lifestyle to account for this new income. If the intent is to create a loyal and dependable (and dependent) informant for the long-haul, this process is a much better "hook" than the promise of one large cash payment. This technique also substitutes a positive motivation for a negative one, something which generally leads to more commitment and a better attitude.

One type of mercenary informant deserves special mention. This is the true professional, who works for one or more law enforcement agencies, traveling from place to place, developing access, making cases, then moving on. Although these people can develop a real affinity for law enforcement and often have a strong egotistical motive, they are in it for the money and are quite good at what they do. The ones with whom I have worked knew almost as much about our procedures and paperwork as I did. Because their livelihood depends on maintaining good will with their law enforcement connections, they follow instructions fairly well and know the legal guidelines better than most lawyers.

Repentance or Desire To Reform

A relatively rare type of informant, these people are sincere in their desire to leave the world of crime behind. This person can be extremely valuable — you have a well-intentioned individual with a very positive motivation who may have tremendous access. This is an exceptional combination in any informant.

This informant is most likely to be addressing needs in the self-esteem and belonging levels of our pyramid. An officer can support this motivation by respecting the difficulties such a choice entails. The informant may be trying to burn bridges to his old life by "burning" his associates. He may perceive these people as standing in his way on the road to reform.

Caution: People who are truly repentant about bad major lifestyle choices in their past are hard to find. If someone comes in saying, "I've done wrong, I'm really sorry, I'm going to do everything I can to make up for it," you should be prepared to help him get what he needs. You should also be skeptical and free with your *cui bono* analysis.

An intelligence community counterpart to Harney's list is known by its acronym, MICE, and describes the typical motivations of spies who betray their countries. This list, which includes all of Harney's categories, is as follows:

1. Money
2. Ideology
3. Compromise
4. Ego

In the CIA's version, "compromise" includes those informants who are essentially fearful of sexual or other blackmail, exposure of violations of law or procedure, or some other skeleton in their closet. It is, for our purposes, synonymous with the fear motive described above. Law enforcement obviously does not use blackmail of any type as a hammer, and sexual blackmail as a motivator may have lost a little of its currency in the current political climate.

The CIA's motivations of ego and money are, for all intents and purposes, the same as Harney's, but the intelligence world sometimes contains people who spy for ideological reasons, something not often seen in law enforcement. The Russians had a great deal of success recruiting idealistic young communists in western countries. These people were highly motivated and most did not see their cooperation with the Soviets as treason. Rather, they were being completely faithful to their ideology.

On the flip side, the Americans and British received quite a bit of assistance from Russian defectors and spies who were abandoning what they saw as a corrupt or morally bankrupt regime for the "better" political system of the west. The motivation of these individuals, too, was ideological.

The closest comparable motivations in law enforcement are repentance and altruism. A truly repentant informant is essentially a defector from the underworld. He is leaving that life behind, not planning to return, and is burning some bridges to make sure he cannot go back. The "good citizen" informant who provides information for altruistic reasons certainly has an ideological motive — he does not approve of crime or criminals. Unfortunately, good citizens usually have little or no access to any valuable information or they would not be good citizens. Their counterparts in the espionage world, on the other hand, may have been entrusted with quite a bit of access.

In addition to the motives described by Harney, other authors have developed their own lists. There is quite a bit of overlap, but while the basic reasons are fairly constant, we have to acknowledge that people may come in for other reasons. A review of some of the literature is encapsulated in the table on page 68.

Several other, less common motives have been described in the literature relating to informants. I am sure most law enforcement officers who have worked with informants can recall some unusual reasons why people agreed to cooperate, and there will always be some really unusual motivation, such as that of Eddie O'Hare, who, as we will see, had an unusual reason for helping the government bring down Al Capone.

Jealousy

This extremely powerful emotion can prompt people to call law enforcement with information about a criminal. Harney included jealousy under his "revenge" category, and, indeed, it is closely related. Whereas those with a revenge motivation generally direct their anger at the person in the relationship who wronged them, such as a boyfriend or a business associate, the jealous person focuses on the person who challenges the relationship.

Jealousy is another one of those transient motives that burns out relatively quickly. The jealous person really wants the love and attention of another and, to eliminate a potential rival for those affections, provides information against that person. Jealous people may have less access to their target. The chances that this information will be stretched, exaggerated, misleading, or outright false are substantial.

Cop Wannabe/James Bond

Some folks just want to "play cop." This may be the closest these people, especially those who have a criminal record, get to living the exciting life of a detective or agent they see on television. Interestingly, some people do initially approach law enforcement for this reason, but many more informants who came for other reasons eventually develop a liking for the work and begin to identify closely with their control. As a narcotics agent, I observed this phenomenon on many occasions, often heralded by the question, "What qualifications do you need for your job?"

This motivation can be very similar to the egotistical informant, but in this case the individual is cooperating because of the perceived excitement of or fascination with police work. He may carry handcuffs or even a badge. He may dress, talk, and look like the officers with whom he works. These are all signs that a control problem may be developing.

Two other categories of individuals do not qualify as informants but do provide information to law enforcement. These are people who call us because of their duty to be good citizens and those who are mentally disturbed.

Good Citizen: Patriotic Motive

The problem with these folks is not their intentions — those are definitely good. The problem here is access. Fortunately for them, but unfortunately for law enforcement, good citizens usually do not have any. The exceptions are people who come into contact with criminals in the course of their occupation or professions. For the most part, these people should have a separate classification as sources of information. Officers should cultivate these sources, especially those who can be expected to have more access than the average citizen. Examples of such people include:

- Taxi drivers
- Motel and hotel clerks or managers
- Airline employees
- Automobile salespeople
- Doormen
- Business operators in the area of interest (e.g., gun dealers, growing supplies, etc.)
- Private investigators
- Apartment managers
- Express and package delivery employees

When trying to locate a fugitive or witness, or if you need information about neighborhood activity, one of these sources can be very helpful. Some of these people may also be willing to work for other reasons; airline employees have reported suspicious activity that led to major drug or drug money seizures, some of which resulted in substantial awards to the employees.

Another type of good citizen source is the "I'm fed up and I'm not going to take it anymore" neighbor. Crime problems, especially those relating to drugs, can cause the type of public outrage that will prompt calls to law enforcement. These callers will report drug trafficking activity, the license plates of vehicles, even the presence of parole violators or wanted persons. While some of these calls can have a nuisance value, good information leading to major cases has come from this type of source. One exception to the above rules was David

Kaczynski, whose "good citizen" motivation is unquestioned. His example demonstrates that nobody should be "written off" until their information is completely evaluated.

Mentally Disturbed Individuals

Mentally disturbed individuals reach out to law enforcement all the time with information that is generally useless. Most investigators have had some contact with these people at some time or another. I received calls from one individual who insisted on being referred to as "Cosmic Cop 709." Fortunately, I was eventually able to convince this person that another agency had jurisdiction over her problem. (I did not feel too bad about this, because I gathered from our conversations that this was approximately how she got my name in the first place.)

These individuals seldom have any real access, are motivated by inner voices or other factors completely incomprehensible to the average law enforcement officer, and are incapable of being properly controlled, even if one wanted to. In the meantime, their efforts to pass along their information consume time and energy that could be better spent on more productive matters. These folks, most of whom are harmless, need to be referred to mental health professionals or counseling or simply discouraged from focusing their attention on law enforcement.

Several other motivations have been noted by other authors. The table below looks at some of the more common motivations identified by several authors who have looked at either informants or espionage agents. You will note that the number of authors who cited fear, money, revenge, and perversity is fairly high.

Survey of the Literature: Common Motivations Attributed to Informants

Motivation	Blum	Copeland	Harney	Jacobson	Lee	O'Hara	Skolnick	Wilson
Fear	X	X	X	X	X	X	X	X
Revenge	X		X	X	X	X		X
Perverse			X	X	X	X		X
Egotistical/vanity		X	X			X	X	
Mercenary	X	X	X	X	X	X	X	X
Repentance	X		X		X			
Mentally disturbed			X					
Ideology								X
Jealousy				X	X	X		
Altruism/good citizen		X	X			X	X	
Cop wannabe	X			X				

Other factors cited by these authors as having some impact on the motivation of informants include:

- Gratitude for gain of special privileges (O'Hara)
- A liking or special trust of the officer (Blum)
- Building up future favors with law enforcement (Blum)
- Bartenders, motel operators, and merchants who want to maintain good relationships with the police (Skolnick)
- Interpersonal rewards, or the reinforcement of self-esteem (Skolnick)
- Protection of the informant's criminal status (Skolnick)
- Assurance of anonymity or non-disclosure (Wilson)

In reviewing the available literature on informants and their motivation, I took special note of three studies which were performed by non-law enforcement researchers. As you can imagine, conducting a survey of officers and informants is a very difficult proposition. A great deal of secrecy surrounds the relationship, with the preference that the informants' identities be kept confidential. This is not the best climate for a researcher with a clipboard and list of probing questions, something the researchers noted.

The three studies were published as parts of books: *The Investigators: Managing FBI and Narcotics Agents,* by James Q. Wilson; *Justice Without Trial: Law Enforcement in a Democratic Society,* by Jerome H. Skolnick; and *Deceivers and Deceived,* by Richard H. Blum and Associates. All of these efforts contain special insights into the informant and his relationship with law enforcement, although they are obviously limited in scope; Wilson's study related to informants at the FBI and DEA, while Blum and Skolnick's were conducted at three California cities.

Some of the findings of these studies will be examined in greater detail in subsequent chapters. All of the studies agreed that the motivation of an informant was a critical factor in the development and management of informants. The story of Anna Sage, whose information led to the end of John Dillinger's crime spree, illustrates the importance of the informant's motivation and how that motivation can be used to achieve law enforcement's ends.

Summing Up

- Motivation is the most critical determinant in the makeup of an informant; the underworld is filled with people who have access to information about criminal activity.
- The incentives against becoming an informant are numerous and powerful. The motivation to provide information must be strong enough to overcome very strong prejudices against betrayal and informants.
- There are several common reasons why people elect to cooperate with law enforcement, all of which relate directly to the informant's perceived needs.
- Most informants have more than one motive for cooperating, and their motive may change as time goes by and their needs fluctuate.
- It is absolutely critical that the officer who is working with an informant fully understand the individual's motivation at all times.

Case Study: John Dillinger

"Never trust a woman or an automatic pistol." —John Dillinger

Almost 65 years after his death, John Dillinger's criminal career still excites popular imagination. Daring, imaginative, smart, and defiant, Dillinger blazed a wide trail throughout the American midwest in the early 1930s, pioneering the use of the automobile as an instrument of crime. His string of bank robberies, escapes, shoot-outs, and confrontations with the police displayed remarkable flair, but his end, which became legend, came as the result of an informant's cooperation with the government.

The story of Dillinger's fatal confrontation with the FBI on the evening of July 22, 1934, outside the Biograph Theater in Chicago, has been widely told in the press and on film. J. Edgar Hoover described this night as the "greatest thrill" in his FBI career. Exhibits at Hoover's headquarters featured Dillinger memorabilia for decades, and the capture of this most notorious of Public Enemies may have been more responsible for the growth and development of the Bureau into the outstanding organization it is today than any other single event. The official version of Dillinger's capture has another, darker rival, but both contain a number of important lessons about informants and their roles in criminal investigation.

Dillinger's crimes were brazen and violent. Specializing in bank robbery, America's "Public Enemy Number One", and the well-armed members of his gang selected likely targets and overpowered the employees, bank security, and even the local police before vanishing in their getaway cars. Improvements in America's network of roads and in the cars themselves made flight away from the crime scene and across state lines a simple task. Once away, Dillinger had a well-developed network of associates and hide-outs to conceal the gang between strikes.

Local law enforcement was largely unable to cope with this new type of highly mobile criminal activity. Traditional methods of apprehension, such as the rounding up of a posse, were ineffective — automobiles made it possible for the criminals to be miles away within a matter of minutes. Dillinger also had a vast number of potential targets from which he could choose, employing a "jugmarker" to reconnoiter likely looking banks or "jugs."

Almost all of the gang members had been positively identified in a number of holdups, with several outstanding warrants on each man, and lawmen across America were involved in the chase. The pursuit was extremely hazardous. Officers tracking the gang located Dillinger and others on several occasions, with spectacular shoot-outs that resulted in the deaths of a number of officers and escape of the criminals. On one highly embarrassing occasion, the FBI shot up a country lodge for hours, killing an innocent bystander before discovering that the gangsters they sought had fled.

It appeared to frustrated police chiefs, the beleaguered FBI, and the fascinated American public that the forces of the law were overmatched. Substantial rewards — $25,000 for Dillinger alone — were offered, and unrelenting publicity kept the gangs' names and faces in the public eye. Despite the notoriety, the crime spree continued; Dillinger robbed more banks in 1933 than did Jesse James in his entire career, but his string was coming to an end.

On January 15, 1934, Officer William P. "Pat" O'Malley and other officers responded to a silent robbery alarm at the First National Bank of East Chicago, IN. Confronting the heavily armed robbers, at least one of whom was carrying machine guns, O'Malley courageously opened fire, hitting Dillinger four times — all into the bandit's bulletproof vest. Dillinger then gunned down the officer, remarking later that he had no choice. "He had it coming. He stood right in the way and kept throwing slugs at me. What else could I do?" Although Dillinger subsequently denied that he was involved in the robbery or Officer O'Malley's killing, the East Chicago Police Department was satisfied that they knew who had killed their fellow officer. Now they just needed to put their hands on him. Dillinger had proved time and again how difficult this task would be, but this time the East Chicago police had an edge — the Woman in Red.

Ana Cumpanas emigrated to the U.S. from Romania in 1909 at the age of 17. Like hundreds of thousands of others who left Eastern Europe, she settled in Chicago, where she kept a small boarding house on the north side and worked as a madam at a brothel, the 42-room Kostur Hotel in nearby Gary, IN. She was also operating other brothels in East Chicago and Chicago.

Cumpanas, whose married name was Sage, was well known as "Katie of the Kostur Hotel" to police officers in northern Indiana, where she had been arrested for prostitution-related violations in the past. One Indiana governor had pardoned two previous convictions, but the reformer currently in office refused to pardon her latest. Although the charge of "operating a disorderly house" was not especially grave, certainly not in the Chicago suburbs, several of which had reputations as "wide-open" towns, they did threaten Sage in a far more serious way.

Twenty-five years after coming to America, Sage was facing deportation by the U.S. Department of Labor, which oversaw the Immigration and Naturalization Service at the time. The prostitution charges gave Immigration authorities the power to deport Sage as an undesirable alien, and, in July 1934, these efforts were well underway. During the proceedings, Sage's brothels continued in full operation, catering to both underworld characters and the more respectable citizens of the Chicago area. This activity gave Sage substantial access to the criminal element, and John Dillinger, who had returned to Chicago after a bankrobbing road trip to Minnesota, South Dakota, Wisconsin, and Iowa, may have been among them. Dillinger, who was "laying low" after changing his appearance with plastic surgery, was seeing 26-year-old Polly Hamilton, a boarder in Sage's Chicago house. Hamilton, recently divorced from her husband, a Gary, IN, police officer, was formerly employed at the Kostur Hotel and was currently working as a waitress at the S & S Sandwich Shop in Chicago. Sage, who desperately wanted to remain in the U.S., recognized the fugitive and saw a way to turn this knowledge to her advantage.

The official version of events states that on July 21, 1934, Sage contacted an acquaintance at the East Chicago Police Department, Detective Sergeant Martin Zarkovich. She told him that Dillinger was living in Chicago and had been visiting his girlfriend, Polly Hamilton, who was a boarder at Sage's house. Sage had talked with Dillinger, recognized him, and even joked with him about his photograph at the local newspaper. Now Sage wanted some help with Immigration and a piece of the reward on Dillinger's head.

Sergeant Zarkovich took this information to his superior, Captain Tim O'Neill. The two police officers were extremely interested in Sage's tip. If true, Sage could lead them directly to Pat O'Malley's killer. They immediately contacted the Chicago office of the FBI and arranged for a meeting with Special Agents Melvin Purvis and Sam Cowley, who headed the team looking for Dillinger.

That evening, Purvis and Zarkovich held a clandestine meeting with Sage in front of the Children's Memorial Hospital in Chicago. With Inspector Sam Cowley and Captain O'Neill following, they drove Sage to the lakefront, where the madam set out the conditions for her cooperation with the government. First and foremost, according to Purvis, was the matter of the Attorney General's $25,000 reward. Purvis promised Sage that she would receive some portion of the reward that was outstanding for Dillinger's capture. He says in his account of the meeting that, "She was agreeable as far as the reward situation was concerned."

Sage also wanted help with her deportation case. Purvis, who had no power in that matter, promised only that he would speak on her behalf to the Department of Labor. These assurances and the promised reward money led Sage to provide the information that would lead the officers to Dillinger. She said that she was planning to accompany Dillinger and Polly Hamilton to the movies in Chicago on the following evening. Sage did not know which film they would be seeing, but she arranged to call the officers when she had that information. This was the first time the police had advance notice of Dillinger's intentions which enabled them to plan his apprehension from a position of strength. As Purvis later said, "I believe that Mrs. Sage has performed an invaluable service, a service ranking among the highest of those needed by our country at that time."

In his initial report to FBI headquarters describing the meeting, Inspector Sam Cowley cabled Hoover:

Late yesterday afternoon Captain Oneal [sic] and Sergeant Zarkovich of the East Chicago Indiana Police Department, called Mr. Purvis and made an appointment to meet Mr. Purvis and myself at the Great Northern Hotel, at which time Sergeant Zarkovich advised that he had a confidential informant who had met and gone to theatres several times with Dillinger and his girl friend. Captain Oneal stated they would like to give the information to the division but requested to work with us which arrangement was accepted. Sergeant Zarkovich had an appointment with the informant last night at 9 o'clock and Mr. Purvis went with him. The informant proved to be a Mrs. Sage, a former prostitute of East Chicago and who has been ordered deported. She is anxious to obtain rewards and not be deported. She was advised that should her assistance bring about the appre-hension of Dillinger we wuld [sic] do all we could for her. She does not know where Dillinger lives and has no way to get in touch with him but has to wait for him to contact her through his girl friend, Betty Keel, of Fargo, North Dakota. She states Dillinger has had his face operated on, removing the mole from between his eyes and the dimple from his chin and that he has also had his fingers operated on, undoubtedly for purpose of chang-ing finger prints.

Sage's service did not end with this first meeting. She agreed to continue in her plan to attend the movie with Dillinger on the following night, Sunday, July 22, 1934. Because she did not know exactly which film they would be attending, the agents had to wait for a call from Sage to lay the trap. This call came at about 5:30 p.m. Sage whispered to Purvis that Dillinger was there and that they planned to leave for either the Biograph or the Marbro theater. She called again around 7:00 p.m. to report that they would be leaving in a few minutes.

Surveillance was quickly established at both locations. Purvis and Zarkovich, who both knew Sage on sight, were sent to the Biograph and the Marbro, respectively. As luck would have it, it was Purvis who saw Dillinger, whose appearance had not changed that much despite the recent plastic surgery, accompany two women to the ticket window of the neighborhood theater only a short walk from Sage's house. As planned, Sage was wearing an orange dress that appeared red in the marquee lights. The film at the Biograph that night was *Manhattan Melodrama*, a gangster film starring Clark Gable. Rather than trying to take Dillinger in the packed theater, the agents waited until the trio emerged at 10:40 p.m. before challenging Dillinger, who made his move and was blasted into history.

This episode, one that did so much to establish the FBI as a professional law enforcement organization in the public eye, appears on its face to involve a substantial amount of luck and indeed, chance was a factor. It would be a mistake, however, to credit Dillinger's demise to luck. Of far greater importance was the critical role played by the officers in the development and handling of their informant, Anna Sage. Further analysis of these actions would be helpful.

Analysis

By all accounts, Anna Sage was a "walk-in" who approached the police to volunteer her extremely valuable information. She initially reached out to Detective Sergeant Martin Zarkovich, with whom she was personally acquainted. Allegations were later made that Sergeant Zarkovich had been a customer at Sage's brothel and had in fact been Sage's paramour for several years. In any event, he had made sufficient personal contact with Sage in the past that when she decided to come forward she had someone in law enforcement in whom she already held some measure of trust.

As noted elsewhere in these pages, the effective law enforcement officer will be both alert to the possibility that individuals will have access to important information and will conduct his or her affairs in such a way that these people will come forward with that information. Whether or not Sergeant Zarkovich had an improper relationship with his informant, he recognized the value of her information and acted upon it by reporting the matter to his superior, Captain O'Neill.

Motivation

Sage's motivations for becoming an informant were well publicized at the time. She received $5000 of the Attorney General's $25,000 reward, although some felt she deserved more.

(Captain O'Neill and Sergeant Zarkovich each received $2500 for their assistance in appre-hending Dillinger, something which would not happen today.) By most accounts, the reward money was the primary reason for Sage's cooperation. According to Purvis, it was the first item on the agenda at her initial meeting with the FBI on July 21. As Cowley reported, "She is anxious to obtain rewards and not be deported." When she was "agreeable as far as the reward situation was concerned" negotiations moved to the subject of her pending deportation. Sage definitely had legal problems with INS which would ultimately lead to her deportation from the U.S. She sought and apparently received assurances from Special Agent Purvis that the appropriate authorities would be contacted and told of her assistance to the government.

At her deportation hearing in 1936, Sage's attorney claimed that Purvis had promised that she would not be deported. Authors have since alleged that J. Edgar Hoover, for reasons of his own, deliberately reneged on this "promise." Purvis, who resigned from the FBI less than a year after Dillinger's death, was widely reported to have left because he disagreed with the bureau's treatment of Sage. Sage, though not especially happy to be leaving the U.S., was interviewed aboard the ship that would take her back to Europe. When asked whether she felt the promise had been made and broken in a government "double cross," she replied, "I have never felt that way."

It seems probable that the need for government assistance in her immigration case was more pressing than a desire for the money, but, in any case, Sage's motivation for assisting law enforcement was positive, powerful and sufficient to keep her in the government's program until the shooting stopped. As is often the case with informants, rather than having one motive for cooperation, Sage had three and possibly four, which can be characterized as follows:

1. Mercenary, as she sought a financial reward
2. Fear, as she wanted assistance with her deportation case
3. Security, as she wanted to protect her identity
4. Possibly a desire for notoriety

If the latter two motives appear to be in conflict, this is not an uncommon phenomenon. Although people will usually act in what they believe to be their best interest, how they *perceive* that interest may change with circumstances. Before Dillinger's death, Sage might have feared his reaction to her betrayal, a fear which could have been diminished by a craving for the spotlight after his demise.

In Sage's case, she extracted a promise from Sergeant Zarkovich that her identity would be kept secret, a promise which was conveyed to Special Agent Purvis, who agreed to honor it. The officers did withhold Sage's identity until she, apparently consumed by the public's fascination with the mysterious "Woman in Red," chose to expose herself by claiming the title. Purvis, writing later about the case, said that he had kept her secret until she herself divulged it to the press. (Sage apparently made this disclosure after being picked up for questioning by the Chicago Police Department.) Whether Sage could have foreseen the incredible amount of publicity that accompanied Dillinger's demise and planned to seize some of it for herself is unknown.

Officers today, especially those in high-profile cases, must be aware that people may come forward in hopes of attaining their own celebrity. Indeed, the FBI had been dealing with a number of would-be informants who claimed knowledge of Dillinger's whereabouts but were found to be angling for personal publicity and were ignorant of any real information on the bandit. Officers should also keep in mind that motivation may change or even disappear with time or circumstances; more than one officer has found himself wondering what happened to the informant whose ardor for the chase suddenly cooled.

Finally, the secondary motivation which is present in most such cases — that of a trust in the law enforcement officers — was also present in this case. An untrustworthy or obviously duplicitous officer will not inspire the confidence of a potential informant. If Sage had been "turned off" by or if she mistrusted Zarkovich or Purvis she might well have decided to keep what she knew to herself, no matter how badly she needed the money or help with her case. As is always the case, investigators must be alert for any perverse motives which might have inspired an informant such as Anna Sage to contact law enforcement. There is substantial evidence that she did indeed have at least one such motive and that it was overlooked in the 24-hour charge to catch Dillinger.

John Dillinger stole a lot of money in his relatively short career, not much of which was ever recovered. At the time of his death he had about $7.70 in his pocket. The large roll of $100 bills — what Dillinger called his "get money" that the robber carried everywhere with him in case of emergency — was never found. There was speculation at the time that Sergeant Zarkovich had lifted the money from Dillinger's dying body. In any event, at least some of the money was likely kept at Dillinger's last hideout. But where was this place? Sage told Purvis she did not know where Dillinger was staying. The secret may have died with Dillinger, but two keys were recovered from his person. One was found to fit the door of Anna Sage's house, the other fit a locked closet in one of the rooms. When opened by police, the closet was empty.

Did police informant Anna Sage plot Dillinger's death or capture in order to gain sole control of the stolen loot she knew was under her roof? It is possible that she did, or that she merely took advantage of the situation to claim more than the government's reward money. In either case, any investigator who is dealing with an informant — *especially a walk-in* — should always be aware that there may be an agenda other than the one on the table. By asking "*cui bono?*" and closely questioning the informant at every opportunity, such perverse motives may reveal themselves. Certainly Purvis would have had no reason to question the motivations expressed by Sage in their meeting. He also had little time in which to evaluate either the informant or her information — less than 24 hours elapsed from the time he met with Sage to her entry into the Biograph theater. He might have wondered a bit after the fact, however.

The Indiana State Police (ISP) advised the FBI on July 27, 1934, five days after the shooting, that Sage, Hamilton, and Zarkovich had conspired to "put Dillinger on the spot in order that they might gain possession of Dillinger's wealth." In something of an ironic twist, this information came to the ISP by way of a confidential informant. The possibility of yet another perverse motivation exists. This will be discussed along with the question of exactly how much access Anna Sage really had to John Dillinger.

Access

Once again, the official version holds that Sage came by her access by accident. She maintained a small boarding house in Chicago in addition to her prostitution-related activity in nearby Gary and East Chicago. One of her boarders was a waitress named Polly Hamilton, who, by sheer coincidence, happened to be dating the man Sage suddenly, and to her great horror, recognized as Dillinger. This was the story told by Sage to Purvis on July 21 and which was reported by Cowley to Hoover on the following day. (In his teletype, Cowley identified Hamilton as "Betty Keel." Hamilton was also known as Rita Keele, her married name.)

Sage was careful to say that her access was extremely limited. She had only known the man who called himself "James Lawrence" for a short time. She did not know where he lived and he never actually confirmed his true identity. She said that Hamilton knew more about "Lawrence" and her own contacts were limited to conversation and an occasional visit to a nearby movie house. As Inspector Cowley reported, "She does not know where Dillinger lives and has no way to get in touch with him but has to wait for him to contact her through his girl friend, Betty Keel, of Fargo, North Dakota."

Although this story was accepted at the time by Purvis and the FBI, it is most probably not true. There is no question that Sage did have the access to Dillinger that she claimed, as shown by his presence with her at the theater on July 22. However, Sage undoubtedly came by this access as a result of her criminal activity and underworld connections, exactly how all good informants are supposed to get their information.

Sage's occupation provided far better access to information of interest to law enforcement. As a brothel keeper and madam, Sage operated on the fringes of both legitimate and underworld societies. Her clientele included criminals and not-so-upright citizens, as well as, by some accounts, law enforcement officers such as Sergeant Zarkovich. Houses of prostitution frequently rely upon organized crime for protection and support, making them information bazaars and good sources for potential informants.

Although information may be available in great abundance under the cat house roof, those possessing it are less often motivated to disclose it to the police. Dillinger, a ladies man, was known to frequent prostitutes — Polly Hamilton was one such. He was also well connected in East Chicago, having maintained hideouts in that town. There were rumors that Dillinger had connections to the East Chicago Police Department, even to the extent that police officers in northern Indiana actively conspired with the gang to "set up" bank robberies.

Sage's story that she learned of Dillinger's identity after a brief relationship with Polly Hamilton is suspect on a couple of counts, although it must have sounded good at the time. Evidence which came to light later on seems to show that Sage's access was much greater than she initially let on. In fact, Dillinger was apparently living in the Sage house, and had been for at least two weeks prior to his death. Keys to the premises and interior rooms were found on his person after the shooting. Several items belonging to Dillinger which were stored at the Sage house were recovered on July 23 from a nearby canal. These included a machine gun and a bulletproof vest. It is now believed that these items were removed by Sage after the shooting, as she had the other keys to the rooms, and were disposed of to prevent the police from concluding that she had been hiding Dillinger.

Sage did not tell the FBI about her ties to Dillinger, something which must always call into question the motivation behind her cooperation with investigators. This question of how much access Sage really had illustrates very clearly the need for investigators to check and recheck the statements of confidential informants. In the Dillinger case, the question of access was not critical; Sage knew Dillinger and knew where he would be at a time when the agents could apprehend him. Even this limited amount of information would prove to be enough to get the job done.

It is *never* good for an informant to lie or deceive his or her handlers, however. This type of deception makes it much more difficult for the investigators to make valid decisions about the case and the uses to which the information may be put. By lying about the extent of her access, Sage could have jeopardized the case and arguably placed members of the public at risk.

If Dillinger really *had* been living at the Sage boarding house and if Sage had truthfully reported this fact, agents could have apprehended him there, or caught him coming to or going from the house. Because Sage had equal access to Dillinger's room, the agents could have even laid a trap inside the room or in an interior hallway. Many more options would have been available, but, as it happened, they were forced to take Dillinger in public, precipitating the gunfire that left two bystanders wounded and Dillinger dead.

The question of Sage's access, then, is a critical one, as it will always be with any informant. "What does she know and how does she know it?" must be answered very early in the officer-informant relationship. This question will be answered by way of a thorough debriefing followed by extensive cross-checking and corroboration. No blame attaches to Purvis or Cowley in this case, as they were relying on a fellow officer, Zarkovich, and had very little time to sort things out.

Many informants derive their value to law enforcement from their intimate association with the subjects of an investigation. Some, such as Joseph Valachi or Sammy "The Bull" Gravano, are long-time associates of top-level mobsters and possess information about criminal activity because of their own participation in it. They have access because of their trusted positions in the gang. This was not the case with Anna Sage. She was not an active participant in the gang's activities and knew nothing of past or future crimes, and even if her access was greater than she allowed, she knew little more than who Dillinger was and where he would be on the night of July 22, 1934. For Public Enemy Number One, who is alleged to have told an associate, "Never trust a woman or an automatic pistol," this was more than enough access and far too much trust. Ironically, on the night he was led to his death by a woman, John Dillinger had a .32-caliber automatic pistol in his pocket.

Control

This was not a long-term investigation or one that was especially complicated. The officers met with Sage on July 21 and confronted Dillinger on the following evening. Control was quickly and reliably established at the initial contact, however, enabling the officers to complete the operation. At the initial meeting, Sage developed the confidence in Purvis and the FBI that would allow her to transfer her loyalty from the criminals to the police. Purvis' assurances led Sage to believe that her best interests would be served by cooperating with the government. All of her subsequent actions furthered her commitment to this change of loyalty.

The officers made it clear to Sage what was required of her in return for their assistance. She was given a means to contact Purvis and instructions about when to call. As a result, Sage was able to call the FBI office even while Dillinger was at her house, relaying the critical information in a timely manner. Despite some last-minute confusion about which film they planned to see, Sage and her controlling agent had an effective plan, in which each carried out his or her part.

Although the informant-officer relationship was relatively short term, what followed indicates that the officers might have had some control problems with this particular informant. She quickly abandoned her desire for anonymity and told the press of her role in Dillinger's demise. This is a situation which most officers would prefer to avoid and which the FBI sought to prevent by moving Sage away from Chicago, first to Michigan, then to Los Angeles.

One of the means available to the officers to control Sage was the promised reward. This was something Sage actively sought and which the agents could withhold until they were satisfied that Sage's end of the bargain had been fulfilled. This conclusion was evidently reached on October 11, 1934, when $5000 was paid to Sage by Inspector Cowley in Los Angeles. Before receiving the funds, Sage was required to sign a receipt, something which should be standard practice in all cases in which law enforcement officers provide informants with any sort of payment. The receipt in this case is worded somewhat differently from those used today and required, in addition to Sage's signature, that she provide a full set of finger-prints. The receipt is reproduced below.

<u>R E L E A S E and R E C E I P T</u>

WHEREAS, THE UNITED STATES DEPARTMENT OF JUSTICE did employ me to secure information leading to the apprehension of JOHN DILLINGER, alias Frank Sullivan, and

WHEREAS, I, ANNA SAGE, did secure and deliver personally to an official of the DIVISION OF INVESTIGATION, UNITED STATES DEPART-MENT OF JUSTICE information as to the whereabouts of the said JOHN DILLINGER at particular time, now therefore,

KNOW YE, ALL WHOM THESE PRESENTS MAY CONCERN, That I, ANNA SAGE, for and in consideration of the sum of five thousand dollars

($5,000) lawful money of the United States of America, to me in hand paid by S. P. Cowley, known to me as an official of the UNITED STATES DEPARTMENT OF JUSTICE, the receipt thereof in full is hereby acknowledged, have remised, released and forever discharged, and by these presents do, for my heirs, executors and administrators, remise, release and forever discharge the UNITED STATES DEPARTMENT OF JUSTICE, or division thereof, and/or any of its officials, employees or the ATTORNEY GENERAL thereof, it, his or their heirs, executors, successors, and administrators, of and from all and all manner of action and actions, cause and causes of actions, suits, debts, dues, sums of money, reckonings, convenants, contracts, controversies, agreements, promises, variances, trespasses, damages, judgments, extents, claims and demands whatsoever, in law or in equity, which against I ever had, now have or which my heirs, executors, or administrators hereafter can, shall or may have be reason of the said employment, or by reason of any other matter resulting therefrom or connected therewith in any manner whatsoever from the beginning of the world to the date of these presents.

IN WITNESS WHEREOF, I have hereunto set my hand, seal and fingerprints this 11th day of October at Los Angeles, Calif., in the year one thousand nine hundred thirty-four.

Modern practice does not require informants to indemnify the government against claims dating back to the "beginning of the world," but a clearly worded receipt is still a good very good idea.

A word about security is also appropriate. Both Sage and the officers were well aware of the potential danger to those giving information against Dillinger. This danger included the possibility that corrupt local police officers might disclose the identity of a potential informant or a planned trap for the bandit. With this in mind, everyone involved took effective security precautions. Their initial rendezvous took place at a neutral location; rather than meeting at the FBI offices or Sage's boarding house, Sage was told to meet the agents in a parked car in front of the Children's Memorial Hospital. Sage approached the parked car occupied by Purvis and Zarkovich, walked past, checking her surroundings, then returned to meet the officers. There were two officers present in the car, always a very wise precaution, and another two in a second car nearby. Security in this case was handled very professionally by everyone concerned, including Sage, which meant the only person to get hurt in this case was John Dillinger.

Purvis did make efforts to preserve the secret of Sage's identity after the fact, although media speculation about the "Woman in Red" was intense. Protection of Sage was critical, because members of Dillinger's gang, notably Lester Gillis (a.k.a. Baby Face Nelson), by everyone's reckoning a vicious killer, were still at large. Public opinion was not universally in Sage's favor, and threats were made that she would be killed to avenge Dillinger. The FBI, which was already facing a storm of criticism for "gunning down" Dillinger without giving him a "fair chance," could ill-afford the revenge killing of their informant. An inability by law enforcement to protect either the identity or the person of individuals who provide confidential information is extremely discouraging for future informants. Sage had insisted that her identity be kept secret, and the FBI did its level best to live up to their commitment. Once the cat was out of the bag, Purvis and Cowley took the steps necessary to keep Sage out of harm's way. She no doubt rested easier after Gillis was killed, although that same shoot-out took the life of Sam Cowley, the man who paid her the $5000.

As to the other promise, the one regarding Sage's deportation, Purvis attempted to honor that one, as well. He spoke on her behalf to his superiors and to the Labor Department, none of which did any good. Sage was deported from Ellis Island to Romania after exhausting her appeals. In one futile effort before she left, she contacted Indiana Governor Paul McNutt, asking for a pardon on the prostitution conviction that underpinned her deportation. The governor inquired whether Sage had done anything to assist the state of Indiana in capturing Dillinger and was told by the Indiana State Police that she had not. Governor McNutt then declined Indiana's help.

In retrospect this seems an unjustified and even spiteful decision. Sage had, all agree, initially provided her information concerning Dillinger to an Indiana officer, Sergeant Zarkovich of the East Chicago Police Department. She was never in control of how the investigation was conducted, as no informant ever should be. It was the decision of Sergeant Zarkovich and his supervisor, Captain Tim O'Neill, to take the case to the FBI, and Dillinger, though wanted in Indiana, was not even living in the state at the time.

In fact, Governor McNutt's decision was probably based in part on the Indiana State Police information that Sage and Zarkovich had "put Dillinger on the spot" to be killed. This information was undoubtedly passed on to Governor McNutt, who would have been less than sympathetic to Sage's appeal. This situation emphasizes the need for officers to refrain from promising more than they can deliver. Purvis promised only to speak to the immigration authorities on Sage's behalf and emphasized that he could make no guarantees. As Inspector Cowley wrote on July 22, "She was advised that should her assistance bring about the apprehension of Dillinger we wuld [sic] do all we could for her." These assurances were enough for Sage at the time.

Summing Up

The Dillinger case still fascinates many in the U.S. and abroad. Several Dillinger-related websites can be found on the Internet, and a number of books have been published about the most notorious American outlaw since Jesse James. As a study in informant handling, the case is also very instructive, although many troubling questions are raised by examining Anna Sage's short but eventful informant career. The answers to those questions may never be known in her case, but they must still be asked by investigators today:

1. What is this individual's motivation for providing information?
2. Who benefits if the information is acted upon?
3. How much access does this individual have to the subject or the activity?
4. What does she know and how does she know it?
5. Can this individual's information be corroborated and how?
6. Can this individual be controlled so that the investigation can be successfully completed?

In sum, Anna Sage was the right person, in the right place, at exactly the right time, which is very fortunate for law enforcement, in general, and the FBI, in particular, though not so fortunate for Mr. Dillinger. The professional manner in which the law enforcement officers, especially Melvin Purvis and Sam Cowley, handled their informant and her information converted a stroke of luck into a victory in the war on crime.

Informant Development

5

> "'I have come to claim the twenty pounds reward offered by the Farmer's Union for information concerning Francis Joseph McPhillip,' he said in a deep low voice." —Liam O'Flaherty, *The Informer*

> "All a man can betray is his conscience." —Joseph Conrad, *Under Western Skies*

Motivation, Trust, and Conscience

In the life of an informant, there is one moment, one fragment in time in which The Decision is made. The process by which this decision is reached will vary from person to person, but every informant has come to this moment of truth. While each arrives at his or her own pace and in a different way, all have three impelling influences acting upon them, all of which must be addressed before the bar can be crossed.

Authors who have written about informants in law enforcement before tend to explain the decision solely in terms of motivation. They propose that if the proper motivation is present, if the appropriate needs are met, the individual will decide to cooperate with the government. In fact, although it is true that motivation is one of the elements (motivation, access, and control) which define an informant, it is only one of the three factors that influence the *decision* to inform.

It will not be enough to merely lay a motivation on the table and expect that someone, however desperately they may need that which is offered, will pick it up. The officer who hopes to develop informants must understand and address the other factors that influence a decision before succeeding in the recruitment. Fortunately, all three influencing factors are something over which the officer has some control. This enables the officer to assist the individual in making the right judgment. (And, from a moral and ethical standpoint, if we don't feel this is the "right" decision, we shouldn't be trying to develop this person in the first place.) Their judgment will be based upon the additional factors of *trust* and *conscience*, neither of which is normally associated with the average informant. Together with *motivation*, however, these forces will combine to influence the outcome.

The process of informant development takes the officer into new areas of human psychology. In many ways this process is much closer to salesmanship than what we would normally think of as "police work." In promoting the cooperation option, we are attempting to influence a major decision on the part of the would-be informant. This conclusion may have life-altering, even fatal consequences; it is certainly as significant to many informants as the purchase of a home or the resolution to marry.

This is a crossing of the Rubicon. Although an individual can be assisted in the crossing, he cannot be forced or carried. Ultimately, he must decide to cross on his own and his judgment to do so will be based upon his trust in the officer and the dictates of his own conscience.

Trust

In the beginning of all human relationships, there is trust. Ironically, the officer-informant relationship, which exists solely because one participant is in the midst of a betrayal, is also built upon trust. And trust plays an important part in the individual's decision to become an informant. Imagine for a moment the position of a person, let's call her Monica, who is being asked to betray some of her allegedly criminal associates. Monica knows that to become an informant, to testify against or wear a body recorder to meetings with these people, is a life-altering step, from which there will be no return to the *status quo ante*. Perhaps she is facing a long prison term and needs the credit for providing substantial assistance to the government to avoid spending many years in jail. She weighs this against the consequences of betrayal.

She has a lot of factors to consider before making such a big judgment. As we saw in an earlier chapter, people rely upon personal experience or the confidence we have in others to make decisions. When Monica is first approached, she knows none of the strangers who are talking to her. She has a tough call to make and she needs more input. Who can she trust?

Melvin Purvis, the FBI agent who got John Dillinger and several other notorious criminals in 1930s Chicago, explained the importance of obtaining an informant's trust in his memoirs, *American Agent*:

> *An informer is an important wellspring of facts. He is often, too, a consummate liar. The brazen individual who comes directly to a special agent's office and proposes to sell information has, more frequently than not, no information to sell. The valuable informer is more cautious than that. He finds out first if he can trust you; he asks you to meet him on a distant corner or in a dark alley; he may even, at a later date, come to your home. But he is always cautious. The reason is obvious; he is risking a bullet in the back.*
>
> *When I came to Chicago, my first job was to build up my own personal sources of information. The most precious asset an investigator may have is a reputation in the underworld as a square shooter; when he gives his word he must keep it. The grapevine of the underworld is pretty accurate about these matters, and it is rather curious to find that the very men who hate you murderously may still have absolute faith in your word. Square shooting is part of the Bureau of Investigation's tradition; it is well known that when the "G" is concerned, confidential information remains confidential information. No one knew the identities of informers with whom I had transactions; and I expected the special agents serving with me to be equally close-mouthed about their own sources. They were."*

In this statement, Purvis touches on three of the keys to confidence: trust in the officer's word, trust in the officer's discretion, and trust in the officer's competence. Think back to

Monica's example. What is she going to do? She does not know yet what her decision will be, but she is dead solid certain that she is *not* going to cooperate with anyone she *doesn't* trust. Would you?

The answer is so obvious that officers sometimes overlook it in their haste to "flip" the would-be informant. If all human relationships begin with trust, how can the relationship the officer proposes begin otherwise? It cannot. For a real-life example, look no farther than a real-life Monica. The now-infamous Ms. Lewinsky was first approached in January 1998, taken to a hotel room, surrounded by agents and attorneys, and asked to cooperate in a case against the President. She refused. Asked later why she made this decision, she testified, "I didn't believe them," and, bluntly, "I didn't trust them."

So, trust was certainly a factor in this situation, as it is in others involving informants. Even from the moment of first contact with the prospective informant, the officer *must* be trustworthy. Comedian Mort Sahl once asked, with reference to Richard Nixon, "Would you buy a second-hand car from this man?" Buying a car is one of those decisions people make, one in which the car salesperson, a total stranger, has quite a bit of input. Furthermore, used-car salesmen do not have the best reputation for trustworthiness, making that buying decision even more difficult. In discussing trust, Samuel Johnson, the British lexicographer, commented, "We are inclined to believe those whom we do not know because they have never deceived us." Even though we may be inclined in this direction, we seek additional information before making a really important decision. If we were really buying a used car (say, a second-hand Yugo), we might not rely so heavily on Mr. Nixon, but instead we may validate his claims by our personal examination, a test drive, or some other employment of our own senses or experience.

We might also obtain the input of a source in whom we already have some confidence. Perhaps we have a copy of *Consumer Reports* which describes that model Yugo as being a good buy. Or, we might take a mechanically inclined friend to the lot to check things out and render a trusted opinion. Finally, we could go to a dependable associate who might recommend "that chap, Dick Nixon," who always does right by his customers.

Some of these alternatives were available to the indecisive Ms. Lewinsky on the afternoon and evening of January 16, 1998. Like many people who are wrestling with the decision to become an informant or not, she knew nothing more about the process than what she had seen on television. Her personal experiences were not going to be much help. She sought the advice of people she already trusted — Linda Tripp, her mother, her father, her father's attorney — before finally making her decision.

The same set of problems confronts anyone who is in Monica's position, whether they are a walk-in drug addict seeking money or a diplomat selling secrets to a foreign power. The key question of "Can I trust this person?" must be answered affirmatively before the person will step over the threshold. The officer answers the question through establishment of a rapport with the informant, something which we will examine more closely later in this chapter. In Ms. Lewinsky's case, the agents and attorneys from the Independent Counsel's office were unable to establish this rapport.

"Trustworthy: deserving of trust or confidence." This is the assurance the decision-maker seeks. She is looking for some evidence that, in this matter of gravest personal importance, the officer is dependable, reliable, and capable — someone she can trust. Once she got some additional advice and assistance in making her decision, Ms. Lewinsky eventually concluded that she could indeed trust the government's representatives.

Trust in the Officer's Word

Purvis said that "The most precious asset an investigator may have is a reputation in the underworld as a square shooter; when he gives his word he must keep it." This is, as any informant would tell you, absolutely correct. Viewing things from the perspective of the informant, nothing could be more important.

Start by telling the truth and not making any promises you cannot or do not intend to keep. Lying to someone to gain his cooperation is a particularly despicable undertaking. Whatever is gained as a result must inevitably be lost to its inherent contradictions. As we have already discussed, getting caught in this sort of treachery is very destructive to relationships. Getting caught in a lie or failing to deliver on a promise will certainly make it very difficult for the informant to trust the officer again.

During World War II, the Germans were approached by Elyesa Bazna, the valet of the British ambassador to Turkey, who offered to sell secrets from the ambassador's safe for money. For an extended period, the spy known as "Cicero" passed along extremely valuable information stolen from the unwitting diplomat. The Nazis paid generously — over $1,200,000 — for the papers, which they initially believed had "almost incalculable value." German trust in their spy's information faded, and, in a bit of treachery of their own, Cicero was paid in counterfeit British pound notes.

Bazna relied upon the Nazis' assurance and was deceived. Not only would he never again trust the Germans' word on anything of importance, any other prospective agent who heard the story about the counterfeit money would doubt that word as well. A betrayal always affects more than the betrayer and the betrayed and in this case could easily damage all future officer-informant relationships.

Assuming that the officer is acting in good faith and that his word is good, how is the prospective informant to know this? Bazna initially walked in late at night to the residence of a German diplomat for whom he had previously worked as a valet. Like many informants, he sought out someone with whom he had a point of common reference. Many informants go to the FBI because they know of the FBI's very well-cultivated reputation for dependability, competence, and discretion. Other potential informants go to a trusted associate, often their attorney, for advice. This was the course Ms. Lewinsky took. After her lawyers negotiated an immunity deal, Monica finally trusted her government enough to take the big step.

In the absence of such common reference points, it essentially comes down to two people across a table. Can I trust this person? Once again, ask yourself how *you* normally answer this question. What is the criteria? Much of the answer has to do with rapport, which we are going to cover in more depth shortly. The rest has to do with being the kind of person *you* would trust.

Trust in the Officer's Discretion

Once again, Purvis says, "Square shooting is part of the Bureau of Investigation's tradition; it is well known that when the 'G' is concerned, confidential information remains confidential information. No one knew the identities of informers with whom I had transactions." Very few informants go to law enforcement knowing, or even suspecting, that their name and information are going to be broadcast to the world. Public exposure is not one of the things most "confidential informants" sign up to achieve, and many are obsessive in their desire that their names be concealed. For good reason. Leaks can get people killed. Premature disclosure of an informant's identity could destroy a case which took months to develop and on which an informant's reward, sentence, freedom, or life may depend. The prospective informant has every right to expect that "confidential" means confidential.

There are legal restrictions on how far law enforcement can go in keeping the informant's identity a complete secret. The filing of criminal charges may require disclosure of the informant, especially if that person will be a witness at trial. Court decisions such as *Brady v. Maryland* (272 U.S. 82, 1963), require production of material that might be exculpatory, and statutes such as the Jencks act force the prosecutor to turn over statements made by witnesses.

Promising that the informant will never, never, never be exposed is very risky and should be avoided unless the officer knows for certain that the promise can be kept.

In a daring robbery on January 2, 1972, five to seven armed men looted safe-deposit boxes at the luxurious Hotel Pierre in New York City. As much as $4 million in jewelry and securities were taken from the boxes. Leads to the robbers were few, but the case was resolved quickly when an FBI informant identified the principals, who were quickly rounded up. Some were found to be in possession of stolen jewelry and it appeared that the case was headed for a successful prosecution.

Ultimately, however, the FBI refused to disclose the identity of the informant or to produce him for any court proceedings. They had made a promise of anonymity, and they intended to keep it (even though the crooks undoubtedly knew who had done them in). Without the informant's testimony, the more serious robbery charges could not be sustained, and all of those apprehended pleaded guilty to lesser crimes such as possession of stolen property and entering a dwelling with a weapon. This was not the result desired by the New York Police Department or the Manhattan district attorney, but it certainly emphasizes the lengths to which the FBI was prepared to go to live up to its word to the informant.

The officer should demonstrate from the moment of first contact with the potential informant that discretion is important. The procedures for registering informants should be explained, with emphasis on the safeguards against disclosure. If the informant is a mercenary type, the officer can emphasize the use of code numbers or pseudonyms on all official documents, including receipts for payment (if that is the department's policy, of course). The officer must never confirm the identity of another informant, even if that person's name is in the newspaper. A defendant-informant will often ask about the informant who cooperated in the case against him. This is a test of the officer's discretion, one the officer must pass.

Informants know they are taking a major step, one filled with physical and emotional hazards. If they believe the officer is going to put their business on the street, they will probably choose to take that business elsewhere. If, in everything the officer says and does, he mirrors the individual's concerns about safety and discretion, this person is much more likely to agree to work with that officer.

Trust in the Officer's Competence

This is another difficult call for someone to make on a first impression in the absence of any other facts. Still, one can see how important the officer's competence might be to someone who is making The Decision. The informant's freedom or some other important need may depend on how well or badly the officer manages the investigation. Would you, if placed in the same situation, want to work with some loser who couldn't do the job right? Can the individual rely on the officer's proficiency?

The prospective informant has a couple of clues on this score, and the officer can provide a couple more. First of all, unless he is a walk-in who is there by luck of the draw, the informant is sitting there in the interview room in front of the officer who has already proven some ability to conduct an investigation. This may be the officer who arrested the would-be informant or some of that person's associates. Second, the officer is usually an investigator or at least a law enforcement professional, who can be presumed to have some training, experience, and proven abilities, or else he or she would not be there in the interview room. Also, by having ready answers to the informant's questions and objections, the officer can prove knowledge of the law, procedure, and how to get the job done.

Real competence shows. Most of us, if we turn on a televised sports event, can immediately tell if those playing are at the high school, college, or professional level. Consider the others in your workplace. Think about the least competent person in the office. This person could be the rookie or the semi-retiree or anyone in between. Now, imagine this person in an interview room, trying to develop an informant. Do you think there might be visual or other clues a potential informant might pick up on that would indicate the officer was lacking in skills or ability? If you were an informant, would you agree to work for that person? Project your own competence. In the presence of the informant, behave at all times as a professional. An assured attitude of self-confidence will inspire similar confidence in the person you are trying to persuade.

A final reminder about establishing trust in these three areas. The officer must not lie to the prospective informant. Lying comes in several forms, all bad from the standpoint of establishing confidence. There may be a temptation to exaggerate the strength of the case against the individual, hoping to convince him it is too powerful to fight. I have done it myself, but it is almost never really necessary. They know what they did, and the fact that you are there and they are in handcuffs usually allows them to conclude that you know it, too. It is a better idea to quietly state the obvious, emphasize your experience in many previous, similar cases, and let the individual draw all the right conclusions. This is especially true if the individual got an attorney, because you may have to deal with the same lawyer for future informants. If the lawyer catches the officer in a lie, word will travel quickly. Establishing trust in this and future cases will be much more difficult.

Conclusion

Trust is the beginning of all human relationships. Without trust in the officer, potential informants who are contemplating the betrayal of one trust will not agree to cooperate. In proving that we are trustworthy, the law enforcement officer is essentially selling himself or herself to the would-be informant. Nothing — not an all-beef hot dog, a used Yugo, or an immunity agreement — gets "sold" until the buyer has some confidence in the seller.

Once again, a short but very telling exchange from Monica Lewinsky's Grand Jury testimony speaks for others in her situation:

A juror: *And did you take them up on that offer?*
The witness: *No.*
A juror: *Why not?*
The witness: *Because I didn't trust them.*

The Area of Conscience

Conscience is defined as the inner sense in every person of what is right or wrong in one's actions or motives. Conscience impels us toward the right action and is one of the obstacles to betrayal. Contrary to what Mr. Conrad said, people can betray more than their conscience, but it is certainly one of the first things to go.

As we have seen, people are conditioned by nature and nurture against treachery. Conscience, H.L. Mencken's "inner voice that tells us someone may be looking," reminds the betrayer of the consequences of the act. An insistent mistress, the conscience commands but everyone responds differently to the voice. What will your conscience allow? Every person will have a different answer. Moreover, their answer will change as the area of their conscience expands or broadens.

The "to talk or not to talk" question obviously troubles the conscience. Although we know that cooperating with the government in its war on crime is almost always in everyone's best interest, the conscience of a criminal, or for that matter anyone who is preparing to betray a trust, can be sorely troubled at the prospect. This puts the officer in something of a dilemma, because we do not want people to do something that is against their conscience. Doing so makes the person stressed and conflicted. These characteristics in an informant are dangerous, as Sarah Jane Moore demonstrated.

What we do want is for the informant to act in accord with his or her conscience — essentially, to search their conscience and receive a message from the inner voice that the proposed action is "right." Once this message is obtained, the informant can act without any of the pangs that trouble someone who is ignoring their still, small voice. This sounds harder than it is, because, in fact, people come to this sort of accommodation every day.

Think of the conscience as an internal barrier on the road to cooperation. In some people, the barrier will be relatively high, maybe even blocking the way. In others, the obstacle, if any, is fairly low, amounting to not much more than a speed bump along the road someone wants to travel. And, for many, the barrier exists as nothing more than a road sign, barely registered in passing. Still, nobody is going to agree to become an informant until they have negotiated the barrier. The officer is not so much trying to break down the barrier as to just move it around a little. Given time and the right motivation, the informant will do all the moving. Mencken also described conscience as "the mother-in-law whose visit never ends." We in law enforcement do not want the visit to end — a conscience is a good thing in any person. We just want the "mother-in-law" to pass along the message that cooperating with the government in the war on crime is "right."

Defining the Area of Conscience

How can we achieve this objective? Think about your own experience. Sure, your conscience nags you about the big things, but you also hear from it on the little ones, reminding you to do right by yourself and others. But none of us does right all the time. Perhaps you know you really *should* go to the gym but you *want* to go out for a couple of beers. Lots of people manage to overcome their conscience and end up at the pub. When they do, two things have happened. First, the conscience has been overcome, though possibly not without some guilt. Second, with the barrier moved, the next time the issue arises it is going to be much easier to make the same decision your conscience told you was "wrong" the first time.

Everyone has an area of conscience that allows them to do certain things and not others. This area is changeable, although it is pretty rare for the area to narrow. Mostly, it just gets broader with every compromise we make with our conscience. Security experts have long known this principle applies to employee theft. Somebody who will steal some small things will have less trouble making the progression to stealing bigger things. The same principle applies to police corruption, which is one of the reasons why accepting small gratuities is forbidden. In both of these examples, the individual's area of conscience for theft or bribe-taking has expanded. That is why the regulators of those crimes like to nip this expansion in the bud.

We define the area of conscience in an informant through a review of word and deed. What the informant *says* and what he or she *does* are equally important in evaluating where that person stands with respect to his or her conscience. Being a good listener always pays dividends in dealing with informants. The informant will often raise objections to actions the officer proposes. The officer must listen carefully to learn whether the objection is based upon conscience or some other concern.

In talking with people about issues where our conscience is consulted, we project echoes of that inner voice. A sensitive listener will hear those echoes and make adjustments for them. One of the most graphic examples is found in the continuing saga of Monica Lewinsky, whose experiences form the basis of the case study for this chapter. When confronted by investigators and asked to cooperate with the government in a case against her lover, Bill Clinton, Monica's conscience spoke. She described her reaction to the Grand Jury:

And I was — I didn't — I didn't want to cooperate. I mean, I didn't — I just kept thinking to myself, well — well, I'll just say I made it all up. I'll just — I'll just — I — I couldn't imagine — I couldn't imagine doing this to the President. And I felt so guilty for having told Linda and that she had done all this.

Her inner voice spoke and Monica listened. Her area of conscience might have allowed her to cooperate in a case against someone else, but, at the time she was approached, it was not going to let her inform against the one she called her "sexual soulmate."

On occasion, an informant may say something to the effect that, "I'll tell you about him, but not about her." The informant's position may be based upon the fact that his or her conscience is not yet prepared to allow the betrayal of that second person. (There could be other reasons, too, such as a desire to protect a connection or business associate.)

Actions speak at least as loud as words. Monica capped her conscience-stricken session with the investigators with a decision to walk out, declining to cooperate. What the informant does, either at the time of the initial approach or later, after agreeing to cooperate allows us to gauge the area of conscience. Monica Lewinsky was presented with a number of possible scenarios which could have arisen as a result of her agreement to work with the investigators. "Cooperation, an interview, telephone calls, body wires, and testimony" were discussed. It is not uncommon for an informant to agree to do one thing in the course of an investigation — make a statement, for example — but refuse to do something else, such as wear a body recorder. Again, the informant may have other reasons for taking this stand, but conscience is often a factor.

The officer cannot allow this situation to continue. For one thing, control is ceded to the informant — she, or rather her conscience, and not the officer is deciding who will be investigated and how, not a decision the informant is supposed to make. Also, this reluctance indicates that the informant is not fully committed to cooperation, something else we need to change. We effect this change, not by forcing someone to act against their conscience, but by broadening the area in which it operates.

Broadening the Area of Conscience

There are two ways to expand the area of conscience in an informant. One is quick and direct, the other takes a little more time. Both are equally effective. The direct approach entails not only the outlining of a motivation to cooperate, but a conscience salving proposal as well. Remember that your conscience does not keep you from doing things, but rather from enjoying them. Someone who *wants* to cooperate may still need something besides the reason on the table. People will justify or rationalize their cooperation based upon the factor which allows them to quiet their conscience.

For example, Nelson Cantellops, who testified against Vito Genovese, had a powerful motivation for doing so; he was facing a lengthy sentence on narcotics charges. He did not agree to cooperate, though, until he felt he and his family had been abandoned by his mob associates. The factor we normally think of as being the prime motivator — fear — got Cantellops on the road, but only his feeling that he had been misused, even betrayed, by those he trusted carried him past the barrier. Something similar happened with Joe Valachi, who thought the same Vito Genovese had put a contract out on him.

In developing an informant, it costs the officer nothing to address both issues at the time the recruitment pitch is made. Explain the motivation: "You're looking at a 20-year sentence with a mandatory minimum of 10 years." This is the reason the individual should agree to cooperate with the government, the need that cooperation can fulfill. Now the officer can propose a rationale (or several) for *why* this cooperation is the "right" thing to do: "Your pals have ditched you." "Who's paying for your lawyer?" "Who's going to go your bail?" "Where are the people who got you in this mess?" "They would do the same thing to you if they were sitting here." "Is it fair for you to have to take this on your own?" "Why should you have to be the only one who has to pay?" "You've got to look out for yourself." These questions give the individual a couple of things to mull over. In Cantellops' case, the narcotics agent put it this way: "You know as well as I do, Nelson, that the mob's letting you go down the drain. No lawyers, no bail. Nobody cares what happens to you. You can go to jail for the rest of your life and they won't raise a finger to help you."

This puts the focus on other people, his associates, rather than on the informant's actions. Those are the people who are the reason why he is in this jam. In this way it is perceived that if there is a betrayal involved here, *they* betrayed *him* first. From this perspective, the informant essentially views himself as a victim.

From a psychological standpoint, it is much easier to betray somebody if they betrayed you first. In fact, the rationalization process for practically every betrayal in world history involves an evening of the score or attempt to achieve some perceived sense of equity or fairness.

In Monica's case, she had plenty of good reasons to "roll" on Bill Clinton. Twenty-seven of them, in fact, the number of years she was facing for perjury, obstruction of justice, and witness tampering. But, when she was originally contacted in January 1998, she declined to cooperate, waiting more than 6 months to come back. What made her change her mind? Not the motivation offered. She got an immunity deal, which she undoubtedly could have gotten in January, given the significance of the target of the investigation. What changed was that her conscience allowed her to betray the President in July, but not in January. She explained it in her Grand Jury testimony: "I had been hurt when he referred to me as 'that woman' in January. And his people — the people who work for him have trashed me … they have smeared me and they called me stupid. I tried to do as much as I could to protect him. … I didn't allow him to be put on tape that night."

In January, Lewinsky was still trying to "do as much as [she] could to protect him." By way of thanks, she was "trashed," "hurt," and "called 'that woman.'" In July, Lewinsky was not only saving herself from possible imprisonment, she was also getting even, a concept that agrees with almost every conscience. If investigators had been able to evoke the same resentment in January, Monica might have gotten on board at that time.

The second means of expanding the area of conscience is the indirect and slower route used by those in espionage, who have more time and money to make it work. In this mode, the officer starts small, obtaining little concessions to the informant's conscience, gradually working the individual to a place of full commitment.

One mechanism used in drug cases is the "confidence buy," which allows the informant to expand his area of conscience. Many recently recruited informants who are going to be active in an investigation are reluctant to take that first big step; introducing an undercover agent to their associates is a very intimidating prospect. They are afraid that the agent is going to give them away. They feel the immediacy and magnitude of their betrayal. They do not fully trust themselves or the agent in their present situation. Their conscience is bothering them. In short, they lack confidence.

One way to give them confidence is to have them make one controlled buy or, better, an undercover introduction. The informant introduces the agent, who makes a small purchase and walks out. To everyone's amazement (or at least the informant's) the sun is still shining, the birds are still singing, and nothing important has changed. Except that, without even realizing it, the barriers have been crossed. If I am the informant, I now have every confidence that the next buy — and there *will* be a next buy — will go just as easily. That agent is really a pretty cool guy. And my conscience? Well, nothing happened; it's not bothering me at all.

The informant's area of conscience has been broadened. It won't be receding, because everything tells him that this is okay.

I generally used throwaway cases for the confidence buys. We never spent much money on them and usually picked someone who was not especially important to the informant for the purchase — someone his conscience would allow him to do. The results were always well worth the minimal amount of money spent on the evidence, even if the case was never referred for prosecution. Having one of these buys under their belts made informants much more prepared to move to the next step, which was usually introductions for bigger purchases from people who were more important to the informant.

The gradual approach or use of little steps instead of one big leap could have been employed in Monica's case, as well. When outlining what they had planned for her, the Independent Counsel listed "cooperation, an interview, telephone calls, body wires, and testimony." They also talked about several people, including the President, Vernon Jordan, and Betty Currie. One possible alternative in a case such as this would be to have the informant commit to cooperation against someone less important to her, such as Jordan, or perhaps somebody she already did not like (there were several of those in the White House), then work from there.

The incremental approach is the one used with Robert Leuci, a New York Police Department (NYPD) detective who initially agreed to cooperate with the federal government to root out corruption in NYPD's Narcotics Division. Leuci, whose story was told in Robert Daley's *Prince of the City*, initially "meant to work primarily against corrupt lawyers, he declared. He wanted to put in jail district attorneys and judges who regularly solicited bribes, and defense lawyers who regularly seduced cops. If the focus was to be strictly on the cops themselves, then he would not take part. Any corrupt cops whom he might, so to speak, stumble over would go to jail too. But they would be incidental to his investigation. And he would not work against cops who had been his friends and partners in SIU."

Leuci was led along, ever deeper into the investigation, his conscience expanding throughout. Ultimately, all of his "friends and partners in SIU" (the Special Investigations Unit of the Narcotics Division) were consumed by the investigation and Leuci's direct or indirect role in it. Almost 30 detectives were indicted, and two, including one of Leuci's partners, committed suicide, but Leuci never got the judges or prosecutors he started out aiming for.

One final word about conscience. Many informants, including almost all of those who walk-in, have already come to some agreeable accommodation with their own consciences. Whatever motivated them to contact law enforcement, they know exactly what they want to do. The Decision has been made, and the officer can assume that whatever process of justification or rationalization that takes place in making that decision has already been completed. In dealing with that person, however, it is still a good idea to listen for clues as to what that justification might be. This will help understand the motivation and will assist the officer in maintaining the proper level of control.

Motivation

We must always remember that in terms of motivation, an informant *never* works for us, only for himself. Even in the case of an informant with a purely altruistic motive, such as David Kaczynski, it is that self-supplied motivation which moves the informant through law enforcement's door. He is there for *his* reasons, not ours.

We have discussed at some length the various reasons or motivations why an informant may cooperate with the government. What remains to be done is to examine the process by which these motivations are employed in making The Decision. As noted before, it is not enough to simply drop the facts on the table and expect them to be picked up. More often than not, the prospective informant has a clear concept of his needs. The officer's role is to present those facts in a way that will allow the informant to make the best use of them in coming to the "right" conclusion.

This process is best handled in a dispassionate accounting of the data. If we return to our second-hand car analogy, this is the point where the benefits of the product, a used Yugo, are outlined. The informant's motivation or needs may involve emotional issues such as revenge or fear, but in the presentation of the facts appeals to emotions should be kept to a minimum. "Just the facts, ma'am," as Jack Webb would have said.

Monica Lewinsky got all the facts she could handle in her recruitment pitch. She was told about the federal charges (perjury, obstruction of justice, witness tampering, conspiracy, as well as similar charges against her mother) the potential penalty (27 years), and the benefits her cooperation might bring her. Given that there were at least six attorneys and four FBI agents or investigators from the Independent Counsel's office present in the room, it can be assumed that the information was presented in an honest, logical, and straightforward way. It was not enough in this instance, but the pitch failed for other reasons.

In order to use motivation effectively in the development of informants, the officer must be able to (1) understand the individual's needs, (2) effectively describe the benefits of the proposed solution, and (3) demonstrate or explain how the proposed solution fits the individual's needs. In some cases, this will be pretty straightforward, as it was for Monica Lewinsky. Let's look at how it worked for her.

Understand the Individual's Needs

The Independent Counsel was focusing on a very specific need in Monica Lewinsky's life — the need to stay out of prison. Any officer who is hoping to develop an informant must first make a needs assessment of that individual and be prepared to address the values identified. (It is important to get this right. The Independent Counsel did not, and Monica failed to respond.) As Monica said, "They knew that I had signed a false affidavit, they had me on tape saying I had committed perjury, that they were going to — that I could go to jail for 27 years, they were going to charge me with perjury and obstruction of justice and subornation of perjury and witness tampering and something else."

Everyone has a different motivation for agreeing to become an informant. Many times an informant will have more than one reason for cooperating. Linda Tripp had at least three and Monica Lewinsky had two or more. The most obvious one may not be the most important to the informant. The officer must understand the needs and properly address them; you cannot sell a used Yugo to somebody who needs a new pickup truck.

Describe the Benefits that Accompany the Proposed Solution

We do not know for sure what was said in the hotel room, but the benefits Ms. Lewinsky was seeking are summed up neatly in the immunity agreement she signed later. It provides that if she "fully complies with the terms and understandings set forth in this Agreement, the Office of the Independent Counsel (OIC): (1) will not prosecute her for any crimes committed prior to the date of the Agreement; (2) will grant her derivative use immunity; and (3) will not prosecute her mother, Marsha Lewis, or her father, Bernard Lewinsky, for any offenses which may have been committed by them prior to this Agreement.

Written agreements are becoming more common features in the officer-informant relationship. They are standard in almost all cases where a prosecutor or government attorney is involved. Whether written or verbal, the benefits of cooperation should be clearly outlined. Honesty is not only the best policy in this situation, it is the only one. The officer must not promise more than he or she can deliver and must be careful not to exceed the scope of his or her authority.

Demonstrate or Explain How the Proposed Solution Fits the Individual's Needs

Finally, the officer has to explain how cooperation is going to work, and why it is the right way to fulfill the individual's needs. The proposed solution includes not just the benefit to the informant but also what she has to do to get that benefit. Monica Lewinsky ultimately learned that the benefit to her included complete immunity, something which must have sounded very attractive to someone facing 27 years in prison. She also learned that the government wanted her to "cooperate," to be debriefed, and to do other things which did not sound so attractive: "I mean, there was, but they — they told me they wanted me to cooperate. I asked them what cooperating meant, it entailed, and they told me that — they had — first they had told me before about that — that they had me on tape saying things from the lunch that I had with Linda at the Ritz Carlton the other day and they — then they told me that I — that I'd have to agree to be debriefed and that I'd have to place calls or wear a wire to see — to call Betty and Mr. Jordan and possibly the President."

There is no such thing as a free lunch, however, and the officer has to explain the whole package. The entire process is conducted in a very direct, very logical way.

1. *Need identification*: "You need (money, revenge, help at sentencing, etc.)."
2. *Benefit identification*: "We have (money, revenge, help at sentencing, etc.)."
3. *Explain how the solution fits the need*: "We will give you (money revenge, help at sentencing, etc.) but only if you are prepared to do the following."

When all of the elements of *trust, conscience,* and *motivation* have been addressed to the individual's satisfaction, The Decision is made and the recruitment is complete. If done properly, the informant is comfortable that he or she has not been dragged to this point against his or her will. The beginnings of commitment are present, as is the establishment of the officer's control of the informant, both of which are key components of success.

Influencing the Decision

Military recruiters have a product (service in the armed forces), of which they are justifiably proud, and a desire to promote the benefits of that product to as many qualified young men and women as they can. The time when people were shanghaied aboard ships is long gone. We no longer draft people in this country and cannot fill the ranks with those who are unwilling to serve. The practice of giving a young person the choice between jail and the military has also gone out of fashion, mostly because military standards have gotten so much higher. Today, people must be persuaded to make this major decision. The recruiter's job is to help the potential service member make the "right" choice. The Navy's manual for recruiting officers has this description of the role of salesmanship in that decision-making process:

> *Navy recruiting is definitely a business of sales, but different in concept and approach than most. Usually, selling involves the exchange of goods or services for a price. In navy recruiting, we are selling the intangible — a Navy enlistment. Our sales do not involve an*

exchange. Instead, we offer opportunities and provide the motivation that will cause our prospects to take advantage of them. Our job is to establish faith, confidence, and belief in our product — the Navy. We use the art of persuasive communication to enable our prospects to see the value of joining our team. Most salespeople with a set product like encyclopedias or vacuum cleaners can use the same approach for all potential buyers. The value and benefits of their products are basically the same for every customer. The Navy means many things to different people. Its value is different for each individual. So, we must use consultative sales to tailor our presentation to our prospects' wants, needs, and dominant buying motives. We ascertain their goals and show them how the Navy will help achieve them. Recruiting is actually the art of diagnosing and solving problems.

This is a very neat summary of what law enforcement attempts in the recruitment of informants. Law enforcement officers who are attempting to develop informants as part of their jobs have a similar goal. Like military recruiters, we use communication to diagnose and solve the problems of our potential recruits. The hope is that each individual will be persuaded of the benefits of cooperation with the government in its war on crime.

The process of achieving this goal is, as the Navy notes, "a business of sales." Because this is not a field in which most law enforcement officers are familiar or especially comfortable, we are going to look at some of the techniques of sales and how these are applied to our special problem — the development of informants.

Rapport

Every sales presentation begins with the establishment of rapport. Rapport is a harmonious, empathetic, and sympathetic relationship, usually between two people, although public speakers try to establish rapport with an entire audience. The word comes from the French *rapporter*, which means "to offer back with grace and elegance." Anyone who hopes to influence a decision must offer back this empathetic relationship. Rapport enables people to understand and agree with each other. Barriers to communication are lowered, and without rapport there will be no true commitment.

We have several commonly used terms for this state. We might say that two people "hit it right off" or that they are "on the same wavelength." We might say that people are simpatico or have charisma, or there is some chemistry between them. We can all think of some individual in our own lives whom this description fits. Achieving this affinity can be accidental, but we can also train ourselves to be better at building rapport. (Incidentally, these techniques will work in other relationships, both business and personal.)

One thing is certain; we are much more likely to listen to and agree with someone with whom we share a rapport. This is because rapport essentially means we are agreeing with ourselves. In human relationships, unlike physics, opposites do *not* attract. People like and empathize with other people whom they perceive to be like themselves. They do not empathize with people who are different.

In wartime, one of the first things the opposing parties do is demonize those on the other side. By convincing soldiers that the enemy is "not like us," armies make it easier for the soldiers to kill those enemies. People in hostage situations are urged to take whatever steps are possible to create empathy in the hostage-takers. The hostage's life may depend on being seen to be "like us."

Why is this important for a law enforcement officer who may not want to be "like" the would-be informant sitting there across the table? Because we are asking someone to make a big, important decision, one they will not make if they do not first have rapport with the officer who is asking. Let's look at some of the ways rapport can be built.

One communication technique originally developed by psychologists is neuro-linguistic programming (NLP). The foundation of NLP is the concept of representational systems, the structure in which people perceive their world. An understanding of these systems is useful in enhancing communication and even in detecting deception, but NLP can also be used to create and strengthen rapport. In fact, NLP, which has been taught for almost 20 years in law enforcement interviewing training, was originally developed for use in psychotherapy, where a rapport between patient and therapist is critical. Because that rapport is equally important to law enforcement officers and informants, we can benefit from some of the same techniques used in the clinical setting.

The pioneers of NLP, Richard Bandler, John Grinder, and Steve Lankton, believed that humans perceive the world primarily through the use of three senses: vision, hearing, and touch or feeling. As we develop in life, one of these sensory systems comes to predominate, and people tend to operate primarily in one of three representational systems — visual, auditory, or kinesthetic.

We need to know which type of person we are dealing with because each type communicates in the "language" of their primary representational system. If they are primarily visual, they will tend to "see" the world and express themselves in visual terms. If asked to recall a specific incident, such as a robbery scene, the visually oriented person might say, "That guy had the biggest gun I've ever seen." Around 60% of the population have visual orientation as their primary representational system.

Auditory people process input and communicate mostly in terms of sound. An auditory witness to the same robbery might say, "He ordered everyone to lie on the floor. I don't know how tall he was, but he had a rough voice." 30% of the people around us are primarily auditory.

This is how the kinesthetic robbery witness would describe her feelings about being there: "I've never been so scared. I felt like it was never going to end." About 10% of the population fits this profile.

How does this knowledge work in enhancing officer-informant rapport? Consider this conversation:

Officer:	*I'm trying to paint a good picture of where you are.*
Informant:	*It sounds like I'm in a lot of trouble.*
Officer:	*Look, I think the facts clearly show where you stand.*
Informant:	*I'm not deaf.*
Officer:	*Can you see why this is in your best interest?*
Informant:	*I guess I better talk to my attorney, hear what he has to say.*

The two people in this conversation are talking, but neither is speaking the other's language. As a result, they are not communicating. No rapport has been developed.

Remember that rapport means to offer back with grace and elegance. By communicating with the individual in the same representational system, we increase their perception that we are empathetic, understanding, similar people. Once the officer has established which primary system the informant uses — in our example, auditory — the officer can consciously communicate in the same system. We will talk more later about how to establish which system someone is using and how to use that information to communicate better.

Other Factors Influencing Rapport

Breathing

As if we did not have enough to do already, now we are supposed to check on the potential informant's breathing. Breathing patterns actually have a relationship to that "he's just like me" factor we talked about. They can also clue you in on the individual's state of mind — and their readiness to accept ideas. Breathing patterns are directly linked to our states of mind. This is a physiological fact of life that we cannot do much about. The polygraph examiner takes advantage of this fact by measuring respiration rates as questions are asked and answered. Breathing patterns will be affected by all sorts of stimuli, including images and sounds, regardless of whether those are generated internally or externally.

We are not polygraph examiners, however, with the benefit of a strap around someone's chest hooked to a machine. We can observe shifts in breathing patterns, though, some of which are manifested in changes in speech, tonal quality, and pace. By evaluating these changes, we can get some kind of an idea as to a person's state of mind, especially their levels of stress or relaxation.

The other reason why breathing is important is its use as a rapport builder. By matching our own breathing patterns to those of the potential informant, we once again create the subconscious impression that "he's like me." This is because breathing patterns are directly linked to the individual's representational system. Visuals tend to breathe high in the chest and shallow. They may actually stop breathing for a moment while they access the information visually. Auditories usually have a more rhythmic, flowing style from lower in the chest or diaphragm. Kinesthetics tend to breathe from very low — what we would call "deep" breathing. Although the informant is unaware of this on a conscious level, our mirroring of his breathing puts us in sync with his representational system — we are in rapport and more "like" the individual. This same "pacing" can be used to match other gestures, movements, even eye blink rates, all of which are good rapport builders.

Kinesics

Body language is one of those nonverbal mechanisms that make up over 60% of communication (some say 80% or more). In building rapport and enhancing communication, body language works for us in two ways. First, we are able to match and mirror the prospective informant's body language. Once again, by presenting a mirror image of the informant, we are demonstrating how amazingly alike we really are. If our posture, movements, and gestures subtly mirror those of the individual, her mind records that she is essentially looking at herself. She is also hearing herself say what a good idea it is to buy a used Yugo or how helpful her cooperation would be in the government's investigation.

The second way in which body language helps is in interpreting the mood of the potential informant. As we work through the process leading up to the individual's decision, we need to understand their needs and address them. The Navy describes this process as using "consultative sales to tailor our presentation to our prospects' wants, needs, and dominant buying motives. We ascertain their goals and show them how the Navy will help achieve them. Recruiting is actually the art of diagnosing and solving problems."

In any sales-type presentation, the customer gives signals that he or she is either receptive or unreceptive. Some of these signals are verbal, while others involve very distinct body language. People in the sales business are taught to recognize these hints, which are known as "buy signals" and resistance indicators. Some are very subtle, while others are fairly obvious, but the officer has to be alert in order not to talk past them. A person who signals "I'm ready to sign up" is only going to be irritated if you keep trying to promote the concept. A person who signals "I've still got some concerns" is going to be irritated if we say, "Fine, that's it, then. I'll sign you up."

Some of the signals that indicate receptivity or acceptance to the proposal include:

- Open posture, uncrossed arms and legs
- Hands on the table, tapping fingers
- Thoughtful gestures, pulling on earlobe, clearing throat, stroking the chin

- Asking again about a point clearly covered earlier
- Leaning more heavily on the table, or leaning forward to ask a question
- Expression changing to one of animation or interest

Some of the signals that indicate resistance or objections include:

- Closed posture, crosses both arms high on the chest
- Closed posture, crosses both arms and legs
- Touching the nose
- Checking a watch or clock
- Showing palms in a "warding off" gesture
- Expressions displaying lack of interest

Someone who is seeking to establish rapport ignores these signs at the risk of losing that rapport.

Proxemics

People are very territorial animals. We tend to establish territories wherever we go, sort of floating zones that surround us in all sorts of social settings. The boundaries of these zones are flexible, depending on the relationship we enjoy with others in that setting, and, although they are invisible, they are very real to the individual. Violation of the territorial imperative can cause stress, tension, even rejection.

Rapport is directly associated with these boundaries, the study of which has been labeled "proxemics." One who is attempting to establish rapport will be very careful not to cross into the other person's territory before being invited, and once there, may be perceived by the other person to be "in sync" or to have rapport.

The intimate zone of communication, normally reserved for extremely close friends and family, extends in Americans to a distance of about one foot. Entry into this zone is very much by invitation only, and extreme discomfort will result if the zone is violated by the uninvited. Touching obviously intrudes into this zone.

A personal zone of communication exists from the edge of the intimate area, about one foot, out to around three feet. This personal zone is where friends and business associates operate. Americans tend to establish themselves in these conversations at a distance of between two and three feet, often slightly offset or at an angle to the other person. In other cultures, this zone may be closer in and head on. This can cause distress in Americans, who will find themselves backing up in a circle to reestablish the "proper" distance and offset, then being "pursued" by the other party, who is also trying to reestablish the proper distance and orientation. Most interviews are conducted in this zone, usually because they are held in some room or interior space which will not allow the parties to get farther apart.

The social zone extends out to around 12 feet. This is also known as "keeping a respectful distance," because we are basically acknowledging and respecting each other's territories until we get to know the other person better. Some business gets transacted in this zone, but normally as a relationship moves forward, two people close the distance between them.

Even though all of this occurs on a very subconscious level, these zones can be very important factors in establishing trust. Someone who trespasses on the territorial imperative is not going to be trusted by the victim of the trespass. On the other hand, an officer who respects the informant's space will be rewarded with a similar respect and possibly an invitation to get closer, because subconsciously the message is received that "this person understands me."

Proxemics can also be used in communicating during the decision-making phase. When the officer is describing the motivation (fear of imprisonment, for example), he or she can gradually move closer, into or very near the intimate space of the potential informant. This will immediately provoke a reaction of distress and discomfort. The officer may see the individual lean back or bring his hands up across his chest. If the meeting is taking place at a restaurant, the individual may move items on the table to create a symbolic barrier or fence defining his space.

When this type of response is observed, the officer should immediately move back and turn the conversation to the benefits of cooperation. The relief on the individual's side will be equally immediate and obvious. This process can be repeated several times, reinforcing the concept that the motivating factor — fear of imprisonment — is stressful and generally "bad" while the proposed solution, providing substantial assistance to the government, is comfortable and "good."

The question of setting also comes up in this context. Some argue that the two people should be seated facing each other with no barriers, such as a table, between them. Others believe that a table allows the distances to be set and the officer's authority to be established. I believe that if a table is to be used, as in a conference room, officer and informant should be seated on the same side of the table with chairs turned to face each other. This imparts a message that "we're both on the same side" and reduces the barrier to communication. In a restaurant or similar, more social setting, the officer and informant should be seated at the corner rather than across from each other. This allows both to be closer, reduces the physical barrier between them, and places each in the slightly offset position favored by Americans in their conversations.

Principles of Influence

Dr. Robert Cialdini, a social psychologist and professor at Arizona State University, is the author of two books (*Influence: Science and Practice* and *Influence: How and Why People Agree to Things*) and is a student of the art of persuasion. As the titles of his books imply, he has examined the process by which people make decisions and how they are influenced in that process. What he discovered is a little unsettling to anyone who likes to believe that he or she is a creature of free will. Cialdini argues very convincingly that many of our decisions are affected by psychological responses over which we have little control. Even more distressing is Cialdini's finding that people he calls "compliance professionals" know all about these responses and use them against us mercilessly.

Do people really have psychological "buttons" which, when pressed, effectively force us to buy Girl Scout cookies we don't want, to give people money because they gave us a flower, or to torture perfect strangers? The very disturbing answer (from an ethical standpoint, at the very least) is probably "yes."

Cialdini's findings have implications for all of us in our everyday lives, but they certainly extend to the officer who is attempting to develop an informant. Are there things the officer can do or say which will, in essence, press these psychological buttons, thereby greatly increasing the chances an individual will agree to cooperate with law enforcement? Again, the answer is "yes." In fact, the application of some of these principles is so effective that the question becomes not whether the informant can be developed but whether it is ethically acceptable to do so.

Cialdini describes six principles of influence that direct human behavior: reciprocation, consistency and commitment, social proof, liking, authority, and scarcity. As we look at each of these principles, try to envision how it works in your daily life. I think you will be surprised and quite possibly shocked to see how you have, at various times, been manipulated by each. You will also see how, often without knowing it, you yourself have used each of the principles in influencing others.

Behavioral psychologists have established in a number of studies that humans and other animals respond to certain situations in a fixed-action pattern which is virtually automatic. When a certain stimulus is received, we react with a fairly standard response. Not every such response is automatic; much of what we do every day is controlled — our reactions are based on analysis of multiple factors — but many human behaviors are reflexive and triggered by one feature.

Certain trigger features that relate to compliance have been ingrained in all of us. We know from past experience that most of the time a response to some requests for agreement will benefit us, triggering our response. If you know what the trigger feature is in that situation, you can have a much easier path to the person's compliance and agreement.

Reciprocation

This is a very old principle and a very powerful one. It essentially holds that when someone provides us with something, we should reciprocate or repay them in kind. Sociologists have found that this rule exists in all cultures around the world; it may be a universal human trait. Under this rule, people not only should reciprocate a gift or favor, they *must*. The act of receiving something triggers an obligation to respond. We see this in our language; people "exchange gifts" at Christmas, "cheerfully return the favor," and engage in "give and take." As we go through life, we assemble a web of favors and obligations, all of which work toward social harmony, just as does trust.

In Mario Puzo's novel, *The Godfather*, people sought opportunities to do favors for the powerful Don Corleone, who, to all appearances, did not need any of the meager offerings of the little people doing the favoring. These people gave because the giving created a powerful social obligation on the Don's part to one day return the favor. A social bond was completed between the two people, cemented with the mutual knowledge of the obligation.

Note that there is no requirement that the favor or gift be large — it is the *act* of giving which triggers the fixed-action pattern response to reciprocate. Many times the automatic response is far disproportionate to the triggering feature. People who are given free samples of a product are much more inclined to buy that product *and* to spend more money generally in the store, which thanks you for your response.

This principle is part of the social glue that binds society as well. Not only does the individual recognize the need to reciprocate, others do, too. Don Corleone would feel compelled to respond to my favor, not because he was afraid of anything I might do if he did not, but because someone who welshes on a debt is not highly regarded, even outside organized crime. In fact, the popular terms for one who takes without reciprocating (*leech, sponge, welsher, mooch, freeloader, bum*) are not much less scornful than those reserved for informants. To avoid feeling bad about not reciprocating (and to avoid having other people disapprove of us) people try very hard to fulfill their obligations, even to the extent of giving up something far more valuable than the original.

How can the reciprocity principle be used in the development of an informant? Start by doing the individual a clear and uninvited favor. Buy the prospective informant a soft drink. Not only does this have a relaxing effect, placing things on a more comfortable social level, this gift creates the need for some reciprocation. You do not have to call unnecessary attention to the gift, but no payment should be accepted. This device has been used for decades by police officers in interrogation settings, though they might not have known why it worked. One officer might say to his partner, "Let's cool things down. Here, go down to the machine and get Jack a Coke," and then gives the money to the other officer. Jack now "owes" a debt, one he can choose to repay with the very next question the officer asks. Watch what happens when the gift is presented. If the individual does not pick it up or drink it immediately, it is not being accepted. As the discussion continues, keep watching to see if it is ever accepted. When it is, the obligation is created.

Many times in discussions with officers, potential informants may make a request. This may be something trivial, such as making a phone call to arrange a babysitter, or it could be something major, such as total immunity from prosecution. We obviously cannot promise the latter, but it is a good idea to grant the small requests ... your gift to the informant.

Hostage negotiators understand this principle. They grant small requests all the time, using another facet of the reciprocation rule, concessions. A concession is basically a gift: "No problem, I'll get you some pizza and have it sent in; what do you want on that?" After the concession is granted, the negotiator can ask for a concession from the hostage-taker, who is now obligated by the reciprocity rule to grant one: "Let all the hostages go." If this concession is too big, the negotiator can retreat again, "Okay, just send out the women." In doing so, the negotiator grants yet another concession, and creates another obligation.

In an interview room with a potential informant, the officer might propose a really spooky scenario: "We want you to wear a wire at your next meeting with the President and testify against him. No? Okay, then, what about making a phone call to his aide?" The officer seems to have made a substantial concession, doing a big favor for the informant by retreating from somewhere she *really* did not want to go. The informant now feels an obligation to repay the favor with a concession of her own, perhaps acceding to the second, much more reasonable-sounding, request and the one the officer wanted in the first place.

Consistency and Commitment

A joke about bacon and eggs for breakfast describes the difference between involvement and commitment. The chicken is involved in the preparation of that breakfast, but the pig, he's *committed*. Commitment is a very positive attribute in an informant. Once someone has agreed to cooperate in an investigation, it is important that they are committed to the whole program. Although we are not going to take things to the pig's extreme, we are looking for commitment, not merely involvement.

People have a deep-seated psychological desire to be consistent in their words, actions, beliefs, and attitudes. Society puts a value on such consistency; people who behave inconsistently are perceived as being erratic, flaky, unpredictable, and even untrustworthy. Few among us want to wear these labels. As we proceed through life, being consistent gives the individual a couple of edges. By maintaining a consistent approach toward certain issues or problems, we no longer have to spend time re-analyzing, evaluating, and formulating responses to them — we just respond in a way that conforms to a decision we made earlier. This makes life a lot easier; you only have to commit to a decision once, rather than having to re-visit it all the time.

From the perspective of one who wants to get someone else to comply with a request or agree to do something, the implications are intriguing. For example, what if I obtain just a small commitment from someone, perhaps something which is barely perceived as a commitment, if at all? Will the person still try to remain consistent with that commitment? The answer is that a journey of a thousand miles begins with a single step. Once on the path, people are very reluctant to move off, at the risk of being inconsistent. Even a small initial commitment has a great deal of power. If you have purchased a car from a dealer, you will recognize one technique often used to get that first, small commitment, one that begins by signing your name.

In an undercover operation involving the purchase of vehicles from a dealership for cash, the agents, who were posing as drug dealers, met with a salesman who bargained hard for their business. As the negotiations progressed, the salesman asked the agents to make an offer, which he then wrote on a piece of paper, asking one of the agents to sign "for the manager." The salesman then left, taking the note to the sales manager.

When the note came back, the manager had written, "Congratulations! You win!" on the paper, along with a figure several thousand dollars higher than the agents' offer. This process was repeated two or three more times, with the agents' number going up and the manager's coming down. Each time, the dealer asked the agent to sign the paper, which eventually got pretty crowded, what with all the "You're a winner!" and "Good Deal!" comments added by the back office.

The paper had no legal significance. It was not an offer to purchase, nor were the agents locked in to buying anything. What the salesman was doing, however, was securing commitment to a decision the agents had apparently made — to purchase the car. He did this by getting them to sign the paper, not once, but several times. Each time, the agents, who were also making an offer, were reconfirming their commitment — "I've made a decision and I'm sticking to it." The manager's remarks congratulated them on what he implied was already a "done deal."

This sort of endorsement reinforces commitment, which is most effective when it is made in a public setting, involves some effort on the part of the one committing, and is perceived as being voluntary or not coerced. Public commitments are much harder to break; you would obviously have to appear inconsistent before more people.

Saturn, a car manufacturer that routinely has extremely high levels of customer satisfaction, gives each customer a Saturn "launch" during which every employee at the dealership assembles around the customer and cheers as a photograph is taken for a display on the wall. Going back on *that* extremely public commitment would be very difficult for anyone, so when the pollsters call to ask how satisfied the customers are with the commitment they have made, a very consistent — and very positive — response is forthcoming.

Effort seems to play a part in the process as well. The harder people have to work for something, the more committed they are. Officers who have completed their basic academy will understand the pride and commitment that come as a result of overcoming the rigors of their training. People who have "paid their dues" say it was all worth it, and the more they suffered to get "it," the more fervently they believe in "its" worth.

Another factor is the power of inner responsibility for a choice. If we believe that we made this choice without being forced or pressured into doing so, our commitment to that decision will be much stronger and last longer. Research of this issue has implications in our development of informants. Psychologists found that both a large reward and a strong threat were viewed as external pressures. These things could, as we have seen, motivate compliance, but the commitment produced was neither strong nor long-term.

This is a problem, because in its approach to informants, law enforcement typically uses things that are obviously perceived as big rewards or strong threats: "Well, Monica, you're looking at 27 years; what are you going to do?" How can we mitigate the effects of this dilemma? Depending on how the recruitment is handled, we may not be able to do so, may not need to, and may not care to. (In Anna Sage's case, once she delivered Dillinger, she had earned her reward and nobody cared if she was still committed to being a friend to law enforcement.)

In an informant recruitment, our interest is in obtaining a commitment to cooperate. In this process, small steps can put the informant on the longer road, and in the rapport-building phase of the interview, opportunities to secure this commitment can be employed. This could include asking the informant to agree in principle to a series of propositions put forward in a conversational setting by the officer: "I think there are more drugs out there than ever before, don't you?" or "Kids are using drugs at earlier ages, don't you think?" These are fairly innocuous and non-threatening statements, but getting tentative agreement on these openers puts a pattern in place. They also serve to break the ice, show the officer's concern, let the informant hear himself saying things like "Yes, I agree, drugs are bad," and give the officer a chance to gauge progress. If you cannot get agreement on something like this, it is going to be a long afternoon.

Best of all, there is no real pressure to respond to these types of requests from the officer, confirming for the potential informant that his or her agreement is voluntary, as is the much stronger commitment which follows. The bottom line is that you can get a commitment from someone to work with you, but, as Samuel Butler wrote 300 years ago, "He who agrees against his will/Is of the same opinion still."

Social Proof

"According to a study by a leading law enforcement agency, nine out of ten people in your situation agree to become informants." The principle of social proof holds that people view a behavior as being correct in a given situation to the degree that they see others performing it. Is everybody else doing it? If so, we are likely to do so, too. If a celebrity endorses a product, people are far more likely to buy that item: "I wanna be like Mike."

As more people are seen to endorse an idea, the perception that it is correct will grow stronger. Police know all about this aspect of social proof. Post-Super Bowl celebrations bring out the worst behavior in some people, and large numbers follow along. The result is that rioting, looting, overturning police cars, and general mayhem are viewed as acceptable because large numbers of people are doing it.

In a now-famous study, a researcher parked a car on the street and left it. The car remained undisturbed for several days, but if the researcher removed something — a mirror or a wheel, the car was quickly stripped. People saw that others were stealing from the car and viewed their own theft as approved or acceptable. Police are now trying to nip these crimes in the bud, stopping small problems from becoming bigger through the power of social proof.

The principle of social proof works even better when the others doing the behavior are seen as being like us. People follow the lead of similar others. This has implications in cases of police corruption. The Knapp Commission in New York City found that certain types of corruption were widely approved while others were not as acceptable. Taking money from gamblers was "okay — everybody does it." Taking money from drug dealers was not socially acceptable under this unwritten code. (Twenty years later, the same department had major scandals involving narcotics-related corruption. Evidently people's consciences expanded in that time.)

So, (truthfully) telling a potential informant that many other people just like him have agreed to cooperate with the government will invoke the principle of social proof and can stimulate one of those fixed-action responses.

Liking

We have already discussed some aspects of this principle, which basically holds that people respond better to others whom they like. Often this liking factor is a product of perceived similarity. In studies, people found themselves liking others who were similar in dress, religion, or age; had similar backgrounds or interests; or even had similar habits, such as smoking. In the face of a request for something such as a donation or a signature on a petition, the request was much more likely to be granted if the person complying liked or felt similar to the requester.

Salespeople are trained to find some point of similarity and work on it. "Oh, you're a golfer? Me, too." The officer can use this same approach, but should be sincere in doing so. We have a big advantage over the car salesman in that, as investigators, we have far more background information available to us, with the opportunity to find many more points of common reference.

In one case, I was attempting to develop a defendant informant who had a 1967 Chevrolet Camaro under a tarp in his garage. By coincidence, I, too, once owned a '67 Camaro. We spent 15 minutes or so talking about our cars and even went out to sit in his car. When we finally got down to business, we were practically old pals.

In the investigation leading up to the initial contact with the potential informant, the officer should be looking for those types of connections. Other informants or witnesses should be asked about background, interests, associates, and employment. Any of these things can be the kind of things two similar people might share.

Authority

While hanging out downtown, some psychologists observed an interesting situation. People waiting to cross at a light were more inclined to jaywalk if others did, too. This sounds like another principle of influence — social proof — at work, and perhaps it is. The psychologists wanted to know more, and tried stationing different instigators at the light. Some people would follow a man in a business suit crossing against the light. Almost nobody jaywalked after a poorly dressed researcher did. By far the most people broke the law by following a man in uniform. It did not matter *what* uniform; a building maintenance man was as likely to get the same positive response as someone dressed like a police officer. People were following the authority represented in the uniform. How much further did this tendency toward adherence with authority go?

Pretty far. In what turned out to be a very disturbing experiment, Yale University psychologist Stanley Milgram studied a phenomenon he called "destructive obedience." In his study, Milgram set up a laboratory in which an unwitting or naïve subject was enlisted to help in a research project. The subject, who was the only person in the room who did not know what was really going on, was assigned to administer an electric shock to a person he was told was participating in a study of learning. On a command from the project director, the shock was to be delivered from a box marked with voltages ranging from 15 to 450 and adorned with labels such as "Danger: Severe Shock." The voltage was increased by 30 volts with every wrong answer. No real charges were being given to the supposed student, who was really a trained assistant.

The results were (if you'll pardon the pun) shocking. Each of the subjects using the "Shock Generator Model ZLB" was first zapped with a real charge of 45 volts, just to convince him that the machine really worked and to give him a taste of what the "student" would be getting. The subject was then instructed to award a shock for every wrong answer and to increase the voltage by one 30 volt notch each time. In behavior which still puzzles anyone who reads about it, 35 of the 40 subjects continued to inflict electrical shocks throughout the scale up to 300 volts, even though the "student" was kicking the wall, screaming, and moaning incoherently about the pain. 26 of the 40 subjects continued to literally shock the spit out of their victims all the way through 450 volts, the top of the scale on the machine and a level clearly marked as being "Dangerous."

Some of the subjects were not in much better shape at that point than the "students." Several had seizures, preventing them from continuing. Others begged and pleaded to be allowed to stop, stuttering, sweating, even weeping at the prospect of having to turn up the voltage again — but when they were told to please continue, they did. Why would otherwise "normal" people torture their fellow humans in such a fashion? Two principles of influence are at work here: (1) commitment and consistency (the subjects had made a decision and were going to stick with it), and (2) obedience to authority. Milgram wrote, "Subjects have learned from childhood that it is a fundamental breach of moral conduct to hurt another person against his will. Yet, 26 subjects abandoned this tenet in following the instructions of an authority who has no special powers to enforce his commands."

We do pay more attention to people with authority than others whom we perceive to have none. As authority figures, law enforcement officers recognize this fact and use it in their dealings with the public. We are taught verbal control tactics and "command voices." We know that our badges represent the authority of our offices. Milgram's experiment clearly shows how someone who voluntarily accepts the authority of another may obey the commands of that individual, even at the risk of trampling his own values.

In dealing with informants, there are a couple of points to be made with regard to the use of our authority. First, in order to get the full effect of the fixed-action pattern response, the individual must *voluntarily* accept the officer's authority. One who believes he is being forced into compliance has no obligation to obey. Second, the effects on the informant of this blind obedience to authority can include, according to Milgram, a "degree of tension reach[ing] extremes that are rarely seen in sociopsychological laboratory studies." By commanding an obedience which revolts against the informant's conscience or sense of values, we can create these enormous stresses — a dangerous, undesirable, and probably unethical situation. Like Sarah Jane Moore, the informant may obey perceived "commands" but only at a high psychological price.

A better solution is to demonstrate the officer's authority as a means of establishing control. In the development process, the officer should clearly identify himself or herself, using badge and credentials. The power of higher authority should be invoked to make clear the officer's role in the vast mechanism for seeking justice. Monica Lewinsky said the officers "told me that — that Janet Reno had sanctioned Ken Starr to investigate my actions in the Paula Jones case." That's taking the authority trip right to the top. As with the other principles of influence, authority needs to be employed with caution, especially since law enforcement officers do have real authority.

Scarcity

Monica Lewinsky was specifically and repeatedly told on January 16 that her decision had to be made that day: "And then they were — they kept saying there was this time constraint, there was a time constraint. I had to make a decision." The government's offer was time sensitive. This feature is common in many instances in which informants are developed. Unlike a car sales pitch, where the salesperson claims to have another potential buyer "coming over," in Monica's case and many others, the decision really does have to be made immediately. Opportunity knocks but once.

Scarcity, the perception that something is rare, infrequent, or in short supply, is another potent tool of influence. People tend to respond automatically if they perceive their chances of losing something are increasing. Scarcity can be real or artificial, like the other customer fabricated by the car salesman. In developing informants, officers frequently use very real scarcities. Often a decision like Monica's does have to be made right now. If word gets out that the would-be informant has been arrested or if that person is due back at her connection's place with the money, the decision cannot be postponed.

In cases involving multiple defendants, the first person who "comes in" will be the one treated most favorably by the prosecuting attorney. This is only logical; that person will be in the position to provide the most timely and useful information, as well as setting an example for others. The decision to "get in early" is at least partly based on scarcity. This last point emphasizes an interesting finding by the researchers. They found that people placed the highest value on things that were newly scarce *and* which were scarce because others were competing for that same item. We can illustrate this by altering Monica Lewinsky's situation slightly.

On January 16, the Independent Counsel approached Ms. Lewinsky, took her to a hotel room, and told her that her cooperation was wanted in a case against the President. Time was short, and her decision was needed immediately. This established the scarcity of the benefit the OIC was offering. If the OIC had added, "Oh, by the way, we're only going to offer one of you this deal, and we've got Linda Tripp in the next room, thinking it over," the value assigned to the benefit by Ms. Lewinsky should, according to the researchers, go up. Would she have prized it enough to grab it on January 16? We will never know.

Influencing Ethically

Sales professionals make no bones about it; they use the principles of influence to manipulate customers into buying things they do not want, even spending money they do not have. The public generally does not have a high regard for the ethical standards of this profession, but they do expect more from law enforcement. Because these principles of influence are so powerful, they can be used to exploit the people we are supposed to serve. Care must be taken to ensure this does not happen.

Life was much simpler when law enforcement could simply force people to provide information, either against themselves or others, but no moral person regrets the passing of those times. In exchange for giving up the ability to coerce confessions or cooperation, law enforcement won the right to become a respected profession. The ethical among us honor our profession by influencing with integrity.

Informant Development

Sun Tzu advised, "Be subtle! be subtle! and use your spies for every kind of business." He valued informants so highly he undoubtedly developed a few himself. We do not know anything about his technique, although he does say that they must be "treated with the utmost liberality," but it probably has not changed much in 2000 years.

Having sat through several hundred interviews with prospective informants, I have concluded that subtlety is not a major factor in the development process. For the most part, these interviews involved either walk-ins (individuals who were volunteering their services) or very hard sales pitches. There is nothing subtle about the appeal of many officers who are after cooperation and want it *now*. These efforts usually succeed or fail on the spot, everyone moving on without much analysis of why the approach did or did not work.

I believe that a more refined approach, one which employs some of the rapport-building and influence principles previously described, can greatly increase an officer's chances of success. This is a difficult theory to prove, as every potential informant's situation is different, but the research conducted by psychologists and the experience of other compliance professionals indicates that the hypothesis has validity. I am, therefore, offering a more systematic approach to informant development, one which requires a little more skill and a lot more subtlety.

There are essentially two settings in which an informant recruitment is attempted. One is the gradual development of someone's cooperation over time. We are going to call this the *progressive approach*. The second is the much more common *determinate approach*. Both of these approaches have common characteristics. Both call for considerable advance preparation, especially in the assembly of background information on the individual. Both require that thought be given to setting, participants, even dialog. In this sense, the interviews used in informant development are not much different from the more carefully structured interrogations which have come to replace those used in olden days.

General Preparation

Know your subject. Get as much background information as possible to help you understand this person. What is the primary motivation? What is the conscience-salving rationale? What interests does the individual have? What do you have in common with this person? What is his or her need structure? Has this person been an informant before? What access does he or she have that you know about already? Make a short summary of all of these factors. Turn this into a checklist to be covered as you conduct the interview. Before the interview, however, consider whether you are the right person to be doing the approach. Is someone else better suited to develop this person? Where, when, and how do you want to make the approach? In many cases, the actual timing of the approach will be dictated by events. Once Monica Lewinsky was approached and made aware of the existence of the investigation, she had to be flipped that day. The Independent Counsel did, however, have plenty of options beforehand as to the where, when, who, and how of this approach.

Flexibility is an asset in dealing with people, and we should always be prepared to chuck the whole program and work with the material we are given. I know an FBI agent who cultivated an organized crime informant for almost 4 years before signing him up. He had the time and the interest to keep trying. Some go much faster. The fastest flip I ever did was an individual from whom I had just bought a fairly large quantity of Quaalude tablets. After an initial meeting at which I placed the order, surveillance followed him to a nearby business which we knew to be operated by a trafficker who had been a target for some time. When the individual came back with the 'ludes, he was quickly arrested and driven away from the scene. As we drove I told him, "I know where you went and who you owe the money to. We want this guy real bad. When I stop talking, you're going to have exactly 30 seconds to decide whether you're going to take me with you to make the payment. If you don't agree to cooperate, we're heading straight for the office and you're history. I'm done talking." He agreed inside of 10 seconds.

Progressive Approach

The progressive method is the one preferred by the intelligence community. Nothing is left to chance in their approach to a potential source. The process is scripted and each contact leading up to the recruitment is analyzed for clues to the source's state of mind, objections, and progress. These techniques can be so subtle that the source may not even realize that he or she has been recruited, or by which intelligence service.

Law enforcement has fewer options (and less money) than the espionage specialists. Time is the important factor in determining whether this method can be used in the context of one of our cases. In the course of our investigation, it comes to our attention that someone has access to information of value. The first step is to profile this person to establish what needs this person has or what might motivate him or her to cooperate in the investigation. This profile should at least look at the potential informant's personal background, family, associates, employment, interests, and some rough idea of his or her finances. Trash covers, the collection and analysis of the individual's rubbish, can be very informative, though not always the most pleasant of jobs. Pen registers can give you an idea of who they are talking to on the phone. Surveillance will let you know who they are meeting. You might get lucky and observe some criminal activity that would provide another motivation.

Before the initial approach is made, the officer has to know which motivation and conscience salve are going to be employed. We also need to know if we can deliver — if money is the motivator, the office needs to know how much is available in this particular instance. It is hard to predict beforehand, but we should have some idea about how long this arrangement is going to continue and what types of things we will be wanting as part of the informant's cooperation.

With all of this in place, the officer can set the initial contact for a place and time most conducive to a positive response. In some cases, this might mean calling the potential informant and asking him to come to the office. In others, the officer might meet the individual in a more social setting or even encounter him or her on the street. Where, when, and how this takes place should be determined by the evaluation of the profile.

It is sometimes possible to use an intermediary for the initial contact. This should always be someone whom the officer controls, and who we are absolutely certain is going to support the development of the informant. In Monica Lewinsky's case, this would have been Linda Tripp, a close confidant who was already under the Independent Counsel's control.

The entire recruitment can take place at the initial contact or over several meetings. The officer must have confidence that the potential informant is not going to "burn" himself, though. Even if the recruitment takes place on the first day, the approach should be gradual and follow a pattern of rapport building, dealing with motivation and conscience and securing commitment. All of the principles of influence can be employed in this process, whereas with the determinate approach, time may not allow this.

The recruitment of NYPD Detective Robert Leuci illustrates the progressive method. Given his state of mind and motivation, the determinate approach would undoubtedly have failed. Leuci's agreement to work in federal investigations of police corruption came slowly. He was deeply committed to his fellow officers on the NYPD. He was an experienced narcotics detective who had seen a lot and done a lot — much of which was illegal. Nicholas Scopetta began developing Leuci as a source by interviewing him, first at the Knapp Commission offices, then at Scopetta's own home, where he cooked Leuci dinner. They talked and Leuci walked, thinking about talking some more.

Over several more informal conversations, Scopetta drew Leuci out, first talking about hypothetical police corruption, then about hypothetical investigations of it. Scopetta brought Leuci to a confession of real misconduct, then to a commitment to work on a far-reaching corruption investigation, one the detective thought he could guide away from his friends and partners.

Leuci's wife saw the picture more clearly. "Do you think they will allow you to do whatever you choose to do? Do you think they will say: Okay, Bob, whoever you want to tell us about. You decide. I don't think they will allow you to do that." She was right; no informant can be allowed to make those decisions, and once Leuci decided to accept the role he gave up the control.

The development of Leuci took a while, days to secure an initial agreement in principle and weeks or even months to obtain a total commitment, but in the end, he was exactly where someone who was arrested and "flipped" would have been. In fact, another detective from Leuci's unit was busted and turned. His cooperation led to even more cases against narcotics officers than did Leuci's.

Determinate Approach

Monica's approach, "determinate" means having defined limits, settled, positive, or conclusive. In the building industry, it also refers to a member of a structure subject only to definite, known stresses. The latter definition actually works pretty well for our purposes, too, if you think about it. The determinate approach has defined boundaries. Conducted in a structured setting under the officer's control, it calls for a positive, conclusive settlement. The outcome is determined in this encounter. The vast majority of informants, both the walk-ins and the ones whose cooperation we solicit, are developed using the determinate method. Once again, time is the key issue. Those "time constraints" of which Ms. Lewinsky spoke exist before and during the initial contact.

Background

In the determinate method, as in the progressive one, the officer should have as much background information as possible. In many cases, there will be less information available, but we still need a good profile of the potential informant. The Independent Counsel had three days to put together the profile on Lewinsky and the assistance of her very close confidante, Linda Tripp. This was enough to formulate a good idea of the motivation which was expected to be the reason for Lewinsky's cooperation. The investigators had nothing for Monica's conscience, though, and this was going to be a problem.

Foundation

In the foundation phase, the actual contact or approach is made, and rapport is established with the potential informant. This is the officer's opportunity to learn a little more about the individual, too. What is their primary representational system (visual, audio, kinesthetic)? Wear a belt badge and evidence a little authority. Obtain some agreement on some trivial matters (commitment). Find some points of common interest or reference (liking and simi-larity). Buy the two of you a soft drink, and accede to any small requests that you can (reciprocity). Spend this time profitably and *listen* to what the individual is saying. This is not the time for the officer to be doing all the talking; that comes next. Listen for any sign that the individual will be receptive to the proposal, because then it is time to make your case.

Construction

In this stage of the development, similar to the body of the case being presented by the prosecutor after opening arguments in a trial, the case for cooperation is set forth. This is make or break time, when the officer's arguments have to be strong and the facts have to be correct. The officer must clearly: (1) understand the individual's needs, (2) effectively describe the benefits of the proposed solution, and (3) demonstrate or explain how the proposed solution fits the individual's needs.

Those needs/benefits include both the primary motivation for cooperation and whatever we have got to address the issue of conscience. The individual will ask questions and voice objections, which the officer must be able to answer with confidence and assurance. If you do not know the answer, say so. This is an indication that the officer is being honest; rather than making something up or sugar-coating an answer, we are saying we do not know, but we will find out.

Major concerns that come up at this point usually involve:

- Assurances that any deals will be honored
- Questions about confidentiality
- Questions about safety and retaliation
- Questions about testifying
- Questions about case development

These are all legitimate points and good news for the officer. They indicate that the individual is interested enough to be giving the idea of cooperation some serious thought. These concerns need to be addressed, though, before we can move to the closing part of this drama. When you answer a question, finish your answer with a question that calls for some agreement, and do not move on until you get a "yes." Following are samples of such answers; you will want to adapt yours to the unique circumstances of each informant's background and situation.

Q. *How do I know you'll keep your promises?*

A. *How do we know you'll keep yours? This is a matter of trust. You and I are going to trust each other. I've given you no reason not to trust my word. I've told you the truth, and when I didn't have an answer or couldn't make you a promise, I told you so. Your safety and my reputation are more important to me than any deal. I have a reputation for keeping the people who work with me safe, and for keeping my word. If I lose that reputation, nobody will ever work for me again. You can see that, can't you?*

Q. *I don't want my name to come out in this. How do I know nobody will find out?*

A. *Well, I'm sure not going to tell anybody. We protect people's identities by not using their names in reports, not telling anybody about you. We'll even use a pseudonym on the receipts for the money we pay you. It's in my interest to keep you confidential; otherwise, we won't be able to get anything done. You understand that, don't you?*

Q. *What about my (or my family's) safety? Can you guarantee I'll be safe?*

A. *No, that's not a guarantee I can make. Look [or listen, if he's an audio], you or I could walk out of here and get hit by a bus. Nobody can guarantee something like that.*

What I can guarantee is that your identity will be safe. We'll keep the bad guys from finding out who you are. If we have to take steps to protect you afterward, we will. My attitude is that no case, no seizure, no crook is worth somebody getting hurt over. I'm not going to put you or anybody else in that kind of situation. It's not in your interest or mine to get you hurt. Can you get a feel for where I'm coming from?

Q. *Am I going to have to testify? I don't want to testify.*

A. *I don't know the answer to that. Nobody does. Until we find out what you know and figure out where to go from there, we won't know. I could say "no, you'll never have to take the stand," but I told you I won't lie to you or try to trick you into anything. I'll promise you this, though, we'll do everything we can to keep you off the stand. I don't want to put you up there any more than you want to go. It discourages people in the future from helping us. You can see why that's so, right?*

Q. *What if I tell you everything and you go out and arrest these people?*

A. *When we do this, we work as a team. I can't do anything without your information, and you don't get [benefit] unless I do a good job with the information you give me. You get me that information and I promise I'll let you know in advance before we do anything like arresting people. We'll both agree to keep each other informed about what's going on, okay?*

All of these types of questions indicate the individual is willing to cooperate if the stated objection can be overcome. The officer's response and his or her manner in responding will either reassure the individual or raise more concerns, which will then have to be addressed in the same fashion. When all of these objections are dealt with, the officer moves to successfully complete the recruitment.

Dos and Don'ts

- *Do* have a witness to all of these discussions. Another officer should always be present during an informant development. As in any other law enforcement interview, this person should be there for support and to act as a witness should there be any dispute about what was said or promised.
- *Don't* bluster, bluff, or threaten. Most law enforcement officers are pretty straightforward people and others tend to see through that sort of thing. Detached professionalism has a much greater impact.
- *Do* use visual aids. The statute book is a good one, as are the Sentencing Guidelines. You can tell people they are looking at 20 years, but showing them in the book makes an impression. If you have photographs or video of the individual doing something relevant, this is a good time to let him or her know it.
- *Don't* get trapped into promises you cannot deliver. People have either objections or conditions to making their decision. Objections you can deal with by answering the questions honestly and openly. Conditions imply a ceding of control to the informant, which is something we cannot allow.
- *Do* prepare yourself in advance. Have the background information available. Discuss the procedure you are going to use with your partner. No surgeon just walks into an operating room and says, "Okay, who is this guy and what's wrong with him?" Plan and prepare for your interview.
- *Don't* give up too much information about your case until the individual has agreed to cooperate in the investigation. There is a temptation to "lay it all out" in the hope that the individual will be so overwhelmed as to surrender immediately. Decide beforehand how much you are willing to give up, then hold to that line. Let his imagination work for you.

- *Do* plan to use the principles of influence and know in advance how this will be done.
- *Don't* forsake your safety to complete this interview. Controlling the site, the participants, and other features of the interview gives the officer more than just a psychological advantage; it also provides a safety edge. Officers have been killed meeting people who claimed they wanted to provide information; don't be the next.
- *Do* use this opportunity to begin establishing control.
- *Don't* joke around with the potential informant. In most cases, and especially if they are motivated by fear of imprisonment, they will not see anything funny about this situation. The fact that you do makes you different, and in this case different is bad.
- *Do* be a professional. Someone in the midst of a betrayal needs the reassurance that a steady, trustworthy, and dependable representative of law enforcement can provide.
- *Don't* give the impression that you are talking around or ignoring an expressed concern. If he says he is worried about his safety, assume this is a real concern and address it directly. Laughing it off or changing the subject is just going to turn him off. Treat his concerns with respect: "It's good that you asked about that. That's a concern many people have. That's a big concern for me, too. Here's how we're going to deal with that." Each objection is an opportunity to understand the individual better and to bolster your argument. Don't waste it.
- *Do* listen. Listen for subtext in the individual's questions. Listen for clues as to his or her primary representational system. Listen for leakage from the conscience. We sometimes tend to get caught up in presenting our case, making our argument. Remember that an informant is someone who provides information to law enforcement. Even before he or she signs up, we can still get information about this person but only if we listen carefully.

Respect

Respect is reciprocal. If you want it, you are going to have to give it. The officer does not have to like the informant, but we must respect the fact that this is a unique human being who has information we need. The oath we take to protect and serve does not say "except for informants." Never use derogatory terms for informants in their presence. This demeans the informant and diminishes the officer in his eyes. From the time of the first contact the informant must understand that the officer values the information and the person providing it.

Closing

Salesmen are taught to work for the close, in which they ask for the sale and receive the customer's commitment. The objective in the determinate approach to informant development is similar — to obtain the individual's agreement. As in sales, there are two steps to reach this point: one, the trial, which allows the officer to find out if the individual is ready to sign up; and two, the actual close.

The trial is an affirmation that the presentation was good, that the facts have been presented, and that the individual's questions and concerns have all been answered. The purpose is to get the individual to the point of saying "yes" without risking his saying "no." For example, in a case like Monica Lewinsky's, the trial might have sounded like this: "Okay, Monica, we've gone over all the facts. I've told you what the downside is — 27 years, right? And you know that when you agree to cooperate with our investigation, we'll give you and your mother immunity, right? You can't ask for more than that. You've asked some really good questions, and I think we've answered them all pretty well, don't you? Based on all that, I think we've both got a good understanding of your situation, don't you?"

The officer has recapped the presentation, has gotten four more agreements, and should move directly to complete the discussion. Be positive and direct in doing so. Ask for the agreement in the same way in which all the other questions have been phrased, so that a "yes" answer is logical and feels "right." If the process has reached this point, your chances of successfully developing this person are excellent. As you look at the following study of Monica Lewinsky and Linda Tripp, evaluate the actions of the investigators in light of the things we have discussed.

Setting (the Interpersonal Relationship)

One final word, this about setting. The perceptive reader will have noticed at this point that every reference to the officer-informant relationship thus far has implied a one-on-one association. Informants are *not* developed by committee. The Decision is a very personal one, and not made easily in a crowd of people. The officer must recognize this fact and structure the interview accordingly. Two officers should be present in the interview. One agent should take the lead, supported by the second. There is a temptation for everyone to "take a crack" at the potential informant, something that happened in Monica Lewinsky's initial meeting with the Independent Counsel, with the usual results. It is far better to select the person who will be able to best establish rapport with the informant and exclude all but one other witness.

The setting for The Decision should be as intimate as circumstances will allow, such as an interview room, private room, or, if the meeting is in public, a place away from the hearing of others. Minimize distractions, especially those caused by other people. The individual who might "flip" in a private setting could be reluctant to do so when his betrayal is taking place so obviously before a crowd of people. The chances that an informant will agree to cooperate are enhanced by your being sensitive to the psychological pressures that accompany betrayal.

Case Study: Why Didn't Monica Flip?

Four people occupy the lead roles in what some call "America's biggest soap opera." Two are informants, one is an investigator, and one is the President of the United States. As this is written, the final act of this tragicomedy has not yet been played out, but regardless of the outcome, the actors' lives have been irrevocably changed by the decisions they made as the drama moved toward its denouement.

On January 7, 1998, Monica Lewinsky, a witness in a civil rights lawsuit brought by Paula Jones against the President of the United States, filed a sworn affidavit in which Lewinsky said she "never had a sexual relationship with the President." As she, and now the world knows, this statement was false. Moreover, the relationship Monica swore she never had was not the deep secret she and the President undoubtedly hoped it was. "That woman, Ms. Lewinsky," as President Clinton would later refer to her, had described her activities with a number of people, one of whom was about to become a government informant.

Linda Tripp, a former staffer in the White House Counsel's office, was not high on the Clinton administration's list of favorite people. She had already given some information to Congress about a previous "scandal." Her access to the White House had been removed with her transfer to a position at the Pentagon. Although her ability to approach, speak with, or enter the White House was now all in the past, Tripp still had current direct access to another former White House employee, one who told Tripp about a plan to conceal evidence of the President's "improper relationship."

Five days after Lewinsky filed her false affidavit, Tripp took her information to Kenneth Starr, the Independent Counsel charged with the investigation of a series of allegations that were generally known to the public as Whitewater. One of the allegations against Clinton was that he and a Washington power broker, attorney Vernon Jordan, had, in effect, obstructed justice by buying the silence of a potential witness, former Justice Department official Webster Hubbell. Tripp's information about Lewinsky's affair with the President did not fall into Starr's Whitewater probe, but the possibility that Jordan had again been employed to "take care of" a potential witness against Clinton must have looked a lot like someone's *modus operandi* at work.

Starr's investigators arranged for a meeting on January 13 between Tripp and Lewinsky at the Ritz-Carlton Hotel in Pentagon City. Linda Tripp came to this 4-hour meeting wired for sound. With the approval of the attorney general to expand the investigation into Tripp's allegations, a second meeting with Lewinsky, who had made all sorts of incriminating statements and generally corroborated much of what Tripp had told the investigators, was set for January 16.

When she arrived at the food court of the Pentagon City Mall, in Arlington, VA, at approximately 1:00 p.m., FBI agents approached the former intern and identified themselves. Monica Lewinsky must have known she was in deep trouble. She had sworn to her affidavit in the Jones case just a week before. Only that afternoon, she had effectively admitted to Tripp, who, it was now obvious, was working with the government, that the affidavit was false. She accompanied the agents to a hotel room nearby, where she was surrounded by FBI agents and government attorneys, all of whom wanted her to cooperate with them in an investigation of the man she believed she loved. The moment of truth had arrived, and it was to be a very long moment, indeed.

Linda Tripp was a walk-in who approached the government only 4 days earlier with startling but believable allegations she backed up with hours of audio tape recorded on her own initiative. Tripp agreed to work with the investigators to make additional recordings and to meet with Lewinsky. Her motivation for cooperating was ostensibly to be a good citizen and to report official corruption in the highest places. Based upon her conversations with Lewinsky, she had every reason to believe her allegations were true.

Lewinsky, on the other hand, was most definitely not a walk-in. She had to be approached and confronted by agents, and her cooperation, if any, would come as a consequence of her fear of incarceration. The Independent Counsel had a perjury hammer to use against Lewinsky, but they needed her cooperation *now*. If she agreed to cooperate, the investigation could be used as an active informant and turned toward other potential witnesses who, unlike Lewinsky, still had direct access to the President: Vernon Jordan and the President's personal secretary, Betty Currie.

Nobody ever needed to turn a witness more than Kenneth Starr on January 16. Given the stakes involved, this was probably one of the biggest flips in American history. Some very experienced agents and attorneys gave Monica Lewinsky their best shot, for almost 12 hours. As we all know, the effort failed. Henry Ford once said that "Failure is the opportunity to begin again, more intelligently." Starr would get another chance to acquire Lewinsky's cooperation, but he would not succeed until her situation had changed. As we try to learn more about the development of informants, Starr's failure gives us a chance to learn "more intelligently."

Analysis

There must be something in human nature that makes it fun to sit back and armchair quarterback the actions of someone else in our own line of work, especially when that someone has just failed spectacularly. In looking at the development and management of Tripp and Lewinsky as informants, however, one cannot help but feel sympathy for the people who handled this case. They did almost everything right and still fell short.

This is a humbling reminder that in dealing with informants we are dealing with people — always a maddeningly fickle lot, whose actions cannot ever be predicted with any degree of accuracy. Although this unpredictability makes life much more interesting, I'm sure Starr and his staff would have settled for more cooperation instead. Let's see why they didn't get it.

The Attempt to Recruit Lewinsky

The Independent Counsel tried for 12 hours to secure Lewinsky's cooperation on January 16. In a remarkable marathon parley that included lengthy sessions in a hotel room, walks, dining, window shopping, and meetings with at least four investigators and six attorneys, Lewinsky's information was sought and ultimately refused. Lewinsky met with her mother, who took the train down from New York. Linda Tripp was in the room for a while. Lewinsky looked for an ATM, paid for her own dinner, and repaid one of the agents $2 for the cost of her coffee. She talked on the phone to her father in California. She had her legal situation outlined for her in impressive detail. "Cooperation, an interview, telephone calls, body wires, and testimony" were discussed: "Monica Lewinsky asked if there was still a chance she would go to jail if she cooperated. …[She] asked, 'What if I partially cooperate?'" Lewinsky talked to an attorney (who specialized in medical malpractice suits), listened as her mother asked about her safety, and told investigators that "this was an emotional experience" for her. She considered double-crossing the investigators. She knew that every word she had spoken to Linda Tripp was now in the hands of the men and women around her.

None of this was enough. She thanked everyone for being "so kind and considerate," and at 12:45 a.m. on January 17, FBI agents walked Lewinsky to her car.

Motivation

Linda Tripp

Several motivations have been identified for Tripp's decision to contact the Independent Counsel. Tripp identified some of these motivations herself, and some were attributed to her by other people.

1. She was a good citizen, coming forward to report corruption in the office of the President (*good citizen*).
2. She wanted to protect herself against allegations that she might be lying or fabricating information; she believed that her government job and possibly even her life might be in danger (*fear of associates*).
3. She resented having been moved from the White House to the Pentagon and wanted to pay back those whom she felt had wronged her (*revenge*).
4. She planned to either write a book herself or develop one with a friend, literary agent Lucianne Goldberg (*perverse/ego*).
5. She hated Bill Clinton and wanted to ruin him politically (*perverse*).

Whatever mix of reasons propelled Tripp through Ken Starr's door on January 12, it was powerful enough that she was solidly with the government's program. She agreed to meet Lewinsky, to wear a recording device, and essentially to betray a fairly close friendship. Because she was a walk-in, the officers had little background available on Tripp, but she was certainly motivated to provide some for herself and for Lewinsky. The process of developing Tripp and any other walk-in is much less complicated than soliciting the cooperation of a non-volunteer.

Lewinsky

"That woman, Ms. Lewinsky" had one primary motivation for cooperating with the government — fear of incarceration. This fear extended to her mother, with whom she had discussed the Presidential relationship, and to her father, who was ultimately immunized in the same agreement Lewinsky signed. The government had an excellent case, built mostly on Lewinsky's own words, for perjury and obstruction of justice. Her alternatives, as her very experienced attorneys must undoubtedly have told her, were fairly limited. Given the strength of the government's case, which was just as impressive on January 16, when she was first contacted, as on July 28, when she signed the immunity agreement, why did she decline to cooperate for over 6 months? Why didn't Monica flip?

There are three main reasons, all of which can be traced directly to Lewinsky's state of mind and the perception of her needs. First, the investigators failed to appreciate and appropriately address those needs. This was a 24-year-old woman whose mother described her as emotionally younger than her age. She was deeply infatuated with the President. Months later, she was still saying she thought she loved him. As she said, hurting Clinton on January 16 was the last thing she wanted to do.

What were her needs on that January afternoon? First, she was living at the luxurious Watergate apartments and was obviously well fed, so it appears that her physiological and security needs were adequately addressed. Her family was hardly impoverished, and she seems to have been secure in her employment; she had Jordan, one of the most powerful men in Washington, bustling about town arranging employment for her. Lewinsky's needs related to love and belonging, things she was not going to get in a room full of agents and attorneys. This was not the sort of need an immunity agreement could fill. She was afraid of going to jail for 27 years, the number thrown at her, but she recognized that betrayal of her "sexual soulmate" would end forever any hope of belonging to the person whose love she wanted. Her commitment to that ideal was too strong.

Second, the investigators failed to gain Lewinsky's trust. This is evident in both her words and her actions on January 16. Referring to the Independent Counsel's staff, she repeatedly says in her grand jury testimony that, "I didn't believe them" or "I didn't trust them." Lewinsky also sought the advice and support of people she *did* trust; Linda Tripp, her mother, her father, her attorney in the Jones case, and her father's friend, California attorney William Ginsburg.

None of this additional input was enough to move Lewinsky toward cooperation. If the investigators could have secured her trust, the outcome would have been quite different. Remember that the process of persuading someone to make the decision to become an informant is, in many respects, identical to selling a big-ticket item. The first part of such a sales process is not selling the product, it is selling the *salesperson*. The investigators in room 1012 of the Ritz-Carlton on January 16, had an excellent product — it was virtually identical to the one Lewinsky bought in July, after all — and there is every reason to suppose that it was well packaged and presented. Unfortunately, they failed to sell *themselves* first.

Finally, Lewinsky was asked to do more than her conscience would permit. She testified that, "I'd have to agree to be debriefed and that I'd have to place calls or wear a wire to see — to call Betty and Mr. Jordan and possibly the President." The investigators were aiming high. They were scrupulously honest about their expectations. Given Lewinsky's devotion to the President and her lack of trust in the investigators, her conscience would not allow her to do the things asked. Again, here is what she said in the grand jury: "And I was — I didn't — I didn't want to cooperate. I mean, I didn't — I just kept thinking to myself, well — well, I'll just say I made it all up. I'll just — I'll just — I — I couldn't imagine — I couldn't imagine doing this to the President. And I felt so guilty for having told Linda and that she had done all this." That's a voice from Monica Lewinsky's conscience speaking.

Note, though, that this attitude changed; her area of conscience broadened. As her emotional bond to the President weakened and when the immunity agreement (and some good attorneys) gave Lewinsky grounds to trust the investigators, she finally bought the program the Independent Counsel was selling. This conversion was 6 months and a million lines of press type too late.

Considering all the facts we have now, I believe there was little or no chance that Lewinsky would flip on the first meeting. Tripp warned the investigators that Lewinsky was infatuated with the President; the taped conversations between Tripp and Lewinsky support the conclusion that the younger woman had at least a crush on President Clinton. There was the possibility that as a jilted lover, she could be motivated to seek revenge, but Lewinsky's own recent, very affirmative actions in signing the false affidavit should have warned of a continuing commitment to the President.

This commitment was what ultimately held Lewinsky back. Only when it weakened was she able to shift her allegiance to the Independent Counsel. ("I had been hurt when he referred to me as 'that woman' in January. And his people — the people who work for him have trashed me ... they have smeared me and they called me stupid. I tried to do as much as I could to protect him ... I didn't allow him to be put on tape that night.") When she finally felt betrayed by Clinton, after his speech in which he failed to acknowledge her, she took up the government's offer of immunity and testified before the grand jury. A copy of Lewinsky's immunity agreement follows.

Summary

The effects of betrayal always reach beyond the betrayed and the betrayer. There can be no clearer example of this principle than the story of Linda, Monica, Ken, and Bill. Links between people are constantly being forged and broken. When betrayal breaks these links, lives (and, in this case, history) are altered. The consequences of their decisions are going to follow these people for the rest of their lives.

Why didn't Monica flip? The bottom line is that she did not have the motivation to do so on January 16; the needs she perceived she had were not addressed by the investigators. When this changed, and when the other elements — trust in the officers and the broadening of her area of conscience — were present, Monica Lewinsky finally got on board.

Office of the Independent Counsel
1001 Pennsylvania Avenue, N.W.
Suite 490-North
Washington, D.C. 20004
(202) 514-8688
Fax (202) 514-8802

AGREEMENT
This is an agreement ("Agreement") between Monica S. Lewinsky and the United States, represented by the Office of the Independent Counsel ("OIC"). The terms of the Agreement are as follows:

1. *Ms. Lewinsky agrees to cooperate fully with the OIC, including special agents of the Federal Bureau of Investigation ("FBI") and any other law enforcement agencies that the OIC may require. This cooperation will include the following:*

    A. *Ms. Lewinsky will provide truthful, complete and accurate information to the OIC. She will provide, upon request, any documents, records, or other tangible evidence within her custody or control relating to the matters within the OIC's jurisdiction. She will assist the OIC in gaining access to such materials that are not within her custody and control, and she will assist in locating and gaining the cooperation of other individuals who possess relevant information. Ms. Lewinsky will not attempt to protect any person or entity through false information or omission, and she will not attempt falsely to implicate any person or entity.*

B.   Ms. Lewinsky will testify truthfully before grand juries in this district and elsewhere, at any trials in this district and elsewhere, and in any other executive, military, judicial, or congressional proceedings. Pending a final resolution of this matter, neither Ms. Lewinsky nor her agents will make any statements about this matter to witnesses, subjects, or targets of the OIC's investigation, or their agents, or to representatives of the news media, without first obtaining the OIC's approval.

C.   Ms. Lewinsky will be fully debriefed concerning her knowledge of and participation in any activities within the OIC's jurisdiction. This debriefing will be conducted by the OIC, including attorneys, law enforcement agents, and representatives of any other institutions as the OIC may require. Ms. Lewinsky will make herself available for any interviews upon reasonable request.

D.   Ms. Lewinsky acknowledges that she has orally proffered information to the OIC on July 27, 1998, pursuant to a proffer agreement. Ms. Lewinsky further represents that the statements she made during that proffer session were truthful and accurate to the best of her knowledge. She agrees that during her cooperation, she will truthfully elaborate with respect to these and other subjects.

E.   Ms. Lewinsky agrees that, upon the OIC's request, she will waive any evidentiary privileges she may have, except for the attorney-client privilege.

2.   If Ms. Lewinsky fully complies with the terms and understandings set forth in this Agreement, the OIC: (1) will not prosecute her for any crimes committed prior to the date of this Agreement arising out of the investigations within the jurisdiction of the OIC. (2) will grant her derivative use immunity within the meaning and subject to the limitations of 18 U.S.C. Section 6002, and will not use, in any criminal prosecution against Ms. Lewinsky, testimony or other information provided by her during the course of her debriefing, testimony, or other cooperation pursuant to this agreement, or any information derived directly or indirectly from such debriefing, testimony, information, or other cooperation; and (3) will not prosecute her mother, Marsha Lewis, or her father, Bernard Lewinsky, for any offenses which may have been committed by them prior to this Agreement arising out of the facts summarized above, provided that Ms. Lewis and Mr. Lewinsky cooperate with the OIC's investigation and provide complete and truthful information regarding those facts.

3.   If the OIC determines that Ms. Lewinsky has intentionally given false, incomplete, or misleading information or testimony, or has otherwise violated any provision of this Agreement, the OIC may move the United States District Court for the District of Columbia which supervised the grand jury investigating this matter for a finding that Ms. Lewinsky has breached this Agreement, and upon such a finding by the Court, Ms. Lewinsky shall be subject to prosecution for any federal criminal violation of which the OIC has knowledge, including but not limited to perjury, obstruction of justice, and making false statements to government agencies. In such a prosecution, the OIC may use information provided by Ms. Lewinsky during the course of her cooperation, and such information, including her statements, will be admissible against her in any grand jury, court, or other official proceedings.

4. *Pending a final resolution of this matter, the OIC will not make any statements about this Agreement to representatives of the news media.*

5. *This is the entire agreement between the parties. There are no other agreements, promises or inducements.*

If the foregoing terms are acceptable, please sign, and have your client sign in the spaces indicated below.

Date: July 22, 1998   *Kenneth W. Starr*
                                                     Independent Counsel

I have read this entire Agreement and I have discussed it with my attorneys. I freely and voluntarily enter into this Agreement. I understand that if I violate any provisions of this Agreement, the Agreement will be null and void, and I will be subject to federal prosecution as outlined in the Agreement.

Date: July 28, 1998   *Monica S. Lewinsky*
Counsel for Ms. Lewinsky:
Jacob A. Stein
Plato Cacheris

Access

6

"Thus, what enables the wise sovereign and the good general to strike and conquer, and achieve things beyond the reach of ordinary men, is foreknowledge. Now this foreknowledge cannot be elicited from spirits; it cannot be obtained inductively from experience, nor by any deductive calculation. Knowledge of the enemy's dispositions can only be obtained from other men. Hence the use of spies." —Sun Tzu, *The Art of War*

"I never forget that when I'm talking with my friend, he's not talking with his friend."

What does the informant know and how does he know it? The answer to this question will always be different; no two informants, even in the same group, will have identical access. Moreover, there may be powerful incentives to lie about or exaggerate the extent to which someone really has access, making the process of getting at the truth more difficult.

The dictionary definition of access is "the ability or permission to approach, enter, speak with, or use." A more splendidly perfect description of an informant's role cannot be imagined. The ability of a cooperating individual to approach or speak with the subject of an investigation is exactly what law enforcement has in mind, but does the informant really have this ability? How did he come by this access? Does he have the access now, or is it a thing of the past? Does he really have more access (or less) than he is saying?

Answering all of these questions and many more will determine how an informant's services will be used and what types of cases will be developed. There are many different types of access, of course. Anna Sage knew only John Dillinger's identity and where he would be at a given moment in time. As we will see in this chapter, Eddie O'Hare had no direct access to the bootlegging, extortion, prostitution, or other crimes committed by Al Capone. He did know one important secret: that Capone was fixing his jury. Other informants, by virtue of their status as long-time mob figures and career criminals, have immense access to all manner of information. Some examples include Joseph Valachi, Vincent Teresa, James Fratianno, and Sammy "The Bull" Gravano.

Access as a Factor of Trust

The key element in acquiring access is trust. People who commit crimes know what will happen if evidence of those crimes gets to the police. This is exactly why their activities take place in relative secrecy and why it is called "the underworld." In order to be admitted to the secret world of crime, a measure of trust is required. We talked about trust and betrayal earlier; now we need to understand that in this world, for the most part, trust equals access. Not all access is created alike. In fact, there are levels of access, delineated by the amount of trust implicit in each relationship.

Who is most likely to know the secrets of some notable crime? The participants, of course, who trusted each other sufficiently to become involved together in the enterprise. Associates of the perpetrators may also have access to information about a crime. They could have acquired this information through hearsay or perhaps through direct observation, as they were trusted enough to "hang around."

As our example, let us suppose that three men decide to rob a New York hotel. Each of these three has full knowledge of the plan and all of the details of the plan's execution. These three have full access to direct evidence of the crime. Even if our three robbers only trusted each other fully, there are others — perhaps many others — who have some limited access to the facts. Associates, friends, and family members can acquire a lot of information in those respective roles, because they have the ability to approach or speak with the principals. Many crimes are solved, not because one of the perpetrators talked to the police, but because one of them told someone else who did.

Those robbers are vulnerable because, as the U.S. Supreme Court ruled in *United States v. Hoffa* (385 U.S. 293, 1966): "Neither this Court nor any member of it has ever expressed the view that the Fourth Amendment protects a wrongdoer's misplaced belief that a person to whom he voluntarily confides his wrongdoing will not reveal it." If a perpetrator talks to the wrong person, tries to fence the stolen jewelry at the wrong pawn shop, or otherwise misplaces his trust, that information may go to the police.

At the lowest level of access are those people who have only a small part of the puzzle. These people may know only that one of the robbers was in town that night or that a week later he paid cash for a new motorcycle. These are folks whose access is created through the coincidence of mere association. Their information is not likely to be as valuable as it would be if provided by someone closer to the action. Anna Sage ascribed to coincidence her knowledge of Dillinger's whereabouts; she supposedly recognized him when he just happened to be dating one of her boarders. Well, maybe; coincidences do happen, but it is more likely that Sage was at the next level up in the levels of access.

In evaluating an informant's access, then, we can characterize it as fitting one of three trust-related categories:

- Direct personal knowledge or participation
- Indirect knowledge through personal association
- Peripheral knowledge through indirect association

Remember that this access does not apply across the board. Just because an informant has direct personal knowledge of one crime does not mean he has that same knowledge about another crime or another criminal. The same access question — "How do you know this?" — needs to be asked about every individual or event described.

Access is also a function of time. It may be current, historical, or both. It may be short or long term. Sage's access to Dillinger was current, but short term. Sammy Gravano developed his access to mob boss John Gotti through a lifetime of criminal activity in the closest association with other criminals. To betray, you must first belong and, boy, did Gravano belong.

If the criminal activity is ongoing, the type of access will be a factor in how the case is investigated. For example, if Sage had gone to the police a week *after* Dillinger accompanied her to the movie, this information would have been far less valuable. As it was, law enforcement was able to use Sage in a proactive way; her access was current. Remember that in the months before the Unabomber case was solved, David Kaczynski, the informant who ultimately identified his brother Ted as the bomber, received a rather nasty letter from his sibling, saying in no uncertain terms that Ted wanted nothing to do with any of his family members. David's access, terminated years before, was strictly historical, but this was good enough, because he still recognized his brother's writings — the key element in the bomber's identification.

We can make up a matrix to describe the various types of access and then relate these to a familiar example:

Access Types and Timing

| | Type of Access | | |
Time	Direct Personal Knowledge or Participation (1)	Indirect Knowledge through Personal Association (2)	Peripheral Knowledge through Indirect Association (3)
Current Access (A)	1A	2A	3A
Historical Access (B)	1B	2B	3B

When Linda Tripp approached Special Prosecutor Kenneth Starr with her information about presidential misconduct, she no longer worked in the White House Counsel's office, so her information about possible criminal activity in that context was historical. Tripp's access probably fit category 2B with regard to this information. She did, however, have current 1A access to Monica Lewinsky, someone who claimed to have some rather special access of her own. Investigators were able to use Tripp's ability to contact Lewinsky to obtain some potentially damaging admissions from her.

Lewinsky's access to President Clinton ("Indeed, I did have an improper relationship with Miss Lewinsky.") was limited by the time she was confronted and asked to cooperate with the government investigation. Although her access to the President was 1B, she supposedly still had 1A access — the ability to approach or speak with Washington power broker Vernon Jordan and the President's personal secretary, Betty Currie. Had Lewinsky agreed to cooperate with the investigators at the time of her initial meeting, there is no doubt that the investigation would have been much different. As it turned out, Lewinsky did not "flip;" publicity destroyed her current access to other potential targets and witnesses, and she ultimately became a purely historical, 1B witness.

Access, rather than motivation, will be the primary determinant in *how* an informant is used. One of the first questions you will want answered in your debriefing of a prospective informant goes back to our original definition of access, "Do you still have the ability to approach, enter, or speak with the subject?" The answer will dictate where you go from there.

As we saw in the last chapter, the recruitment or development of the informant begins a chain of events that, one hopes, will end in a criminal prosecution Whether that informant will be a success or a failure will depend upon everything that follows the initial interview or debriefing, where the tone is set.

The highest grade of olive oil, known as "extra virgin," comes from the first cold pressing of the olives. Subsequent pressings yield progressively lower grades of oil. More often than not, with informants, however, the best information may not always come from the interview equivalent of the first cold press. Even more important than the information itself is the fact that this is the first opportunity for the officer to establish the control necessary to make an effective informant.

Determining Access

As we have seen, the level and type of access are going to vary widely from one informant to another. They are even going to vary with a single informant, who will, during his career, probably pass along good, first-hand information, the rankest gossip, and everything in between. It is important for the officer to establish which is which.

One of the best ways to do this is to continually ask the informant, "How do you know this?" It is very easy, especially in a lengthy debriefing, for the informant to present Fact A, Fact B, Fact C, and Conclusion (or Conjecture) D. Because these are exactly the elements of Joseph Goebbels' "Big Lie," officers can be deceived by such statements. By determining how an informant came by the information, then evaluating each statement on the matrix we used above, we accomplish two things. First, we increase our confidence in the informant's material. By learning *how* the informant knows something we gain a better idea about *what* he knows (as opposed to what he is just guessing about). Second, this information allows us to prioritize our investigations. We may want to focus on those events described by the informant that are within his personal knowledge. It may be desirable to send the informant back for more corroboration in a given area.

A side benefit to the continual asking of the "How do you know this?" question is that within a relatively short time, the informant will begin telling you without being asked. He is probably tired of hearing the same question and wants to save a little time, so you will find he is qualifying all of his statements with, "I heard this, but I didn't see it myself." Congratulations, you have succeeded in training the informant to do a better job and you have asserted a measure of control you may not have had before.

Another aid in this effort is rating the informant's statements after they have been reduced to writing, using something like the access matrix, above. I've used an excerpt from the Monica Lewinsky's written proffer to Independent Counsel Starr to illustrate how this process might work (note that Lewinsky refers to herself in the third person at various points in the proffer):

> After Ms. Lewinsky was informed she was being transferred to the Pentagon, Mr. Clinton told her that (a) he promised to bring her back to the WH after the election and (in a subsequent conversation), (b) Evelyn Lieberman spearheaded the transfer because she felt the President paid too much attention to me and vice versa. Ms. Lieberman told the Pres. that she didn't care who worked there after the election but they needed to be careful until then.
>
> After the election, Ms. Lewinsky asked the Pres. to bring her back to the WH. In the following months, Mr. Clinton told Ms. Lewinsky that Bob Nash was handling it and then Marsha Scott became the contact person. Ms. L met with Ms. Scott twice. In the second meeting, Ms. Scott told Ms. L she would detail her from the Pentagon to her [Ms. Scott's] office, so people could see Ms. L's good work and stop referring to her as "The Stalker." Ms. Scott told Ms. L they had to be careful and protect the Pres. Ms. Scott later rescinded her offer to detail Ms. Lewinsky to her office.
>
> Ms. Betty Currie asked Mr. John Podesta to take over placing me in the WH. Three weeks after that, Ms. Linda Tripp informed Ms. L that a friend of Ms. Tripp's in the NSC,

Kate, had heard rumors about Ms. L; Ms. L would never work at the WH with a blue pass; and suggested to Ms. Tripp that Ms. L leave Washington, D.C.

Following this conversation, Ms. Lewinsky requested of the Pres. that he ask Vernon Jordan to help secure her a non-government position in NY. He agreed to ask Mr. Jordan.

Ms. Lewinsky had, at one point or another, direct, personal access to and knowledge of the facts relating to the President, Betty Currie, Vernon Jordan, and Linda Tripp. She had personal access to Marsha Scott and John Podesta, but no direct knowledge as to what they actually did for her. She has neither direct access to "Kate" nor personal knowledge of Kate's statements. Her access to all of these people was historical, except for Linda Tripp.

In reviewing the informant's statement, the officer might conclude that all of the historical material would keep for later investigation, while the 1A direct contact with Tripp might bear more immediate scrutiny. As the statement is reviewed, omissions or additional "how do you know this?" questions will be uncovered.

Another way to evaluate access in the review of the informant's statement is to list all of the people identified in the statement, then rate each by the type of access and whether it is current or historical. Lewinsky's list would have looked like this:

The President	1B
Bob Nash	Unknown
Marsha Scott	2B
Betty Currie	1B
John Podesta	Unknown
Linda Tripp	1A
Kate	3B
Vernon Jordan	2B

Using a list like this, we have a better idea of Lewinsky's access to each person. It can quickly be seen that the only person to whom she has current access is Linda Tripp. The direction of the investigation may be dictated by how and when Lewinsky's access to these various individuals can be exploited. (Note that the rankings above are based on the excerpt from Lewinsky's proffer only. In fact, when she was first approached by investigators, she still had current access to both Currie and Jordan, as well as Tripp.)

Creating Access

Most informants who first approach law enforcement, and all of those who are approached *by* law enforcement, already have some access to criminal activity. If they do not, we should not be wasting our time on this person. In some cases, however, we may want to place these informants in situations where their motivation can be used to create new contacts.

This is a very sensitive situation, because a highly motivated informant may use this opportunity to entrap innocent people or make false allegations. If the informant has a fear of incarceration and is facing a 20- or 30-year prison sentence, he may go looking for someone to "give up." If a decision is made to put the informant in a situation where he had no previous access, the officer, *not* the informant, should be the one selecting the targets.

For example, the FBI, in its use of Sarah Jane Moore, directed her to make contact with a San Francisco radical she identified as "Tom." Prior to the FBI's instruction, Moore, who had access to other radicals in the Bay Area, had no relationship with Tom. Because her FBI controllers (presumably) had some valid reason, based upon prior intelligence, to monitor

Tom's activity, they undoubtedly had more confidence in her reports — or at least that she was not focusing on a completely innocent bystander.

Espionage agencies may be able to place "sleeper" agents in place for long periods of time, in the hope that they will eventually gain access to some worthwhile target, but law enforcement seldom has the time or the money for this luxury. Keeping an informant motivated for that type of operation is problematic. Even the Russians are known to have placed sleepers in the West, where they were left for long periods of time and finally lost when the agents' commitment weakened.

Sun Tzu's "surviving spies" are examples of informants who have limited access but go and acquire information in something of a "scouting" process. On one occasion, I sent an informant who was a known heroin addict onto a city block where several heroin dealers were working. The informant could not buy directly from the dealers but was acquainted with other customers who could. His dual purpose for being there was to identify other people buying at the locations and to assist in getting probable cause for search warrants. This was information that would have been much more difficult for me to obtain directly via surveillance.

Summing Up

How much access the informant has is going to be a major factor in his success or failure. Those who have a lot of access — either to many criminals or to one or two high-level ones — are resources that need to be carefully developed. Not all access is alike, however. Because it is a function of trust, the informant who is most trusted by his or her criminal associates is usually going to have the best ability to approach, speak with, use, or enter. Of course, this makes the betrayal much greater, requiring a stronger motivation. Understanding the type and level of access enjoyed by the informant is the first step in developing cases with his information. Once this is established, generally through one or more interviews with the informant, plans can be made to exploit the information, which is, coincidentally, what we will be looking at next.

Case Study: Artful Eddie and His Mechanical Rabbit

A key feature in greyhound racing is the mechanical rabbit that leaps from its box at the starting line then zips around the edge of the track, pursued, but never caught, by the speedy dogs. In 1919, Oliver P. Smith and Edward J. O'Hare, Sr., formed a partnership to market the rabbit, which Smith had invented. As greyhound racing grew in popularity, especially in states where horse racing had been prohibited, the value of Smith's patent and the Smith-O'Hare partnership also grew. In 1927 Smith died, leaving O'Hare with the sole patent rights to the rabbit, which by then was a fixture at every dog track in America. You had to have the rabbit if you wanted to race greyhounds, and, by coincidence, this was exactly what a Chicago businessman named Alphonse Capone wanted to do.

Capone's interest in greyhound racing was substantial, though well concealed through a series of front men and cut-outs. It was well known that Capone owned the Hawthorne Kennel Club in the Chicago suburb of Cicero. O'Hare's mechanical rabbit was used at this track, just as it was at others in the Capone empire, a fact which had first brought the attorney and businessman into contact with the Chicago mobster.

This was not O'Hare's first brush with the underworld. Dog racing was initially illegal in Illinois and elsewhere, which meant that criminals ran the illicit dog tracks which flourished despite the ban. O'Hare, known as "Artful Eddie," prospered through his association with these individuals and grew wealthy as racing was legalized in America and Europe. O'Hare claimed that, "You can make money through business associations with gangsters but you will run no risk if you don't personally associate with them. Keep it on a business basis and there's nothing to fear." O'Hare's association with Capone eventually went far beyond business and, as it turned out, he had quite a bit to fear.

The Lawndale Kennel Club, opened by O'Hare only a short distance from Capone's Hawthorne Kennel Club, was a thorn in Capone's side and a threat to his gambling profits. When Capone proposed a merger of the two tracks, O'Hare agreed, making him a partner to the gangster and bringing him deeper into the Chicago outfit and its operations. Although he was not actively involved in Capone's criminal activity, O'Hare had been convicted of a Prohibition law violation, receiving a 1-year sentence that was later overturned on appeal. The barrier between business and personal association was disappearing.

As O'Hare became more involved in the Capone empire, the government was taking an increased interest in Scarface Al. An investigation headed by Frank Wilson of the Intelligence Unit of the Bureau of Internal Revenue was underway, though it was making little progress. One reason for this lack of headway was a nearly complete lack of informants. Almost no one, it seemed, was willing to cooperate with the government against Capone. This was understandable; Chicago had, under Capone's reign, dozens of gang-related killings, virtually none of which had been solved by the police. The police themselves were notoriously corrupt, with entire squads on the Capone payroll. Neither witnesses nor informants survived long in such a climate.

One of the objectives of Wilson's investigation was to demonstrate that Capone was receiving income from such operations as the Hawthorne Kennel Club. In pursuit of that objective Wilson sought the identities of those affiliated with Capone businesses, one of whom was Capone's partner, Artful Eddie O'Hare.

Wilson was introduced to O'Hare by John T. Rogers, a reporter with the *St. Louis Post-Dispatch*. Rogers arranged for a meeting at the Missouri Athletic Club, at which the three men had lunch but did not discuss Capone. Later, Rogers called Wilson to say that O'Hare wanted to provide information to the government and this meeting had been a chance for O'Hare to evaluate Wilson's trustworthiness. Rogers told Wilson that O'Hare had been sucked into the Capone organization and now could not leave until Capone himself was gone.

O'Hare became an excellent source of information for the Treasury agents, although his knowledge of Capone's operations was somewhat limited. He was not an active participant in the bootlegging or other criminal activities, but O'Hare was nevertheless trusted with management of dog tracks in Illinois and Florida and was the recipient of substantial underworld gossip. Security within the Capone organization seems to have been somewhat haphazard. On the one hand, anyone caught double-crossing the syndicate was dealt with harshly, a policy that included preemptive termination of potential informants. On the other hand, important information was evidently discussed widely among those people who were part of the rather large, trusted, inner circle. For example, O'Hare was able to learn in advance of a plot to kill Frank Wilson. This was information which someone in his position should never have possessed.

Even more critical was the vital information O'Hare provided just before Capone's trial for income tax evasion got underway. O'Hare had continued his contacts with Wilson even after Capone was indicted for the tax crimes that would eventually send him to prison for 11 years. On the eve of the trial, O'Hare called to report that every member of the panel of potential jurors was being bought or bribed by Capone's henchmen. Members of the Capone organization had been assigned to reach out to everyone on the panel, O'Hare said, offering "$1000 bills" or making threats so that no impartial jurors would be seated.

At first the agents scoffed. No one, not even the U.S. Attorney or Judge James Wilkerson had the names of the venire men on the panel. O'Hare was insistent and as proof he produced a list of ten names, numbers 30 to 39 on the jury panel roster. O'Hare said that the gang had the entire list, which was parceled out in lots of five and ten names, each of whom was to be contacted by a Capone "big shot." The agents were shocked to the core. If O'Hare was correct, the Capone case was lost before the trial even began. Years of work would have been wasted and Capone would emerge from the courtroom more powerful than ever, having triumphed over the federal government.

When they approached Judge Wilkerson with the information, the judge did not appear to be especially concerned. "Bring your case to court and leave the rest to me" was the judge's advice to the worried prosecutors. Their concerns grew when they received the government's copy of the jury panel list; names 30 to 39 on the list were identical to those provided by O'Hare.

At 10:00 a.m. on Monday, October 5, 1931, the trial of Alphonse Capone on charges that he had evaded taxes on $1,038,654 in illegal income began in federal court. Capone was looking smug, secure in the knowledge that every one of the "peers" who would sit on his jury was also in effect his employee. This confidence lasted less than 5 minutes, when Judge Wilkerson told the bailiff, "Judge Edwards has another trial commencing today. Go to his courtroom and bring me his entire panel of jurors. Take my entire panel to Judge Edwards." All of Capone's efforts to manipulate the outcome of his trial ended in this one shattering moment of betrayal. It would not be a moment he or his associates would forget or forgive.

An informant's timely warning allowed the government to put on its case in an environment untainted by Capone's power. The un-bought jury ultimately convicted Capone, who received an 11-year sentence from Judge Wilkerson. Suffering from advanced syphilis, which he had contracted as a youth, Capone was released from prison on November 16, 1939, having served over 7 years.

O'Hare was not there to see Capone's release. Only 8 days before, while driving on Ogden Avenue in Chicago, a car drew alongside and two men with shotguns blasted O'Hare, killing him instantly. His death was seen as a "get out of jail gift" to Capone. The murder, like so many others in Chicago at the time, was unsolved.

In the years since Capone's conviction, O'Hare had become a wealthy and successful businessman, one of the most respected in Chicago. He developed legal dog tracks in Illinois, Massachusetts, and Florida, then diversified into real estate, insurance, advertising, and professional sports, becoming a secret director of the Chicago Cardinals professional football team. It appeared that Artful Eddie had gotten his wish — to free himself of his mob connections and become a completely legitimate member of society. Or perhaps not. On his person at the time of his death was a note bearing the names of two FBI agents to whom O'Hare was providing information about criminal activity.

Analysis of the O'Hare Case

Eddie O'Hare was a long-term informant who remained in place, actively providing information to the Treasury agents from a position of trust within the Capone organization. Although he was not a member of Capone's ruling councils, O'Hare did have access to sensitive information which was faithfully passed along to Frank Wilson throughout the Capone investigation. O'Hare never testified in the trial, nor was his identity ever disclosed by the Treasury agents. What is perhaps most interesting about O'Hare's case is the motivation behind his cooperation with the government.

Motivation

When he first reached out to Frank Wilson, Eddie O'Hare was already a successful businessman with connections to legitimate and not-so-legitimate enterprises in two states. He effectively held all of the rights to a very valuable patent and was apparently bright, talented, and charming. His associations with gangsters — including Al Capone — had been extremely profitable and promised him even more wealth. Furthermore, O'Hare was well aware of the penalties for betrayal of someone like Capone. (At a banquet held in their honor, three who did betray Scarface Al were tied up and then beaten to death by a bat-wielding Capone.)

What on earth would have compelled O'Hare to provide information to law enforcement under those conditions or to act in a way which appeared to be so obviously against his own self interest? As is the case with many informants, O'Hare undoubtedly had more than one motive for acting as he did, and his motives did not easily fit any of our established categories. O'Hare had married young and was the father of three. His oldest son, Edward J. O'Hare, Jr., known as "Butch," dreamed of attending the U.S. Naval Academy. John Rogers, the reporter who introduced O'Hare to Wilson, said that if O'Hare had ten lives, he would have given them all for his son Butch. Artful Eddie wanted his son's dream to come true.

Although this is not a matter in which law enforcement officers normally have much say, Frank Wilson and his boss, Elmer Irey, did assist in securing Butch O'Hare's Annapolis appointment. As we will see, this would ultimately turn out to be a very good deed, indeed. O'Hare did live to see his son graduate from the Academy and become a naval aviator, something which might not have been possible for the son of a convicted bootlegger and mob associate had it not been for the intercession of the Treasury agents.

O'Hare's request, though unusual, emphasizes that just as informants come in all shapes and sizes, so do their needs and desires. Flexibility in dealing with these requests is essential. Had Wilson shrugged off O'Hare's request, he might have been deprived of the information which ultimately led to Capone's conviction.

Another motive had darker implications. Artful Eddie walked a continual tightrope between legitimate society and the underworld. He may have enjoyed this role, as many performers do, but the assurance that O'Hare had a government safety net must have comforted him. These situations allow informants to manipulate their situation, to exploit their underworld connections, even to break the law without fearing the full legal consequences. There is some evidence that O'Hare, who continued to associate with gangsters until his death, also continued to provide information to law enforcement, which of course means he still had access to criminals and their activity.

This is a potentially hazardous situation for all concerned. Law enforcement officers who are working with an informant in this category must constantly be alert to the possibility that the information being provided is a cover for the informant's own illegal activities or is being "banked" against a future arrest. The informant may feel "immune" from prosecution by virtue of his assistance to the government and may commit crimes, secure in the belief that he will not have to pay for them. O'Hare's motives may well have been more altruistic, but it is difficult to believe that he did not see the advantages in a continuing relationship with federal law enforcement.

Access

O'Hare acquired his access through business connections with organized crime. Because he was convicted on Prohibition charges, had associated with notorious bootlegger George Remus, and had entered into a partnership with Al Capone undoubtedly provided him with more access than a completely "straight" businessman. O'Hare's ownership of the patent for the mechanical rabbit made him a valuable asset to the dog track owners.

As he came to be more trusted O'Hare collected and reported more information, much of which came to him as a result of sloppy security by Capone's organization. The value of underworld gossip should not be overlooked by officers who are debriefing informants. While he possessed a great deal of knowledge about the workings of the Hawthorne Kennel Club (later Sportsman's Park), it does not appear that this information was used extensively in the case against Capone. This was probably an effort on Wilson's part to protect the identity of his informant.

Investigators must also be alert to the possibility that an informant will provide information about some illegal activities while withholding information about others. This situation could have existed in O'Hare's case if he had furnished (admittedly valuable) information about such things as the tainted jury pool while concealing information about the dog tracks that might have harmed O'Hare's own business interests.

The potential for such double-dealing is particularly high when the informant's motivation for cooperating with the government is not clearly established or when the informant is not completely committed to the government's program. In cases where the informant has a business relationship with the target, the informant may attempt to use a law enforcement connection to gain a competitive advantage, eliminate competition, or cement a relationship with an associate. Officers who are used in this manner may not find out about the informant's double role or the perverse motivation until it is too late.

There were plenty of people in Chicago who had access to more information about Capone than Eddie O'Hare. The government's problem was that none of these people wanted to come forward and talk about it. Those in the innermost circle around Capone would and some literally did, go to the grave before discussing the many crimes he had committed. The fact that the government was forced to bring tax charges against Capone rather than charging him with the hundreds of other murders, assaults, arsons, bootlegging violations, or conspiracies he had committed illustrates the difficulty of finding witnesses against such a person. O'Hare was a good fit for the type of case which was brought and was almost perfectly placed in the organization to provide the type of information needed for that charge.

Control

Frank Wilson reported regular contacts with O'Hare, who developed a solid working relationship with the Treasury agent. He appears to have begun identifying with the government agents, seeing himself as an extension of the government's efforts to nab Capone. Wilson encouraged frequent contact by O'Hare, which took place in clandestine meetings or over the telephone. In doing so, Wilson undoubtedly subjected himself to many hours of seemingly pointless conversation in which no information of real importance was conveyed by O'Hare. Wilson did not regard this as time wasted, however. Instead, he was providing a receptive ear for O'Hare, creating a climate in which the really significant information would be passed.

Control of an informant such as O'Hare, who has an unusual and possibly perverse motivation for cooperating with law enforcement, is problematic. In O'Hare's case, he was not being asked to take any special actions, introduce undercover agents, or actively seek out certain information; his role was that of a relatively passive observer and reporter. Generally speaking, the more passive the informant's role, the less opportunity they will have for getting into serious trouble. An officer who is working with such an informant should, as Wilson undoubtedly did, instruct the informant not to take any unnecessary risks in getting information and especially not to commit any illegal acts in doing so. As is the case with intelligence assets, a protracted relationship in which information is passed over a long period of time is usually preferable to a sudden "coup" that ends the informant's access to the target (see the Dillinger case example in Chapter 4 for a notable exception).

Wilson did meet with O'Hare alone, something which is not recommended for reasons described elsewhere in this book. This decision probably had a lot to do with Wilson's concern for O'Hare's safety, but as numerous other cases have shown, this is not a practice in which investigators or their superiors should feel comfortable.

O'Hare's security was well protected by the Intelligence Unit, a factor which, given the penalties for a mistake, no doubt increased O'Hare's confidence in his handler. Frank Wilson carefully kept O'Hare's name out of all of his reports, and only Elmer Irey, the unit's chief, and reporter John Rogers knew O'Hare's identity. Although they met frequently, Wilson was careful not to expose O'Hare in a town where gangsters and police would be extremely interested in a meeting between Wilson and any potential informant. This cover wore thin in the years after Capone went to prison, with the newspapers speculating about O'Hare's role in the case, even identifying him as an informant, something which was never confirmed by the Treasury agents.

Ironically, O'Hare was probably killed because his role as an informant became known. It appears that he was furnishing information to the Chicago office of the FBI immediately before his death. A note reading "Mr. Wolz phoned" was found on O'Hare's body. The note indicated that Mr. Wolz wanted some information about a former bootlegger and bank robber named Clyde Nimerick. The note asked O'Hare to contact Mr. Bennett with the information. Both Wolz and Bennett were FBI agents who relayed this message through Antoinette "Toni" Cavaretta, O'Hare's confidential secretary. Any confidence which O'Hare (or the FBI agents for that matter) might have had in Cavaretta's discretion was probably badly misplaced. After O'Hare's death, the "confidential secretary" married Frank "The Enforcer" Nitti, the man who took Capone's place as head of the Chicago syndicate.

The U.S. government gained a tremendous victory in its case against Al Capone. Never before or since has the mighty fallen farther or harder. This was a time when the government most needed to defeat the corrupting influence of organized crime, reestablish the rule of law in the nation's second largest city, and demonstrate the effectiveness of federal law enforcement. At this moment, informant Eddie O'Hare came forward with the information that made it possible.

The people of the United States also benefited indirectly from Eddie O'Hare's cooperation. The Treasury agents' support enabled Edward, Jr., to fulfill his dream of attending the Naval Academy. Upon graduation, Butch O'Hare entered flight school, becoming a naval aviator just prior to the outbreak of World War II. Flying from the deck of the aircraft carrier *Lexington* on February 20, 1942, Butch O'Hare single-handedly took on nine Japanese bombers that were attacking his ship. He shot down five planes and drove off the remaining four, the first naval aviator to become an ace and the first to win the Medal of Honor. Returning to combat, Butch O'Hare was killed in action on November 26, 1943. In tribute to his heroism, Chicago's international airport was named for Butch O'Hare, the son of the informant who helped bring down Al Capone.

Informant
Management

7

"*Spies cannot be usefully employed without a certain intuitive sagacity. They cannot be properly managed without benevolence and straightforwardness. Without subtle ingenuity of mind, one cannot make certain of the truth of their reports. Be subtle! be subtle! and use your spies for every kind of business.*" —Sun Tzu, *The Art of War*

"*...a good citizen, an upright man, and an ardent patriot, but of limited information regarding circular saws.*" —From the obituary of a man killed by a circular saw

Motivation, access, and control are the strategic triad of the informant system. We have spent quite a bit of time looking at motivation — *why* informants cooperate with the government. Now we need to understand how the other two elements complete the informant, for only an individual who has all three can succeed in this business.

In this chapter, we will look at how informants can be managed to increase the chances of their success. A valuable weapon in the war on crime, the informant is like a sharp sword, capable of inflicting great damage but only if properly wielded. This is the function of the law enforcement officer, who must control and direct the informant's efforts. We will look at the different types of informants and their motivations to see how each type can best be handled.

Although most of us might not view it in these terms, the handling of an informant is a management function, using the same sort of skills as a first-line supervisor would, with some key differences. The biggest difference is the very autocratic management style required. The biggest similarity is the need for mutual respect on the parts of both officer and informant. Informant management is not an easy job.

Some years ago, a muted controversy surfaced in the ranks of a major intelligence agency, where most controversies are muted. The source of the dissension was the view by some officers that the agency's promotional process favored officers who recruited sources over those who managed them. In the institutional culture of the agency, a premium has always been placed on the recruitment of spies. This seems logical enough; without spies you have nothing for the analysts to analyze and no intelligence to pass along to the decision-makers. Officers' careers reflected this preference. The more spies an officer developed, the higher he or she rose in the agency's esteem.

This formed a schism between people who developed the sources (recruiters) and those who managed the sources after recruitment (handlers). It is all well and good, the handlers said, to develop sources, but only skillful handling — effective management of that source — will allow the source's potential to be fully realized. This day-to-day management often takes place under difficult, even dangerous conditions for years on end. The handlers felt that their efforts — though quite different from the recruiters'— should receive equal consideration at promotion time.

Both sides have valid points. In law enforcement, the officer who develops the informant generally continues to work with the individual, placing the officer in both roles as recruiter and handler. The controversy at the intelligence agency reminds us that different skills are required for both of these very different functions. Recruiting is a lot like sales in its objective to influence an important decision in a person's life. Officers who are good recruiters (and who would probably be successful salespeople) may not be as suited for the equally important role of managing the informant as cases are developed and prosecutions planned.

In law enforcement, unlike the intelligence business, the credit usually goes, not to the person who developed the informant, but to the one who manages him or her and brings the cases to a successful conclusion. You can be a good recruiter, but our product is not intelligence; rather, it is something much more tangible — a conviction or a forfeiture. To achieve that goal the informant has to be successfully managed.

Management

Management styles have changed quite a bit over the centuries. Flogging, keel-hauling, and chaining people to their machines have pretty much gone out of fashion. This does not mean that the boss is no longer the boss and the worker no longer a worker; it means that the way this relationship is conducted has changed. The overall trend has been toward management that is more democratic and less autocratic, more participatory and less dictatorial. A search at your local library will find dozens of titles reflecting the modern management styles — Quality Circles, Management by Objectives, Team Building — but, as we will see, nothing much that will help us in our situation, which is really something of an anachronism.

Management is a process by which the goals of an organization are set and achieved. This description applies to organizations as small as a family or as large as a multi-national corporation. In some respects, managing an informant is no different from managing IBM. The management process consists of three principal elements:

1. Policy
2. Methods
3. People

Policy relates to where we are going — the direction or goals of the organization. We often hear that "management sets policy," and it does, but not in a vacuum. There will always be external factors that pressure policy decisions. In the management of informants, these outside influences include the courts, who dictate how evidence can be obtained; the legislature, who enacts the laws to be enforced; and the public, which can voice its approval or disapproval of how informants are employed by law enforcement. In the officer-informant relationship, policy is set by the officer, though external forces are at work on his or her decisions. Information provided by the informant will have an impact on the goals set by the officer — what cases will be pursued, what access will be exploited.

Methods are the organizational structure and the resources necessary to get the job done. How will the policies be carried out? Let's suppose that our organizational goal is to utilize informant A to make a conspiracy case against drug dealers B, C, and D. This goal cannot be achieved by wishing it so. What resources are available? Is there money to purchase evidence? Is there money to pay the informant? Are there resources for surveillance or evidence gathering? Can records be subpoenaed? Is drug dealing even a crime? Does the law permit us to offer an incentive to the informant in exchange for his cooperation? All of these questions are answered in the form of an organizational structure which is already in place. It need only be applied to this case. If policy is what we are going to do, methods are *how* we are going to do it. Again, this is something that has traditionally been a management prerogative. In many organizations workers have little say in this area. So it is with informants. The idea that the informant would come in and say, "Here's what we're going to do, and this is how we'll do it," should be (if it is not already) utterly preposterous.

People are the final element in the management process. No organization is complete without them, after all. We obviously need at least two people — an officer and informant A — and probably many more to use the methods available to lock up the three drug dealers (our goal). People have a very significant influence on how goals are achieved and even the methods that are employed. In fact, all three elements interact with each other and influence action. In our example, the goal is busting B, C, and D. The manager can impose conditions on the people who are working toward this goal — no entrapment, for instance, or 24-hour shifts. The people in turn, influence the methods. They have physical, mental, and other limitations that can keep them from functioning in the process.

The Manager's Role

The manager obviously participates in this program, playing an important role in achieving the goals of the organization. Some of the most important functions of the manager (who, for our purposes is synonymous with the officer) include:

- Developing objectives
- Planning
- Coordinating financing
- Obtaining personnel
- Coordinating and informing
- Guiding and leading
- Monitoring, testing, and evaluating
- Maintaining external relationships

There are other functions, but these are the ones most important in the context of the officer-informant relationship. Note that all of these tasks are the exclusive purview of the officer. The informant's sole responsibility is to provide information and whatever assistance the officer directs. In this, the relationship is very different from others in modern management.

Management Styles

For about 80 years now, scientific methods have been applied in earnest to the study of management. This is a big deal for business — there is a lot of money at stake and they want the most efficient, effective organization possible, a goal which requires good management. What these studies found was that good management is largely a function of good leadership. They also found that a good leader was one who helped a group become more productive and

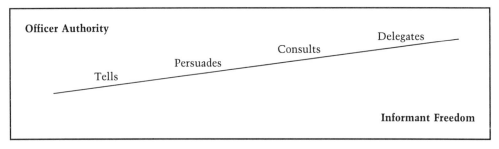

Figure 1. Leadership styles.

creative. Very rigid, autocratic, and controlling management styles which had predominated throughout history gave way to more democratic and permissive styles. These styles fostered commitment and motivation among the members of the group because the members were involved in the decision-making process on a democratic basis. (Remember the commitment and consistency principle from Chapter 5.)

Four leadership styles are typical of how the leader influences the group. These styles can be characterized as Telling, Persuading, Consulting, and Delegating (see Figure 1). The officer's authority is balanced against the informant's autonomy in the decision-making process:

1. *Telling:* The leader identifies problems, weighs alternatives, decides, and tells the group what to do. The group has substantial input in the problem-identification phase, but little or none in the rest of the process.
2. *Persuading:* Again, the leader identifies the problem, considers the alternatives, and makes the decision but tries to persuade the group that the decision is in the best interest of both the group and the organization. The group has some more input, though not in the decision itself, only as to whether or not they are going to execute it.
3. *Consulting:* The leader involves the group in the entire process, presenting the problem and asking for input and possible solutions. The group can provide alternatives, but the leader makes the final decision about how the problem will be solved.
4. *Delegating:* The leader identifies a problem and the conditions under which it must be solved. The group comes up with a solution that works for everyone. The leader agrees in advance to support the solution as long as it meets the conditions.

Delegating: A Good Idea and Why It Will Not Work

Delegating is a dandy idea for employee empowerment and motivation. By involving the employee in a decision from the beginning, that decision *becomes* his or hers. People who work under those conditions tend to have very high levels of commitment and motivation, with accompanying high productivity. These are all things we would like to see in an informant or any employee.

Delegating also works well for the manager. Nobody can do everything, after all, so some of the work is shared with someone else. Delegation allows managers to share the work among many individuals at many different levels of an organization. Knowing that the work is being done, the supervisor can focus on other management chores.

There is absolutely no room for that sort of thing in the handling of informants. Control is the essence of informant management. At all times in the relationship, the officer, *not* the informant, must be in control of the decision-making process. No authority is ever delegated by the officer, directly or indirectly.

A Leadership Style for Informants

What is to be done with the informant's information? Who is to be investigated or prosecuted? What types of cases, if any, are to be initiated, and how are we to proceed? None of these questions must ever be left to an informant to answer. This is not their responsibility. Informants are not trained, emotionally prepared, legally empowered, or in any other way qualified to make these calls. In almost every case, the informant has an inherent conflict of interest and cannot make an impartial decision. That is the job of the informant's first-line manager, his case officer.

There is only one acceptable leadership style in the officer-informant relationship. The officer *tells* the informant what the decision is and how it will be carried out. This does *not* mean that the informant is not consulted, that his feelings or information are ignored, or that his opinions are not respected. Quite the opposite is true. A wise officer will go to great lengths to learn exactly what the informant thinks about the situation, the problems, possible solutions, and every available alternative. People's lives may be at stake. Why would we ignore input that could prevent a bad decision or foster a good one?

As in the military, however, once the decision is made, the informant is expected to salute smartly and move out. The informant possesses the information we need to make the correct decisions; the officer must respect this fact of life. At the same time, the informant must respect the officer's prerogative to make those decisions. This mutual respect is the foundation of good informant management.

Informant Management

Like the man whose obituary appears at the head of this chapter, I, too, am a person of limited information regarding circular saws. I have a great deal of respect for them, however. I understand that in the right hands they are very useful. I also know that in the wrong hands they can *remove* hands. For a circular saw to be of any use whatsoever, it will have to be controlled, and the same is true of informants. In skillful hands and with other tools, a circular saw will produce beautiful things, even entire buildings. What the informant will produce will depend upon the case officer.

An informant is not an inanimate tool, however. He or she is a sentient human being, with needs, ambitions, emotions, failings, strengths, and weaknesses. Managing a person is much different from wielding a tool. Managing a person who is carrying the weight of betrayal around with him is a challenge few in society could either appreciate or fulfill. Managing such a person is about control.

The Basis of Control

Informant management is a one-on-one proposition. The organizational chart for this particular organization looks like this:

$$\text{Officer} \quad \rightarrow \quad \text{Informant}$$

One officer is the primary contact for the informant. This person should have the authority to make decisions affecting the informant and case development, together with the knowledge and ability necessary to address the informant's questions or problems. With this authority goes responsibility. The officer is responsible for receiving full value from the informant, developing cases, and communicating up the chain of command.

One officer can manage multiple informants, but informants should not report to more than one case officer. There are obviously situations in which the informant has to speak with someone else, as when the case officer leaves town for work or vacation. Make arrangements for a designated back-up contact, preferably someone who is known to the informant through meetings or the case officer.

Informant contacts with other officers should be formalized. If the case officer is transferred, retires, or is otherwise prevented from dealing with the informant, a formal reassignment of the informant to a new case officer resets the relationship. With this transfer, the new case officer assumes the responsibility for the informant's management and the informant knows to whom he will be reporting. Continuity is maintained without confusion or disruption. It is a good idea to have the outgoing case officer, in whom the informant already has trust, assist in the transition, introducing the new officer and emphasizing the continued commitment of the agency to the informant.

Having an informant report to more than one officer or provide information to whomever he or she pleases is an abdication of control. It enables the informant to play officers off against each other, promotes confusion, and greatly increases the chances of conflict among the officers; everyone talking to the informant will have their own priorities and interests and will issue their own instructions. Chaos will ensue.

An informant who cooperates with more than one agency at a time are under even less control. Where does his first loyalty lie? (Who knows?) Which instructions will the informant follow? (Whichever the informant feels like.) Will the officers in the different agencies communicate effectively with each other? (Highly doubtful.) Is the informant angling for rewards or benefits from both, perhaps shopping information to the highest bidder? (Most probably.) Who is in control here? (The informant.) If it is determined that the informant is in contact with more than one agency, the informant should be offered a clear choice and made to stick to it. Save yourself a lot of aggravation and follow the basic rule: *One officer manages the informant.*

Share Information, Not the Informant

One mistake often made in law enforcement agencies is underutilizing a source. This might happen when a case officer focuses too intensely on one investigation or issue. Perhaps the officer and informant have grown too close, or the officer is merely trying to protect his source for some future operation. Management cannot allow this to happen. An informant is a very valuable agency resource, *not* the personal property of an officer. The officer's role is not to hoard the information provided by the informant, but to make sure that every little bit of it is used in the most productive way possible.

If this means referring information to another agency with jurisdiction, make the necessary arrangements. If the informant has information about burglaries and the officer works narcotics, the officer is still responsible for making certain that the burglary information is exploited to the fullest. Is this sometimes a difficult pill for officers to swallow? You bet. I once had an informant who had terrific information about a major, very high-profile crime which was completely unrelated to narcotics. I knew full well that if I gave this information over, some officer from another department was going to get the credit for solving the case. My responsibility as the informant's case officer, however, was to make sure that every lead that person had was developed.

This does not mean that *everything* gets shared. Although some means must be found to get the information to the appropriate parties, this does not automatically require that the informant's identity is disclosed or that anyone else will have access to the source. In many cases, part of the deal with the informant may be that his or her identity will not be disclosed.

The Hotel Pierre robbery case, in which the FBI managed to get the important information to the police but ultimately refused access to the informant, is an excellent example. The

NYPD and the Manhattan District Attorney were very upset with the Bureau over their recalcitrance, but the Feds were within their rights, and one suspects if the situation was reversed and NYPD had made the promise to their informant, they might have taken the same line. At any rate, the ultimate decision to disclose the informant under these circumstances will take place far above the case officer's head.

Establishing Control

The relationship between officer and informant is one of business and must always be kept on a professional basis. Promulgation of a clear set of rules sets the tone. These rules establish the authority of the officer. After all, the officer is the one putting them forward. The rules also let the informant know in no uncertain terms exactly what he can and cannot do in his new situation. This process should be familiar to most people who have held a job. Most employers start a new employee out with an employee handbook and a clearly written job description. There is no such description of an informant's duties, but the rules can still be set forth. The other thing that happens when we apply for or begin a new job is a small blizzard of paperwork, and so it is with informants. Keeping the relationship on a professional basis means the old, informal way of documenting the informant is no longer acceptable to management.

Rules and the Informant Agreement

Most law enforcement agencies (and all of the federal ones) have a set of written guidelines for informants. These rules are outlined at the time the informant is documented or registered. In most cases, the informant is required to sign the form, acknowledging his understanding. This form is then kept in the informant's file.

The presentation of the rules can be a good opportunity to start establishing control. First, the informant agreement should be presented and signed in a formal setting, such as at the law enforcement agency offices. Each paragraph should be initialed by both the officer and the informant as it is read. This has the psychological effect of signing something significant, like a contract, as indeed it is. As with a legal contract, this implies a commitment on the part of both parties and reinforces the correct perception that the officer and informant are "in this together."

Second, the two-way nature of the contract should also be stressed. If the informant agrees to behave in a certain, officially approved manner, the law enforcement officer agrees to fulfill his or her end of the arrangement. At all times it should be emphasized that this is a business relationship.

Some directions for informants are included in the Attorney General's guidelines in the Appendices together with a form used by a federal law enforcement agency. I usually include a personal caution in addition to the printed warning. This is an acknowledgment that we are not going to be living with each other and while he is out of my sight, he is, for all practical purposes, able to break the rules. I am not going to take it personally if he does, but if he gets caught, he should not take it personally if I immediately void the agreement. Nothing personal; this is business.

Documentation

The second means of establishing control is also a requirement at almost all law enforcement agencies. This is the formal documentation of the informant. In all cases, the officer should know as much as possible about the informant *before* the relationship gets underway. There are many instances of wanted persons, impostors, and other undesirable characters walking in with information. These people are discovered when the background check has been completed. I know of one case in which a man wanted for murder in another jurisdiction was detected by the background check. This check should always include at least the following:

- Personal history
- Fingerprint card
- Photographs
- NCIC check
- Criminal history
- Local records checks

Copies of a personal history form are included in the Appendices, along with other forms used in documenting an informant. Do not feel constrained to stick to the form, however. Get enough information from the informant about his background to make yourself comfortable that you (1) know exactly who this person is, (2) you can find him again if you need to, and (3) you have a good idea about his possible motivations for informing. A thorough personal history includes names and addresses of relatives, present and former employers, and even financial information, if it is that type of case. Law enforcement often starts working with an informant with less information about that person than a fast-food place would get from a burger flipper. Do not make this mistake. *Know* this person.

Evaluation and Assessment

From the first moment of contact with an informant until the day he walks away for the last time, the officer is assessing and evaluating the informant and his information. While you are doing this, the informant, who has a big stake in this game, is doing the same. Can I trust this person? Should I believe what he or she is telling me? Is he or she telling me everything I need to know? These are significant questions for the officer, but they have huge importance for the informant.

The evaluation and assessment process is not scientific. There is no way, for example, to objectively measure someone's cooperation or to get the answers to those important questions. Everyone tends to make their evaluations subjectively, based on "feel," which is exactly why it is so important that the relationship be kept on a one-on-one basis. Only someone who is really knowledgeable about the informant and his situation can get the proper feel for progress and problems.

Even though the process is non-scientific, there are a couple of tools that can be used successfully to assess the informant's motivation, evaluate his access, judge his truthfulness, and appraise the level of control. This information is every bit as important as those things the informant is saying about crime.

Initial Debriefing. Much information will come out in the all-important initial debriefing. This is covered in some detail in the chapter on interviewing, but now is a good time to remind everyone how critical the "first cold press" is. It is at this interview that the officer must establish the informant's motivation. Do not leave the room until you are confident you have got it right. Do not assume that because the informant is "working off a beef" that this alone motivates him. Perhaps he sees this as a good chance to nail an enemy or protect some friends. Maybe he only wants to pretend to cooperate or he is too afraid to talk about the things he *really* knows. The initial interview is the officer's chance to sort all of this out.

It is also another opportunity to assert control. Because it takes time, this debriefing should be held at the office or in some private and official setting, always on the officer's turf. Although many officers prefer not to meet with informants at the office, an exception is the initial debriefing. Because we are required to take fingerprints and photographs anyway, the office is a logical choice. This is probably the first extended period in which officer and informant will be together. By placing officers in a setting in which they can be seen as professionals in a position of authority, the superior-subordinate role can be reinforced.

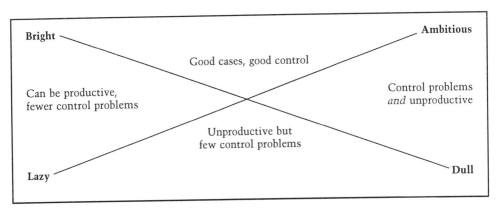

Figure 2. Rating system for evaluating informants.

One final note: Informants (or prospective informants at this stage) are at an extremely stressful and emotionally conflicted point in their lives. They may not be fully committed to a decision that leads them toward betrayal and all that it entails. They have, as yet, no reason to trust the case officer, and this distrust may be coupled with a long-time dislike, fear, or even hatred of law enforcement. In short, the officer should consider the initial debriefing a time for extreme caution. "Informants" have killed law enforcement officers before. At least two such cases are described in this book. No doubt they will do so again. The debriefing should be held in a place where the officer is in full control.

Rating Scales. We looked at a way of appraising access in Chapter 6, and we have discussed motivation at some length. Creating a rating scale for control is difficult, because it is based largely upon individual personalities. A narcotics agent with whom I worked developed a rating system for evaluating informants which I thought was quite useful as a predictor of control (Figure 2). He evaluated the informant on two scales, the criteria being intelligence and ambition. This produced four different types of informants.

1. *Bright and Ambitious:* An ideal combination; understands his role and accepts control well. Good cases.
2. *Bright and Lazy:* Good news/bad news. The good news is that these folks can make good cases. The bad news is that the officer has to work much harder. These informants are not going to do anything (good or bad) on their own, so control problems are minimized.
3. *Dull and Lazy:* You are not going to make many cases, but you are not going to have many control problems, either. Such a waste of time.
4. *Dull and Ambitious:* This informant can cause major control problems, and bad cases are the result. A dangerous combination.

While we are obviously generalizing here, in our highly unscientific chart, it helps us get a feel for the informant. It might also explain why we may be having difficulty in controlling someone or developing cases. Looking back, I would have to say that the best informants with whom I worked were all bright, motivated, and ambitious. The ones who caused the most trouble were generally not too swift and were trying too hard. Those are the ones who are out entrapping people or not following instructions because they have worked out a "better" plan on their own.

Maintaining Control

Control is an ongoing process that involves three elements: contact, corroboration, and communication. Control is established with the first contact, the initial debriefing, and through documentation of the informant. Subsequent contacts reaffirm the officer's control. The frequency of such contacts and their nature — telephone or personal — will be determined on a case-by-case basis, but a regular schedule is important for several reasons. First, the officer is attempting to assert control. By setting a regular schedule for contacts, the officer is requiring the informant to conform to some structure instituted by the officer.

Telephone Contacts

A daily schedule of telephone contacts is desirable. At least once each day, you will know exactly where the informant is (on the phone) and what he is doing (talking to you). This is good for the officer's peace of mind, if nothing else. I usually ask a new informant to call in daily even if only to report that the sun rose as usual. Take the opportunity to ask questions, even old ones to which you already have his answers. This repetition is a good way to check that the story is still straight.

A flat contact time — "10:00 a.m. every day except Sunday" may be a good way to require dependability, but beware; some informants, especially walk-ins with fuzzy motives, may be using their calls to check on the officer's whereabouts (they know where *you* are once a day, too). Thanks to beepers and cellular phones, this is not as big a concern as it once might have been.

Another benefit of regular, if not daily, communication is that it gives the officer a chance to pass along directions or instructions. The officer's role is to provide guidance. Remember, in this leadership style, we are *telling* them what to do. We cannot do that if we are not talking. Even telephone contacts allow the officer to direct the informant and to check on whether previous instructions were followed. Incidentally, except in an emergency, the officer should always *take*, not *make* the scheduled phone calls. The informant is the one who is being held to the schedule, not the other way around.

Finally, the dependability of the informant can be gauged by how well or poorly he follows the schedule he is given. If he succeeds at this relatively simple task, we may have more confidence that he'll succeed at other, harder assignments. The fact that an informant was instructed to make regular contact and did so can also be used in establishing credibility for purposes of later search warrant affidavits.

Some informants may not like being on this short a leash, but they must accept the officer's control, and this is not an unreasonable place to start. Having the informant call the officer makes him work for the officer, rather than the other way around. It sets a good precedent and is well worth the hassle of taking all those calls.

Home Telephone Contact. Some officers give their home phone numbers to informants with instructions to call in emergencies or even under routine circumstances. Do *not* do this. You are trying to establish a business relationship with the informant, one characterized by professional detachment. Giving the informant access to your home and, by implication, your personal life threatens this detachment. Familiarity breeds contempt for rules and roles. This weakens the respect necessary for the relationship to function. If you are going to be working with informants, get a pager or a wireless phone and an unlisted home telephone number. You have to be able to accept emergency calls — it is part of the deal you made with the informant. Make the distinction clear for the informant — the pager, cell phone, or dispatcher is for work.

Personal Contacts

The notation "meeting a CI" is written on sign-out boards in police stations and squad bays all over the world every day. This activity is so common that it can become dangerously routine. No one will argue that personal contacts with informants are not necessary; in fact, they are indispensable. Like everything else in an officer's relationship with an informant, however, they should be carefully controlled. There is no substitute for face-to-face contact, at which questions can be asked and answers evaluated. If the informant is actively developing cases by introducing an undercover agent or contacting potential defendants directly, additional meetings will be required. Some questions will arise about when and how these meetings should take place.

Frequency. How often do you meet with an informant? It depends, but the general rule should be not more often than you need to. If there is some pressing reason to meet, a personal contact should be arranged. Pressing reasons may include the need for a detailed interview on a specific subject, general debriefing, or just the desire by the officer to reassert control. There might also be the need to make a regular payment or meet some other obligation.

Unnecessary meetings should be avoided. They increase the risk to officer and informant, create unwanted or superfluous paperwork, and promote familiarity, which, as the saying goes, breeds contempt. Every time the officer meets with the informant, some information is conveyed to him, even if it is only what car the officer is driving or where the officer prefers to meet informants. A little remoteness will not harm the relationship, as long as the informant knows the officer will meet when needed.

In the intelligence business, where officers meet with the people who are doing the spying, actual face-to-face contacts may be rare. There are documented cases in which, once a communications channel was established, the source never met again directly with his case officer. In other cases, arrangements were made for periodic meetings in foreign countries, reducing the risk to the source.

Aldrich Ames, the CIA officer who betrayed American secrets to the KGB for years before the FBI caught him, regularly used a set of dead drops to communicate with his handlers. This reduced the need for more dangerous personal contacts, but the Russians still felt the need to meet with Ames. These get-togethers took place overseas, in South America or Europe, where the risk of detection was far lower. At these meetings, Ames, who was a mercenary and egotistical informant, was paid large sums of cash, was questioned extensively about CIA activity, and had his motivation to betray recharged. The KGB used these opportunities to issue instructions, focus their spy's efforts, and generally assert control.

How To Meet an Informant. *Not alone.* This rule should be engraved on the consciousness of every law enforcement officer everywhere in letters 9 feet high. There are a dozen rationalizations for violating this rule. I have heard all of them and used most, but the bottom line is that it is *never* a good idea to meet an informant alone. In fact, it is a disaster waiting to happen.

Joe Petrosino found this out the hard way. A Detective Lieutenant on the New York Police Department, Petrosino was selected to travel to Sicily to conduct an investigation of the links between Mafia gangsters in Sicily and their counterparts in New York City. On March 12, 1909, Lieutenant Petrosino spoke briefly with some unidentified men in a Palermo café. Leaving the restaurant, he walked alone through the Piazza Marina, apparently planning to meet there with a man who had offered information about the Mafia. When he arrived at the rendezvous, he was gunned down by two or more assailants. Lieutenant Petrosino's murder was never solved.

Murder is only the most extreme bad outcome of a violation of the rule against meeting alone. Informants have "set up" officers for assaults and robberies, made false claims of physical or sexual abuse, and alleged that the officer shook the informant down, extorted the informant for drugs or money, or sold or gave drugs to the informant. Without a witness, the officer has no defense against such claims but his own credibility.

The temptation to meet alone with an informant, especially one of long-standing, is great, but it should always be resisted. Some informants, especially walk-ins, will say to their prospective case officer, "I'll talk, but only to you, nobody else." Being selected for this position of trust is highly flattering, particularly if the officer has worked long and hard on developing this source. At this moment, with the prize almost in hand, the officer need only make one small, seemingly reasonable concession.

Here's why this "little" concession is a bad plan. First, at the exact moment when the officer needs to assert his control, he relinquishes some to the informant. He sets a bad precedent, virtually guaranteeing that the informant will try to get some more control later. Second, communication is always two way. By agreeing to this condition, the officer sends a message that he values the informant's information more highly than perhaps he should. This is a particular problem when the informant has shopped that information around or previously worked with another agency. In that case, he knows exactly what sort of edge he has.

Finally, this is a matter of trust. By agreeing to meet alone, the officer is trusting the informant with his position, his career, even his life. Placing these things most precious in the hands of someone who is in the process of betraying some other trusting individuals does not seem to be the most logical (or sensible) course of action one could take.

How can we avoid this situation? The officer must be up-front with the condition. "These are the rules of my agency. They are non-negotiable, and anyway, they are for your own good. If something happens to me, if I'm on vacation or out of town, you've got someone to call in an emergency." Offer other assurances — pseudonyms, code numbers, or covert meeting locations — but do not succumb to the temptation now, or you will regret it later. Make no mistake, this is not a motivation question: "He'll be motivated to work with me if I fulfill this need." No, this is a control issue: "He is usurping the authority I need to do my job." The conditions for the informant's cooperation are clear. If he cannot take "no" for an answer at this point, what is there that would make one believe he will take "no" for anything else?

Where To Meet an Informant. You would think the choices for where to meet would be endless, but they are actually fairly limited. Because we have already agreed that we are only meeting when necessary to serve some important purpose, the location of the meeting must also support that objective. If the officer plans a lengthy debriefing, the meeting will need to be in a place where notes can be taken and questions answered in private. If a payment is to be made, the officer might want to meet in a car "on the fly."

The main consideration in setting a meeting location is security. The informant's identity needs to be protected and both the officers and the informant need to be safe at the meeting site. These sites generally fall into six categories:

1. Office
2. Car
3. Safe house or controlled meeting location
4. Public place
5. Semi-public place
6. Informant's residence or business

Each location has advantages and disadvantages. With the exception of the informant's residence or business, the officer will probably use all at various times:

- **Office** — *Advantages*: Most secure; private spaces, interviews rooms, etc. Files and computers are available for immediate corroboration of statements. Office has the trappings of authority. *Disadvantages*: Criminals who know the informant may be coming or going. Some informants do not like to go to law enforcement offices, fearing disclosure of their identity. *Comments:* The office is the best place for the initial debriefing and any subsequent lengthy interviews.

- **Car** — *Advantages:* Mobile, private, convenient, secure. *Disadvantages:* Not really suited for long interviews, although you can take notes. *Comments:* A car is a good alternative for short meetings, payments to the informant, or other focused contacts. The officer's car should always be used to pick up the informant, *not* the other way around.

- **Safe house or controlled meeting place** — *Advantages:* Private; no connection to law enforcement; can be secured; available for extended interviews. Recording equipment can be used in private. *Disadvantages:* Can be expensive. No resources (files, computers) available for research. *Comments:* This was the alternative used for the first contact with Monica Lewinsky. She was taken to one of three adjoining hotel rooms that were rented for this purpose. Because it can be costly and because supervisors say "Why don't you just use the interview room?" this alternative does not get used much. If an officer can develop contacts at local hotels, motels, or executive conference centers, or even city convention centers, the cost factor might be reduced, making this alternative more attractive.

- **Public places (restaurants, bars)** — *Advantages:* Convenient, casual, and inconspicuous; no overt connection to law enforcement; good for short meetings, payments, development meetings. *Disadvantages:* Difficult to take notes; privacy is limited; possibility exists that the officer or the informant will be recognized. *Comments:* Selected with care, these locations are good for established informants. They are also good for those informants whom you do not want to expose to other officers who might be coming or going from the office. For security reasons, it is best not to use the same place for more than one informant.

- **Semi-public places (parks, mall parking lots, open areas)** — *Advantages:* Less chance of encountering people known to the informant; fairly private; can be secured with additional surveillance; can take notes. *Disadvantages:* Not set up for long-term meetings; possible recognition of the officer or informant by others. *Comments:* Better for relatively short meetings, payment of the informant, and pre-operational briefings. You can improve security by having additional surveillance officers covering the meeting.

- **Informant territory (residence or business)** — *Advantages:* The informant feels comfortable in this setting. *Disadvantages:* Insecure; high risk of being "burned;" presence of family members or friends of the informant. *Comments:* There are very few occasions when meeting on the informant's territory should even be considered. The risks to all concerned far outweigh the benefits, if any. One occasion when this may be necessary is when a juvenile informant's parents need to be consulted or their permission obtained.

There are so many perils in this last situation that they cannot all be recounted here, but an example may illustrate just one. In an ongoing task force investigation, we received information that one of the subjects was boasting about having a "Fed" on the payroll. This was obviously a major concern and something that should be looked into. It turned out not to be an integrity problem, but a violation of the rule against meeting an informant alone and not on his turf.

The subject owned a night club in addition to his drug-trafficking activity, and the agent thought he had developed the subject as an informant. The agent frequented the club and was rewarded with tidbits of (probably) useless information from the "informant." In the meantime, the informant was pointing out the agent to other patrons in the bar and telling them he was "the Fed who keeps me posted on what the cops are doing." One of these patrons was a real informant for the local police department, who passed the word along. The agent had good intentions but bad technique. He placed himself in a compromising situation for no good reason and was predictably compromised as a result.

Emergency Contacts

In dealing with informants there are always going to be emergencies, real and imagined, to which the officer must respond. It is possible that the informant is "crying wolf" or is unnecessarily concerned about something that has come up, but part of the officer's pact with the informant is to respond to these calls. An emergency contact procedure should be outlined for the informant at the time he begins his cooperation. The use of cellular telephones and pagers makes this process much easier, but some reliable means of getting a message quickly to the agent must be found.

The agent should emphasize what types of situations qualify as "emergencies." Threats or violence against the informant obviously fit the bill. Information about an impending crime of violence against others should also prompt a call. Beyond that, the officer should specify what needs to be reported immediately. There is a balance to be struck. One does not want to be getting calls at 2:00 a.m. about a deal that is not supposed to happen until next week, but we also do not want to hear something like, "The connection dropped off a load at my place last night," at our next regularly scheduled call.

Even emergency calls can be a source of additional control. The officer, by praising appropriate calls and discouraging the unnecessary ones, is training the informant to respond correctly to situations that arise in the course of his cooperation. There will probably be some false starts and confusion about priorities at first, but effective communication will smooth the path.

Searches

Consider requiring the informant to agree to be searched at any interview. In all cases where the informant is working under the hammer of a criminal charge, this should be a condition. An informant who knows he or she might be searched at a meeting will be less likely to possess contraband or weapons. (Not always, however, which poses new problems for the officer.) This condition does not need to be included in the informant agreement, but if this is something you choose to do, be up front about the requirement.

Corroboration

One of the many irksome things defense attorneys say is that the jury is being asked to convict their client "on the uncorroborated word of an informant." It is probably nonsense and such a case should never get to a jury in the first place, of course, but at least they, too, recognize the sensible need for corroboration of the informant's statements. Corroboration is not just good sense; it is also an important means of controlling an informant and his information. Absolutely everything reported by the informant should be subject to corroboration by the officer. This ideal can never be fully met in the real world, but that should not stop us from trying. Corroboration is our guarantee of the truth in what the informant is advertising. We will examine this issue in somewhat more detail in the chapter on case development, but here we need to emphasize the value of corroboration as a mechanism for control. If the informant knows that everything he says is going to be checked, that every detail is subject to independent corroboration, he is far less likely to lie to the officer.

I told an informant this on one occasion and was rewarded with a sincerely offended reply: "What's the matter, don't you trust me?" Well, the truth was that, no, I did not, but my (also true) response was to remind him that it did not matter whether I trusted him or not. I said his job was to tell me everything he knew and my job was to check everything he told me.

Try to find some way to corroborate everything. Finding the means to corroborate the informant's statements is what the officer is paid to do. There are a number of choices:

- *Informant self-corroboration:* The informant's statements are cross-checked against each other to establish whether the story remains consistent over time. Monica Lewinsky made numerous statements over time to the Independent Counsel and the Grand Jury. Her story hung together consistently throughout.
- *Background checking:* Details of the informant's statements are checked against databases or other sources of information. Joe Valachi's statements regarding 30-year-old murders were checked against the files of the New York Police Department, which often found that, yes, a body had been found in the place and under the circumstances Valachi described.
- *Other informants:* If the officer is lucky enough to have two informants who have access to the same information, the statements of one can be checked against those of the other. This only works if the neither knows the other is cooperating.
- *Surveillance:* Surveillance, either with or without the informant's knowledge, can provide good corroboration. Linda Tripp knew she was under surveillance on the day she met with Monica Lewinsky. Knowing this, she would hardly be likely to lie about what happened. Surveillance of the activity described by the informant can also be useful. If the informant says drug dealing is taking place at a certain location, surveillance can verify the accuracy of the information.
- *Consensual monitoring:* Recording the informant's telephone calls or personal contacts with defendants is another good method to corroborate statements. Tripp was wired for her meeting with Lewinsky. If John Condon had been wired for his meeting with Hauptmann, the prosecution would have looked much different and there would be no controversy today over the "true" identity of the Lindbergh kidnapper.
- *Non-consensual monitoring:* Wiretapping or bugging can provide great corroboration of the informant's statements. Quite a bit of what mob informants such as Sammy "The Bull" Gravano say can be verified by going back over intercepted conversations.
- *Undercover agents:* Another good way to verify information, either with or without the informant's knowledge.

Corroboration is a means of keeping everybody honest. Even if you do not intend to use the information in a criminal prosecution (where corroboration would be essential), you can still gain confidence in the informant's word by checking out the things he says. It is not a matter of trust or lack thereof, simply good business.

Communication

The informant must communicate the information which the officer will convert into a successful prosecution. The officer, in turn, must clearly communicate his expectations of the informant, issuing instructions that can be understood and acted upon. This is what is going on in all those contacts we just talked about. Once again, it is incumbent on the officer to manage this communication process effectively, controlling the flow of information sent and received. Start by remembering that all communication is two way. Just by asking a question you communicate your interest in the answer or your ignorance or knowledge of the subject and can give the other person information of interest.

Two-Way Communication

Informants are extremely interested observers. We operate on a "need to know" principle in dealing with informants, telling them as little as they absolutely must know to do their jobs.

Even so, informants are constantly processing the messages, both spoken and unspoken, they receive from the officer. In the intelligence business, the person actually doing the spying will probably never know what, if anything, is done with the information he provides. Certainly his handlers are not going to tell him much. (The KGB officer handling a research scientist who provides the Russians with information about a new jet engine would never tell his spy, "Oh, we incorporated your data into our new XJ-19 fighter jet. Thanks to you, the top speed was increased from 800 mph to over 1000! Here's how we did it...") In law enforcement there is always more feedback, because criminal cases will be developed, people arrested, seizures made. These actions all directly impact on the informant, whose future and perhaps freedom depend on how well or poorly these decisions or actions are carried out.

Communication and Management
Managing the informant through this case development process can be facilitated through the use of several rules:

- *Listen carefully.* The only reason the informant is there is because we need his information. Asking the right questions helps, but the officer has to be a good listener. Listen with all your senses, as 60% or more of communication is non-verbal. The informant transmits information through body language, gestures, attitude, and actions. These provide clues for the alert officer.
- *Transmit information cautiously.* Does the informant really need to know what you know? The only reason for telling an informant anything, either verbally or through non-verbal communication of your own, is if the informant needs the information to do his job better. It is acceptable, for example, to tell the informant that the subject of the investigation is frequenting a certain location and that is where the informant should go to look for him to make contact. It is unnecessary to tell the informant that the subject has five prior arrests; the informant does not need that information to fulfill his role.
- *Train wisely.* Life is for learning, and informants learn quickly. We need to communicate information which will help the informant be a better informant, *not* a better criminal. Teach the informant how to make a better statement, not how our technical equipment or surveillance techniques work. Do not expose the informant to law enforcement officers, operations, or techniques unless this is absolutely essential. Only under the most extraordinary circumstances should the officer expose the informant to another informant or even confirm the identity of an informant.
- *Show no weakness.* Especially the moral sort — the informant needs to have absolute trust and confidence in the officer. The officer must communicate confidence, competence, and dependability.
- *Document everything.* Document the informant's statements, payments made, your efforts to corroborate the information, anything that might be important later.
- *Respect the informant's role.* The informant is there to provide you with information. By listening to him, responding to his information, and paying attention, you are communicating that you respect his role and reinforce the message that his information is important. You also ignore the informant at your own peril.

Barriers to Effective Communication
Gender, age, and race may be factors that can cause problems in the management of informants. It would be extremely difficult for a female officer to control a male informant effectively who was from certain Asian and Middle-Eastern cultures. In these societies, the traditionally subservient role of the female would make it difficult for a male informant to accept the control of a female officer. Not always, however, as Emad Salem, the informant in the FBI's World Trade Center bombing case, was managed very capably by a female FBI agent.

Nevertheless, this problem is recognized in such organizations as the Israeli intelligence service, which reportedly has no female case officers. According to one ex-Israeli agent, almost all of the targets of the Israeli service are Arab males whom he says could be recruited or handled only with the greatest difficulty by a woman. As time goes by and women are assimilated into positions of authority in these societies, this problem will diminish. At present, it is a concern for female officers and those who supervise them.

Age is another important factor in relationships in certain cultures around the world. Role expectations may exist in which a younger person must display a marked deference to his or her elders. Some accommodation must be made for these attitudes, because the case officer who defers to the informant for whatever reason risks losing control. In a narcotics case some years ago, I was attempting to establish a rapport with a defendant informant who was about 10 years older than I. He clearly understood the need for me to control the case and make decisions about the investigation, but it was equally clear that he was uncomfortable with the discrepancy in our ages. In his culture (Korean), age is a major consideration in interpersonal relationships. Males often refer to each other in conversation as "older brother" and "younger brother," with suitable deference paid to the elder of the two. The translator alerted me to the problem after the informant asked about my age. I gave my correct age, to which he responded that I "looked much older, maybe 55 or 60." This would not be much of a compliment in our culture, but in his way he was at least trying to accommodate himself to the reality of a clash in cultural values.

One way this age-related problem can be resolved is to have an older officer participate in the investigation, even occasionally, to remind the informant that a respected elder is involved in the decision-making process. This can also be a very useful technique in recruiting an older informant from an Asian culture. All other factors being equal, the chances of a 25-year-old officer in blue jeans recruiting a 55-year-old Asian male as an informant are far lower than those of a 57-year-old officer in a three-piece suit doing the recruiting. The younger officer will be able to manage the informant, but should keep in mind the difference in their ages.

Race unfortunately also plays a part in some officer-informant relationships. In his study of FBI and DEA agents, James Q. Wilson described a black agent who was known and respected for the quality of his informants, many of whom were also black. This agent no doubt benefited from the affinity people have for others like themselves, but many officers are successful at developing and managing informants of other races, creeds, and colors. These same officers are probably equally successful in their other interpersonal relationships.

Obviously, there is no room for prejudice or outdated stereotypes in the management of informants (or anyone else, for that matter). The best managers are probably those who can appreciate ethnic and cultural diversity while still focusing on the requirements of the job at hand. In order to manage the informant, the case officer must establish his or her trustworthiness, something that will never happen if the informant believes the officer to be racist, sexist, or in some other way bigoted.

Once again, respect plays a most important part. If an officer's prejudice cannot allow him or her to respect someone who is gay or lesbian, Jewish, or addicted to narcotics, that officer should refer that informant to someone who can. Access has no color, ethnic background, religion, or sexual orientation.

Language is another potential barrier to establishing that trustworthiness. Because communication is so essential to maintenance of the officer-informant relationship, it is desirable, if not essential, that both have at least one common language. Working through a translator, especially one who is not a law enforcement officer, places a heavy strain on all concerned. The potential for misunderstanding and confusion is too great. If the informant speaks only Spanish or Korean, the officer assigned to manage his case should also speak Spanish or Korean.

Documentation

Any significant informant contact must be documented. Quite a few people have an interest in what the informant has to say, and because the officer and his or her partner are the only ones who hear it, they have to report the contacts to the interested parties. These include others involved in the cases being developed, the officer's supervisors, and the prosecuting attorney.

Telephone contacts should be logged, with memos or reports written on meetings. The informant's code number or name should be used in these reports, which should contain only the information provided by the informant. Operational information beyond the date, time, general location, and persons present should not be included.

Let informants know at the outset that their information will be duly reported. Some are nervous about this, but once again, the officer can emphasize the business nature of the relationship and paperwork is how things get done in business. Explain the protections used by the agency — code names or numbers, restricted distribution, security, etc., but do not share the reports with informants unless they are something they are required to sign.

Officers should also document contacts with potential informants or persons they are trying to develop. This is mostly for the officers' protection — charges have been leveled that officers were seen "consorting with known criminals." If your job includes working with informants, you *should* be consorting with criminals, but only on approved terms and with the support of the administration. This means those development contacts should be documented in writing.

Management Review

The officer is not a lone actor in this drama. The law enforcement agency has a major role as well. In addition to reviewing the reports submitted by the case officer and records of payments, management should conduct periodic reviews of the informant's status. Are cases being developed? Is the information being exploited? Is the case officer doing everything necessary to get full value from the informant? Are there any integrity problems? A management review every 3 to 6 months can answer these questions. Reports of each management review can be included in the informant's file. Unless there is some perceived problem, management should not interfere with the officer-informant relationship. Contact should be through the case officers, who should know that their actions are subject to management oversight. Everyone in this situation should be accountable for behavior and results.

Payment

Informants who are being paid for their information or expenses will always sign for the money. Large payments should be made by check and smaller ones in cash. The officer must not cash the informant's check, and should only assist the informant in cashing a check if the chain of command approves in advance. Informant payments must always be witnessed by another officer. Some departments require the informant's thumbprint for verification. At minimum, the standard receipt should be signed.

Payments are taxable, something mentioned in the informant agreement but frequently "forgotten" later by the informant. Failing to report payments as income will be brought up by defense attorneys at trial if the informant is to testify. Jurors will take appropriate notice.

Informant payments are generally of two sorts: expense payments and awards or rewards. Both are something officer and informant should discuss before getting started. If it is agreed that the informant's expenses in cooperating are to be reimbursed, the informant must also clear these expenses in advance with the officer. If he comes in after the fact with a bill for some expense and asks for payment, the answer should always be a firm "no." Make the rules clear up front, agree upon what expenses you will cover, and do not deviate or you will be getting (ever more bizarre) requests daily.

Awards and rewards are obviously in a different category. For one thing, they get paid out at the end of a case, when the officers are satisfied that they have gotten full value from the informant. This is very much a C.O.D. proposition, something else that should be made absolutely clear up front. We have to be careful about the promises we make in this area to avoid contingent payments, but the limits of the award can be described. Check with legal counsel about how to word these descriptions, then stick to the script.

The bottom line on the payment issue is that they are for value received — not value promised or value in the pipeline, but value received, examined, evaluated, and approved. Informants must know that their needs, whether they relate to money or lenience, will not be fulfilled until the officer is satisfied. *That* will be a motivated informant.

Relinquishing Control

All good (and, it is hoped, most bad) things must come to an end. No informant should ever be on a lifetime contract. When the terms of his agreement are fulfilled, when his motivation is gone, when his access no longer exists, it is time to terminate the relationship. In most cases, the informant will be more than ready to go his separate way, but some informants may want to cling to the commitment made months, even years before. Some informants grow to like the work and thrive in the relationship with the officer. This is a business relationship, however, dominated not by emotional satisfaction but by legal concerns and practical considerations. The time comes when it is time to move on. When that time comes, the informant moves on.

Termination

Most informants are terminated when their access is gone. Some lose motivation and drift off. Some go out of our control and are terminated with prejudice. Others get locked up for some new offense and no longer have the motivation, access, or control to continue. When any of the above occurs, the agency that developed the informant should reverse the process and terminate his services. Termination is a clean break on paper. As of the date of termination, that informant is no longer cooperating; the agreement is ended. While there may be some additional contacts with the informant, such as a court appearance or award payment, everyone should be clear that the party is over. It is not uncommon for a terminated informant to get arrested and claim that he was "working for officer A." This is why the break is clean on paper, and why the officer should not have further dealings with the informant unless the file is reopened.

Termination with Prejudice

Some informants do not make the grade, perhaps through no fault of their own or through circumstances beyond their control. Others lie, cheat, steal, or generally behave like the criminals they once were and will be again. Those informants should be terminated with prejudice, a process sometimes known as "blackballing."

A blackballed informant is removed from the register and cannot be reactivated or used without extraordinary permission. Management should also take whatever steps are necessary to protect officers from other agencies from becoming entangled with this problem. Occasionally officers or their bosses are reluctant to disclose details of a problem informant; maybe they feel this is a poor reflection on the officer or the agency. This attitude is unwarranted, as anyone can be "burned" by a bad informant and there is no shame in being burned once.

Informants should be terminated with prejudice for the following offenses:

- Assaulting or threatening an officer
- Endangering an officer

- Failing to report a threat to an officer's safety
- Engaging in entrapment or other illegal evidence gathering
- Committing perjury
- Stealing from the agency
- Providing information about agency operations to criminals

There may be some other transgressions which merit a blackball, but these should earn a swift exit for the perpetrator. Any of the above should void the agreement and even subject the former informer to prosecution. Most officers have little patience for this sort of behavior; it usually means a lot of time and money have been wasted. The officer and his department may have been opened up to some civil liability, and cases may be lost. Making sure that the informant will not be able to repeat the process with another officer is the least we can do. A blackballed informant should be told of his status. He should also be told that other agencies will be told of the problem. The agreement is void and the informant is on his own.

Contact after Termination

There may be some need to continue official contacts with informants after they have been terminated. If court cases are still pending, the prosecutor may require that the informant keep law enforcement posted on his whereabouts. This may be true even if the prosecutor does not intend to call the informant as a witness, because some courts have ruled that potential witnesses must be available to the defense. To avoid charges that we are "hiding" witnesses, the officer should at least keep track of the informant after termination.

Termination of the official relationship is not the opportunity to go into business with the informant or to start some personal relationship. "Hey, she is not an informant anymore, so now we can date" is not something a supervisor especially wants to hear. Officers have become business partners with ex-informants, married ex-informants, and lent money to or borrowed money from ex-informants. They have even collaborated with informants on books. None of these activities is acceptable behavior. For these purposes, an informant is never terminated. The conflict of interest should be obvious to everyone.

Summing Up

It may seem ridiculous to ask a career criminal to respect a law enforcement officer. Perhaps it is just as improbable to ask that law enforcement officer respect someone who makes her living as a junkie prostitute. If the officer-informant relationship is to succeed, each will have to find the ability to respect, if not the individual, then their position.

Throughout this chapter I have emphasized the importance of control Obtaining this control requires the intuitive sagacity and subtle ingenuity of which Sun Tzu spoke. The officer must be in control of the decision-making process, yes, but this does not mean that an informant must be kept on the ground under the officer's heel. That approach, aside from being inhumane and inappropriate, is also unproductive and unnecessary. Brute force — the physical abuse of informants to coerce their cooperation — was once an all too common practice. Thankfully, that era is over. The officer who behaves in that fashion is not only rightly seen as a criminal, he is also plain stupid. An informant, in addition to being a human being with rights and feelings, is a valuable resource. He is not going to see much from the ground with a boot at his neck and is going to say even less. No, to borrow a management phrase, the officer is going to have to manage smarter, not harder.

Case Study: World Trade Center Bombing

The bomb that blew apart the underground garage in New York's World Trade Center weighed 1500 pounds and cost a few hundred dollars to build. When it exploded on February 26, 1993, it killed six people and the damage cost $700 million to clean up. The investigation of this bombing would cost many millions more, as the FBI, NYPD, ATF, and other agencies sought answers in the rubble of a tragedy that could have been much, much worse.

Within days of the explosion, the first of the bombers, Mohammad Salameh, was in custody. ATF and NYPD bomb experts working in the ruined garage had found a part of the truck that had contained the bomb. The part bore a vehicle identification number which was quickly traced to a Ryder truck rental agency in Jersey City, NJ. Salameh, who had rented the van, had reported it stolen the day before the bombing and wanted his $400 deposit back. The FBI was waiting.

The World Trade Center case began as all cases do, with a criminal act. Investigators begin by following leads and employing as many of the seven basic investigative techniques that might apply. In such a major crime, there were thousands of leads to run down. The collection and preservation of physical evidence from the crime scene yielded hundreds of clues. Interviews of witnesses produced more information. Even surveillance tapes from the security cameras in the building contained information the investigators could use. As valuable as this massive quantity of data would be in convicting the perpetrators, none of it would yield the identities of the bombers. To get this information the investigators needed to start with a name. One name, they knew, would lead to others. "Mohammad Salameh" was the first name.

In addition to his name, Mohammed Salameh gave his address to the attentive Ryder representative, who was really an undercover FBI agent. A search of the residence in Jersey City yielded Salameh's cooperative roommate and other information. One item of extreme interest to the investigators was a photograph of Salameh and another man. The photograph was good news and bad news for the FBI.

The good news was that agents knew the man with Salameh; he was El Sayyid Nosair, the accused assassin of the radical Zionist rabbi Meir Kahane three years earlier. The bad news was, although Nosair was in prison, his associates had been under FBI surveillance prior to the bombing. Even worse, up until a few months before, the FBI had had an informant in the group, someone who told them Nosair was planning a bombing campaign from his prison cell. "You better hope it was not those guys who did it," an NYPD anti-terrorism detective told his FBI counterpart.

Emad Salem, the informant in question, heard about the bombing like everyone else. His ties to Nosair's group were still very strong, but he had no access to the inner workings of the cell of terrorists who planned and executed the actual bombing. He figured the FBI would be calling him, however, and he was right. Salem had been a difficult informant to manage. He was a volunteer, who offered his assistance to an FBI agent he met while working as a security guard. A former colonel in the Egyptian army, the 44-year-old Salem claimed to have been a member of the Egyptian president's personal guard, an intelligence operative, and a security expert. Some of his stories were undoubtedly exaggerations. Since coming to the U.S., he had worked as a taxi driver

During Nosair's trial, his supporters were joined by a relative newcomer, one who would become a close confidant of Nosair's cousin, Ibrahim El-Gabrowny. Emad Salem's assignment was to keep track of Nosair and El-Gabrowny, who were in contact during the trial, and afterward, when El-Gabrowney and Salem went to visit Nosair at the Attica State Correctional Facility. Salem gave the FBI several pieces of critical information concerning these meetings. He said that Nosair was directing his supporters to wage a *jihad* or holy war, the purpose of which was to free Nosair from prison. He also said that Nosair's group, including El-Gabrowney and Mahmud Aboulhalima, another Attica visitor, planned to wage a terror campaign, including the bombing of public buildings in New York City.

The FBI, unsure of its informant, who had trouble on polygraph tests and tended toward hyperbole, wanted more corroboration before taking any action. They instructed Salem to continue watching El-Gabrowney while the Bureau worked with other informants in Nosair's group.

In any event, corroboration for Salem's allegations was already in government hands. On the day after Rabbi Meir Kahane was killed, officers searched Nosair's home, seizing boxes of documents. Among these papers was a formula, written in Arabic, for a urea nitrate bomb, the explosive substance used in the World Trade Center device 2 years later. In the same boxes were speeches by Salem's boss, the radical Sheik Omar Abdel-Rahman, urging followers to "destroy the edifices of capitalism." Some of these edifices were also featured in photographs in the Nosair papers. The photographs depicted, among other famous buildings, the World Trade Center. While Nosair's formula and photographs languished in the FBI's evidence room, Salem moved toward a falling-out with the FBI.

The FBI had sought to use their informant to develop a case against El-Gabrowney and Nosair. They wanted Salem to wear a recording device and tape the prison meetings; tapes would provide corroboration for Salem's allegations. The Bureau also wanted Salem to testify against the conspirators, something the ex-colonel vehemently refused to do. This was not part of the original deal. The FBI had promised, Salem said, that his secret role would never be revealed.

Too bad, the FBI replied, no play, no pay. The Bureau was paying Salem $500 a week plus expenses, and they did not feel they were getting their money's worth. Salem was volatile, tended to exaggerate, and had received inconclusive results on FBI polygraph tests. There was a lack of confidence in the relationship, and it was mutual.

Salem, the walk-in informant, walked out. Now, 7 months later, after the massive shock of the World Trade Center bombing, the FBI was back. Salem's original handler, Special Agent Nancy Floyd of the Intelligence Division, was in contact with him, as was Special Agent John Anticev, of the Anti-Terrorist Task Force. The task was not to convince the prickly Salem to cooperate — he wanted to do that; liked it, in fact. The problem was getting him to do it on the Bureau's terms.

Salem's background made this an even bigger problem than it would have been for most informants. He was an experienced informant, after all, having worked not only for the FBI but also for the Immigration and Naturalization Service, the CIA, and other intelligence agencies the FBI could only guess at. They knew he was in contact with Egyptian military intelligence, even as he reported to Nancy Floyd. He was also smart and knowledgeable about how investigations were conducted. In short, Salem knew exactly how valuable a commodity he had just become to the FBI. He figured that his access to the people who had executed the bombing made him worth, say, about $2 million.

As the clean-up costs, which would eventually top $700 million, began to climb, a couple of million did not seem like such a big deal. It was very clear that they would not be going back to the original $500 a week deal, but there were still those who questioned the need for Salem's assistance. One FBI supervisor called him a "buffoon;" perhaps they did not require his services after all.

The investigation had had some successes and was proceeding well without Salem. After only a couple of weeks, the FBI had four people in custody, not counting Nosair, the instigator. The cases against El-Gabrowney and Salameh were strong; the one against Aboulhalima, less so. There was always the possibility that one of these subjects would "flip" on the others; all were facing life sentences. The FBI also had some other informants, one of whom had been asked by the conspirators to acquire explosives just before the bombing.

On the other hand, the confidence and credibility issues remained unresolved with regard to Salem, although the bomb had emphasized rather dramatically that those already in the FBI's net were capable of doing the things he had alleged. Three factors combined to bring the colonel back into the fold. The first was Salem's role as bodyguard and security adviser to Sheik Omar Abdel-Rahman, the spiritual guide and, the FBI believed, the true instigator of the World Trade Center bombing. Second, Salem was alleging that the bombers were not finished. The FBI knew that they had not gotten everyone involved in the plot; the terrorists claimed to have 150 soldiers ready to die for Islam. If Salem was right, more terrorist attacks could be in the offing. The FBI had not prevented the World Trade Center blast, with devastating consequences. They could not afford to miss the next time.

The last reason bore directly on the mercurial colonel and would-be informant. Salem was telling the agents that he had warned them that the World Trade Center was a target. He had identified the conspirators beforehand, some of whom were in custody for doing exactly what he had said they were going to do. Because the FBI had not trusted him, Salem said, six people were dead and hundreds of millions of dollars in damage had been done. This was not an opinion the FBI wanted to hear expressed on the six o'clock news. To borrow an old, but appropriately Arab, saying, the FBI could have the camel outside the tent, spitting in, or they could have the camel inside the tent, spitting out. Perhaps it would be better for all concerned if the colonel were inside the tent.

This was unquestionably the correct decision, made for all the right reasons. The sticking point was motivation. For $500 a week, Salem was motivated to be an intelligence source of the FBI, remaining at the Sheik's side and furnishing the type of information which would not put him on the witness stand. For more money — a lot more money — Salem would go the full distance. The FBI talked about $200,000 and Salem scoffed. Two million sounded much better. Ultimately, Salem and the Bureau agreed on $1.5 million and a promise that he would not be made to testify unless there was no alternative. Emad Salem went to work.

He met with a friend of Nosair and Aboulhalima, Siddig Ali, who boasted of helping with the World Trade Center bomb. Ali had a plan for another bomb, this one to be detonated in the underground parking garage beneath the United Nations building. He had contacts in the Sudanese mission that could get the diplomatic plates necessary for access to the garage.

Later, Siddig Ali produced detailed diagrams of the building at 26 Federal Plaza, which housed the FBI and the U.S. Attorney's office. The building could be assaulted, Ali said, and the government employees held hostage, to be traded for the release of the Trade Center bombers.

Siddig Ali, Salem, and others visited Attica, where the jailed Nosair advised Salem to seek "spiritual guidance" about the new plans. Salem, wired by the FBI for the meeting, recorded the conversation. Salem interpreted Nosair's advice to be an instruction to consult with Sheik Omar Abdel-Rahman. The Sheik counseled against the United Nations' plan and caution in the Federal Plaza assault. In the meantime, the plot acquired new targets, all of which were duly reported by Salem to the FBI. This time, there was no doubting Salem's information — he was recording everything.

The targets were shocking. One bomb on the George Washington bridge. One each in the Holland and Lincoln tunnels. Federal Plaza and the United Nations building had been reconnoitered. The Statute of Liberty was on the list, as was New York's diamond district. The bombers were not going to use the more sophisticated, but harder to obtain chemicals used in the World Trade Center blast. This time they were going to use ANFO (ammonium nitrate and fuel oil), the same explosive mixture that would bring down the Murrah Federal Building in Oklahoma City. Casualties from these assaults would be heavy, especially if the tunnels could be collapsed or the bridge brought down.

With Salem's help, the FBI sought to "sting" the bombers. Salem showed the bombers a warehouse in Queens that could be used for preparation of the explosive. The unit was rented, and the bombers moved in with their supplies, watched around the clock by FBI agents who had wired the building with concealed television cameras.

When the FBI moved in on June 23, 1993, they caught 12 people mixing the chemicals that would have brought Manhattan to its knees. Salem, who thoughtfully left the door unlocked, was taken too, then released to the protection of the Witness Security Program. The would-be bombers, caught red-handed and on videotape, went quietly.

Analysis

A typical informant in a very atypical case, Emad Salem was a control problem from the outset but the access he possessed was so valuable he could not simply be dismissed. After the World Trade Center bomb went off, the FBI and NYPD quickly apprehended several of the perpetrators and identified others without Salem's assistance. They did not, however, get to the part of the conspiracy that might have produced many more terrorist acts and chaos in New York City. Salem led law enforcement to that part.

Salem had all of the attributes of a good informant — and many of those we might find in a bad one. He was intelligent and ambitious. Based on our rating scale, we could expect an informant in those categories to make some high-value cases. He had current, 1A access to targets who planned to blow up bridges, tunnels, and the New York headquarters of the FBI, an orgy of destruction which would have made the Oklahoma City bombing look small-time by comparison. He was highly motivated and, in the end, his information proved accurate.

On the bad side, Salem played his FBI handlers off on each other, worked for more than one agency, had all sorts of private agendas, tended to be volatile, and was prone to exaggeration. He was negotiating for big money — he waved off $200,000 as "pennies." As a walk-in mercenary he could walk out any time he felt the urge; he occasionally reminded his handlers of this fact, usually when the subject of money came up.

On balance, Salem was a good informant, and he ultimately proved the conventional wisdom in law enforcement: "Good informant, good case. Bad informant, bad case. No informant, no case." The case that Salem made was very good, indeed.

Motivation

Emad Salem had exactly 1.5 million good reasons to cooperate with the FBI. A mercenary informant from the word go, Salem exploited his connections to the Muslim extremists for the money he knew he would need to hide from those people for the rest of his life. From his statements, one can discern the usual mix of motives in this money-oriented informant.

Money was the big factor, though. He originally volunteered to work in a covert role, receiving $500 a week plus his expenses. Later, after the value of his information was demonstrated, Salem was able to command a much higher price. Salem, who was entering the Witness Security Program, claimed he needed the money to be able to avoid revenge by the victims of his betrayal. Those were a particularly ruthless group of people, so the money would seem to be well spent. As a motivating factor for Salem, it clearly had a galvanizing effect, and it is highly improbable that he would have agreed to the FBI's requests that he surface from his covert role had the money package not been sweet.

Salem's ego was also a factor. He was bright and experienced in the intelligence business. He liked the secret role and his affiliation with the FBI. He clearly did not like at least some of the people he was betraying. He played the mysterious secret agent role with his acquaintances, but he wanted to be a hero with the FBI. He reminded them often that they had missed the boat on the first bomb plot and sought out ways to convince them of the reality of the second.

Also, Salem had the other elements necessary in an informant. He had confidence in his FBI handlers, though the Bureau did not always share this confidence in their informant. Salem did believe that the government would live up to its promises; when the money offer was put on the table, Salem picked it up, assured that after the case was over, the government would come through.

He was confident of the government's ability to protect him after his role was disclosed. Remember that nobody is going to cooperate with law enforcement if their life or the lives of their family are in serious jeopardy. To do so would ignore another of Maslow's needs, that of security. Salem originally agreed to inform on the condition that he would not be required to testify. He knew that to surface as an informant and testify would place him at extreme risk. This was a risk he literally could not afford to take, simply because he would not have had the means to hide from anyone seeking revenge. After the FBI agreed to pay Salem a rather handsome (though well worth the price) reward and to place Salem in the government's Witness Security Program, attitudes changed. Salem's confidence in the FBI was apparently justified. His role as informant and witness over, he has disappeared, taking with him the thanks of his handlers and the people of New York City.

Motivation was the key to this case, as it always is for all informants. Salem's access did not change much over time. What did change was his motivation. When that changed, the results were dramatic. Before, when Salem was motivated by a $500 weekly payment and a chance to play spy, he produced good intelligence about some very bad people. This was not enough to prevent the World Trade Center bombing, mostly because Salem was not motivated to play a larger role in a criminal investigation.

When he was motivated by a $1.5 million payment, Salem cooperated fully in a criminal case that averted several terrorist acts and led to the prosecution of several bomb makers. Motivation had a direct impact on Salem's actions and a corresponding impact on the type of investigation conducted and, ultimately, on the outcome of two different bomb plots.

Access

Salem was Sheik Omar Abdel-Rahman's personal bodyguard and security adviser. He had access to most of the inner workings of the Sheik's group, as well as that of Nosair and Aboulhalima. These groups were compartmentalized to prevent the leakage of secret information, and Salem's access to the World Trade Center bomb plot was limited. He claimed afterward that he had warned the FBI specifically about the Trade Center, something his handlers did not recall. It is more probable that he knew that a terror campaign was being planned, who was planning it, the general targets, and objectives.

This is a lot of access. Unfortunately, the FBI did not follow up on Salem's information in time to prevent the bombing. Afterward, there was no question about Salem's access, which was worth right around $1.5 million.

Salem originally got his access through connections in the Muslim community and those involved in the Nosair trial: El-Gabrowney and Aboulhalima. As both of these men were key figures in the World Trade Center bombing, Salem was well placed to know about the bomb plot beforehand. Salem increased his access by using his background as a colonel in the Egyptian army and as a security and intelligence specialist. It was these attributes, plus his pose as a loyal follower of Abdel-Rahman, that enabled Salem to penetrate the group more deeply.

Officers should look for both kinds of access in handling an informant. Not only must the informant appear to be loyal and trustworthy to those he is informing against, he can often improve his access by possessing a special skill, knowledge, or ability. Aldrich Ames, the spy who betrayed the CIA for the Russians, was not only trusted by those in the CIA, he had special access by virtue of his position as a counterintelligence specialist (on the Russian desk, no less).

Some of Salem's access was historical. In the second phase of his informant career, El-Gabrowney, Aboulhalima, and others in the World Trade Center case were in custody and represented by attorneys; Salem had no ongoing access to these people. He did have current access to the plotters in the second *Jihad*. By using this access, Salem was able to assist in the FBI's "sting" at the explosives factory.

The bottom-line on access is that Salem, unlike even the other informants the FBI had in the same group, was perfectly placed to deliver both the World Trade Center bombers and those in the second *Jihad*, too. Had he been motivated to do so, he probably could have been persuaded to become a part of a sting of the El-Gabrowney and Aboulhalima, which could have prevented the bombing. The access was definitely there; all that was lacking was motivation. Because the FBI questioned Salem's veracity as well as his access, the case was not developed.

Control

There was quite a bit of discussion about the fact that Salem was not under FBI control prior to the bombing. His refusal to testify or take additional investigative steps to corroborate his information was also an issue. After the bombing (and after getting a promise of big money), Salem did agree to testify, if necessary, and to wear a recording device.

The FBI's control of Salem was actually not bad, but it has to be viewed in the context of Salem's two distinct informant careers. In his first incarnation, Salem was an intelligence asset, working for Nancy Floyd in the FBI's Intelligence Division. Salem was getting paid $500 each week to furnish information from inside Nosair's group. Neither he nor Floyd were concentrating on the development of criminal cases at that point.

As a walk-in mercenary informant, Salem was free to walk back out at any time. When pressed to move toward criminal prosecutions, he declined. The FBI, knowing that it had other informants within the same group, though not as well placed as Salem, opted to continue their investigation without him.

In his second career, the one that began after the bombing, Salem and the FBI changed focus. No longer was he needed as a source of intelligence; now the FBI had one of the biggest criminal investigations in their history underway and Salem was talking about additional terrorist acts which would have made the Trade Center bombing look like kindergarten. The informant who before was not worth $500 a week suddenly became cheap at $1.5 million.

Salem agreed to testify, to wear a wire, and to work in a proactive way to "sting" the second *Jihad* plotters. In return, he was promised entry into the Witness Security Program and a lot of money. The FBI's control over their informant at this point was excellent. He was highly motivated, knew there was absolutely no turning back, and accepted the direction of the agents who handled him. Virtually everything Salem did was monitored electronically by the FBI, which had the bomb factory wired for video and Salem wired with a recorder or transmitter. Corroboration of his statements was a breeze, as the agents had Salem's full cooperation in making the recordings.

Salem seems to have developed a good working relationship with his handlers, Nancy Floyd and John Anticev, though FBI management appears to have had less confidence in him. This lack of confidence flows down to informants, who, like Salem, can sense when their information is distrusted or they are being disrespected. Salem certainly knew. On one visit to the FBI offices, he saw his picture on the wall amidst those of all the other plotters. He interpreted this as lack of trust by the FBI.

In truth, Salem had given the FBI reason to mistrust him. He had taken a polygraph test, the results of which were inconclusive. He was prone to hyperbolize, a not uncommon trait in many informants. He was providing information which could not be readily corroborated without further action by Salem, something he was unwilling to do. Ultimately his information was borne out in a rather explosive way, resolving any doubts that might have lingered.

We need to get used to the idea that some things the informant tells us will never be proved beyond a reasonable doubt, and other things will be verified only after something bad happens. No informant's word should ever be taken for any material fact (and not for most of the immaterial ones, either).

One potential control problem which was never resolved was Salem's conflicting loyalty. The FBI knew that he was providing information to Egyptian military intelligence, and they had word that he was in contact with other law enforcement and intelligence agencies, as well as private groups. This sort of thing should never come as a surprise to an informant handler; someone who is informing for money will look for the best deal and may try to sell the same information twice.

This is a control issue, however, and must be discouraged. Informants should be told, in effect, that they must "dance with the one who brung you." In some cases such as Salem's, the value of the information is so great that some double-dipping can be tolerated. With most informants, the officer is asking for trouble by allowing the informant leeway to work with more than one agency at a time, and no informant working under a hammer should be allowed to double-dip. This causes all kinds of problems at trial, and when the informant is claiming that one officer promised this and the other promised that.

Finally, Salem's taping of his conversations with the FBI agents is something which should concern any informant handler. The agents in this case knew that Salem was recording them, and they conducted themselves accordingly. Most of the time, the officer will not know because, unlike Salem, the informant will not tell. Keeping this sort of secret from the officer demonstrates a lack of trust on the informant's part and a lack of control on the officer's.

The informant, who once again is acting in what he perceives to be his best interest, is effectively saying, "I don't trust your word. I need some insurance." He may be trying to get some blackmail material on the officer or just document a promise. Unguarded or incautious statements by the officer can bounce back hard on an audio tape. I know of one agent who was caught in this sort of trap and it almost cost him his job. Recently, an FBI agent was convicted in a corruption case, partly because the drug dealer with whom he was talking taped their conversations and had some good evidence to take to the prosecutor.

When dealing with an informant it is always a good idea to assume that he or she is taping the conversation. It happens often enough that, if you work with enough informants, your assumption will be right on occasion. If you know the informant is taping conversations, either on the phone or in person, you need to get him or her to stop. First resolve the trust issue by finding and fixing whatever is causing the mistrust. Next, explain that the informant is making life more difficult for himself by creating material which may have to be turned over to the defense at the time the informant testifies. Do not let this, or any other control problem fester — deal with it quickly and efficiently.

Summing Up

The objective of the World Trade Center bombers was to knock one of the 107-story buildings into the second, dropping both and killing at least 50,000 people. The next phase of the bombing campaign called for more death and destruction, a buffet of horror which would have exceeded even Hollywood's imagination. This campaign was averted by the intervention of an informant and skillful investigative work by the FBI and NYPD. Emad Salem's story is one of effective informant management — not perfect, but good enough to get a very important job done just in time. Informant management involves dealing with people — unpredictable, imperfect, emotional people who make the management process much more of an art than a science. As Emad Salem's experience proves, mastery of this art is a worthwhile endeavor that can pay enormous dividends.

Interviewing and Communications Skills

8

"Have you brought any letters — any documents — any proofs that you are trustworthy and truthful?"

"Of a surety, no; and wherefore should I? Have I not a tongue, and cannot I say all that myself?"

"But you're saying it, you know, and somebody else's saying it, is different."

—Mark Twain, A Connecticut Yankee in King Arthur's Court

"Spies cannot be usefully employed without a certain intuitive sagacity. They cannot be properly managed without benevolence and straightforwardness. Without subtle ingenuity of mind, one cannot make certain of the truth of their reports." —Sun Tzu, The Art of War

An informant is someone with access to information about crime and a motivation to give that information to the police. No matter how this person arrives on our doorstep, it remains for the law enforcement officer to obtain all of the information the individual is willing or able to provide. This debriefing process may consist of a single meeting or hundreds of hours of interviews. There may be one short encounter in a restaurant or bar, or dozens of sessions closeted in interview rooms. In any case, the objective of the interview is always the same — to learn what the informant knows, and how he or she knows it.

If cases are to be developed using the informant's information, questions must be asked, instructions will have to be issued, directions given, and the results of all this activity reported to management. Communication is the means by which this task is accomplished, and the process of communication is controlled by the officer. The officer, not the informant, decides what information is required, what questions are asked, where and when the informant will be questioned, and who will be present. The officer also decides what information will be communicated *to* the informant, a very critical determination, as all communication is two way, even in a law enforcement interview or interrogation.

The interview or debriefing serves as the officer's vehicle for receiving information and is always directed toward three objectives:

1. Establish the informant's motivation.
2. Determine the extent of the informant's access.
3. Explore possibilities for case development.

Basic Interviewing Rules

A few basic rules serve to put the interviewing process in context. Some of these rules appear in other parts of the book but bear repeating here.

Safety First

No information the informant is likely to possess is more valuable than the safety of the officers, the informant, or others. No interview should ever be conducted in an environment which is unsafe or places the interviewers or interviewee in legal or physical jeopardy. I generally recommend against interviews at the informant's residence, in dark alleys at midnight, or in any circumstances which would place people at unacceptable risk. A minimum of two officers should always be present during interviews with informants.

Remember Motivation

The informant's motivation must be clearly understood throughout the duration of his or her cooperation. Because this motivation may change over time, it is not enough merely to make some determination at the initial debriefing and then assume the *status quo* continues. Missing a change in attitude could be costly. Each time the informant is interviewed the officer should listen for clues about motivation.

Minimize

Contact with informants should be kept to the minimum necessary to get the job done. Minimal contact means making the most of the time you do spend in an interview. Spend time on the "W" questions — who, what, when, where, how, and why — and ask how the individual knows this information. Minimize your reports. All reports connected with an informant should contain the least amount of information required by law and procedure. You cannot leave important information out, but you should not include the trivial or irrelevant.

Write for the Jury

Assume that everything the informant says and you write will end up in front of a jury. This does not mean fudging or shading reports or informant statements, but it does mean making sure the truth is reported in a way that 12 people who are ignorant of the facts will be able to understand it.

All Communication Is Two Way

An officer cannot ask a question without imparting some information. Remember that as you are interviewing the informant, he or she is interviewing you. Your words, body language, attitude, and approach may speak volumes to someone who is desperately interested.

Corroboration Is the Key

Every interview should be conducted with independent corroboration in mind. Knowing what the informant knows or thinks is fine, but proving it is something else entirely. Countless hours are wasted by officers who never ask, "How can I *prove* this allegation?"

Interviewing Techniques

Considering how vital interviewing skills are to the criminal investigator, it is surprising how little time is spent in police academies or other law enforcement training in their study. Several really good interviewing schools have attempted to fill the gap, but in dealing with informants we are in a somewhat unique situation. Most training deals with interrogations or hostile interviews in which the objective is a confession. Some time may be devoted to the interview of crime victims or witnesses. None of these situations fits the informant precisely.

At this stage of the game, we are assuming that the individual has made the decision to cooperate and that rapport between officer and informant is established. What we have here is a cooperative witness who wants to impart information for a variety of reasons important to the individual. The objective here is generally not to wrangle a confession out of an unwilling subject, although some informants do need to be prodded in the right direction. This was the case with Joe Valachi, the subject of the case study for this chapter.

Setting the Stage

The objective of an informant interview is to get as much accurate information from a cooperative witness in as short a period as possible. Sometimes the interview will take two minutes and cover a single short subject. Other interviews, such as Valachi's, may take months and cover a lifetime of crime. Some interviews take place on the fly, with the informant passing along information in a car or in a brief contact on the street. Others may be formal statements or depositions, made in a conference room with a stenographer present.

Developing a stage plan for such a wide variety of possible circumstances is plainly impossible. Nevertheless, because we can control most aspects of the interview, we can, within the framework of our basic rules, follow a general pattern. Informant interviews, no matter what the setting, should involve three related steps:

1. Planning
2. Execution
3. Follow-up

Plan the Interview

Because the officer controls the interview process, he or she can plan how each interview will be conducted. This is true to some extent even in initial interviews where a would-be informant walks in off the street. Having a plan allows the officer to establish and maintain control over this process.

Have the information you need to get the job done. Other than at the very first contact with the informant, you should already know the general direction of the case or the information. Take a look at the last debriefing report. If you have follow-up questions or areas that were uncovered in previous sessions, these can be made into a short list to be covered at the next. You may also have photographs, a photo lineup, or something else to show the informant.

Always have one or two questions prepared that show you checked on something the informant said last time you talked. This lets informants know that you are following through on the information they have provided. It is also a good idea to re-cover one or two issues, just to make sure last week's story is the same as this week's.

Execution

Time is always a factor in these interviews. Nobody wants to spend any more time than necessary in this type of meeting. If the informant is actively working on cases, time in the interview room is time away from his associates. Lengthy meetings in public places increase the chances of the informant or the officer getting "burned."

The length and structure of each interview will be dictated by the type of information that is being conveyed. If the informant is just passing along a tip about the whereabouts of a wanted person, the meeting can be brief and unstructured. If we are in the middle of a complex debriefing which is being made into a written statement, the meeting will take longer. Joe Valachi's took more than 8 months.

The case officer should ask the questions while the support officer takes the notes. Because so much of communication is non-verbal, the case officer needs to observe the informant's eyes, demeanor, gestures, posture, and facial expressions as the statements are made. The case officer knows the informant better than anyone and is attuned to subtle differences between previous interviews. Feedback is a big part of the communication cycle, no less so for the informant. If information checks out, or if the informant performs well, the officer must reinforce the desired behavior. If there is some problem, the interview, where both people are face-to-face, is the place to discuss and remedy it.

Follow-Up

The process is not over when the interview ends. In fact, the officer's work is just beginning. There are leads to run down, statements to check, and corroboration to obtain. Questions will be formatted for the next meeting. Reports are prepared from the notes of the meeting, and (one can hope) enforcement actions are planned. Work with informants should always be directed at a clear-cut goal or objective. Interviews lead toward that goal, but the investigative follow-up is equally as important. Without the product of this follow-up, there can be no prosecutions.

Interview and Communication Skills

These interviews are unlike others in law enforcement. There is no need for hostile questioning or interrogation techniques; informants are friendly (or at least cooperative) witnesses. There is more confidence in these interviews; the informant is a known quantity, unlike a victim or witness to a crime whom we are meeting for the first time. The elaborate rapport-building phase of most interviews and interrogations has already been dealt with. In all but the initial interview, the officer can cut right to the chase.

How To Interview an Informant

Our purpose is to obtain the informant's information and the means is the interview. In meeting with an informant, the officer should follow some standard procedures which we might not use in a hostile interrogation or the interview of a crime victim.

Ask Open-Ended Questions

Open-ended questions such as "What happened?" allow the informant to tell a story in his or her own words. There are a couple of good reasons why this is a good place to start. First, we are not giving very much information *to* the informant. We are finding out what he or she knows, rather than describing what we know. Second, we are giving the informant the opportunity to answer the question in whatever way he or she chooses. This could be completely and honestly, or something less. This is a test the informant must pass.

Move From the General to the Specific
The answers to open-ended questions are often broad descriptions. The devil is in the details, which the officer elicits with a series of ever more specific questions. Again, this is a way of asking questions without providing too much information to the informant. He already told us about the event (what happened); now we are asking about the finer points. The details are generally found in specific answers to the standard "who, what, when, where, why, and how" questions. The officer asks these questions until he is completely satisfied as to the accuracy and completeness of the information.

Make the Informant Commit
"How do you know this?" is a critical question. After over 30 years in the Mafia, Joe Valachi knew all sorts of juicy gossip, hearsay, buzz, and scandal. He had also participated in a murder or two. Separating one from the other is the beginning of the case-development process. The informant should commit to how he or she came by the information. You may be able to train the informant, as the agents did with Valachi, to provide this information without being asked.

Check the Answers Against Known Information or Previous Statements
I tell informants right off the bat that I already know the answers to some of the questions I ask, though they will have to guess which questions these are. I also try to ask at least one or two questions that were covered in a previous statement, mainly to see whether the answer changes at all. Corroboration of the informant's statement begins during the informant's statement.

Train the Informant
Provide positive feedback for the type of answers you want and negative feedback for the ones you do not. Some people, given an open-ended question to answer, will talk for 10 minutes, wandering ever further from the original subject. Unlike other witnesses, informants can be trained to provide their information in the form the officer prefers. The informant can also be trained to be more observant or to focus on certain things of interest to the officer. If, every time you meet an informant, you ask for some specific detail, such as license plates or telephone numbers, the informant will eventually get the picture and start looking for these things. Feedback is important in this effort. If you finally get the individual trained to bring you the right information in the right form, this should be the subject of praise and reward.

Deal Effectively with Discrepancies
Everybody makes mistakes. In a complicated case, or in a debriefing covering several years' worth of activity, there are bound to be discrepancies. Distinguishing between the inevitable disagreement and outright deception is a difficult, but essential, task. The officer must decide in advance how discrepancies will be handled. One of the better ways is to dissect a problem to the very finest detail. While this is going on, the officer should remain detached and non-judgmental, sending the message that we could have a problem here, and we are not leaving until it is solved. The informant who is confused about the facts will want to help clear things up. Someone who is deceptive will react differently. Outright deception must also be dealt with in a decisive fashion. Catching an informant in a lie can void their agreement and could even be grounds for criminal prosecution. This fact should be emphasized to the informant *before* the problem comes up, in the hope that deception can be prevented.

Use the Power of Association

Memory experts rely upon association to achieve their amazing feats of recollection. The officer can do this, too, in exploring issues with an informant. Questioning the informant about historical events is much easier if the incidents can be linked to some important date or circumstance. For example, I questioned an informant in a historical drug conspiracy about events which took place several years before. When we began, he could not even recall the exact year the overt acts took place. By associating the acts with other important circumstances of his life — "Where were you living?" "What car were you driving?" "Was it before or after you got arrested on the burglary charge?" — we were able to narrow the date down to within a few weeks. This makes all the difference in the world when you are trying to corroborate a witness statement and need to locate documents or other evidence. Not only does association help the informant remember things during an interview, but the event is also forever fixed in their memory by that association. If and when the informant ever goes to court, he will remember that that particular shipment occurred before he sold the Corvette and after he got arrested for burglary.

Be Respectful

The informant has information we need. He deserves our respect for doing his job and providing this information. If the officer shows disrespect or contempt for the informant or his efforts, count on it, productivity is going to go into a steep decline. Put yourself in the informant's shoes. You have a job that is filled with emotional and physical hazards. You are betraying your close friends. You are taking big risks to get information that other people are trying hard to keep secret. Would you prefer to work for someone who understood these pressures and respected your accomplishments, or someone who blew them (and you) off as a "snitch" or a "rat?"

The Initial Debriefing

The first interview with an informant is the contact that most resembles a regular investigative interview. If the informant is a walk-in, the officer will be working to establish rapport and determine the informant's motivation for coming in. At this early stage of the game, little or nothing may be known about the informant. We may be hearing the information for the first time. The accuracy, truthfulness, and value of the information may be unknown. What is worse, this may be the officer's only chance at this informant, who may choose, after an initial contact with the officer, not to go forward with the cooperation.

In other cases, the officer has more extensive knowledge of the informant or the information. Perhaps the informant is someone developed through an ongoing investigation. The officer knows the individual and has a pretty good idea about what this person knows, as well. Or the informant could be someone who walks in with information about a subject already familiar to the officer.

In situations where we have more background information available, we are able to make a better judgment of the value of the informant's cooperation, but it is still vital that the officer get as much done as possible in this initial debriefing. This is what I referred to earlier as the "first cold press." In olive oil manufacture as well as informant development, it is the stage where the best work gets done.

The initial debriefing has three primary objectives, all of which operate throughout the interview. Every question asked is directed at all three aims.

1. Establish the informant's motivation.
2. Determine the nature and extent of the informant's access.
3. Assess the possibilities for control of the informant's information and for case development.

The officer is also trying to evaluate the informant's personality. Is this person someone I can work with or should I thank him and see him to the door? There is a lot going on in one of these interviews. Because there is so much happening, the officer may need some help. A source debriefing guide such as the one in the Appendices can be a good tool to cover the bases. Officers can develop debriefing guides of their own, basing the questions on their particular interest or specialty (e.g., narcotics, burglary, telemarketing). Having two or three pages of ready-mix questions moves the discussion right along and allows the officer to make a much better judgment about where the informant stands.

The initial debriefing may be a short session or one concluded over a period of several days. Monica Lewinsky's debriefing was not completed in a single day, but the investigators had a lot to go over and a signed agreement with her attorneys. They knew she would be available over the long term, so they could afford to spread the questioning out. Even so, it is a good idea to get the most important matters cleared up first. Later sessions can be used to fill in blanks, bring out details, and test for accuracy.

I always felt that the initial debriefing of any informant was a challenge, but also an exciting event. It is a lot like opening a birthday gift; sometimes you get a bow-tie. Most of the time what is inside is something practical or useful; however, on very rare occasions, it can be the key to a new Ferrari. As Forrest Gump said, it's like a box of chocolates; you never know what you're going to get.

Dealing with Deception

In the 25 years I have been in this business, I have worked with hundreds of informants. I believe that exactly one of them was completely truthful, and there is no way to be 100% sure about him. People do not always tell the truth, the whole truth, and nothing but the truth. Sometimes they are wrong. Sometimes they lie. The practice is universal enough for us to be able to say that everyone lies sometimes. Perhaps the lie is a little thing or only to oneself. We probably deceive ourselves much more than we mislead others, but because important decisions are based upon the informant's statements, there is no room for deception of any sort.

This does not mean that one lie is grounds for instant dismissal and referral of the false statement to the prosecutor for criminal charges. Understanding, not haste, is required. If we are absolutely certain that the statement in issue is intentionally false, the first order of business is to find out why the informant felt compelled to deceive. The reason, perhaps more than the deception itself, will determine what, if anything, we are to do about the matter.

People need a motivation to cooperate with law enforcement as informants. As we have seen, these motivations vary, but they all relate in some way to the informant's interest or needs. If we assume that people generally act in what they perceive to be their own self interest, it logically follows that a lie is told under the same conditions. An informant may lie to protect himself from being detected in an illegal act, to hide a previous lie, to protect (or falsely implicate) someone else. These are all bad reasons to lie, although the informant may not see it that way when he is doing it.

There are other reasons for lying which are less clear cut and perhaps less corrupt. Informants sometimes lie because they think that is what the officer wants to hear. They may deceive themselves into thinking what they are saying is true. Witnesses (not just informants) may exaggerate the extent of their knowledge: "I saw the whole thing, officer." They might fill in a few gaps with guesses or conjecture, then swear to it as fact. The officer bears some responsibility for preventing these lies, which can be avoided by being very clear about what constitutes the whole truth and nothing but, and by carefully questioning the details of the informant's statements.

Informants should be asked in advance to consent to a polygraph examination in the event of any discrepancy. This consent is a part of some informant agreement forms and serves to remind the informant that the government has the means and the intention to verify the informant's statements.

No effort should be made by the officer to conceal a false statement by an informant. Not only does protection of the informant under such circumstances send exactly the wrong message, but it also makes the officer an accomplice to the deception, something of which the courts strongly disapprove. Instead, the facts relating to the deception should be referred by the officer to his or her superiors for a decision about further action. Those decisions should not be made by the officer, who has a conflict of interest in the outcome.

Informant Statements and the Law

If you never take a case to court, you will never have to worry about the informant's statements becoming a part of the trial record. Of course, you are not using the informant properly or getting your job done, either. Informants are not entirely trusted by the courts, who issue special instructions to jurors about what the informant is saying. This lack of trust follows many betrayals by informants, who, the courts know, often have a motivation to lie.

Quite often, too, the statement of an informant may be the main thing standing between a defendant and freedom. Defense attorney Alan Dershowitz calls the word of a paid informant "simply worthless," but it is not. The true value of any witness statement is the sum of the credibility of the witness *and* any corroboration the officer can locate. Courts are caught in a bind, though, between protecting the rights of the defendant and allowing introduction of the evidence of their guilt, especially when this evidence comes from a sometimes questionable source.

Balancing these interests, the courts have decided not to prevent informants from testifying as some have urged, but to allow extensive cross-examination of the informant. In order to assist the defense in their cross-examination, the courts and the legislature provide ammunition in the form of access to things such as the informant's prior statements, the officer's notes, and any exculpatory information in the government's protection. Knowing these materials will have to be produced dictates, to some extent, how law enforcement does business with an informant.

Discovery

Title 18, U.S. Code, Sec. 3500, relating to "demands for production of statements and reports of witnesses," reads:

> (a) *In any criminal prosecution brought by the United States, no statement or report in the possession of the United States which was made by a Government witness or prospective Government witness (other than the defendant) shall be the subject of a subpoena, discovery, or inspection until said witness has testified on direct examination in the trial of the case.*

> (b) *After a witness called by the United States has testified on direct examination, the court shall, on motion of the defendant, order the United States to produce any statement (as hereinafter defined) of the witness in the possession of the United States which relates to the subject matter as to which the witness has testified. If the entire contents of any such statement relate to the subject matter of the testimony of the witness, the court shall order it to be delivered directly to the defendant for his examination and use.*

(c) *If the United States claims that any statement ordered to be produced under this section contains matter which does not relate to the subject matter of the testimony of the witness, the court shall order the United States to deliver such statement for the inspection of the court in camera. Upon such delivery the court shall excise the portions of such statement which do not relate to the subject matter of the testimony of the witness. . .*

(d) *If the United States elects not to comply with an order of the court under subsection (b) or (c) hereof to deliver the defendant any such statement, or such portion thereof as the court may direct, the court shall strike from the record the testimony of the witness and the trial shall proceed unless the court in its discretion shall determine that the interests of justice require that a mistrial be declared.*

(e) *The term "statement" as used in subsections (b), (c), and (d) of this section in relation to any witness called by the United States means —*

  (1) *a written statement made by said witness and signed or otherwise adopted or approved by him;*

  (2) *a stenographic, mechanical, electrical, or other recording, or a transcription thereof, which is a substantially verbatim recital of an oral statement made by said witness and recorded contemporaneously with the making of such oral statement; or*

  (3) *a statement, however taken or recorded, or a transcription thereof, if any, made by said witness to a grand jury.*

This statute, also known as the Jencks Act, was passed by Congress in response to a Supreme Court decision which gave the defense access to government reports. The Jencks Act was designed to prevent unfettered access to the government's records, while still protecting the rights of criminal defendants to material needed for effective cross-examination. There is some counterpart for the Jencks Act (many of which are more liberal) in every state.

The Law Regarding False Statements

Making a false statement to a law enforcement officer may be more than a credibility issue for the informant. It could also be perjury or some other criminal offense. Title 18, U.S. Code, Sec. 1001, relating to fraud and false statements, provides in part:

(a) *Except as otherwise provided in this section, whoever, in any matter within the jurisdiction of the executive, legislative, or judicial branch of the Government of the United States, knowingly and willfully —*

  (1) *falsifies, conceals, or covers up by any trick, scheme, or device a material fact;*

  (2) *makes any materially false, fictitious, or fraudulent statement or representation; or*

  (3) *makes or uses any false writing or document knowing the same to contain any materially false, fictitious, or fraudulent statement or entry;*

  (4) *shall be fined under this title or imprisoned not more than 5 years or both.*

Once again, prevention is the better alternative. Let the informant know at the outset that the provisions of Section 1001 (or any equivalent state statute) apply to statements made to the officer. Prosecutions of informants under this section are rare, but, given the consequences false statements can have on the lives of innocent people or in the disruption of a criminal investigation, they are not something which should be tolerated.

Written Reports

Once the information has been imparted by the informant, an equally critical step must be taken by the officer. This is, of course, the bane of all law enforcement officers: the written report. It sometimes seems like there is a form for every occasion. Some examples of the forms used in connection with informants are included in the Appendices. The use of other reports will be dictated by agency policy. All written reports have the purpose of communicating information to the reader; in this case, the information is that provided by the informant, either in the form of a statement or a memorandum or report of the interview. Many informants will never see the inside of a courtroom or appear as a witness. Others are being interviewed with the full expectation that they will be testifying for the prosecution. Thanks to the Jencks Act, we need to assume that.

Officers' Notes

Very few people have the sort of photographic memory that allows them to recite verbatim the entire contents of a lengthy conversation. Those of us who are not so gifted must rely on notes taken at the time the words are spoken. Notes can take different forms, from jottings on a napkin to transcribed tapes of lengthy meetings.

Tape-Recorded Notes

Some departments require interviews to be taped, even videotaped. Some officers like to tape a meeting with an informant because the recorder frees them from having to write while they are listening or asking questions. Still others want the security of having the informant's exact words on tape in case of a future dispute or disagreement. While there is some merit in each of these arguments (especially, orders being orders, the first one), tape recording is not a good idea for informant interviews or debriefings.

There are a couple of reasons why officers should not rely on tapes. First, there is a security concern. We protect informants with numbers and code names and conceal their identity, even their gender, in our reports. Having a debriefing on tape exposes the informant. I know of one incident in which an officer taped an informal conversation with an informant, then accidentally allowed the cassette to fall into the hands of a second informant — who promptly gave it to the criminals named by the first. This admittedly rare, but very dangerous, incident could have been prevented by not relying so heavily on tape.

A second reason relates to the law and discovery. Because this tape is a prior statement of the witness, it must be produced if that witness is called to testify. This means the officer has to safeguard that tape just like a piece of evidence — with all its wrinkles, background noise, extraneous comments, and unrelated or irrelevant conversation. The officers who were sued in *Pleasant v. Lovell* (876 F. 2d 787, 10th Cir., 1989) taped some of their meetings with an informant and undoubtedly regretted doing so, as the tapes were played back and every word analyzed in the most minute detail by opposing counsel.

There is no legal requirement that meetings with informants be recorded, only that relevant statements be preserved in some fashion. For these reasons, the old-fashioned way of recording a statement — using notes to prepare a written statement — is much preferable when dealing with a cooperative witness such as an informant.

Good Note-Taking Procedure

One person takes notes during the interview. There is absolutely no need for two sets of notes for the same interview. In fact, this is undesirable. The informant's case officer or primary handler should ask the questions, listen to the answers, and gauge the informant's attitude and demeanor. This in itself is a full-time job in any interview. The other officer present serves as a recorder, taking all the notes. I usually take a pad along and will make notations about additional questions to ask or areas to cover, but these are never more than two or three words, usually abbreviated (e.g., "Bob — last name?").

The exception to this rule is if a formal statement, such as the initial debriefing is being prepared. I highly recommend preparing these statements on a laptop computer as the informant is speaking. There is no need for notes, and the statement can be revised and amended as the interview progresses. The final result is the informant's one and only statement on the matters covered. Either officer can do the data input, but no notes are required.

Whether you will be taking a lot of notes may dictate the choice of the interview location. For a long debriefing when lots of notes would be required, you might want to meet at the office or some other private location. Short notes can be taken in a short meeting of limited scope, as in a restaurant or coffee shop setting. The information passed at many a meet has been recorded on a restaurant napkin. Remember, though, those original notes are subject to discovery by the defense if the informant testifies.

The notes should contain the date, time, and location of the interview; the persons present (though not the informant's name); and the relevant information. Notes should be as brief as possible, while including the substance of the informant's statement. If you want to avoid embarrassment, do not include material from other cases, grocery lists, your girlfriend's phone number, doodling, or any other personal data with the notes.

The Law on Notes

Cases have been lost because the officer "lost" or "destroyed" his or her original notes. At the very least, this looks highly suspicious to a jury, and when the notes relate to something an informant supposedly said, suspicion can easily turn into reasonable doubt. Case law varies from state to state, but a good rule generally is to keep the notes. There are several court cases which required officers to produce notes under certain circumstances. *United States v. Harris* (543 F. 2d 1247, 9th Cir., 1976) is one such. The court ruled that the FBI must preserve the original notes taken by agents during interviews with prospective witnesses to enable the court to play their proper role in determining what evidence must be produced pursuant to the Jencks Act.

Although the officer's rough notes are generally not considered Jencks Act materials, mostly because the informant or witness has not subscribed to them, the notes may still be necessary to determine whether the witness said something that might be exculpatory to the defendant. Under *Brady v. Maryland* (272 U.S. 82, 1963), "the suppression by the prosecution of evidence favorable to an accused upon request violates due process where the evidence is material either to guilt or to punishment, irrespective of the good faith or bad faith of the prosecution."

If the officer's notes go missing or are destroyed, questions will be raised as to whether they contained exculpatory information, perhaps a false statement by the informant, or some conflicting information that the officer wanted concealed. This problem can be avoided simply by making accurate notes, then preserving them for possible future use.

Written Statements, Affidavits, or Reports

Law enforcement officers do quite a bit of communicating via the written report. Reports go to our superiors, to other agencies, and to the prosecuting attorney. The management of an informant should generate quite a few of these reports, and the better the informant, the more reports, perhaps something of a mixed blessing. General rules for written statements or reports made in connection with an informant include the following:

1. Every significant contact with an informant should be reported in some form. This includes all face-to-face meetings and any telephone calls in which consequential information is provided.
2. Administrative matters should not be combined with the informant's statement. This includes references to payments or other details not connected with an investigation.
3. The form of the report should be consistent. If you start by having the informant hand-write his statements, follow that pattern throughout. If you make any changes, you should have a good explanation, because inconsistencies will be exploited by the defendant's attorney.
4. Decide early on how the content of each statement will be reported. At any meeting the informant may have information about more than one individual or case. This can either be reported in separate reports or in one comprehensive statement. The initial debriefing should be comprehensive, but subsequent reports can be focused on a single subject. Again, this is a decision that you may have to explain to the jury under cross-examination.

Types of Statements

Many different types of reports are used to document informant statements. All contain the declarations of the informant or a summary, but the form may vary. Some of the more common types of statements include:

1. *Handwritten statements:* The informant prepares a narrative statement, which he or she signs. There is no question that these are the informant's words, but such statements may not cover all the points that need covering.
2. *Tape-recorded statements and transcripts:* Verbatim records of an interview, memorialized on tape. A court stenographer can also be used to record an entire interview. They are complete and accurate, but they require more preparation and more time and often are not worth the trouble.
3. *Affidavits:* A legal document, the statement is made under penalty of perjury and sworn to by the affiant/informant. The affidavit can be in either narrative form or prepared in a question-and-answer format. An affidavit might be used if the officer wanted to "lock the informant in" to a specific statement. It is presumably more reliable because it was made under oath and the penalty of perjury.
4. *Signed statements:* A statement signed by the informant but prepared by the officer; these statements are standard in many departments. This statement can be in narrative form or question-and-answer format. The officer has more flexibility in recording the information in a manner that can be less confusing. The statement can be organized in chronological order or by topic, and extraneous or irrelevant material omitted.
5. *Report or memorandum of interview:* Also prepared by the officer, the report or memo is generally not seen by or subscribed to by the informant. This is a recounting of what the officer heard the informant say. The report can be made on a form specially developed for the purpose (see forms in the Appendices) or as part of a regular investigative report. In either case, it does not pretend to be a verbatim recitation of the informant's words and may include notes about corroboration, other information, or leads for follow-up.

The last two documents are the only ones most officers really need when dealing with informants. There is usually no need to swear a cooperative informant to a statement, and the handwritten types seem to be invariably messy, hard to read, and incomplete. The word processor is a very helpful tool in preparing any of these statements.

The Law on Statements

The two doctrines which apply most often to informant statements are Jencks and Brady, both of which we discussed a bit earlier. Jencks requires that statements which have been adopted by the witness be turned over to the defense after the witness testifies in court. In federal court, accepted practice is to turn the Jencks material over a week or so before trial. This avoids the disruption of the trial as the defense attorney asks for time to review the statements. Of the five types of statements we just covered, the first four would almost invariably be Jencks material.

Under the Supreme Court's decision in *Brady v. Maryland* (272 U.S. 82, 1963), any "evidence favorable to an accused … where the evidence is material either to guilt or to punishment" must be disclosed to the defense. Brady material is turned over in advance of the trial in order to give the defense a chance to evaluate it.

The defense has a right to receive everything that reflects on the credibility of the government's witnesses. Conflicting or inconsistent statements, the fact that the informant lied in the past, and impeachment evidence all must be turned over. See *Kyles v. Whitley* (115 S. Ct. 1555, 1995), a case in which substantial evidence existed that the informant, not the defendant, was the killer in question.

Summing Up

Information is communicated by the informant to the officer, who communicates it to his or her superiors and the prosecutor. The information is used to make decisions in case development and to advance investigations. Ultimately, the information may be communicated to a jury by the informant. Obtaining this information is the officer's job. Effective communication, in the form of interview techniques, is the means of accomplishing this task. It is also the officer's responsibility to make use of the information, also achieved by effective communication. The officer provides instructions to the informant, conveys information to the prosecutor, and adapts the information for prosecution.

Learning to communicate well with an individual who may be from a much different world than our own is not easy. The case study that follows illustrates the value of the education, however. In it, a college-educated, Irish-American law enforcement officer found a way to communicate effectively with a high-school dropout, Italian-American career criminal, with results that would shake the entire country.

Case Study: Introduction to Cosa Nostra — The Interview of Joseph Valachi

"He told me to make a cup out of my hands. Then he put a piece of paper in them and lit it with a match and told me to say after him, as I was moving the paper back and forth, 'This is the way I will burn if I betray the secret of this organization.'" With these words, Joseph Michael Valachi became a part of American lore and quite possibly the best known informant in U.S. history. He was an unlikely informant. Almost 33 of his 58 years had been spent in the organization he described, the Cosa Nostra, or "this thing of ours" that he said "comes before everything — our blood family, our religion, our country." Cosa Nostra was Joe Valachi's home, yet he betrayed its secrets, first to federal investigators, then on national television at a Senate hearing.

His story began in the 1920s, when he had a ringside seat for the creation of America's national crime syndicate. A violent and dangerous hoodlum, Valachi associated with others like himself, first- or second-generation Italian-Americans in Prohibition-era New York City. By 1929, he had been arrested for carrying a weapon, burglary, attempted extortion, assault, and robbery. A short prison term was followed by a brief period on parole, which he violated, landing him back in Sing Sing. By age 27, he was a career criminal.

Valachi's direction seemed to change in 1930 with his initiation into the secret society he later described as Cosa Nostra. He was not going straight, however, just getting better organized. He earned his way into the secret society by participating in several murders and acting as a soldier in the Mafia war between Salvatore Maranzano and Giuseppe "Joe the Boss" Masseria. Maranzano administered the oath at Valachi's induction, which he described as taking place at a large house in upstate New York.

Also present at the ceremony were Mafia notables Thomas Lucchese, Tom Gagliano, Joe Profaci, and Joe Bonanno, Valachi's "goombah" or sponsor. Valachi eventually became a member of the family of Vito Genovese, as ruthless an individual as could be found anywhere in America. Genovese, who offered to be the best man at Valachi's wedding, and Valachi, the loyal soldier, would eventually have a falling out that would put their family on the front page of every newspaper in America.

Valachi never rose in the ranks of the Mafia; he lacked the family connections and the "right stuff" to make it in the mob. He soldiered on through the '30s, '40s, and '50s, running a variety of small-time scams on his own and getting into some bigger operations that were run by others. During the war, Valachi trafficked in gasoline rationing coupons. He also began buying and selling heroin, which brought him to the attention of the Treasury Department's Federal Bureau of Narcotics (FBN).

Federal Bureau of Narcotics agents encountered Valachi along the heroin trail no less than five times between 1944 and 1959. Although he later claimed that all of his drug charges were either exaggerated or "frame-ups," Valachi was eventually convicted three times, receiving 5-, 15-, and 20-year terms. He was known by FBN to supply several large Harlem traffickers, one of whom sold three kilos of heroin to an undercover FBN agent. Valachi admitted to having connections for morphine in Mexico and heroin in Europe.

On June 17, 1960, Joseph Valachi arrived at the United States Penitentiary at Atlanta, GA. He had 15 years to do on his latest narcotics conviction, and he was 55 years old. The future did not look good. Also incarcerated in Atlanta was Vito Genovese. By coincidence, the boss of the family was also doing 15 years for narcotics trafficking. Genovese was not especially warm toward his soldier, believing Valachi to be associated with Anthony "Tony Bender" Strollo, a Genovese *capo* whom Don Vito thought was an informant. After Strollo disappeared, undoubtedly at Genovese's command, the boss did accept Valachi back into the fold, eventually inviting him to move into Genovese's cell.

The relationship soured as Genovese came to believe that Valachi, too, was informing to the hated FBN. Valachi claimed later that another Atlanta inmate had identified him as an informant to divert attention from himself, but Genovese somehow concluded that Valachi was a threat. This, Valachi knew, was very bad news indeed. Genovese was still running his organization from within Atlanta's walls, passing instructions to people inside and outside the facility. He could, and no doubt did, have people killed while he was incarcerated, Strollo being only one of many.

One evening in June of 1962, Genovese began talking to Valachi in a way that convinced him the boss had murder on his mind. "Vito starts saying to me, 'You know, we take a barrel of apples, and in this barrel of apples there might be a bad apple. Well, this apple has to be removed, and if it ain't removed, it would hurt the rest of the apples.' Then he said to me that we had known each other for a long time, and he wanted to give me a kiss for old time's sake. Okay, I said to myself, two can play the game. So I grabbed Vito and kissed him back." Another inmate warned Valachi that this was "the kiss of death," but he needed no warning. He had just received a sentence of death from which there was no appeal.

Valachi ran for cover, but running in prison is difficult. He asked to be put in protective custody and was placed in "the hole" for a week. Upon release and still fearing Genovese, he prepared himself for a confrontation with the men Don Vito would send to kill him. Spying one, Joseph DiPalermo, Valachi grabbed an iron pipe left from some prison construction and beat the man to death in full view of guards and other inmates. Valachi learned too late that the man he had killed was not DiPalermo at all, but Joseph Saupp, a forger not tied to Genovese in any way. Now Joe Valachi faced the death penalty for capital murder.

The Interview

While in solitary, Valachi reached out to George Gaffney, the supervisor of FBN's New York office. FBN was putting together another conspiracy case on Valachi and had been pressuring the harried mobster for information. Valachi admitted giving some information to the narcotics agents, but denied telling them anything about the Mafia. Now facing a murder charge, he again sought out Gaffney, who moved Valachi back to New York.

The results of the initial debriefings were mixed. While Valachi was forthcoming on some issues, he was obviously withholding information on others. Narcotics agent Frank Selvaggi, who knew of Valachi's association with people like Genovese and Strollo, pressed for more details about the Mafia which the FBN knew existed. Valachi was not going there, and a stalemate ensued, one broken by the entry of another agency, the FBI.

Special Agent James P. Flynn was assigned to debrief Valachi jointly with Agent Selvaggi. Flynn, a well-respected and well-liked agent who was assigned to the FBI's squad charged with investigating the organized crime it had only recently discovered existed. He turned out to be the perfect choice to work with the reluctant informant, Joe Valachi.

Although the interviews began as a joint FBN-FBI affair, Valachi was eventually placed in the exclusive care of Agent Flynn and the FBI. Flynn recognized that Valachi was not fully committed to his defection, but he also understood that an irrevocable step had been taken; Valachi could not go back or sideways, he could only go forward. Flynn set out to win the trust of the man he would call an unrepentant killer. It would take months.

He began by trying to gain Valachi's confidence. Flynn expressed concern for Valachi's health — he was 40 pounds overweight, a chronic smoker, and in poor physical condition. Flynn brought Valachi some exercise devices, such as a chest expander, and proposed a training program for the little Mafioso to follow. Flynn also brought in Italian delicacies — Provolone cheese, pasta, and Genoa sausage — and shared the meals Valachi prepared. The two men handicapped horse races, studying the racing forms Flynn brought and following the results of the races. They competed to see who could pick the most winners — a game Valachi usually won, as he had previously owned and trained race horses and was a lifelong horse player.

There was little questioning in the early sessions. Flynn let Valachi talk about subjects that interested him, and he proved to be a willing listener. When the topic turned from food or the ponies to people and places, Flynn was able to display some knowledge of his own, talking about people he knew who frequented the places Valachi described. This all must have been very reassuring and comforting to Valachi, who had to have been feeling very abandoned at that point. He had been cast completely out by his criminal associates, been given the kiss of death by his boss, killed the wrong man, and could never resume anything like his former life again. He found relief for the anxiety this caused in his new friend, Special Agent Flynn.

Gradually, Flynn's patience paid off. Discussions became more specific. More and more individuals were identified and connections were made. Valachi was providing the context the FBI needed to make sense of the thousands of hours of tapes they had made from wiretaps and bugs they had installed around the country. Although he paused frequently to rail at Vito Genovese, whom he blamed for all his troubles, Valachi was also providing details about hundreds of other members of the secret syndicate he described.

Valachi's memory for names and events was outstanding. After the interviews, which took place for three hours or more each day, four days every week, agents would go through police and FBI files to link Valachi's memory with crimes two or even three decades old. Through Valachi, the perpetrators in a number of unsolved homicides were identified. He knew of crimes that had been notorious for 20 years, and he had up-to-date information from inside Genovese's Atlanta cell.

Best of all, Valachi could describe the structure of the Cosa Nostra, dating practically from its inception in America. He had been present during the Maranzano-Masseria wars, which led directly to the formation of the national crime syndicate organized by Lucky Luciano and Meyer Lansky. He knew Vito Genovese, who had been angling to be the *capo di tutti capi* ("boss of bosses") prior to his incarceration, and he could describe every detail of the Genovese family.

Joe Valachi was a gold mine of information for the FBI, even though none would ever be used to make any criminal cases. Valachi proved in these interviews that the thing that had always been rumor was really fact. That he provided this information at all is a tribute to the interviewing skill of Special Agent Flynn and others who worked with a very reluctant defector. These were difficult, stressful interviews, conducted across the cultural gulf between an Italian killer and Mafiosi and an Irish investigator. Credit should go to both men, who somehow found a way to communicate the information.

Analysis

Valachi's initial debriefing lasted over 8 months. He continued to be a resource available to law enforcement for years after his Senate appearance. During this time Valachi spent hundreds of hours in interviews with agents from the FBI, FBN, the Justice Department, the McClellan committee, even his ghostwriter. Nobody ever caught Valachi in a lie. It is possible that he withheld some information or protected a few friends, but even this seems unlikely, given the extent of his debriefing.

From a pure law enforcement perspective, the Valachi interviews resulted in absolutely nothing. No indictments, no convictions, no seizures or arrests. Nevertheless, Valachi's information had a tremendous impact on criminal justice and organized crime. The public consciousness of the Mafia which came as a result of Valachi's testimony resulted in new laws, an increased federal effort against organized crime, and more pressure on the mob. The fact that Valachi's associates were never able to exact their revenge on him for his betrayal encouraged others to follow in his footsteps. None of this would have been possible had the information inside Joe Valachi's head not been retrieved by the federal investigators assigned to work with him. These interviews are textbook descriptions of how to develop and manage an underworld defector-informant.

Motivation

James Flynn, the FBI agent who managed Joseph Valachi as an informant, described his motives. "Revenge was a large part of it, but it was also a cold, calculated move for survival. Don't think for a moment that this was a repentant sinner. He was a killer capable of extreme violence. He was devious, rebellious against all constituted authority, and he lived in a world of fear and suspicion. Fear especially marked him. Fear of what he was doing and at the same time fear that nobody would believe him."

Special Agent Flynn spent a good deal of time with Joe Valachi, much of which was devoted to understanding the little gangster's motivation for cooperating. It should have been obvious from the beginning why Valachi had turned — he had bludgeoned to death a fellow inmate within plain view of dozens of witnesses; Valachi, already serving a 15-year term on one drug sentence, was looking at a 20-year term on another, and now he was facing the death penalty as well.

Although one would suppose the desire to avoid the electric chair would be enough to motivate anyone, it was really only sufficient to get Valachi through the door. Most observers agree that he initially intended to give the appearance of cooperating in hopes of getting the best deal possible. He definitely did not begin his cooperation with the idea of testifying on television about the Mafia's blood oath.

Most probably, Valachi had a mixture of motives in deciding to cooperate:

1.   Fear of the death penalty for the Saupp murder
2.   Fear of additional incarceration on the new narcotics charges
3.   Fear of associates, particularly Vito Genovese
4.   Desire for revenge against Genovese

When all of these motivations were combined with the development of a trusting relationship with Special Agent Flynn, Joseph Valachi's defection was complete. Asked at the Senate hearings why he decided to cooperate, Valachi identified his own motivation:

Mr. Valachi:	*The main answer to that is very simple. Number one, it is to destroy them.*
The Chairman:	*To what?*
Mr. Valachi:	*To destroy them.*
The Chairman:	*Destroy who?*
Mr. Valachi:	*The Cosa Nostra leaders, or the bosses. The whole — how would you explain it — that exists.*
The Chairman:	*You want to destroy the whole syndicate or the whole organization?*
Mr. Valachi:	*That is right; yes, sir.*
The Chairman:	*Why do you feel like it should be destroyed?*
Mr. Valachi:	*Well, through the years, first of all I was concerned, and second, they have been very bad to the soldiers and they have been thinking for themselves, all through the years. It is all put together, and I put together so many things that it all comes to that, to destroy them.*

This is a pretty incoherent statement, but the desire for revenge certainly rings out loud and clear. Valachi, the soldier, blamed his current sorry situation on a breach of faith by his boss, Genovese. Having been wronged and betrayed, Valachi was able to justify his own betrayal of the secrets of the Cosa Nostra.

As is so often the case, a mix of motivations brought the informant to the table. Valachi had a *bona fide* fear of his associates, particularly the vicious Genovese. He did not want to die, either in the electric chair or at the hands of his boss. The "kiss of death" was a sentence Valachi sought desperately to avoid, first by going to solitary, then by lashing out at the threat and killing the wrong man. Unable to accept any responsibility for his own actions, Valachi blamed others, then took his revenge on them.

In this chapter's discussion of interviewing, we noted that the officer should be alert for clues to the informant's motives for cooperation, and for any changes which might be taking place in that motivation. Valachi's motivation did change with time. He began by agreeing to cooperate from fear of his associates and fear of the chair. Over a period of some months, and with the skillful support of Special Agent Flynn, Valachi developed a burning desire for revenge. At the end, he probably continued to cooperate from his "fear that nobody would believe him" and his trusting relationship with his handlers. It appears that this process of transformation was understood by Special Agent Flynn, who also knew how to manage this very volatile and complex individual.

Access

Somewhat surprisingly, the question of Valachi's access is still openly debated. There is no doubt that he was a "made member" of the Mafia or Cosa Nostra, a fairly elite group consisting of 2500 to 5000 individuals in 24 American cities. Moreover, Valachi was affiliated with the Genovese family, then one of, if not the, most powerful of the various crime groups.

Valachi's lengthy criminal history and involvement in drug trafficking and multiple murders gave him a certain level of trust within the family, but he was far from being a major player. He always described himself as a "soldier" who carried out the orders of his superiors. The structure of the organization he outlined for the Senate included many layers of insulation between soldiers like Valachi and people like Genovese. As a result, much of Valachi's information came second- or third-hand through other members of the not-so-secret society. Quite a bit of gossip floated around the organization. Valachi and other insiders spent a good deal of time trading rumors and putting two and two together.

Ironically, Valachi's access probably increased after his incarceration at Atlanta. When Valachi arrived, he was eventually invited by Genovese to move into the godfather's eight-man cell. Because Genovese was still running his family from within the prison, Valachi was in a position to collect much more of the family gossip. As a result, Valachi was able in debriefings to lay bare the entire Genovese family. The organizational charts of the other families presented at the Senate hearings were much less detailed than that for Genovese's outfit — something which might have prompted the $100,000 contract the Don is supposed to have let on Valachi.

In his access and control, Valachi was much more like a defector from a foreign intelligence service than a law enforcement informant. Most intelligence services are tightly compartmentalized so that no one has access to too many secrets. A defector such as Valachi knows something about the general workings of his organization, much less about specific operations or individuals (unless, like Valachi, he was personally involved), and almost all of the goings-on in his own compartment.

Valachi's status as a "made member" of a vast, shadowy conspiracy and his shocking betrayal of the secret ritual had a galvanizing impact on law enforcement and public opinion. This knowledge did not require access to the highest councils of the Cosa Nostra's national commission; those at Valachi's more pedestrian level had enough access to spill those beans. What made Valachi different was his willingness to describe his access to the world. As a result, though others who followed Valachi had much better access, few have had the same impact.

Control

Valachi was in federal custody during the entire time he was cooperating with the government. This did not preclude a number of control problems from arising in connection with that cooperation. Control did not come easily to Valachi, a career criminal and multiple murderer. There is considerable evidence that Valachi had no intention of "giving it all up" when he first sought the FBN's protection. It is more likely that he began cooperating with the intention of getting the best possible deal, protecting himself from Genovese, and then taking revenge against Don Vito, the man Valachi saw as being responsible for his predicament.

The initial interviews with Valachi were difficult and the relationship strained. He resented the FBN agents who "flipped" him but did not want to be turned over to the FBI. When joint FBN-FBI debriefings began, Valachi played narcotics agent Frank Selvaggi off against FBI agent James Flynn. Only later did patient questioning by Flynn bring Valachi, whom Flynn described as a "killer, capable of extreme violence," to break his ties completely with the organization that was his home for decades.

Flynn took a gradual approach to the development of Valachi, who, thanks to the FBN, already had one foot in the door. He moved carefully, building personal rapport and never asking more from Valachi than the gangster's conscience would allow him to give. As more details emerged, Valachi's conscience expanded to a point where he was telling the agents, if not everything, a reasonable facsimile thereof. By taking a lot of small, though still difficult, steps, Flynn moved Valachi to a place no Mafiosi had ever been before. It was, by all accounts, an impressive piece of investigative work.

Valachi had a tremendous memory for names and events dating back 30 years. As the interviews progressed, both the agents and their informant trained each other. Valachi taught the agents to let him tell his story in a rambling, stream-of-consciousness fashion, filling in the details later. This process took over 8 months, 3 hours a day, 4 days a week. The agents taught Valachi to specify how he knew what he was saying. If he had seen it himself, he told the agents so. If the information was hearsay, he prefaced the remark with "one of the boys told me." If he considered the information reliable, he pronounced it "solid."

Two control problems were rather peculiar to the Valachi case. First, everyone wanted a piece of his action. He eventually wound up testifying in front of a Senate committee, an experience not shared by most informants. Second, Valachi wanted to write a book, eventually coming up with a 300,000 word manuscript describing his more than 30 years in the Mafia. The Justice Department got into a nasty dispute with author Peter Maas and Valachi, eventually winding up in court. Maas, with Valachi's assistance, published *The Valachi Papers* in 1968. Most informants do not seek to publicize their activity, but Valachi was unique. He wanted revenge, and he got it by exposing every secret thing he could remember.

These extraneous activities detracted from law enforcement's ability to use Valachi as an active informant. (His incarceration for narcotics trafficking and the prison murder, coupled with his appalling criminal history, would have made him an awful witness at any trial which depended on Valachi's testimony.) The FBI appears to have wanted to keep word of Valachi's cooperation a secret long enough that they could employ wiretaps or other investigative techniques against some of Valachi's former associates. This was not possible, thanks to his exposure at the Senate hearings.

Summing Up

People remember Joseph Valachi as the first person to break with the American Mafia or Cosa Nostra. He is sometimes described as the most important of the many mob informants who followed, because he broke the ice, shattering the code of *omerta* which had previously kept even the existence of the national crime syndicate from the public eye. In becoming an informant, Valachi, it is said, did incalculable harm to the Cosa Nostra.

There is a good deal of myth in this analysis. Valachi was hardly the first Mafiosi to turn informant. By the time Valachi came in, the FBN had already worked with a long list of mob informants, some of whom came from quite high in the ranks, both in the U.S. and in Italy. Valachi was not even the first mobster to provide information about Vito Genovese. Informant Nelson Cantellops, though not a "made member" of the organization, was close enough to provide the information that put Don Vitone in Atlanta for 15 years.

The great value of Joe Valachi, the informant, was his Senate testimony and his willingness to expose the secret workings of Cosa Nostra. Years later, some members were overheard musing that they could understand Valachi informing against Genovese, even giving up some of his narcotics connections, but why did he have to describe the initiation ritual and all the organizational secrets of the crime group? That was unforgivable, because it exposed the organization and everyone in it in a way that had never happened before. Thanks to Valachi, there was no longer any doubt about the existence of the Cosa Nostra.

Ironically, although Valachi's information heralded the belated arrival of the FBI into the fight against organized crime, not one person was ever sent to prison as a direct result of his cooperation. He was never called to testify against Vito Genovese, who died in prison in 1969. Outliving the man who gave him the kiss of death must have given Joe Valachi considerable satisfaction. He served out his own life sentence in the federal prison at La Tuna, TX, dying in 1971. No one claimed the body of the informant who put the Mafia on the front page.

Case
Development

9

"*The dust that Poncho bit down south, ended up in Lefty's mouth./The day they laid poor Poncho low, Lefty split for Ohio;/Where he got the bread to go, there ain't nobody knows.*"— Townes Van Zandt, *Poncho and Lefty* (as sung by Willie Nelson and Merle Haggard)

"*Be subtle! be subtle! and use your spies for every kind of business. Whether the object be to crush an army, to storm a city, or to assassinate an individual, it is always necessary to begin by finding out the names of the attendants, the aides-de-camp, and door-keepers and sentries of the general in command. Our spies must be commissioned to ascertain these.*" —Sun Tzu, *The Art of War*

In the world of espionage, a spy like Kim Philby may work for years, even decades, passing along information which is presumably of interest to those paying for it. In times of peace or even "cold war" it could be that this information will never be used for the significant (or even visible) purposes Sun Tzu describes. For those running the intelligence agencies, to "know the enemy" is a worthy objective in and of itself.

Law enforcement has little use for this objective, however. We do not care what color underwear *el presidente* is wearing, or which model tank he is buying this week. Our goals are more immediate and substantive. We need to know where the criminal is so we can put our hands on him. We need to know who committed a particular act so that person can be held accountable for it in court. In our world, someone is going to have to bite some legal dust.

Sun Tzu advocates using spies for "every kind of business," but he clearly has some very tangible (and rather bloody-minded) objectives in mind. Those of us in law enforcement are not in the army-crushing, city-storming, or assassination business, but informants *are* used to break criminal organizations, to obtain search warrants, and to develop the probable cause for the arrest of criminals — all modern counterparts in the criminal justice system. Great care — the subtlety Sun Tzu urges — is still required to accomplish any of these goals, but the objective should be clear to every officer; the end result of an informant's tip should be a criminal prosecution.

I worked once with a district attorney's investigator in a smaller county who had the most amazing network of informants I have ever seen. He aggressively collected intelligence; interviewed victims, witnesses, and defendants; and developed dozens of informants. He had his own filing system in a set of three-ring binders, cross-referenced and indexed so that he could quickly identify any criminal by name or description. Most of the crimes committed in the county were also indexed so he could put a name to a crime very quickly.

Riding with this investigator was like a fantasy trip to the informant bazaar. Over the course of one evening, he arranged to meet with six or seven individuals, gathering more information from each person for the binders. He said he had between 40 and 60 informants active at any given time. I was frankly astonished at the depth of the man's knowledge and at the number of people in this relatively small community who were willing to "give up" information to him. I later marveled at this to the narcotics detective for the local police department. "Oh, yeah, he knows everything there is to know, all right," he responded, in what I thought was a rather bitter tone. "Knows everything, does nothing."

I quickly gained some new insights into how informants should and should not be used. The "marvel" of the informant network turned out not to be so marvelous. The detective explained to me (using one- or two-syllable words so this city boy would get it) how the miracle came to be. The investigator, he said, never, never, never burned an informant. No matter what information was provided, the investigator never made use of it if it meant disclosure of the informant's identity. Furthermore, because he worked for the district attorney, the investigator had access to every person arrested or prosecuted in that county and had some influence over the "hammer" on each informant. He could, the detective said, "make their case go away" in exchange for the information he prized.

This was more than the detective could do. In fact, it was apparent that the investigator had developed more than a few informants from among those the detective had arrested, which may have accounted for some of the bitterness. In doing so, the investigator effectively spoiled the market for everybody else. No potential informant in that county wanted to provide information to people like me or the detective; we were going to use it to make cases, after all, and expose the informant in the process.

Somewhere along the line, the investigator had lost sight of the main purpose of the informant in law enforcement. It is never enough merely to *know*. Our function is to use informants as a tool for conducting criminal investigations. The misuse of informants in this instance actually had the effect of hampering effective law enforcement in that county, because not only was the investigator not making any cases, other officers could not do so, either.

Case development is the goal, but how we work toward that objective will vary with every informant. Sammy "The Bull" Gravano had historical access to his crime boss, John Gotti. The case that grew from Gravano's access was far different from the one Linda Tripp might have made against Monica Lewinsky. In both situations, though, the investigators were focused on a very clear end result — a criminal prosecution. Because everyone's access is different, the approach used to reach the end result will differ in every case. Some of the paths are fixed by statute, by case law, and by convention, and, of course, officers who are investigating computer fraud will have a completely different approach to case development than those investigating drug trafficking. There are some common threads, however.

Rules for Case Development

Case development is all about corroboration. In trying to convict a criminal, can we rely upon the word of an informant, one who has an interest in the outcome and a myriad of possible motivations to lie? This sort of reliance is not only unwise, it is downright foolish. Only the relentless corroboration of the informant's statements will provide the foundation for a successful prosecution.

In constructing this case we must certainly follow the legal processes set by the legislature and the courts, but there are some guidelines we can establish for ourselves as well. I have listed a few that seem to work in most situations, but every officer should develop a set that fits his or her own situation.

1. Buy the informant, not the information, *but ...*
2. ...Build your case around the information, *not* the informant.
3. Do not rely on the informant to "make the case;" this is *your* responsibility.
4. Always assume every case will end up before a jury.
5. Corroborate and evaluate.

Buy the Informant, Not the Information, *But ...*

This is an old saying in the espionage business, one which translates neatly for our purposes. Deals with informants should always be for the entire package rather than for some piece of information or evidence. Two bad things can happen when the officer negotiates for a snippet of the whole string. First, you will have to re-negotiate every time you need anything. Every piece of information the informant collects will be subject to a bargaining process which may include the informant's seeking out other agencies for a higher bid. Control is nonexistent, and nobody can develop a good case under these conditions.

Second, this sort of arrangement affects case development because the informant is in a position to determine what information is forthcoming and what is not. Without having access to the entire package, the officer cannot make the decisions necessary to move the case forward. Jurors are uncomfortable with the notion that some informant was in a position to say who got arrested and who did not.

At the time the informant is initially developed, the entire package should be explained so that there is no room for confusion. One former CIA officer describes this as the "bittersweet talk." This is essentially an assurance that as long as the informant follows the terms and conditions of his commission, which include a 100% commitment to full disclosure, the informant can expect to receive 100% of whatever benefit was offered. If, on the other hand, the informant provides anything less than 100%, he can expect to receive nothing. Completely truthful statements and an honest answer to every question put by the officer are important parts of the 100% obligation; it's an all or nothing deal.

Understand that when you are negotiating with an informant for his or her cooperation, you are buying *full* cooperation or nothing. Once you have that commitment to full cooperation, you can move forward to develop cases with the assistance of the informant, keeping in mind that cases are made, not with informants, but with their information.

Build Your Case Around the Information, *Not* the Informant

Although you want to "buy" the informant rather than his information, it is unwise to build a case around the individual. Cases — during both the investigation and the prosecution phases — should instead be constructed around the *information* provided by the informant. Why is this? Because we cannot count on a jury to believe informants. Reliance on the uncorroborated word of an informant is the surest way to an acquittal one can conjure up. It is also the route to charges of misconduct, perjury, and assorted other scandals.

Remember that in our previous discussions of betrayal, we learned that people value trust and confidence and reject those who betray. The *Bible* (Proverbs 11:13) says: "A talebearer revealeth secrets: but he that is of a faithful spirit concealeth the matter." In considering the word of an informant, jurors are going to consider whether that person is "of a faithful spirit," and most times they will conclude he is not. A second biblical expression (Ecclesiastes 21:28) then comes into play, "A talebearer defileth his own soul, and is hated wheresoever he dwelleth." In order to get around these biases, it is best not to place the informant in anything like a key role in an investigation.

Ideally, the informant functions as a signpost along the road to conviction. We use that signpost for direction or guidance, but it is not the vehicle which carries us to the end of the road, or even the road itself. Unfortunately, we do not live in an ideal world, and for various reasons the informant may become more than merely a guidepost.

One of these reasons is that crime takes place in an atmosphere of secrecy. The idea of a burglar leaving a calling card with his name and address at each burgled home is ridiculous, even though he may have left more subtle clues, such as fingerprints, tool marks, or even a piece of clothing. Although they might tell a few trusted associates, almost nobody broadcasts their involvement in a criminal act. This secrecy means that when one of those trusted associates comes in to provide information about the crime, corroboration of the statement may be difficult.

We build our case on what we *know*, as opposed to what the informant *says*, because the defendant is going to say just the opposite. A classic example is the Independent Counsel's perjury and obstruction of justice case against Bill Clinton. The investigators had an informant, Linda Tripp, who told them about a former intern who said she had been having a sexual relationship with the President. Although Tripp seemed credible and came with far less baggage than the usual informant, the investigators did not simply stop with her statement. Steps were taken to corroborate her information, including a meeting with Monica Lewinsky, at which the two women's conversation was recorded.

At this point, Tripp's statements took on a whole different flavor. As a witness in the case against the President, Tripp was no longer especially important. The information she had provided, however, was very significant, and the case was being developed around this information. The attention turned to Lewinsky, who initially refused to cooperate. The investigators still had hours of her statements to Tripp on tape, statements which could be corroborated independently. Even before Lewinsky finally agreed to cooperate, the Independent Counsel had spent a great deal of time subpoenaing records, calling Secret Service personnel, and generally trying to verify the information it already had from her. When she finally provided a written proffer, much of it was already corroborated.

One of the hottest debates in the Senate trial of President Clinton was over the question of whether witnesses would be called. This probably seemed somewhat surreal to most in law enforcement; witnesses in court are, after all, the end product of an investigation. This issue was political, but it did serve to illustrate a basic fact with regard to the Independent Counsel's case. The cry that "we do not need witnesses" really meant that the case had been built around the *information*, not the informants. The Independent Counsel had Monica Lewinsky's statement that she had had sex with the President, but he also had the navy blue dress. She said she met a certain number of times at the White House, but the Independent Counsel had other witnesses, logs, and other evidence that would have proved that fact, even if Lewinsky had never agreed to cooperate. When she finally did appear in a videotaped deposition, the standard reaction was "nothing new." This is a tribute to the efforts of the much-maligned staff of the Independent Counsel's office.

The only questions that really remained unanswered were those facts in Lewinsky's proffer which could not be corroborated. What was said, for example, in her breakfast meeting with Vernon Jordan? Did Clinton tell Lewinsky to lie in her affidavit? Only two people were privy to each of those conversations, and ultimately a case may come down to which of them is being truthful. Both may have reasons to lie and reasons to tell the truth. Without a tape recording or the testimony of a third party, there will be no direct evidence supporting one or the other. Any conclusions we might make will probably be based, as they were in Lewinsky's situation, upon circumstantial evidence.

Thanks to the credibility problems that accompany informants, we have to corroborate their direct testimony even more than that of a regular witness. Corroboration is even more important when the evidence is circumstantial. Often, an informant's statement will be a mix of direct and circumstantial evidence, as was the case in Monica Lewinsky's proffer. The heart of the obstruction of justice case against President Clinton was the attempt to conceal gifts that he had given Ms. Lewinsky. In order to develop a prosecutable case involving this attempt, the prosecutors had this statement by Lewinsky to work with:

> *Ms. L then asked if she should put away (outside her home) the gifts he had given her or, maybe, give them to someone else. (Ms. Currie called Ms. L later that afternoon and said that the Pres. had told her Ms. L wanted her to hold onto something for her. Ms. L boxed up most of the gifts she had received and gave them to Ms. Currie. It is unknown if Ms. Currie knew the contents of the box.)*

In corroborating this statement, investigators could possibly document the phone call by Currie, obtain Currie's statement about the conversation, retrieve the gifts from Currie's home (they were under her bed), and then confirm through purchase records that the President had bought all the items. All of this information, even without Lewinsky's statement, is fairly strong circumstantial evidence that might (but in this case did not) lead a jury to conclude that the obstruction had taken place. The original informant (Tripp) and even Lewinsky are much less central to the ultimate conclusion.

Judge Stephen Trott, a former Justice Department official and prosecutor, writes of his technique in presenting informant or accomplice testimony (*Lecture Supplement*, 1996):

> *One of my favorite tactics was to suggest to the jurors that they set aside at the outset of their deliberation the testimony of the accomplice for the purpose of testing the case on the basis of the rest of the evidence. The jury will do this anyway, and it enables you to argue that the case is "there" without his testimony. "Let's suppose that Terry Miller [the accomplice witness], himself, was killed during the shooting and never ever made it into this courtroom," I told them, "and let's see what the rest of the evidence shows." Then I took a Sherlock Holmes approach to "solving the case," and the jurors usually loved it. They want to be detectives, not just the jurors. Invite them to solve it with you. Dwell on the strength of the circumstantial evidence. I then told the jurors to add the accomplice's testimony into the mix and the defendant's guilt is established not only beyond a reasonable doubt but to an absolute certainty.*

This case is built around the information, not the informant. Even when you have a weaker set of circumstances, it still pays to use the informant to support the evidence rather than the other way around.

Do Not Rely on the Informant To Make the Case; This Is Your Responsibility

Case development is not something that should ever be left to the informant. The cooperating individual *has no say* in whether a case is initiated, who is to be targeted, how the case will be investigated, or who will work on the case. All of these things are within the exclusive purview of the person who is being paid to make these decisions — the investigating officer.

All manner of bad things can happen when the officer abdicates this responsibility. The control that is essential to a successful officer-informant relationship is lost and probably cannot be retrieved. Here is one example from Robert Daley's *Prince of the City:*

> *It is said that The Baron can work with any narcotics team he chooses. He is a fantastic informant who works off and on for the Bureau of Narcotics, for the Treasury Depart-ment, and for the Police Safe and Loft Squad, as well as for Police Narcotics. Leuci will have to sell himself to this man. ...Finally, The Baron agrees — and then he spends the next hour lecturing Leuci on how to put the case together. He knows where the Italian comes from, how he operates, and suspects who his Mafia contact must be. Leuci listens with his mouth open, marveling at the Baron's knowledge and skill.*

It is quite natural to want to rely upon the informant in making these types of decisions. After all, who knows the targets, their method of operation, or all the intimate details better than the informant? Furthermore, some informants like the Baron are vastly more experienced than even some officers with whom they work. Nevertheless, a crystal-clear distinction should be drawn between the *information* and the *corroboration.* Providing the information is the responsibility of the informant. Obtaining the corroboration is the responsibility of the investigator. These roles should never be reversed.

Always Assume Every Case Will End Up Before a Jury

It is usually not a good idea to make assumptions, but this one is not only safe, it is harmless and almost inevitably beneficial. We all know that most criminal cases result in a plea. In the federal system, more than 90% of those indicted eventually wind up pleading guilty to something. In the face of these statistics, it is extremely tempting to make a bad assumption — that the individual is going to plead out. Nine out ten times, you'll be right.

It is the other 10% we need to be worried about. The bigger the case, the more important the defendant, or the more money the defendant has for his defense, the better your odds that this particular prosecution will fall in the 10% that go to trial. If you start off with the assumption that you are going to have to fight this thing all the way to the Supreme Court, you may find that you have gained a whole new perspective on that informant.

The next time you are in an interview room with the informant, try visualizing this person on the witness stand with twelve strangers looking on while the defense attorney pounds on him. Visualize a multiple-defendant trial with six or seven defense attorneys cross-examining the informant with information on his background they have dug up through a private investigator.

Not a pretty picture? Now, rather than after the jury is seated, would be a good time to develop a case which does *not* rely on this individual as the linchpin of the entire prosecution. What is the cost of this strategy? The officer may have to work a little harder, prepare a little better, and produce some more corroboration. This will make the prosecutor happy and, coincidentally, make the case stronger and more likely to end in a guilty plea, in which case you will have been wrong in your assumption that the case would go to court, but you will be satisfied with the outcome. Best of all, that informant never had to take the stand.

Corroborate and Evaluate

In the development of a case with an informant, an investigation consists of the actual obtaining of the information, the corroboration of this information, and the evaluation of the end product. This process should be continuous and the officer should try to be objective.

Corroborate

Richard Nossen, a Treasury agent and administrator, lists in his handbook, *The Seventh Basic Investigative Technique,* those investigative steps or methods which have traditionally been used to investigate crime:

1. Development of informants
2. Use of undercover agents
3. Laboratory analysis of physical evidence
4. Physical and electronic surveillance
5. Interrogation
6. Wiretapping, where permitted by law
7. Financial investigation

Note that informants are listed first. Everything else is corroboration.

In developing a case with an informant, we start with the statements made. These invariably take us to some individual or group of individuals against whom there is some allegation of criminal wrongdoing. We evaluate the informant's access: Is it ongoing or historical? Is it direct personal contact or indirect through some third party? We assess the informant's motivation for cooperating and how this relates to the allegation and the person implicated. Now an investigation can be conducted.

How will the statements be corroborated? How will the crime be proved? We are going to use one or more of the other six of Nossen's basic investigative techniques. Which ones or how many we use will depend on the crime, the informant's access, the circumstances, and a variety of other factors. Because these situations are all different, it makes little sense to try to apply some universal rule for every case, but a brief discussion of how each relates to the informant might be helpful.

Development of Informants. Informants can be used to corroborate the statements of other informants. Having two or more people actively providing information about a certain group or individual is a rare but wonderful luxury. This is especially true if they do not know about each other. The officer has the opportunity to test statements, monitor the informants' actions, and generally get a unique, multi-perspective look at the case as it develops. If they do know about each other, as when a husband and wife or boyfriend and girlfriend are working together on a case, the chances that both are being deceptive are higher if one is lying. In this case, the officer has to treat the information from both as coming from one, and corroborate it independently.

Use of Undercover Agents. Undercover agents are basically a means of inserting a good witness in the place of the (possibly not so good) informant. By introducing an undercover agent, the informant can positively demonstrate the veracity of his information and perhaps move one step away from the witness stand. There are obvious advantages to having an undercover agent, rather than the informant, make the buy, observe the activity, or listen to what the defendant has to say. For one thing, the undercover agent is a trained observer with a very focused perspective. For another, the undercover agent has none of what the prosecutors like to call the informant's "baggage" — a criminal record, participation in crimes, and such. Finally, the undercover agent has experience testifying in court, is much less likely to face the sort of attack an informant would undergo on the stand, and can, if it is still necessary to put the informant on, corroborate those facts described by the informant which the undercover agent witnessed.

Laboratory Analysis of Physical Evidence. Very good corroborative evidence, the scientific analysis of fingerprints, DNA, ballistics, or documents can have a real impact on a jury. This type of evidence is objective and persuasive — as opposed to the subjective and often unpersuasive testimony of the informant. When the informant says, "I got the heroin from John," and a fingerprint specialist says John's prints were on the package, juries tend to believe both people are telling the truth. For an even better example, look no further than Monica Lewinsky, who said she had sex with the President. This statement might have been in dispute, except that Lewinsky also had that stained dress. The FBI's DNA analysis was rather conclusive, making Clinton's finger-wagging "I did not have sexual relations with that woman, Ms. Lewinsky" denial utterly inoperative. Officers should look for opportunities to bring this type of dispassionate and objective evidence into the courtroom in support of an informant. It is not perfect, as the prosecutors in the O.J. Simpson murder case will tell us, but coupled with the testimony of an informant, both types of evidence are bolstered.

Physical and Electronic Surveillance. This is another example of substituting the observations of an officer for those of the informant. Asking the informant to "wear a wire" is so common that it is practically standard procedure. Linda Tripp wore one to her meeting with Lewinsky, who was asked to wear one if she cooperated against Betty Currie or Vernon Jordan. Both physical and electronic surveillance can be the best corroboration available for an informant statement. They should always be used in any case in which the informant's word is going to be questioned. (That would be *every* case.) By having the officer take the stand and say, "I saw the informant enter the restaurant, I saw her meet with the defendant for three hours, and here is a tape recording of that conversation," we take a great deal of pressure off the informant. (Though not all the pressure, as Tripp found out.) The facts in such an admittedly ideal situation are really no longer in doubt. The informant's statement concerning the meeting does not carry much weight any more — the jurors can hear for themselves what was said, ending any dispute about the facts. There is a dangerous flip side, however. This is the prospect that any statement made by the informant which is *not* supported by physical or electronic surveillance can be doubly suspect by the jury. It may not work that way; the jurors might decide that the informant was truthful on ten occasions where we have tape, so we can conclude that he is probably being truthful on the eleventh, when we do not. I would not count on this response, though. Physical and electronic surveillance are relatively easy means of corroborating an informant's statements, though they obviously work best if the informant still has some current access. Surveillance is absolutely mandatory if the informant is actively working — making purchases of evidence or introducing an undercover agent. You also want to do surveillance to protect the informant from harm or detection.

Interrogation. This relates to interviews of the informant, but also of the defendant, who can, by way of confessions or admissions, corroborate the informant's statements. I would include interviews of third-party witnesses in this category also. The informant's associates may have useful information which can be obtained in interviews. Business partners, crime victims, even unrelated persons who happened to witness part of some activity described by the informant can be useful in obtaining corroboration. Documents provided by witnesses can also corroborate informant statements, though usually with some limitations. Hotel, travel, and phone records are very commonly employed in drug conspiracy prosecutions. These records may verify an informant's statement that on a certain date he and the defendant traveled to a city, stayed at a hotel, and made telephone calls to the connection. They do not tell us what was said in that conversation, however, so the value may be restricted.

Interviews of the informant may afford a sort of self-corroboration. This is the reasoning used in most "jailhouse confession" cases. The thinking is that only the criminal would know the details of the crime. If an informant comes in, saying he has gotten a confession from his cell mate, the informant may or may not be telling the truth. If the informant has details about a crime which he could not have gotten except from someone who had been there when it was committed, this is better evidence of the informant's veracity. Because this type of evidence rests on not one, but two rather questionable assumptions, it is rightly regarded with a good deal of suspicion. (Assumption 1: The informant is telling the truth. Assumption 2: He could only have gotten the details from the perpetrator.)

Wiretapping, Where Permitted by Law. Wiretapping is great corroboration. It is relatively difficult to get the court order needed to put in a wiretap or a room bug. Still, there is nothing like having a complete record of an entire conversation, including the defendant's own statements to back up the informant. Wiretaps often provide good *ex post facto* corroboration. In this situation, the police get a wiretap and overhear all sorts of incriminating statements. Some of these statements might not mean much because, while wiretaps do make a complete record, they may not provide the context of the conversation. For example, in this conversation, two wiseguys, Ray DeCarlo and Anthony "Tony Boy" Boiardo, are talking business in DeCarlo's hangout, which the FBI has bugged:

> Ray DeCarlo: *He do not want that job no more than the man in the moon. But he has gotta keep it; you know why he wants to keep it? Because he figures if someone else becomes boss, then the boss can turn to him and say "How many points you got? Thirty points from all the joints? Well, fifteen we need for the boys." That's the only reason why he wants to keep it because he knows the boss can do that to him. Where does he figure to have thirty points — that means thirty G's a month. Does he need that much money to live on? Thirty points? Maybe he has got fifty, maybe he has got seventy. Who knows? Frank's piece of the Tropicana — that had to go to somebody. Frank's piece in the other joint. Abe's piece. Where do they go now?*

An informant could provide context by identifying the "joints" (Las Vegas casinos) and the players, "Frank" (mob boss Frank Costello) and "Abe." An informant, even coming in long after these tapes were made, could provide investigators with the context that would allow the conversation to make sense to a jury. As evidence, both the statement of the informant and the taped conversation gain in this transaction.

On October 29, 1989, FBI agents listened as a bug they had placed at 34 Guild Street in Medford, MA, captured the induction ceremony for several new Mafia members. The recording was used in the trials of over 20 of those who attended and is now available as proof of the existence of the criminal organization known as the Cosa Nostra. Valuable though this tape may be, it would not have been possible without the information provided by Angelo "Sonny" Mercurio, an FBI informant. Mercurio, who was among those present in the room during the ceremony, was available to provide the full context to the FBI and to identify all the speakers, even though he never surfaced at any of the trials.

Financial Investigation. Analysis of financial evidence is one of the newest of investigative techniques and one of the most persuasive to jurors. Jurors are comfortable with the concept that while an informant might lie, numbers do not. For instance, an informant might say that he paid a drug trafficker over a million dollars over a period of two years. This might or might not be true. If an analysis of the trafficker's finances shows bank deposits of over a million dollars in the same period, jurors may conclude that the informant might have been right about the source of those funds.

The power of financial investigation is its objectivity. Careful records are kept of almost all financial activities (even the illegal ones), especially by banks and legitimate businesses.

Using several indirect methods of proving income, a financial investigator can demonstrate conclusively that a person received money from some source. The records used in this analysis may come from the defendant, who may keep "pay and owe sheets" or other documents. More often, the records are obtained from a bank or financial institution, or from some other third party. These third-party records are almost always accurate and complete (banks are especially obsessive about thoroughly documenting every transaction, no matter how small).

An informant provides the one thing that a financial investigation may not be able to do — identifying the source of the funds. This is particularly true when the defendant's income is in cash. Large amounts of cash could come from anywhere; all the financial investigation will tell us is that the cash was deposited or spent. An informant can explain that cash: "It came from drug sales."

Jurors appreciate this sort of evidence. Defense attorneys hate it because the conclusions are so obvious. "Well, no, my client hasn't had a legitimate job or filed a tax return for the last ten years, and yes, he did buy a new house, some cars, and deposit all that money in the bank, but you can't really believe the informant when he says my client is a drug dealer!" Yes, as a matter of fact, that is usually what they will believe when the investigator has corroborated the informant's statement using one or more of the other investigative techniques.

Evaluate

The officer should be engaged in a continuous process of evaluation where the informant is concerned. The informant guidelines included in the Appendices provide several reviews of the informant by first-line supervisors and higher level management. This is the minimum evaluation that should be taking place. The officer should be constantly evaluating statements and activities to determine whether the informant's motivation is unchanged, whether investigative objectives are being attained, and whether any possibility exists for "double dealing."

One way of evaluating informant statements is to analyze the status of your corroboration. The officer can review a statement by numbering each "fact" provided by the informant in the margin of the report, then go back through the statement and check off each number that has been corroborated independently. Put a minus sign next to each fact which can be independently corroborated but has not been corroborated yet, then circle those numbers for which no corroboration is possible.

Several conclusions will become immediately obvious using this review. First, if you have a high percentage of numbers with check marks, you also have a case which is heading toward prosecution. The chances that your informant is reliably reporting the facts are obviously much better if you have been able to verify the things he or she is saying. If you have a lot of minus signs, there is still some investigation to do. Take heart; at least the informant is telling you things for which corroboration is possible. This is not the case if you have a lot of circled numbers. In that situation, you have an informant who is telling you things you cannot prove. Although this might mean you have been asking the wrong questions, it might also mean that the informant is fabricating information; if there is no way it can be checked, it does not have to be true.

This system works best on successive statements. If you take one statement and wind up with all zeros, another statement is definitely in order. If, after asking new questions, you still come up with nothing verifiable, two possibilities exist: (1) the informant has no access to any actionable information, or (2) the informant has access but is not sufficiently motivated to give it up. In either case — no access or no motivation — you do not have an informant, only trouble.

The following excerpt is from Monica Lewinsky's written proffer to the Office of the Independent Counsel. Review this statement with an eye toward corroborating the things Lewinsky is saying. You should see that some of the things she says can be confirmed fairly easily, others may take some work, and several of the most important will need to be verified by other players — Vernon Jordan or Betty Currie. As we know, this did not happen, but the statement does provide the investigator with quite a bit to work with:

> On the day Mr. Jordan drove Ms. L to Mr. Carter's office, she showed Mr. Jordan the items she was producing in response to the subpoena. Ms. L believes she made it clear this was not everything she had that could respond to the subpoena, but she thought it was enough to satisfy. Mr. Jordan made no comment about whether or not what Ms. L brought was right or wrong. Mr. J drove Ms. L to Mr. Carter's office; introduced them; and left.
>
> The Pres., through Ms. Currie, invited Ms. L to come see him to get her Christmas presents. They played with Buddy, he gave her the presents, they talked casually and spoke for a few minutes about the case. Ms. L asked him how he thought the attorneys for Paula Jones found out about her. He thought it was probably "that woman from the summer … Kathleen Willey" (Linda Tripp) who led them to Ms. L or possibly the uniformed agents. He shared Ms. L's concern about the hat pin. He asked Ms. L if she had told anyone that he had given it to her and she replied, "no."
>
> Ms. L then asked if she should put away (outside her home) the gifts he had given her or, maybe, give them to someone else. (Ms. Currie called Ms. L later that afternoon and said that the Pres. had told her Ms. L wanted her to hold onto something for her. Ms. L boxed up most of the gifts she had received and gave them to Ms. Currie. It is unknown if Ms. Currie knew the contents of the box.
>
> Ms L told the Pres. she was planning to sign an affidavit. When Ms. L and the Pres. discussed when Ms. L was moving to NY the Pres. thought it might be possible that they would not seek her deposition if she was in NY.
>
> Ms. Lewinsky called Mr. Jordan several times concerning her employment in NY. When she called one day especially concerned about the case, Mr. Jordan suggested they meet for breakfast.
>
> At breakfast, Ms. L expressed concern about Ms. Tripp saying she (Ms. L) had trusted her before, but was now suspicious of her. Ms. L said Ms. Tripp may have seen notes when she was in Ms. L's home. Mr. Jordan asked if the notes were from Ms. L, who said they were notes to the Pres. Mr. Jordan suggested to Ms. L she check to make sure they are not there (something to that effect). Ms. L interpreted that to mean she should get rid of whatever is there.

We also need to evaluate actions. In the course of corroborating the informant's information, some affirmative steps are taken, such as the introduction of an undercover agent, the controlled purchase of evidence, the execution of search warrants, the arrest of wanted persons, or the seizure of evidence. Each of these actions should be evaluated to determine whether they did in fact corroborate the informant's statement as advertised. If not, steps should be taken to find out why not. The possibility always exists that the informant is double dealing or not being fully cooperative.

Summing Up

Case development is the end result of an informant's cooperation. Knowledge for knowledge's sake is a luxury for which law enforcement has little time. The process of developing cases will vary depending on a number of factors, but when an informant is involved, the process should flow from the information provided, rather than centering on the informant. Corroboration via a number of other investigative techniques is the key to case development.

Case Study: Betraying the Boss of Bosses

Vito Genovese was not the sort of man one wanted to cross. By 1960, law enforcement officers believed Genovese had been directly or indirectly responsible for dozens of murders, including at least one man who was scheduled to testify against the man who wanted to be the *capo di tutti capi*, or "boss of bosses," of the Cosa Nostra. In the late 1950s, the Cosa Nostra was in a period of flux. Some of the older, established family heads were out of the picture, either deported or dead. Those in the second tier were moving up the corporate ladder, and the most ambitious of these men was the short, stocky Italian immigrant, Vito Genovese.

A close associate of Charles "Lucky" Luciano, Genovese rose through the ranks to command his own family, one of five that dominated organized crime in New York City. His climb to the top was marked by violence that claimed the lives of several rivals. Anyone who represented a threat to "Don Vitone," real or imagined, needed to check his life insurance policy. You would not think that people would betray a man like this, but the don had his share of problems in the disloyalty department. The first to turn were Ernest "The Hawk" Rupolo and Peter La Tempa, two hoodlums from Genovese's group, whose testimony linked Genovese to the killing of his lieutenant, Ferdinand "The Shadow" Boccia. Genovese fled to Europe, living in Italy during World War II, waiting for things to cool down in New York.

Extradited to the U.S. in 1945, Genovese was held for trial for the Boccia murder. Also in police custody were the informants La Tempa and Rupolo. La Tempa was the first to go. Someone who was never identified substituted "enough poison to kill eight horses" for La Tempa's pain medication. Lacking corroboration for Rupolo's statement, the government was forced to free Genovese. The judge scolded, "I believe if there were even a shred of corroborating evidence you would have been condemned to the electric chair. By devious means, among which were the terrorizing of witnesses, kidnapping them, yes, even murdering those who could give evidence against you, you have thwarted justice time and again."

The next betrayal must have really cut Genovese to the quick. His second wife, Anna, filed for divorce in 1950. Unable to get any child support from the notoriously tight-fisted Genovese, she sued, taking Genovese's very private business before the court of public opinion. Anna accused Genovese of blacking her eyes and breaking her nose. She described his sexual peccadilloes, his mistresses, and intimate details of her own marriage. Worse, she outlined Genovese's finances in great detail, trying to prove that he did indeed have the resources to pay her child support. Anna described the locations of his bank accounts and safe deposit boxes, his overseas banking activity, and his possession of large amounts of cash. She detailed his involvement in the rackets, particularly gambling and extortion. All in all, it was about as bad as it could get in terms of exposure, and Genovese's associates wondered for years afterward why he had not planted Anna as he had so many others who displeased little Don Vitone.

Surprisingly, given the extent of Anna's betrayal, Genovese not only survived the disclosures but prospered, enduring the Kefauver hearings and the furor following the abortive Apalachin conference. Held at the estate of Mafia boss Joseph Barbara in Apalachin, NY, the meeting called by Genovese in November 1957 brought over 100 mobsters from around the country to cement his power over the national crime syndicate. Barely underway before being interrupted by the New York State Police, who apprehended 45 of Mr. Barbara's guests, the discovery of all these criminals in one place appeared very ominous to the public. Law enforcement agencies, including the FBI and the Federal Bureau of Narcotics (FBN), intensified their efforts to penetrate the crime syndicate. At the top of the list of targets was the man who fancied himself the boss of all bosses, Vito Genovese.

The FBN had been eyeing Genovese for years. He was reported to have gotten into the heroin business in the early 1920s, a long run for any drug trafficker. Although he had been arrested numerous times for carrying a concealed weapon, assault, robbery, and several murders, he had never been convicted of anything serious. FBN believed that, with Luciano, Genovese controlled the importation of most of the heroin consumed in the U.S. and virtually all of the drugs that came to America via the infamous "French Connection." Proving this allegation, especially against someone as dangerous and as well insulated as Don Vitone was a daunting task. The New York office of the FBN began looking for an informant. The one they found remains controversial to this day.

Nelson Silva Cantellops, born in Puerto Rico in 1923, was, by every account, a small-time crook. He had been convicted previously for fraud in 1949, which earned him a 3-year sentence, forgery in 1952 (1 to 3 years), and possession of marijuana in 1956 (6 months). All of these convictions were in New Jersey, but Cantellops moved to New York and got involved in the heroin business. In 1957, Cantellops was arrested for selling heroin on Manhattan's West Side. A four-time loser, Cantellops pleaded guilty and received a 4- to 5-year term at New York's Sing Sing prison. Feeling that he had been abandoned by the gangsters who had promised to pay for his attorney and make his bail, Cantellops turned to the FBN, which had already sought out his assistance. Cantellops had a wife, children, and a mistress to worry about, and he was upset at being treated as "a slob" by the kings of organized crime.

Cantellops said that he began working for the Genovese organization as a courier in 1955. Owing money to a Genovese soldier, Joe Barcellona, Cantellops agreed to deliver ten pounds of heroin to Las Vegas for Barcellona's associates, Joe DiPalermo and Carmine Polizzano. Cantellops performed this assignment, then took on others, transporting heroin for Polizanno to or from Chicago, Cleveland, Philadelphia, Miami, Tampa, Los Angeles, Key West, El Paso, and the Virgin Islands.

As Cantellops got more involved with the organization, he was introduced to more players, among them John Ormento and Vincent "The Chin" Gigante. Both of these men were known to FBN as major heroin traffickers and ranking Cosa Nostra members. Cantellops described one heroin delivery to Cleveland in 1956, in which Gigante accompanied him with the heroin as far as Lorain, OH. This trip was made on Ormento's behalf, Cantellops was told.

Cantellops testified that he saw Vito Genovese exactly four times prior to the trial. He first saw the boss in December 1955 in Greenwich Village. Genovese was "sitting in a car with Carmine Polizzano. I went over to the car and Polizanno told me to beat it. When I saw Polizanno later, he bawled me out. He said, 'You should know better than to interrupt me when I am talking to the Right Man.'" Cantellops knew that the "Right Man" was a reference to the individual who made the decisions for the heroin distribution operation.

This was not an auspicious introduction to the boss of bosses, but Cantellops would cross paths with Don Vitone again. Their next encounter was 7 months later in a restaurant on East 86th Street. "I was with Ormento and Evola [both of whom were ranking members of the Lucchese family] and Genovese was seated at a table with a woman. Ormento went over to speak with him for a few minutes. When we left, Ormento told me Genovese got a good look at me and told him I seemed all right." Three weeks later, Cantellops finally met the aspiring boss. This would be the only time, by Cantellops' own admission, that he ever spoke directly with Don Vitone. The meet began at the same German restaurant, where Cantellops was again accompanied by Ormento and Natale Evola. Following is Cantellops account of that meeting:

Ormento made a phone call while I had a drink with Evola. When Ormento came back to the bar, we left. We went with Evola in his car to the West Side Highway. I noticed that another car was following us. When I told Evola about this, he told me not to worry about it. A few minutes later, he pulled off the highway into an emergency parking area. The car that was behind us also stopped.

Ormento told me to get out of the car with him. We went over to this other car. Gigante was driving and Genovese was sitting in the back. Ormento introduced me to Genovese. We got in Gigante's car and Genovese said we were going to a meeting where territorial control would be discussed.

At the home of Rocco Mazzie in the Bronx, Gigante and Genovese waited in the car while Ormento and Cantellops went inside to meet with Evola and Mazzie. The men discussed the takeover of some territory in the East Bronx. Genovese entered the room during the discussion. "He wanted to know what we decided," reported Cantellops. "Ormento told him it would cost a hundred and fifty thousand to move into the East Bronx, and he thought it would be worthwhile. Genovese told him, 'All right, set it up as soon as possible and let me know when I can send the boys in.'"

This was the last time Cantellops saw Genovese, who was ultimately convicted on the strength of this testimony. The case was weak, but the jury had much more evidence against the other conspirators and evidently decided Vito was guilty, too. Cantellops' testimony did more damage to the Cosa Nostra than any other single case up to that point. In addition to Vito Genovese, the highest ranking Cosa Nostra figure ever to fall on a narcotics rap, 14 others went to prison for varying terms. These people represented a substantial slice of the American heroin business and were a much more important catch than those arrested in the more famous French Connection case in 1964. Genovese's co-defendants included:

- *Vincent "The Chin" Gigante* received 7 years. He would later head operations for one of the New York families and achieve fame by affecting incompetence and wandering outside in his bathrobe. Gigante was the man who was alleged to have attempted to assassinate Frank Costello on Genovese's orders.
- *Natale Evola*, an attendee at the Apalachin conference and a *capo* in the Lucchese family, got 10 years and a $20,000 fine.
- *Carmine* and *Ralph Polizanno*, brothers and Genovese associates, received 8- and 7-year terms, respectively.
- *Salvatore Santora*, a.k.a. "Tom Mix" and considered by FBN to be a major importer heroin importer with ties to Europe and Latin America, received 20 years.
- *Joseph* and *Charles DiPalermo*, also soldiers in the Lucchese family and also brothers, drew 15 and 12 years, respectively.
- *Daniel Lessa, Nicholas Lessa, Rocco Mazzie, Alfredo Aviles, Benjamin Rodrigues, Charles Barcellona,* and *Jean Capece* all went to prison based on Cantellops' information.

Two others were indicted with Genovese but tried later. One of these was Carmine "Lilo" Galante, underboss of the Bonanno family and believed by the FBN to be one of the biggest heroin traffickers in the world. He would head the Bonanno family before being gunned down in 1979, in the narcotics business to the end. The other man, "Big John" Ormento, was a Lucchese *capo* and major trafficker. Both Galante and Ormento later went to prison for narcotics trafficking, making the final score in the Cantellops indictment 17-0: one boss, one underboss, two *capos*, five buttons, and an assortment of other traffickers. This was a very good case for 1958, and a commendable record for any informant.

Analysis

Vito Genovese certainly had his problems with betrayal. Although he managed to dodge the worst effects of the earlier treachery by his associates and his wife, Cantellops' testimony put

Genovese away for what would amount to a life sentence. Joe Valachi also turned on Genovese, making Don Vitone possibly the Godfather most likely to be informed on. In examining how and why this came about, it is best to look at each of the three informants separately. Each had different motivation and access. The uses to which the information was put also differed. The impact of these betrayals was felt far beyond the life of the would-be "boss of bosses."

Motivation

Ernest "The Hawk" Rupolo: Like so many other informants we have discussed here, Rupolo had more than one motivation to turn on his Mafia pals. The primary and most obvious motivation was the 48-year sentence he was facing for the attempted murder of another mobster. Rupolo wound up doing 9 years on this charge, much better than the original alternative. He probably would not have talked had it not been for a betrayal by his Mafia associates. Rupolo had tried to kill another mob figure who somehow managed to survive The Hawk's bullets. This individual then complained to the police, something which seems to have shocked and offended Rupolo, who was now facing even more prison time. Assured by his mob buddies that the complainant would eventually claim to have made a mistake, Rupolo relaxed and went to court, where the witness pointed at The Hawk, saying, "There's the contract killer." Feeling he had been used and sold out, Rupolo took his revenge by cutting up the mob's business. Years before Valachi, Rupolo described the foundation of the national crime syndicate and how the enterprise functioned. His information provided an intelligence foundation from which investigations could grow. In sum, Rupolo was motivated by fear of incarceration, accompanied by a desire for revenge and a feeling of betrayal. His conscience was clear regarding giving up Genovese and others, though it is not recorded that much more came from Rupolo's cooperation besides Genovese's indictment.

Anna Genovese: Here we have a straight revenge motivation. Anna wanted to get some money out of Vito; she was eventually awarded $350 per week in support. If money had been the sole motivation, however, she probably would not have had to expose the family secrets to the extent she did. Her story certainly made interesting reading, and the general public learned all about Vito Genovese. Ex-spouses and ex-paramours can make good informants because of their access. Anna claimed that Genovese had actually allowed her to handle the proceeds of some of his operations, including the Italian lottery, which grossed $20,000 to $30,000 each week. Anna knew where the bodies were buried — literally, in the case of her former husband, Gerard Vernotico, found strangled to death in 1932. She had married Genovese a short time after Gerard's demise, and her knowledge about the killing might have been what kept Genovese from shutting Anna up permanently. Anna was not motivated to give any of this information up for years, until after she had taken all the physical and emotional abuse she could handle. Although she testified to her knowledge of Genovese's mob activity in open court, she was never really a police informant in the truest sense of the word.

Nelson Cantellops: Cantellops was an informant/witness who came to the FBN after his incarceration on drug charges. Cantellops, too, had more than one motive for cooperating. Like Rupolo, Cantellops was facing a lengthy, though not as severe, prison sentence, from which he wanted some relief. Although Cantellops was questioned at length, agents believe he did not decide to cooperate in the investigation until after he was abandoned by his underworld associates. One of the narcotic agents told him, "No lawyers, no bail. Nobody cares what happens to you. You can go to jail for the rest of your life and they won't raise a finger to help you." When this prophesy came true in court, Cantellops agreed to provide the information he had been withholding.

One author, who claimed to have obtained the information from Charles "Lucky" Luciano before his death, said that Cantellops was part of an elaborate frame-up by the mob, who wanted Genovese out of the picture for a while. Cantellops was supposedly paid $100,000 to testify falsely about Genovese's role in the heroin conspiracy. If true, this would mean Cantellops had a perverse motivation for informing, a possibility the law enforcement officer should always consider and never rule out. A *cui bono* question about who would have benefited from Genovese's incarceration might have detected connections between Cantellops and rivals for Don Vitone's job. He certainly had plenty of enemies. Cantellops was "flipped" by a capable narcotic agent, who worked on developing Cantellops' motivation. Even so, the small-time criminal did not turn until he felt betrayed by those he was protecting by his silence. Then all hell broke loose.

Interestingly, after the Genovese trial, "Big John" Ormento, who had been a fugitive, approached the terrified Cantellops and persuaded him to recant his testimony about Genovese and the others. If he agreed, Genovese would get a new trial and Ormento would be home free. Cantellops did agree, then recanted his recantation after the narcotics agents reminded him that his original 5-year sentence was waiting and he faced prosecution for participating in the Genovese conspiracy, as well. In any event, the agents said, Genovese would undoubtedly kill Cantellops for the initial betrayal. Genovese stayed in prison, but this incident should remind all law enforcement officers that motivation to cooperate cuts both ways. Fear of incarceration might motivate cooperation with law enforcement, but fear of retaliation might motivate cooperation with the criminals.

Access

Ernest "The Hawk" Rupolo: Rupolo had terrific access, at one level. He had literally killed for Genovese, his loyalty was unquestioned, and he, too, knew where the bodies were buried. Rupolo was close enough to Genovese in the late 1930s that he claimed to be taking murder contracts directly from the boss. At another level, however, Rupolo's access was limited. He was not privy to the inner secrets of Genovese's organization; like Joe Valachi, he was a soldier. Still, there is no statute of limitations on murder, and Ernest Rupolo knew enough to be a bad guy to have hanging around, ticked off at the boss.

Anna Genovese: If *The Godfather* author Mario Puzo is to be believed, Mafia wives are supposed to be kept in the dark about the family business. This was not true of Anna Genovese, who claimed she knew much more than Vito should have told her. Some of the most graphic testimony at the support hearing related to the regular Tuesday and Thursday "board meetings" held at the Genovese residence. High-ranking mobsters attended these meetings, Anna said, where payoffs were made and cuts distributed in bushel baskets full of money. Afterward, there was entertainment, including food, drink, and women for the boys. "They were wild parties. You should see the kissing and the sex. The drunkenness, the awful games. It was disgusting." More damaging to Genovese than revelations about kissing and awful games was Anna's itemized knowledge of his financial affairs. She knew of the bank accounts overseas, the safety deposit vaults in American banks, and financial transactions by the score. She described in excruciating detail his assets, which included dogtracks, lotteries, nightclubs, liquor and beer distribution companies, vending machine businesses, and a steamboat used as a floating casino. All of this information would have made a slam-dunk money laundering case against Genovese under current statutes.

Anna Genovese had all the access one would expect from someone in an intimate relationship with a criminal. Actually, she had more, thanks to Genovese's indiscretion. He was very heavily insulated from the day-to-day operation of his illegal enterprises and was notoriously ruthless about tidying up loose ends. His trademark was to dispatch a killer to deal with a potential problem, then follow up by having a trusted someone kill the killer. This could, and occasionally did, turn into a (quite literally) vicious cycle, but it definitely reduced the number of witnesses to the contract murders. For someone as calculating and utterly merciless as Genovese to leave his wife as a loose end is hard to understand. She had too much access. Or did she? In point of fact, not much Anna alleged was ever proven. The tax investigators were unable to make a case, and none of the cash hoards she claimed were scattered about were located. Nothing really came of Anna's allegations that Genovese had a lot of money. She knew about the "board meetings" that took place at her house, but the rest of it could have been conjecture, gleaned from hints dropped here and there or conversations overheard. Maybe Mario Puzo was right after all about Mafia wives.

Nelson Cantellops: People still question how much access Nelson Cantellops *really* had. I spoke about this case with noted organized crime expert and former NYPD Lieutenant Ralph Salerno, who told me he believed it almost inconceivable that Genovese would behave in the manner alleged in dealing with someone like Cantellops. "This is just not how these people acted," he said. The idea that a small-time Puerto Rican courier could gain direct access to "The Right Man" is questionable. As noted, Genovese was obsessive about insulating himself from the operational details of his business. He knew he was under intense scrutiny by the FBN and the Intelligence Unit of the Internal Revenue Service. Knowing this, would Genovese have risked giving any sort of directions to an outsider? One wonders.

In Cantellops' favor, he did not actually have a lot of access to Genovese, and never really claimed much. He did have some access to Genovese associates who were involved in narcotics and against whom Cantellops testified. If he had wanted to lie (and especially if he had been given $100,000 to lie), Cantellops probably could have come up with a better story than his tale of the one meeting with Genovese. Also, Genovese was pretty arrogant in using his power. He knew that he could squash a person such as Nelson Cantellops like a bug, and so did everyone else. This knowledge could have made Genovese careless, although Lieutenant Salerno did not think so. The question of Cantellops' access will go forever unresolved. I do not believe his information would be sufficient to get a conviction today, but those were different times.

Control

Ernest "The Hawk" Rupolo: Rupolo was incarcerated during his cooperation and for some time afterward. While locked up, Rupolo evidently caused no control problems of note. He eventually testified against Genovese in the pre-trial phases of the government's murder case, then went into hiding. Corroborating Rupolo's story was very difficult. The key elements relating to Genovese involved conversations which had allegedly taken place in private, so it was really Rupolo's word (and La Tempa's) against Don Vitone's. The police were able to corroborate many of the collateral details, so they could be sure Rupolo was telling the truth about those. This, too, would have been a tough case to prove, although Vito thought enough of it to flee to Europe for 6 years.

Anna Genovese: Law enforcement had little or no control over Anna, who was acting more or less independently. She had her own agenda, which included making Vito's life miserable, an objective shared by some in law enforcement. How this mutual goal was to be met was never the subject of much agreement between Anna and the government. She was willing to use the police or whomever to achieve her objectives. Several years after her divorce, Anna was called before a New Jersey grand jury investigating organized crime. She claimed no knowledge of the subject and wanted to be left alone.

Nelson Cantellops: Also in custody throughout the investigation, Cantellops appears to have been a compliant witness/informant … perhaps *too* compliant for those who subscribe to the "frame-up" theory. He was obviously well prepared by the agents and Assistant U.S. Attorneys, undergoing a week on the witness stand on direct examination and four full weeks on cross-examination. He appears to have been a good witness — the jury believed him — and his answers speak of the extensive pre-trial preparation that went into this case.

Summing Up

Ernest Rupolo did not survive his bout with Don Vitone, although he lived much longer than anyone expected him to in 1946. Genovese had a long memory, though, and did not forget The Hawk. After winning the reduction in his sentence Rupolo was released from prison and tried (not very hard) to fade out of sight. A newspaper article weighed his chances: "All concerned in the release, including 'The Hawk' himself, agreed he is now marked for murder and cannot expect to survive long. Rupolo will make a desperate effort to disappear completely." He survived almost 18 years before washing up, weighted down with chains, in Jamaica Bay in 1964: "Cause of death: bullet wounds of head, brain, neck, and spine. Multiple stab wounds of the chest, lungs, heart, and abdomen."

Anna Genovese lived on quietly in New Jersey, undisturbed by her ex-husband. Vito apparently still carried a torch for the woman who caused him so much embarrassment. In Atlanta, one of the toughest penitentiaries in America, one of the coldest men in America used to speak of his ex-wife with blubbering affection, tears rolling down the don's cheeks as he talked of his "little Anna." Other hardened criminals watched these displays in amazement. Joe Valachi could not believe it himself.

Nelson Cantellops saw "The Right Man" go off to prison but did not live to see him die there. By what could be a coincidence, Cantellops, like Rupolo, was killed while Genovese was still in Atlanta, dying in a bar fight in 1965. His killer was never identified.

Betrayal always affects more than the betrayer and the betrayed. In Genovese's case, Cantellops' testimony began a chain of events which would have profound consequences for organized crime across America. By turning on the "boss of bosses," Cantellops put Genovese in Atlanta, where he would soon be joined by Joe Valachi. Vito's attitude toward informants was not improved by Cantellops' treachery, something which would carry over into his dealings with others, including Valachi. As a result, Valachi, feeling threatened, would act on his own and become the informant who would expose the face of the Cosa Nostra to the world.

Special Situations

10

"Well, I understand that they get five pounds if they can give information."

"Yes, sir, but the chance of five pounds is but a poor thing compared to the chance of having your throat cut. You see, it isn't like any ordinary convict. This is a man that would stick at nothing." —Sir Arthur Conan Doyle, *The Hound of the Baskervilles*

"Hence, thou suborned informer! A true soul when most impeached stands least in thy control." —William Shakespeare, *Sonnet 125*

In one sense, management of every informant is a special situation. There are some categories of informants, though, that do present particular problems or hazards. The law or official procedures may dictate how informants in these categories are handled, but common sense should not be forgotten, either.

High Risk: Hazardous Situations

Working with certain informants carries extra risk. Although they may have valuable information which cannot be ignored, the officer is required to take special care in dealing with these persons. In these situations, an officer's life, health, career, marriage, and standing with his or her peers are at stake. Taking a few common-sense precautions does not seem to be too high a price to pay for peace of mind.

Opposite Sex Informants

Law enforcement takes its informants where it can find them and one of these places is on the other side of the gender barrier. Malachi Harney and John Cross, writing over 30 years ago, commented on the additional caution needed when an officer is dealing with an informant of the opposite sex: "There is a particular danger to the law enforcement officer in the case where protracted association with a female informer is required. We feel impelled to stress this fact bluntly, even to mature officers, for the simple reason that hard experience has proved this risk."

185

That risk is still proved with depressing regularity, as officers continue to ignore the simple precautions which should prevent problems of this nature. An article from the *National Law Journal*, dated April 17, 1995, illustrates only one of the hazards: "The love affair started after the federal agent and her informant joked about having a fling. It ended when they were caught stealing a kiss in a federal prison and were overheard cooing on taped jailhouse phone calls. The dangerous liaison between Synda Smith, IRS criminal investigator, and Charles Goldman, convicted marijuana smuggler turned government informant, included having sex in a prosecutor's lounge known as the "igloo" in the federal courthouse in Miami." This dangerous liaison led to predictable consequences. Smith left her job with the IRS, and the defendants convicted in the money laundering case developed by Smith and Goldman asked for a new trial, based upon the misconduct represented by the illicit affair: "They argued that Mr. Goldman manipulated a federal agent to win a reduced sentence and likewise deceived the jury." After hearing the motions and the testimony of the former agent and informant, the judge denied the defense motion for a new trial.

The professional detachment which should have protected Smith broke down, effectively costing her a job and a marriage. "We just became friends on top of the agent stuff," she testified. "I'm sure I told him how bad my marriage was. He would tell me what went on at the prison." The officer is not supposed to have *any* sort of relationship with an informant other than "the agent stuff," as Smith so quaintly puts it. Whenever another relationship is established, be it friendship, business, or sexual, control is ceded by the officer to the informant. Once lost, control is difficult, if not impossible, to reacquire, as Smith discovered. "He would bug me and bug me," she recalled. 'Would you do this? Would you do this?' And sometimes I would do stuff just to get him to quit asking."

Claims of sexual abuse or harassment against officers by informants are not uncommon. Not only will state and federal laws protect informants against this type of harassment by officers, in some jurisdictions the officer's misconduct might even be considered rape. Because police officers hold positions of authority and can exercise control over informants, a sexual relationship could be viewed as inherently coercive. Such claims have been made against police officers, prison guards, and federal agents. No officer (or his supervisor) wants to hear some informant say, "He told me if I would sleep with him he would see that the charges were dropped, so I did." Unscrupulous individuals may deliberately entrap an officer in this type of situation in order to blackmail or otherwise control him or her.

On other occasions, the sexual relationship is only alleged, although this can have equally traumatic results for the officer falsely accused. Prevention of false accusations is the reason why male police officers routinely record the mileage on their patrol cars when transporting female prisoners. If, however, the officer puts himself or herself in a position to be vulnerable to false accusations, control is again transferred to the informant.

Informants come in all shapes and sizes. We can obtain valuable information from those of the opposite sex — but only if routine precautions are rigidly adhered to. The rules against meeting an informant alone apply with added emphasis in any situation where the informant is of the opposite sex. Under no circumstances should an officer *ever* meet alone with such a person, no matter how reliable or how long-standing the relationship. Contacts should be documented with care, and the professional detachment which is the officer's best defense should be maintained at all times.

Addicted Persons

More than any other informant, addicts *need*. Maslow, who knew a thing or two about human needs, would have designed a completely different pyramid if he had been studying addicts instead of gorillas. Addict priorities are always straightforward; physiological, security, ego, even self-actualization needs can be fulfilled in the same place at the same time, every day, so long as there are drugs to fill the syringe. Ensuring that this condition is met will always be the primary focus of the drug addict's life.

Informants who are also addicted to narcotics pose other problems for the officer who is required to deal with them. Robert Leuci, the NPYD narcotics detective whose story was told in *Prince of the City*, described the relationship between addict-informants and officers who worked with them: "Inevitably, addict-informants become almost a part of Leuci's family. They are as dependent on him as his own children. He becomes convinced it is his responsibility to take care of them. After a day's work, each addict crawls back into some hovel. It seems heartless to leave him without anything, to be sick, when he has been with you for weeks."

Most law enforcement officers are not unsympathetic to the addict's plight. Certainly those of us who have had experience with this condition know the compulsive nature of the disease. Many got into the profession in hopes of helping others or making the world a better place. Confronted with an addict's need, a misguided sense of compassion may lead officers to provide informants with the narcotics wanted to stave off withdrawal. This decision can also be rationalized on grounds of practicality; a sick informant is unable to work.

Regardless of the motive, the officer who aids the informant in this fashion is taking the world's worst gamble. Not only is the officer committing a felony, he is also (rather stupidly, in my opinion) betting that the informant will not turn and use this information against the officer in the future. Anyone expecting such loyalty should speak with Detective Leuci. To impeach Leuci, defense attorneys brought many of his former informants (the ones he had made "almost a part of his family") to court, all of whom testified that he had given them heroin in the past. One lawyer claimed to have a line of such witnesses that would reach "around the block."

It is not the officer's responsibility to care for the addict informant, any more than it is our responsibility to treat an informant who has cancer or athlete's foot. Once again, a professional detachment, established early and reinforced often, is the best defense against the temptation of making addict-informants dependent on the officer. The officer should behave toward an addicted informant in exactly the same way as one who is not addicted, while still recognizing that the addict has a medical condition which requires some attention.

A compassionate alternative is to refer addicted informants for treatment or detoxification, although funding can be a problem. It can be helpful for the officer to maintain a cordial relationship with the administrators of methadone or other drug treatment programs. If the officer arranges for treatment, and especially if the government pays for the treatment, this fact should be reported to the prosecutor as a benefit received by the informant in exchange for his cooperation.

Payment to addict-informants puts the officer in something of a moral quandary. We can be reasonably certain that monies given to an addicted person are going to be used to support that addiction. Because the addiction can only be maintained by violating the law, this places the officer in the position of tolerating or at least knowing of ongoing criminal activity — something we are paid to stop. Payment should therefore be conditioned on the informant's enrolling in some treatment program. Non-addicted drug users should receive the standard admonishment against engaging in any illegal activity and told that this includes drug possession.

The intensity of addict-informant needs is such that courts recognize the special care that must be taken in evaluating their information. In *United States v. Fletcher* (334 F.2d 584, 1964), one court stated, "A drug addict is inherently a perjurer where his own interests are concerned; it is manifest either that some corroboration of his testimony should be required, or at least that it should be received with suspicion and acted upon with caution." These strong words were echoed in a second decision from the same circuit in which Judge Miller, writing in dissent in *Godfrey v. United States* (122 U.S. App. D.C. at 289, 353 F.2d at 460), stated: "During the last fifty years I have had many opportunities to observe the way drug addicts testify in criminal cases about matters which concern their own interests. On the basis of that experience, I believe [Judge Pine] was correct in saying they are inherently perjurers and I see no reason why a jury should not be told this fact of life."

These are powerful sentiments expressed from the bench. Although the courts seem to recognize the need for informants, even those addicted, particularly in cases involving the drug laws, they do not seem especially happy about the idea. Their caution — and the insistence that insofar as possible the statements of the addict-informant should corroborated — should be echoed in the officer. The following is an excerpt from *United States v. Kinnard* (465 F.2d 566, 1972):

> *We believe that a government informer's addiction to narcotic drugs and his indictment for narcotics violations so increase the danger that he will color his testimony to place guilt on the defendant for his own benefit that this special danger should be recognized by courts and flagged by a special charge to the jury.*
>
> *This belief is grounded in the hard realities of narcotics law enforcement. The use of informers is the primary police technique in this field since addicts are the primary sources of information about the drug trade. Law enforcement officials are open about their use of informants, but there is less discussion about why their informers perform. The addict's habit makes him uniquely subject to constant surveillance and susceptible to arrest — he is in a perpetual status of violating the law. For the addict, arrest is harassment of a special sort, for he is forced to undergo the beginnings of withdrawal symptoms. At this stage, a bribe of heroin or the promise of immediate release and return to the habit seem irresistible. The deliberate harassment of addicts for information, through illegal searches, arrests and general intimidation by police and other officials, has been reported.*

Many cases involving entrapment or perjury by addict-informants have been resolved in the appellate courts. Because the addict is presumed to have an even greater need to obtain results, he or she is also presumed to have a greater motivation to lie or fabricate evidence, extending to the entrapment of otherwise innocent persons. This prejudice is something with which the officer must contend. In a notable decision relating to entrapment, Chief Justice Warren, in *United States v. Sherman* (356 U.S. 372), said:

> *The case at bar illustrates an evil which the defense of entrapment is designed to overcome. The government informer entices someone attempting to avoid narcotics not only into carrying out an illegal sale but also into returning to the habit of use. Selecting the proper time, the informer then tells the government agent. The set-up is accepted by the agent without even a question as to the manner in which the informer encountered the seller. Thus the Government plays on the weaknesses of an innocent party and beguiles him into committing crimes which he otherwise would not have attempted. Law enforcement does not require methods such as this.*

Forewarned is forearmed. The courts have clearly placed their mistrust of the addict-informer on the record. Whether or not he or she is inherently a perjurer or one who would entrap an innocent party, thorough investigation of the informant's claims and corroboration of every facet of the informant's statements will be even more important in cases when addiction is present.

Persons with Mental Health Problems

Even a paranoid can have real enemies, and people who have mental health problems may also have real information about criminal activity. These people represent special hazards for the officer, who is not ordinarily trained as a psychologist. The degree to which these problems can be addressed will depend upon the nature and severity of the informant's condition. Someone who is paranoid and delusional about imagined plots or contrived schemes is not going to be a very successful informant.

An informant's success is determined by his or her motivation, access, and control. Establishing *any* of these three elements in the mentally disturbed person could be a problem. The more severe the personality disorder, the more difficult it can be to discern the reason why the informant is cooperating or how much she really knows. These individuals should not be used as informants.

One type of individual we should expect to encounter regularly, both as a criminal and an informant, is the anti-social personality, also known as the sociopath or psychopath. James T. Reese, a Special Agent assigned to the Behavioral Science Unit at the FBI Academy, wrote about the psychopath as an informant for the May 1980 *FBI Law Enforcement Bulletin*. He noted that the psychopath possesses both "good and bad informant qualities" and asked "Should he be targeted and developed as an informant? The answer is yes; however, this answer must be qualified. He is a good informant so long as the officer is aware of the characteristics of his personality and his motivations for informing…"

Exploring these personality characteristics, Reese cited the American Psychiatric Association's description of the anti-social personality as "individuals who are basically unsocialized and whose behavior patterns bring them repeatedly into conflict with society. They are incapable of significant loyalty to individuals, groups, or social values. They are grossly selfish, callous, irresponsible, impulsive, and unable to feel guilt or to learn from experience and punishment. Frustration tolerance is low. They tend to blame others or offer plausible rationalizations for their behavior." An individual of this same personality type is also known as a sociopath, and, most officers would agree, is fairly common in the criminal world.

Hervey Cleckley, in the *Mask of Sanity*, lists 16 characteristics or traits of the psychopath. The officer should keep in mind the possible use of this type of individual as a criminal informant and interpret these characteristics accordingly, evaluating the effect each characteristic will have on the way the informant is handled and the purpose and usefulness of the information provided by him. These characteristics are

1. Superficial charm and good "intelligence"
2. Absence of delusions and other signs of irrational thinking
3. Absence of "nervousness" or psychoneurotic manifestations
4. Unreliability
5. Untruthfulness and insincerity
6. Lack of remorse or shame
7. Inadequately motivated antisocial behavior
8. Poor judgment and failure to learn by experience
9. Pathologic egocentricity and incapacity for love
10. General poverty in major affective reactions
11. Specific loss of insight
12. Unresponsiveness in general interpersonal relations
13. Fantastic and uninviting behavior with drink and sometimes without
14. Suicide rarely carried out
15. Sex life impersonal, trivial, and poorly integrated
16. Failure to follow any life plan

Most of us would recognize these characteristics in persons we might have arrested or even developed as an informant. (A few of us immediately recognize an ex-spouse.) Because we can expect to find this person in the ranks of the informant we must develop methods of dealing with the psychopath's personality characteristics.

One of the key features of a psychopathic personality is the lack of conscience or guilt feelings accompanying their bad acts. As we have discussed, betrayal has a strong impact on the normal conscience; because the anti-social personality has a much diminished, if not completely absent, conscience, he or she is likely to be a walk-in, volunteering information. "Flipping" someone with this personality is also going to be easier, as they are more self-centered, "incapable of significant loyalty to others," and relatively untroubled by the prospects of betraying a confidence.

Once motivated to cooperate, the psychopath may actually be a pretty good informant — if properly controlled. Their lack of loyalty means they are inclined to give up their associates more readily; this is perceived as no great loss because they have never established any emotional ties to those people, anyway. They may also like to talk, emphasizing, even exaggerating their own knowledge or importance, although the officer has to remember that the characteristics of a psychopath are also those of a confidence man — seemingly intelligent, articulate, manipulative, amoral, and a facile liar.

Corroboration is one of our best means for controlling informants. They should always be told that their information will be checked and given good reason to believe that it is being checked. Red flags should be going up if an officer is unable to corroborate a high percentage of the informant's statements. Verification is even more important with the anti-social personality type, who will take advantage of a perceived opportunity to "get over" on the officer.

Is it worth it to cultivate this type of informant? Any informant's value will depend to a large extent on his access. If an evaluation shows that the prospective informant has useful information, the officer may want to develop the source — with caution. As Reese noted, "He is a good informant so long as the officer is aware of the characteristics of his personality and his motivations for informing. Nothing he says can be taken at 'face value' but must be corroborated by active investigation. In a good and thorough investigation, even false information, examined carefully, can become valuable and steer the officer in the proper direction."

Legal Problems

The law may impose some restrictions on whether and how an informant can be developed by law enforcement. Some classes of persons, notably those who are under the supervision of the courts or a paroling authority may be constrained from working as an informant.

Persons on Parole or Probation

There are two types of restrictions on law enforcement's use of parolees or probationers as informants. One involves the conditions of the individual's parole or probation that restrict his activities or associations. The second restriction is contained in law enforcement's own rules and procedures concerning such people. Both must be adhered to in conducting our business.

Both parole and probation are essentially contracts between the individual and a government authority. The parolee agrees to abide by certain terms and conditions of his parole. Almost all such terms and conditions include a requirement that the parolee notify his probation officer of any contacts with law enforcement. Furthermore, these binding agreements prohibit the parolee from associating with convicted felons or other criminals. Because

a violation of this agreement can lead to revocation and a return to prison, these are conditions the parolee ignores at his peril.

Nevertheless, those under some form of supervision frequently find themselves in contact with law enforcement, often because they have already violated the terms of their parole or probation by associating with other criminals and committing new crimes. This situation is not as uncommon as it used to be, mostly because of the huge numbers of Americans currently under some form of supervision. Over four million people have probation or parole officers, and substantial numbers of those now incarcerated are there, not as a result of the original sentence, but because they violated some of those terms and conditions.

While the individual may have a requirement to notify his parole or probation officer in the event of a contact with law enforcement, the police officer is not always under the same restriction. Federal policy, as outlined in Resolution 18 concerning Utilization of Cooperating Individuals and Confidential Informants, states:

> *Prior to utilizing a Federal or State probationer, parolee, or supervised releasee as a Cooperating Individual/Confidential Informant, a supervisor of a Federal Law Enforcement Agency shall determine if the use of that person in such a capacity would violate the terms and conditions of the person's probation, parole, or supervised release. The Federal Law Enforcement Agencies are encouraged to consult with appropriate prosecutors prior to making such a determination. The determination shall be documented in the Federal Law Enforcement Agency's files. If it is determined that there would be a violation of probation, parole, or supervised release, prior to using the person as a Cooperating Individual/Confidential Informant, a representative of the Federal Law Enforcement Agency must obtain the permission of the relevant probation, parole, or supervised release official which, likewise, shall be documented in the Federal Law Enforcement Agency's files. If permission is denied or it is inappropriate to contact the appropriate official, the Federal Law Enforcement Agency may, nevertheless, obtain authorization for such use from the court or a supervisor of a probation, parole or supervised release official.*

This policy makes it clear that Federal officers must obtain permission before using someone on probation or parole as an informant. State officers may have similar restrictions in their policies.

This is a good policy, or at least a well-intentioned one. Although it may interfere with law enforcement's ability to develop an informant, the primary purpose of parole or probation is supposed to be the rehabilitation of the offender. Rehabilitation is impeded by the criminal association someone needs to function effectively as an informant. On the other hand, these are exactly the types of people who are likely to have good information. In general, law enforcement should not "troll" for informants in the ranks of those under supervision. If someone from this category comes into the net voluntarily or in the course of an investigation, the officer and her management will have to evaluate whether the individual should be used and how.

Officers should try to maintain good relationships with parole and probation authorities. It is extremely important that law enforcement officers not betray the confidences of these people. Because parole boards and probation departments have immense power over their clients, their assistance in future cases cannot be jeopardized by going around or behind them today. Let them know what you want to do. Honor the conditions they may impose. Keep them informed about their client's status. Assist them when possible with information about others' violations. Do not conceal conduct by the informant that violates the conditions of his parole or probation. Treat the parole or probation officer as a fellow professional who has a difficult and challenging job to do. The fact that so many Americans are under supervision

means that more contacts between law enforcement offices and parole or probation authorities are inevitable in the future.

Juveniles

Juveniles are another exceptional category of informants. As anyone who has been in law enforcement knows, juveniles have all the same access to criminal activity that their adult counterparts have. In some cases, the juveniles actually have more access. Some law enforcement agencies routinely use juveniles to make cases against merchants who are illegally selling alcohol or tobacco products to minors. They also may have the same motivations to become informants, but caution is required.

Because they are minors, the permission of a parent or legal guardian will be required before juveniles can be used as informants. Even with a signed permission in hand, the officer should think long and hard before using any juvenile as an informant. This is mostly because of the potential for extreme public relations problems which will invariably accompany any harm that comes to the juvenile.

In a recent case, officers received substantial criticism for failing to protect an 8-year-old witness to a homicide. Both the 8-year-old and his mother were murdered after their cooperation became known to the alleged perpetrator. This sort of publicity has a very negative effect on the willingness of others to come forward with information and opens the police up to censure for failing to protect their asset. They will probably also face some substantial civil lawsuits as well.

At least one such lawsuit is currently pending in California, where a 17-year-old informant was killed after assisting in a police investigation. A local paper wrote about this case: "The lawsuit alleges that Brea police misled MacDonald into working as an informant, then failed to protect him. MacDonald, 17, agreed to work as a drug informant for Brea police in January after his arrest for methamphetamine possession. He was found strangled in a Los Angeles alley in March. At a preliminary hearing, MacDonald's girlfriend testified that the teen was slain after the two visited a Norwalk house frequented by drug users and dealers. She also testified that the three defendants in the case thought MacDonald was working for the police."

In Virginia, a mother sued police after her son committed suicide after becoming an informant. Claims such as these and the publicity which accompanies such tragic events have prompted the legislature or the courts in several states to take additional action to protect juvenile informants. In California, the governor signed legislation which requires law enforcement to have the approval of a judge before using a juvenile as an informant.

Involving a juvenile as an informant means that everything has to be done at least twice: once for the young informant, once for her parents, and possibly once more for the courts. In addition to the standard CI agreement, the officer should prepare a second form advising the parents of all of the rules and requirements for their son or daughter. The background check may also require more work, as regular files and those of the juvenile justice system must be reviewed.

Juvenile informants represent additional problems and additional risk for the officer. Whether the results will justify using a juvenile in this capacity will depend upon the individual's access, but management should always review requests to employ juveniles as informants and should view these requests with an eye toward the worst case scenario.

A final word about the practical (as opposed to the legal) aspects of developing juvenile informants: Most of the time we are talking about teenagers, people who have all of the problems, attitudes, and values of others in their age group. They are self-centered, immature in their judgment, and subject to misguided loyalty to their peers, and they have not developed the values common to older people (importance of job, career, children, etc.). They also have

a belief in their own invincibility, thinking that nothing *really* bad can happen, or that the bad things will go away. All of these factors make teenagers much more difficult to "flip."

Exceptional Categories

Two categories of informants bear special mention because of the special handling required. "Jailhouse snitches" are one of the most reviled classes of informants, one which can bring extreme discredit to law enforcement. We should also be on the lookout for the super-informant, a rare bird who can make cases like no other, but represents control problems of his own.

Jailhouse Informants

Jails are about where you would expect to find informants. After all, nobody has more access to criminals and information about criminal activity than a jail inmate. Jailhouse informants — those who provide information while incarcerated — excite considerable comment and not a little distaste. Defense attorneys understand, even if their clients do not, how much information is essentially for sale inside the cellblock walls.

Jails, prisons, and correctional institutions of all sorts are virtual warehouses of information. Filled to the rafters with criminals, all of whom have little to do but sit around talking about crime, under conditions of little or no privacy, jails are full of knowledge of interest to law enforcement. Getting this information, however, can be a problem. Motivation is generally not the obstacle. Everybody who is *in* prison, with very few exceptions, shares a common desire to be *out* of prison. If they can't get out now, they would like to get out as soon as possible. Even those who have no chance at parole or early release have the desire for special treatment, transfer to another facility, or some other reason for trading the most valuable thing they still possess — information.

Some inmates will provide information to law enforcement about ongoing criminal activity within the facility. They may have knowledge of drug trafficking, weapons possession, or illegal acts by prison personnel. Those inmates may even be able to arrange for drug transactions, introduce undercover agents, or provide leads to thefts or other crimes. The inmate who acts in this capacity is really a traditional informant who happens to be incarcerated. Although the officer is going to have to take special precautions in communicating with this informant, and in protecting his or her identity, much of the development and management of this source will be very similar to any other.

Communication is one of the most difficult aspects of working with incarcerated informants. Telephone calls are monitored at many facilities, and mail may be opened and inspected. Visits to the facility by law enforcement are sufficiently interesting that everyone on both sides of the bars knows about them even before the inmate returns to his cell. Getting the inmate out of the institution for a visit requires quite a bit of finesse and usually some help from the staff. If an officer is planning to do this sort of thing on a regular basis, he or she should develop a cover in advance for these types of meetings.

Jailhouse informants are another breed, with a whole different set of problems. The traditional "jailhouse snitch" is one who is either awaiting trial or already sentenced and who is offering information gleaned from conversations with other inmates about the crimes they committed on the outside. These conversations frequently do contain admissions and confessions which would ordinarily be quite valuable to law enforcement. This is not an ordinary situation, however.

There are two major problems with jailhouse informants. First, they usually have an enormous and immediate motivation to lie about their access. Second, having the informant conversing with people who are awaiting trial and represented by attorneys may be trampling on the Sixth Amendment right to counsel, something which could taint the case. These two factors combined make the jailhouse informant a very questionable asset for law enforcement.

Reliability and Credibility Issues

From a reliability standpoint, the jailhouse informant ranks with addicts in the courts' and the public's estimation. One story in the *Los Angeles Times* described activities of Leslie White, a jailhouse informant in Los Angeles County who demonstrated for the reporters how, using only a prison telephone, he was able to collect enough information to manufacture the "confession" of a murder suspect White had never even met. Other inmates, in a process they laughingly refer to as "testi-lying," collect files of newspaper clippings, legal documents stolen from other inmates' cells, or information purchased from other inmates with candy or cigarettes in order to fabricate confessions.

None of this inspires great confidence in the word of the jailhouse informant. One prosecutor commented that jailhouse informants are the "scum of the earth. Outright conscienceless sociopaths to whom truth is a wholly meaningless concept." And that is a remark from the government's point of view. Extreme skepticism, coupled with earnest attempts to corroborate every detail of a jailhouse informant's statement, should be standard procedure in this type of situation.

Fifth and Sixth Amendment Issues

The other issue concerns interference by the jailhouse informant with the defendant's rights under the Fifth and Sixth Amendments. Whether this is the case will usually depend on what the informant *did* to obtain the confession or admission. The jailhouse informant is uniquely placed to hear the confessions of other criminals. Whether these confessions will be admissible in court will depend on several factors, including when the informant heard the statements and what the informant did or said to obtain the confession. Juries and the courts will look hard at these statements. Famous decisions such as *Miranda v. Arizona* (384 U.S. 436, 1966) and *Escobedo v. Illinois* (378 U.S. 478, 1964) raise Constitutional issues with respect to police interrogations, but less well-known is the fact that these decisions also apply to jailhouse informants who are effectively working as agents of the government.

A set of five jailhouse scenarios may help us better identify some of the problems relating to these Constitutional issues. In these scenarios, John is the informant and Bob is the subject. Both are awaiting trial and represented by counsel.

Scenario 1. *Bob is charged with murder. John, his cellmate, approaches law enforcement with information about the murder that he claims to have obtained from Bob.*

A classic jailhouse informant scenario: There is no police involvement in soliciting the informant to come forward or in the informant's eliciting of Bob's confession. Even though he made the statements in a custodial setting, *Miranda* does not apply because Bob's statements cannot be considered to have been coerced as he was not being questioned by an agent of law enforcement. In *Kuhlmann v. Wilson* (106 S. Ct. 2616, 1986), the U.S. Supreme Court held that when someone makes incriminating statements to a jailhouse informant which are later admitted in evidence at trial, that person must show that the police and the informant did something that was deliberately intended to elicit the incriminating remarks. If the police or the informant — who is essentially acting as an agent of the police — take some affirmative action to question the person or elicit the incriminating statements, a claim can be made that the accused person's Sixth Amendment right to counsel was violated. When the informant's role is primarily that of a passive listener, no interrogation is taking place.

And even though Bob was represented by counsel at the time he foolishly told John about the killing, his Sixth Amendment rights were not violated because John was not acting on behalf of the government when the statements were made. The big question in this scenario is not whether anyone's rights were violated, it's whether we can believe John's claims.

Scenario 2. *John, who is already an informant, is in pre-trial detention but still talking to his case officer. He overhears Bob describing a murder he committed and "got away with." Bob is charged with burglary in a completely unrelated case.*

Although John is already working with the police, he has done nothing to elicit Bob's statement. In another Supreme Court decision, *United States v. Henry* (447 U.S. 264, 1980), the Court ruled that Henry's statements had effectively been "deliberately elicited" by the government, which had created a situation which was likely to "induce the defendant to make incriminating statements." This Court defined the extent to which an informant could go before conducting the "functional equivalent of an interrogation:"

> *Similarly, the mere presence of a jailhouse informant who had been instructed to overhear conversations and to engage a criminal defendant in some conversations would not necessarily be unconstitutional. In such a case, the question would be whether the informant's actions constituted deliberate and "surreptitious [interrogation]" of the defendant. If they did not, then there would be no interference with the relationship between client and counsel.*

John did not question Bob; he merely overheard the statements in his role as a passive listener. The facts in our scenario are similar to those in *Illinois v. Perkins* (110 S. Ct. 2394, 1990). In that case, an informant (Charlton) reported conversations he had had with Perkins about a homicide Perkins boasted about committing. (Perkins was proud of his role in the crime and apparently happy to talk about it, although up to that point he had not been connected with the murder.) An officer recognized the facts, and an undercover agent accompanied Charlton to Perkins' cell, where he elicited statements concerning the murder.

In *Perkins,* the Court ruled that *Miranda* did not apply to situations in which an undercover law enforcement officer posing as an inmate did not give Miranda warnings to an incarcerated suspect before asking questions likely to elicit an incriminating response. *Miranda* was concerned with a "police-dominated atmosphere" and compulsion, both of which were absent in Perkins' jail cell.

In our example, John's questioning of Bob about the murder is non-coercive, but does it violate Bob's right to counsel? Probably not. First of all, John did not actively elicit the confession; he merely overheard it in the course of normal jailhouse business. Bob's confidence in John's discretion was misplaced, but as the Court ruled in *Hoffa,* that is not the government's problem, but the defendant's. Second, Bob is not represented in the murder case. In fact, he was not even a suspect in the homicide until he confessed about that crime to John. He is represented in the burglary, so John would have to be very careful about eliciting confessions about that crime.

Scenario 3. *John, who is an informant, is moved from his cell into Bob's, where officers hope that John will be able to overhear Bob in some admission about the crime in which he is charged. John is told not to question Bob, but just listen for any interesting statements Bob might make.*

The police are taking an affirmative step to elicit Bob's confession, moving John into direct proximity for that purpose. While this does not create the sort of coercive atmosphere of an official interrogation that would bring *Miranda* into play, the right to counsel may be infringed, depending on what John does or says to elicit Bob's statement.

In *Kuhlmann v. Wilson,* the Supreme Court decided that "the Sixth Amendment is not violated whenever — by luck or happenstance — the State obtains incriminating statements from the accused after the right to counsel has attached." The Court said that it was not enough for an accused person merely to show that a jailhouse informant had reported some incriminating statements to the authorities. Instead, the person who claims the Sixth Amendment violation must show that the police and their informant took some affirmative steps, beyond passive activity, that were intended to deliberately elicit incriminating statements.

One example of an affirmative step could be the movement of the informant into a situation where he was more likely to obtain that confession. Another Supreme Court decision, *United States v. Henry,* described some of the circumstances in which a jailhouse informant could violate the defendant's Sixth Amendment rights. In this case, Nichols, a paid FBI informant, was told by the FBI of Henry's presence in the same cellblock and instructed not to question him but to be alert for any statements Henry might make about the bank robbery.

Sure enough, Henry did make some incriminating statements in several conversations with Nichols, who passed these along to the FBI and was paid for his assistance. Henry got 20 years for the bank robbery. He appealed after learning that his confidante was a paid informant and that he had been intentionally moved into the same cellblock with the informant. The Supreme Court held that Nichols had deliberately used his position to secure incriminating statements from the respondent when Henry's counsel was not present. The Court noted that the conversation between the respondent and informant was staged so that the accused would disclose certain information not otherwise likely to be revealed. Thus, the Court concluded that "deliberate elicitation" within the meaning of Massiah arises when the police "intentionally create a situation [that is] likely to induce … incriminating statements."

In *Henry,* the informant was actually serving as a "jail plant," something that distinguished this case from others in which the informant is essentially a "listening post." Because the informant's conduct (and the government's in placing him in that situation) increased the probability that Henry would incriminate himself, the Sixth Amendment rights were violated.

Scenario 4. *John and Bob, who are both charged in the same conspiracy, are housed together at the local jail. Unbeknownst to Bob, John has already "turned" and is talking with law enforcement. He sets up a meeting in which the officers record Bob's statements about the conspiracy.*

This is roughly the fact pattern from *Massiah v. United States* (377 U.S. 201, 1964), a landmark decision on the right to counsel. In the *Massiah* decision, the Court held that "the Government violated the Sixth Amendment when it deliberately elicited incriminating information from an indicted defendant who was entitled to assistance of counsel. Government agents outfitted an informant's automobile with radio transmitting equipment and instructed the informant to engage the defendant in conversation relating to the crimes." Subsequent decisions have confirmed the "deliberately elicited" standard set by *Massiah.*

Scenario 5. *John and Bob are both charged in a conspiracy to distribute drugs and John has already come to a secret arrangement with the government to plead guilty and cooperate. He learns of Bob's plans to escape from jail, passes this information to the police, and is instructed to go back and find out more about this plan.*

This is information about a new crime, one which has yet to occur but is in the planning stages. John is not questioning Bob about the drug conspiracy. Because Bob is represented in that case, none of his statements could be used against him, but anything he might say about the escape could be used in a prosecution of that crime. The police have an obligation to investigate and prevent a planned crime such as escape, and the perpetrators have no right to hide behind the Sixth Amendment in such circumstances.

It can depend on the situation, however. In *Maine v. Moulton* (469 U.S. 1206, 1985), police had evidence of new crimes — a plot to kill witnesses and threatening phone calls to other witnesses — and they obtained the assistance of an informant, Colson, in investigating these crimes. Moulton and Colson were both indicted in a theft case and had retained counsel, but Colson entered into a plea deal to cooperate in the case against Moulton. He described plans to kill one witness and to intimidate or influence others. The government recorded telephone conversations between Colson and Moulton, as well as one meeting in which details of the original crime were discussed.

The Court said that the government knew that Moulton was likely to make incriminating statements to his co-defendant, and by "knowingly circumventing the accused's right to have counsel present" during the confrontation, Moulton's Sixth Amendment rights had been violated. Although the State had a concern about its witnesses and the investigation of additional offenses, this interest was outweighed by the knowing circumvention of Moulton's right to have counsel present when he was confessing to his crime partner.

Extreme caution is required in situations where an informant is describing new crimes being planned or which are attributed to an indicted defendant. The officer must not seek information about the crimes for which the defendant is represented by counsel. Any questioning by the informant about this past activity, or anything which could be construed as an attempt to "deliberately elicit" statements about those crimes will bring a Sixth Amendment challenge. This caution extends beyond the jailhouse to any person who is under indictment or charged with a crime and represented by counsel.

Lest we condemn all jailhouse informants out of hand, remember that under some circumstances the information they furnish can prove very valuable. I received information from one jailhouse informant who described a plan by a fellow inmate to escape from a correctional institution. The informant provided corroboration of her information with a map drawn by the would-be escapee, a map that included the position of a guard whom the escapee's accomplices were supposed to kill. Thanks to the informant, a jail break (and possibly a murder) was prevented.

The Super-Informant

Every once in a while an informant comes along whose information is so amazingly good that even the most cynical law enforcement officers sit up and take notice. These informants can take officers to dozens, even scores of cases, perhaps involving the seizure of huge amounts of contraband or the recovery of valuable stolen property. Possibly this informant can penetrate the highest levels of one or more crime groups, bringing down people who have been on law enforcement radar screens for years. Careers can be made on the strength of this type of information — and the super-informant usually knows it.

This informant is extremely rare; perhaps one in ten thousand meets the qualifications. Above all, they are characterized by the best possible access. They are the people who, if one was sitting around looking at an organizational chart of the opposition, would be in the one key position to know as much as possible about the largest number of people.

Joseph Valachi was such an informant. He was not the first Cosa Nostra member to provide information, but he was, through his long affiliation with the mob, extremely well connected. He literally knew where the bodies were buried (and who put them there). Valachi's access was cut off when law enforcement finally turned him, but others have penetrated deeply before surfacing in a blizzard of arrests and seizures.

The super-informant has other characteristics, as well. They are highly motivated to work with law enforcement and invariably are of above-average intelligence. They are confident, calculating, and may develop a strong relationship with their case officer. They are popular in their circles and completely trusted by their peers. This is the type of person one would want for a friend, if one had friends who were criminals (or informants).

Where do you find this most desirable of all informants? At or close to the top. Rarely will you find one of these folks in the lower echelons of a criminal operation. Logic alone should tell us that if they make good informants, they probably made pretty successful criminals, as well. The officer must go looking for this informant in the upper ranks, not among the foot soldiers. One approach is to map out an organized crime group or other organization, identifying as many of the important players in the group as possible. Pick the one person who, if the informant fairy granted you one wish, could do the most damage to this group and any other criminal enterprise he or she touched. Then, because the informant fairy appears to be off duty 12 months of the year, go to work on this person, either by cultivating him or her, or by developing a case which can be used to turn the individual.

As always, motivation will be critical, but the super-informant is intelligent enough to immediately recognize where his or her interests lie. Finding the right motivation is trickier, but the lengthy sentences and high mandatory minimums in drug cases have prompted more of these people to come forward. The government is usually willing to pay much more for the information these people have, and, indeed, some feel this is the only type of informant who should be getting paid. They certainly deliver much more bang for the buck.

The FBI's Top Echelon Informant Program is designed to develop this type of cooperative witness. Excellent in concept, the program rewards agents and their managers for production of informants in this category. A Top Echelon Informant — one who has access to significant organized crime activity — can be a career booster for the agents who develop and work him. There may also be control problems with these people, as the FBI discovered in recent cases in Boston. These problems will be discussed at greater length in the chapter on ethics, but they do emphasize the additional risks that can accompany work with the super-informant.

Simply put, these people are prizes almost beyond measure. They often realize their value to law enforcement and to those officers who are working with them. Safe in the belief that "he needs me more than I need him," the informant may make requests for favors, special treatment, or other benefits which ordinarily would not be considered. The officer, smack in the midst of what might be the biggest cases of his or her career, may bend over backward to keep the informant happy and working. With eyes locked solidly on the prize, the officer may also be tempted to overlook criminal activity in which the informant may be engaged on the side.

More than one officer has been trapped in this very deadly game. I will freely admit that professional detachment is extremely difficult to maintain under such circumstances. The officer probably has the best of intentions; compromising a little on the rules may seem a small price to pay for the outstanding results almost within reach. Here, however, is where professional detachment is most needed. Who does this person work for? Is he or she following the officer's instructions or is it the other way around? One simple question can provide the best guidance. Would I grant this request from or tolerate this behavior in an addict-informant working at street level? If the answer is "no" for the addict, it should be "no" for the super-informant as well.

Mel Weinberg, the informant who assisted the FBI in the so-called "Abscam" investigations, is the stereotype of the super-informant. Weinberg, a professional confidence man, came to the FBI after he and a female associate were charged in a Pennsylvania swindling case. He stayed to make cases against mobsters, mayors, congressmen, and a U.S. Senator. Weinberg had all of the characteristics necessary to be a good informant. He was intelligent, confident, and very knowledgeable about criminal behavior. After decades of operating on the fringes of organized crime, he was well connected to hundreds of people; he would exploit these connections in his work for the government.

The FBI appears to have handled Weinberg very professionally. Although these cases led to the formulation of guidelines concerning informants and undercover operations which are still with us today, these rules were not promulgated as a result of abuses or misconduct by Weinberg or his case officers. Weinberg was fully aware of his value to the investigators and prosecutors with whom he worked, and he sounds like a very pushy and demanding informant who knew exactly how *he* thought the investigation should be run. The FBI did not let their super-informant run the case, however, with the result that those high-level defendants who fell into Abscam's net were all convicted after trials in which Weinberg testified. Abscam worked because the officers did their jobs and the informant — in this case a super-informant — did his.

Post-Trial Relocation and the Witness Security Program

Law enforcement has an obligation to protect the people who provide us with information. If we are perceived to be abandoning informants to the retribution of the street, sources of information will dry up. In many cases, the informant's identity can be concealed, affording the protection of anonymity. Other informants, particularly those who are required to testify in open court, may need additional protection.

The Federal government and many states have established witness security or protection programs to relocate or otherwise safeguard trial witnesses. Congress sets aside $50 to 60 million for witness protection and security each year, and many of those who receive this assistance are informants who have testified at trial.

The U.S. Marshals Service operates the Federal Witness Security Program, known as "WitSec." This program has successfully relocated thousands of individuals whose lives have been threatened by virtue of their cooperation with the government. Although WitSec is not without its problems, the overall result has been good; people who testify against really dangerous criminals have a place to go, and no one has ever been killed while in the WitSec program.

WitSec is shrouded in secrecy. Much about the program is concealed to keep those who would harm witnesses from learning the methods and procedures used by the marshals. It is known that over 6800 witnesses and their families — more than 16,000 people altogether — have entered the program. Some very prominent names have enjoyed WitSec protection, including Sammy "The Bull" Gravano, James "The Weasel" Fratianno, Henry Hill, Joseph "Joe Dogs" Iannuzzi, and John Dean of Watergate fame. An average of 150 to 170 witnesses enter the program each year. Witnesses who are taken into the WitSec program can be provided with new identities, housed at government expense, protected by Deputy U.S. Marshals, and, above all, kept safe from retaliation by their former associates.

WitSec was created by the Organized Crime Control Act of 1970 (Public Law 91-452). Subsequent legislation, now codified at Title 18 U.S. Code, Sec. 3521 et seq., provides that the Attorney General may:

(A)   Provide suitable documents to enable the person to establish a new identity or otherwise protect the person.
(B)   Provide housing for the person.
(C)   Provide for the transportation of household furniture and other personal property to a new residence of the person.
(D)   Provide to the person a payment to meet basic living expenses, in a sum established in accordance with regulations issued by the Attorney General, for such times as the Attorney General determines to be warranted.

(E)   Assist the person in obtaining employment.

(F)   Provide other services necessary to assist the person in becoming self-sustaining.

WitSec is not a free ride, however, nor is every witness a shoo-in to enter the program. Before accepting someone, an assessment is performed evaluating the person's information, testimony, risk of danger, criminal history, even the results of psychological examinations. Some people simply are not good candidates for the program, while others may not qualify because the threat against them is not sufficient to warrant such extraordinary protective measures.

Before WitSec protection is provided to anyone, they must sign a memorandum of understanding with the Attorney General in which the witness' own responsibilities are set forth. These include:

(A)   The agreement of the person, if a witness or potential witness, to testify in and provide information to all appropriate law enforcement officials concerning all appropriate proceedings

(B)   The agreement of the person not to commit any crime

(C)   The agreement of the person to take all necessary steps to avoid detection by others of the facts concerning the protection provided to that person

(D)   The agreement of the person to comply with legal obligations and civil judgments

(E)   The agreement of the person to cooperate with all reasonable requests of officers and employees of the Government who are providing protection

(F)   The agreement of the person to designate another person to act as agent for the service of process

(G)   The agreement of the person to make a sworn statement of all outstanding legal obligations, including obligations concerning child custody and visitation

(H)   The agreement of the person to disclose any probation or parole responsibilities and, if the person is on probation or parole under State law, to consent to Federal supervision in accordance with section 3522

(I)   The agreement of the person to regularly inform the appropriate program official of the activities and current address of such person

With that, the protected witness can effectively disappear and many do, living under new names in new towns. Many protected witnesses are living in anonymity in communities around the country, their true identities known only to program officials in the Marshals Service.

Law enforcement has an obligation to protect those who agree to cooperate in investigations or testify in criminal cases. This obligation is sometimes fulfilled by preserving the confidentiality of the information. If the informant's identity or even his existence can be concealed, the possibility of retaliation is greatly reduced. In other cases, informants may be given enough funds to relocate or stay out of the reach of those they betrayed. The last resort may be WitSec; with all its restrictions and conditions, it is still a very effective means of keeping important witnesses safe. This has a very positive effect on future informants and witnesses who can depend upon the government to protect them from harm.

One other aspect of WitSec is not so positive and relates to our look at informants. Some of the people relocated under new identities in the program have returned to crime and come again under the scrutiny of law enforcement. The officer who encounters one of these people may first learn of the person's true identity when he or she gets a call from the local U.S. Marshal. Protected witnesses can be arrested and charged with crimes they have committed while in the program, but the investigating officer should still coordinate with the Marshals Service. After all, it is in every officer's interest to keep a witness safe, even if they are going to have to spend some time being protected in prison.

Finally, protected witnesses can be used as informants, but only with the prior approval of the Office of Enforcement Operations (OEO) of the U.S. Department of Justice. This rule applies to current *and* former participants in the Witness Security Program. OEO will be coordinating requests to use the protected witness with the Marshals Service.

Case Study: A Trust Betrayed

On December 13, 1976, Octavio Gonzalez, Special Agent in Charge (SAIC) of the Drug Enforcement Administration's Bogota, Colombia, District Office had an appointment to meet in his office with an established confidential informant. As this was a routine occurrence taking place within the DEA's own offices, SAIC Gonzalez met alone with the informant in an interview room. After a brief conversation, the informant, a U.S. citizen, produced a .38-caliber handgun and shot SAIC Gonzalez three times before turning the gun on himself. Both men were killed instantly. SAIC Gonzalez was not armed at the time of his death.

SAIC Gonzalez was the fourth DEA Special Agent to be killed in the line of duty within a year. He was survived by his wife Mariella and four children: Mariella, 16; Dennis, 14; Sandra, 12; and Catherine, 7. At the time of his death, Gonzalez, who was 38 years old, had been a federal narcotics agent for 8 years. He was a 5-year veteran of the U.S. Air Force and a graduate of Florida Atlantic University in Boca Raton, FL.

There are *no* routine meetings with informants. There is *never* a time when an officer should be relaxed and comfortable in the company of a confidential informant. I would wager that every investigator who is reading this has broken this fundamental rule — I certainly have, but Special Agent Gonzalez's death is a sobering reminder of the inherent dangers that accompany work with confidential informants. The penalties for breaking the rules can be severe. Other examples in this book demonstrate the moral, ethical, and professional hazards that attend informant development and management. Special Agent Gonzalez died because there are physical dangers as well.

Could his death have been prevented? It is impossible, not to mention unfair, to second-guess one who gave his life in the service of his nation. If Mr. Gonzalez had been accompanied in the interview by another agent his obviously determined assailant might have killed two, rather than only one DEA agent. If he had been armed, he might still have been surprised by the informant's sudden turnabout. It is always difficult to protect oneself against an assailant who is prepared for and, in this case, has planned his own death.

I have been unable to establish the reasons why Mr. Gonzalez's assailant acted as he did. It appears that he was upset because he believed that information he had previously provided to DEA had not been acted upon. This hardly seems a reason for killing, but then murder often makes no sense. In one sense, the precise reason is irrelevant. I believe *any* informant is capable of this act, due largely to the psychological pressures that accompany the decision to switch loyalties and cooperate with the government. As investigators who are hoping to maintain control of this cooperation, we cannot lose sight of the fact that:

1. Informants are complex and conflicted individuals, frequently torn by contradictory motivations and often under a great deal of psychological stress.
2. Informants are often emotionally unstable, sometimes even psychopathic, individuals who may be incapable of dealing with the additional complications that accompany life as an informant.
3. Most informants were criminals before they became informants and will be criminals again after they cease their cooperation with the government.

This combination of factors is a recipe for control problems. The consequences of a loss of control can include the informant's resuming his former loyalty to the other side and, in the most extreme case, even a fatal assault on the informant's handler.

A law enforcement officer never has complete control over an informant, even in a situation in which the informant is incarcerated in jail or prison. During the time that the informant is out of the officer's immediate control, his already conflicted loyalties are subject to more emotional battering, and more than one has re-aligned his priorities.

A couple of important rules should be reemphasized.

1. Never meet with an informant alone.
2. Remember that if the informant changed loyalty once, he can and, in the case of criminal informants, almost certainly will change loyalties again. Be prepared for this possibility.

The informant's motivation for cooperating is the strongest means available for control and for the prevention of problems such as that faced by Special Agent Gonzalez.

Legal Issues

11

"This sour informer, this bate-breeding spy./This canker that eats up loves tender spring,/ This carry-tale, disentious Jealousy,/That sometimes true news, sometimes false doth bring."
—William Shakespeare, *Venus and Adonis*

"He had been accused by an anonymous informer of having killed a stag in the royal preserves. I said: 'Anonymous testimony isn't just the right thing, your Highness. It were fairer to confront the accused with the accuser.'"—Mark Twain, *A Connecticut Yankee in King Arthur's Court*

Legal issues surround informants like debris in a tornado. The ultra-high winds are generated by those members of the legal profession who see advantage in attacking every aspect of an informant's cooperation. In this they are blameless, because it is their job to do the best they can for their clients, many of whom would not *be* clients were it not for the intervention of an informant.

Attacks on the informant are particularly ferocious because they resonate well with other people, such as jurors, who generally distrust "sour informers" and "bate-breeding spies." The case law is filled with judicial rulings dealing with every aspect of the informant's role, from search and seizure issues to the payment of rewards. Every criminal defense attorney worthy of the name will have boilerplate motions relating to informants on the hard drives of the office computers. Some of these motions might relate to disclosure of the informant's existence, identity, and background. Prior statements, records of payments, or other benefits provided to the informant will also be sought with persistence.

Throughout all these maneuverings and despite numerous attacks, courts have consistently recognized the continuing need for this investigative resource. That there is a concurrent need for strict controls and careful judicial review of informant-related practices is repeated often in the case law. Perhaps the most accurate phrase which describes the courts' attitude toward police use of informants is they "approve of the practice, but…" In this chapter we will examine some of the "buts" and find some ways to avoid the pitfalls that concern those who sit in judgment of law enforcement's actions in dealing with its most valuable (and dangerous) tool.

Legal Definitions

Black's Law Dictionary defines an informant or informer as "a person who informs or proffers an accusation against another whom he suspects of the violation of some penal statute. An undisclosed person who confidentially volunteers material information of law violation to officers and does not include persons who supply information only after being interviewed by police officers or who give information as witnesses during the course of investigation."

Another definition is even simpler (76 A.L.R. 2d. 262, 267–268, 1961): "Informants, or informers, are people who voluntarily furnish information of violations of the law to law enforcement officials." This definition conforms closely to the common perception about the voluntary and confidential nature of informants. It excludes crime victims and witnesses who are interviewed after the fact in connection with a crime. It obviously excludes law enforcement officers, essentially describing a distinct class of people who come to law enforcement with their information.

"It Is the Duty and Right..."

For over 100 years, courts have recognized that citizens have the right and the duty to report information about violations of the law to those who are charged with law enforcement. Many decisions refer to the common law duty of citizens in medieval England to report crimes to the proper authority, a tradition which has been inherited by American jurisprudence.

In *Vogel v. Gruaz* (110 U.S. 311, 1884), the Supreme Court recognized that a privilege existed for people who reported crimes; they could not be held civilly liable for notifying the proper authorities. In this case, Rudolph Bircher went to the Illinois State's Attorney to complain that Timothy Gruaz had stolen from him. Bircher followed up his complaint by testifying before the grand jury, all in the apparently honest belief that a crime had been committed and Gruaz had committed it.

Gruaz sued, claiming that he had been defamed by Bircher when he made his complaint with the State's Attorney. The Court ruled that it was "of the opinion that what was said by Bircher to Mr. Cook was an absolutely privileged communication." Under Illinois law, the Court said, "It was the province and the privilege of any person who knew of facts tending to show the commission of a crime, to lay those facts before the public officer whose duty it was to commence a prosecution for the crime. Public policy will protect all such communications, absolutely, and without reference to the motive or intent of the informer or the question of probable cause."

The implications of this decision are clear; if victims, complainants, witnesses, or informants could be successfully sued for talking to the police, the number of reported crimes would undoubtedly drop dramatically. The Court made this point emphatically:

> It is the duty of every citizen to communicate to his government any information which he has of the commission of an offence against its laws; and that a court of justice will not compel or allow such information to be disclosed, either by the subordinate officer to whom it was given, by the informer himself, or by any other person, without the permission of the government, the evidence being excluded not for the protection of the witness or of the party in the particular case, but upon general grounds of public policy, because of the confidential nature of such communications.

The duty to report an offense described in *Vogel* was given the status of a civil right in another 19th-century decision, *In re Quarles and Butler; In re McEntire and Goble* (158 U.S.

532, 1895). Henry Worley reported a violation of the Internal Revenue laws to a Deputy U.S. Marshal in Georgia, information which led to the arrests of several moonshiners. They were rather annoyed with Mr. Worley and "took him from his house and beat, bruised and otherwise ill-treated him, and shot at him with guns and pistols with intent to kill and murder him."

The defendants were convicted of violating Worley's civil rights, and the Supreme Court upheld the convictions, saying:

> *The necessary conclusion is that it is the right of every private citizen of the United States to inform a marshal of the United States, or his deputy, of a violation of the internal revenue laws of the United States; that this right is secured to the citizen by the Constitution of the United States; and that a conspiracy to injure, oppress, threaten, or intimidate him in the free exercise or enjoyment of this right, or because of his having exercised it, is punishable under section 5508 of the Revised Statutes.*

The Court likened the right to inform to the right to vote or petition the government for redress of grievances, both guaranteed by the Constitution. The logic in the Court's decisions is apparent; if people are prevented from reporting criminal activity or are retaliated against for doing so, criminals, not the government, will determine how the laws are enforced, if at all. We are all in this together, the Court found, not just the officer whose duty it is to keep the peace, but the citizen who has knowledge of a breach and a duty to report it (*In re Quarles and Butler; In re McEntire and Goble*):

> *It is the duty and right, not only of every peace officer of the United States, but of every citizen, to assist in the prosecuting, and in securing the punishment of, any breach of the peace of the United States. It is the right, as well as the duty, of every citizen, when called upon by the proper officer, to act as part of the* posse comitatus *in upholding the laws of his country. It is likewise his right and his duty to communicate to the executive officers any information which he has of the commission of an offence against those laws; and such information, given by a private citizen, is a privileged and confidential communication, for which no action of libel or slander will lie; and the disclosure of which cannot be compelled without the assent of the government.*

Constitutional Issues — Informants in Law Enforcement

The question of whether law enforcement has the right to use informants is fairly well settled. Repeated challenges to the general practice of seeking out and employing informants have all failed, though not without some serious soul-searching by the courts. Law enforcement should pay attention to the reservations expressed by the judiciary, as these reflect popular discomfort with the concept that betrayal and deception are law enforcement tools.

One of the definitive cases on informants was *United States v. Dennis et al.* (183 F.2d 201, 1950). In this decision, Judge Learned Hand, writing about informants in particular and deception generally, said: "Courts have countenanced the use of informers from time immemorial; in cases of conspiracy, or in other cases when the crime consists of preparing for another crime, it is usually necessary to rely upon them or upon accomplices because the criminals will almost certainly proceed covertly. Entrapment excluded, of which there was none here, decoys and other deception are always permissible."

In *Dennis*, the defendants were appealing a conviction for violation of the Smith Act relating to "willfully and knowingly conspiring to organize the Communist Party of the United

States as a group to teach and advocate the overthrow and destruction of the government by force and violence." An informant described the words and writings of the defendants which enabled the government to show they were doing more than merely exercising their First Amendment rights to political speech.

As Judge Hand noted, conspiracy was the type of crime which was apt to be committed "covertly." Perhaps only those participating in the crime or their closest associates would be aware of the criminals' activity. In *Dennis*, the informant brought information to the government about the words or statements of the accused, as opposed to descriptions of actions taken by those individuals. Conspiracy is the type of crime in which the statements of the participants are essential

The government's prosecution of labor leader Jimmy Hoffa also focused on the words of the defendant, as conveyed to the court by a confidential informant. Hoffa was already involved in one criminal case when the FBI, suspecting that he was planning to bribe jurors, received assistance from Edward Partin. The question of how Partin came to assist the government was hotly disputed. He was a Louisiana local union official who was under state and federal indictment at the time of Hoffa's difficulties. Released from jail on bail, Partin traveled to Tennessee and began hanging out with Hoffa, with whom he had a previous association.

Although the defense claimed that Partin had been "inserted" into the Hoffa camp by the FBI and was subsequently "paid off" for this assistance by having his own criminal cases dropped, the Supreme Court did not find these claims to be supported by the record. In any event, Hoffa's assertion that his Constitutional rights had been violated by Partin's betrayal of his confidences was soundly rejected by the Court.

Hoffa actually based his challenge on three contentions, all of which bear directly on the use of informants by law enforcement. First, he complained that the informant had failed to disclose his role as a government informer. Because of this deception, Hoffa had unknowingly allowed an agent of the government, Partin, to enter his hotel room and other constitutionally protected areas, where Partin overheard Hoffa's incriminating statements. This, Hoffa said, was a violation of his Fourth Amendment protections against illegal search and seizure. The Court disagreed, saying "No rights under the Fourth Amendment were violated by the failure of Partin to disclose his role as a government informer. When Hoffa made incriminating statements to or in the presence of Partin, his invitee, he relied, not on the security of the hotel room, but on his 'misplaced confidence' that Partin would not reveal his wrongdoing."

Second, Hoffa claimed that the Fifth Amendment should prevent the government from making use of his conversations with Partin. These conversations were clearly incriminating to Hoffa, but the Court pointed out that Hoffa had not been compelled in any way to make those statements. Compulsion being a key part of the protection against self-incrimination afforded by the Fifth Amendment, the Court found that the amendment did not shield Hoffa in this instance.

Finally, the government's use of the informant in the midst of an ongoing trial was alleged to have violated Hoffa's Sixth Amendment right to counsel. Partin was active in the midst of Hoffa's trial for violating provisions of the Taft-Hartley Act, a time when Hoffa was represented by counsel. Although Partin was, by his own admission, present when Hoffa was meeting with his attorneys, the Court held that there was no violation of any Sixth Amendment right to counsel in this case.

The facts did not support Hoffa's allegations about Partin's interference with his defense. This is, however, a very serious issue, both for law enforcement and prosecuting attorneys. Courts have repeatedly held in cases subsequent to *Hoffa* that informants may be used only with the greatest care in contacting represented parties or intruding into a protected relationship. Since this issue can arise in multiple defendant and conspiracy cases — exactly the ones Justice Hand described — these are situations in which great caution should be employed.

The *Hoffa* decision placed the courts firmly in the position of once again supporting a practice which, as Justice Hand said, courts had "countenanced ... from time immemorial." This support was qualified, however. Chief Justice Earl Warren, dissenting in *Hoffa* (385 U.S. 293, 1966), wrote that:

> *This type of informer and the uses to which he was put in this case evidence a serious potential for undermining the integrity of the truth-finding process in the federal courts. Given the incentives and background of Partin, no conviction should be allowed to stand when based heavily on his testimony. And that is exactly the quicksand upon which these convictions rest, because without Partin, who was the principal government witness, there would probably have been no convictions here. Thus, although petitioners make their main arguments on constitutional grounds and raise serious Fourth and Sixth Amendment questions, it should not even be necessary for the Court to reach those questions. For the affront to the quality and fairness of federal law enforcement which this case presents is sufficient to require an exercise of our supervisory powers.*

These concerns have been echoed in other cases in the years since *Hoffa* was decided. Law enforcement must always remember the unease with which informants are greeted, not just by judges — who are well aware of their value — but by the jurors who actually try the facts of each case. The defense may argue that government deception, overreaching, or improper insertion of an informant into someone's private conversations may have made the solution worse than the crime. This argument, Chief Justice Warren's dissent reminds us, may find receptive ears.

The Informant in Law Enforcement: Taking a More Active Role

Both *Hoffa* and *Dennis* clearly affirmed judicial support for the concept of law enforcement use of informants in their most traditional role, that of providing information about a crime to the police. But, just as Sun Tzu exhorts us to "use our spies for every purpose," so has law enforcement turned to the informant in a variety of far more active roles. It is common enough today for informants to participate directly in crimes and report the facts of this participation back to the police. Thanks to advances in audio and video technology, it is now possible for informants to report instantaneously by transmitting the details of meetings directly to their case officers.

Court decisions that have addressed the question of how far the informant can go in pursuing evidence of a crime generally take the position that they are effectively acting as agents of the government. As such, the informant can go to the same lengths and employ the same techniques as a police officer or criminal investigator.

The courts are nervous about this one, too. The prospect of allowing an untrained, possibly criminal, individual to run about loose, doing the job of a police officer, is something that has intimidated magistrates since the time of Vidocq. Reassurance, in the form of strong police control over the informant's activity, will be sought. Visible attempts by the officer to independently corroborate all aspects of the informant's statements are good indicators of that control.

In his dissent to the *Hoffa* decision, Chief Justice Warren said, "Given the incentives and background of Partin, no conviction should be allowed to stand when based heavily on his testimony. And that is exactly the quicksand upon which these convictions rest, because without Partin, who was the principal government witness, there would probably have been no convictions here." Law enforcement recognizes that criminal cases will not be won on the strength of informant testimony alone, which is why corroboration is always sought. This quest for corroboration can place the informant in a more active role.

A narcotics investigation by the Treasury Department raised the issue of whether an informant could participate in a more active capacity in the enforcement of the law. As part of the operation, Chin Poy went to the laundry of a suspected drug trafficker, On Lee, in Hoboken, NJ. Unbeknownst to On Lee, his former hired hand was actually an informant or "special employee" for the Federal Bureau of Narcotics. Chin Poy was also wired for sound, carrying a transmitter in his pocket and broadcasting his conversation to a Chinese-speaking narcotic agent, Lawrence Lee, who was stationed just outside with a receiver.

In the traditional role of informants and under the reasoning in *Hoffa*, Chin Poy could come forward to describe the statements On Lee had made during their previous conversations. Recognizing the need to corroborate the word of their informant, FBN took additional steps — having Chin Poy contact the suspect to obtain new information and tape recording or overhearing the conversations electronically so that a (presumably more credible) second witness could testify to the contents.

The Supreme Court in *On Lee v. United States* (343 U.S. 747, 1952) ruled in the government's favor on the question of its use of the informant under the circumstances:

The use of informers, accessories, accomplices, false friends, or any of the other betrayals which are "dirty business" may raise serious questions of credibility. To the extent that they do, a defendant is entitled to broad latitude to probe credibility by cross-examination and to have the issues submitted to the jury with careful instructions. But to the extent that the argument for exclusion departs from such orthodox evidentiary canons as relevancy and credibility, it rests solely on the proposition that the Government shall be arbitrarily penalized for the low morals of its informers. However unwilling we as individuals may be to approve conduct such as that of Chin Poy, such disapproval must not be thought to justify a social policy of the magnitude necessary to arbitrarily exclude otherwise relevant evidence.

The court was deeply divided, though, on the issue of Chin Poy's use of the transmitter. Four of the justices felt that this consensual monitoring constituted wiretapping, an unconstitutional invasion of privacy. Justice Felix Frankfurter, who dissented in no uncertain terms, called it a "dirty business" and a "short-cut in the detection and prosecution of crime that [is] as self-defeating as [it is] immoral."

A lengthy list of cases following *On Lee* has confirmed the government's ability to use informants in a variety of capacities. Today, informants are used to make controlled purchases of evidence, introduce undercover agents, and obtain the probable cause for search warrants and wiretaps. We have come a long way since the informant's tip put the police on a criminal's trail or identified the location of some stolen property. Today, in the effort to corroborate an informant's statement, he or she may be called upon to take a more active role in the investigation, sometimes with negative consequences.

Entrapment and the Informant

This active role has led to a new problem. Throughout the history of law enforcement, police had concentrated on solving historical crimes. The evidence necessary to solve these cases was mostly testimonial, although modern science began providing new tools, such as fingerprints and ballistics, which could be used to support the live witnesses. The police, who were looking for better ways to link suspects to crimes, found the informant could be of special help in resolving a new class of offenses, something which might be termed a continuing criminal enterprise. The legislative branch, seeing a number of social problems, reacted by passing laws that criminalized a broad spectrum of behavior. Narcotics trafficking, gambling, commercialized vice and prostitution, counterfeiting, bootlegging, moonshining, smuggling, fencing, and some kinds of fraud were all organized, ongoing, conspiratorial, commercial operations. They almost invariably involved multiple participants in a network or hierarchy. An informant may not be much help in a robbery case involving a lone gunman or even a serial killing spree, but they were perfectly suited for these new crimes.

As police began to move beyond using informants solely as a source of tips or leads to past activity, the issue of entrapment arose. Thanks to the evidence supplied by the informant or undercover agent, there was no doubt that the subject of the investigation was involved in the commission of the crime. In their defense to the charge, however, some of these people claimed that their involvement was a result of the informants' actions; they had been induced or coerced into committing their crimes.

This contention became known as the entrapment defense. Current law on entrapment follows two standards: a subjective one used in the federal system, which relies upon a determination of the defendant's predisposition, and an objective standard used in many states, which looks at the government's conduct in making the case.

The entrapment defense was first recognized in federal law in *Sorrells v. United States* (287 U.S. 435, 1932). In case law since *Sorrells*, the principal question is whether the individual has a predisposition to commit the offense charged. This standard was articulated in *Sherman v. United States* (356 U.S. 369, 1958), in which the court said that:

> *Entrapment occurs only when the criminal conduct is the product of the creative activity of law-enforcement officials; that is, when the criminal design originates with the officials of the government and they implant in the mind of an innocent person the disposition to commit the alleged offense and induce its commission in order that they may prosecute; on the other hand, the fact that government agents merely afford opportunities or facilities for the commission of the offense does not constitute entrapment.*
>
> *To determine whether the defense of entrapment has been established, a line must be drawn between the trap for the unwary innocent and the trap for the unwary criminal; to make this determination the accused at trial may examine the conduct of the government agent involved and will himself be subjected to an appropriate and searching inquiry into his own conduct and predisposition as bearing on his claim of innocence.*

In the *Sherman* case, an informant approached an old acquaintance and fellow narcotics user when both were undergoing drug treatment. The informant persistently asked Sherman to get narcotics for him, although there was no evidence that Sherman was in the business of selling drugs or willing to sell drugs in this instance. He was, the Court felt, "otherwise unwilling" and not predisposed to comply with the informant's repeated requests.

The actions of the informant came under fire in the *Sherman* decision. Before he brought the agents into the scenario, the informant made multiple requests for drugs, played on Sherman's sympathy, obtained a source of heroin, and got Sherman to resume his own drug use. "Finally, assured of a catch, [he] informed the authorities so that they could close the net." The fact that none of this had taken place with the government's knowledge cut no ice with the Court, which ruled that:

> *As regards the defense of entrapment in a prosecution for violation of the narcotics laws, the government is responsible for the actions of an active confidential informer who, before instigating the prosecution, instigated at least two other prosecutions and who was*

himself under criminal charges for illegally selling narcotics and had not yet been sentenced, it being immaterial that he was not paid for his services by the government.

The entrapment defense has been raised in many thousands of cases since *Sherman* was decided. Case law on the subject varies from state to state, and we need not explore the issue at great length here. It is sufficient for our purposes that the officer who is working with an active informant *must*:

- Be aware of local laws on entrapment.
- Caution the informant against practices which might constitute entrapment.
- Advise the informant that entrapment will not be tolerated.
- Monitor the informant's activities to prevent entrapment.
- Gather whatever evidence might counter an entrapment defense.

An informant who is highly motivated to obtain results can very easily cross the line between legitimate evidence gathering and entrapment. It is the officer's responsibility to prevent this from happening. Blame for a failure will always be laid, not at the door of the informant, but at that of his or her case officer.

Credibility and the Question of Payment

In *Hoffa*, the informant received two forms of compensation. After Hoffa's first trial, Edward Partin's wife received four payments from the FBI totaling $1200. The federal and state charges pending against Partin himself were either dropped or not actively pursued. The prosecutors claimed that the money paid to Partin's wife was simply partial reimbursement of Partin's out-of-pocket expenses and that there was "no necessary connection" between Partin's services as an informant and the fact that the charges against him were dropped.

Thirty years later, the question of whether paid informants can be used has taken on new intensity. Professor Alan Dershowitz, a dean of the criminal defense establishment, says of paid informants, "The word of a bought witness is simply worthless. ...If a defense attorney were to pay a witness or informant for the defendant, he would be immediately jailed . ...Tell me that is a fair system."

Of course, defense attorneys have roles which do not require them to investigate crime, bring criminal charges against anyone, or prove those charges beyond a reasonable doubt, but the professor does raise a valid point about the interest paid witnesses have in the outcome of a case. This type of testimony, though accepted in the courts, is the subject of strong admonitions to the jury. One instruction given to jurors, which can be found in *Federal Jury Practice and Instructions — Civil and Criminal* (Devitt et al., 4th ed., West Group, St. Paul, MN, 1987), reads:

> *The testimony of an informant, someone who provides evidence against someone else for money, or to escape punishment for [his] [her] own misdeeds or crimes, or for other personal reason or advantage, must be examined and weighed by the jury with greater care than the testimony of a witness who is not so motivated. _____ may be considered an informant in this case.*
>
> *The jury must determine whether the informer's testimony has been affected by self-interest, or by the agreement [he] [she] has with the government, or [his own] [her own] interest in the outcome of the case, or by prejudice against the defendant.*

Although it may be unclear whether the informant has been paid for actions leading up to his testimony or for the testimony itself, in cases where an informant has been paid and testifies in court, issuance of such an instruction is appropriate. Refer to *U.S. v. Brooks* (928 F. 2d 1403, 1409, 4th Cir.; cert. denied 112 S. Ct. 140, 1991).

A recent case in the Ninth Circuit discusses the problems connected with informant payments and credibility. Judge Stephen S. Trott wrote in *United States v. Bernal-Obeso* (989 F. 2d 331, 9th Cir., 1993) that informants have provided valuable information in many cases, and their testimony should not be summarily excluded or discounted merely because they were paid. He proposed a system that involved four checks or balances to gauge the credibility of the testimony offered by a paid informant:

> *Thus, we have decided on balance not to prohibit, as some have suggested, the practice of rewarding self-confessed criminals for their cooperation, or to outlaw the testimony in court of those who receive something in return for their testimony. Instead, we have chosen to rely on (1) the integrity of government agents and prosecutors not to introduce untrustworthy evidence into the system,* Berger v. United States *(295 U.S. 78, 1935),* United States v. Agurs *(427 U.S. 97, 1976); (2) trial judges and stringent discovery rules to subject the process to close scrutiny,* United States v. Heath *(260 F. 2d 623, 626, 9th Cir., 1958); (3) defense counsel to test such evidence with vigorous cross examination,* Davis v. Alaska *(415 U.S. 308, 316, 1974; "Cross examination is the principle means by which the believability of a witness and the truth of his testimony are tested."),* United States v. Butler *(567 F. 2d 885, 890, 9th Cir., 1978); and (4) the wisdom of a properly instructed jury whose duty it is to assess each witness's credibility and not to convict unless persuaded beyond a reasonable doubt of the accused's guilt,* On Lee v. United States *(343 U.S. at 757). To quote the Supreme Court, "The established safeguards of the Anglo-American legal system leave the veracity of a witness to be tested by cross-examination, and the credibility of his testimony to be determined by a properly instructed jury."* Hoffa v. United States *(385 U.S. 293, 311–312, 17 L. Ed. 2d 374, 87 S. Ct. 408, 1966); see also* United States v. Cervantes-Pacheco *(826 F. 2d 310, 315, 5th Cir., 1987; cert. denied sub nom* Nelson v. United States *(484 U.S. 1026, 98 L. Ed. 2d 762, 108 S. Ct. 749, 1988; "An informant who is promised a contingent fee by the government is not disqualified from testifying in a federal criminal trial."). Because we have made this choice, it is essential that relevant evidence bearing on the credibility of an informant-witness be timely revealed (1) to defense counsel as required by Giglio, and (2) to the ultimate trier of fact, unless clearly cumulative or attenuated. See Fed. R. Evid. 403;* Delaware v. Van Arsdall *(475 U.S. 673, 679, 89 L. Ed. 2d 674, 106 S. Ct. 1431, 1986; "Trial judges retain wide latitude insofar as the Confrontation Clause is concerned to impose reasonable limits on such cross-examination…").*

In other words, the determination as to whether "the word of a bought witness is simply worthless" is going to be left to the jury. Paid informants are a fact of life in law enforcement. How their actions will be received and whether their testimony will be accepted will largely depend upon "the integrity of the government agents and prosecutors" who work with the informants.

Trading Leniency for Cooperation

The practice of rewarding someone's cooperation with leniency at sentencing is not a new one. Francois Vidocq employed it frequently in his efforts to develop informants in the early 19th century. Today, given the very heavy penalties which can be imposed in some federal and many state cases, the practice is alive and well. More people than ever are seeking to make this trade, which the courts rightly recognize as a form of payment.

The policy is not so popular with defense attorneys, who must cope with the evidence produced by hordes of eager co-defendants, all eager to be the first on board the prosecution's train. The practice raises some doubts in the public's mind as well. Regarding a scandal involving FBI informants in Boston, one commentator in the *Washington Times* wrote recently that, "Allowing an Irish thug to get away with murder so you can catch an Italian one hardly seems a reasonable policy."

The courts have examined this question in a pair of well-publicized appellate decisions which will probably find their way to the Supreme Court. In the case of *United States v. Singleton* (10th Cir., 1998) *en banc* (10th Cir., 1999), Sonya Singleton's money laundering and drug conspiracy convictions were initially overturned, then reinstated by a panel of the 10th Circuit Court of Appeals, then by the entire Court *en banc*. The issue was whether the government had violated Title 18 U.S. Code, Sec. 201(c)(2), by promising leniency to a witness against her. The statute, which relates to bribery of witnesses, provides for a 2-year prison sentence for anyone who:

> *...directly or indirectly, gives, offers or promises anything of value to any person, for or because of the testimony under oath or affirmation given or to be given by such person as a witness upon a trial, hearing, or other proceeding, before any court, any committee of either House or both Houses of Congress, or any agency, commission, or officer authorized by the laws of the United States to hear evidence or take testimony, or for or because of such person's absence therefrom.*

Singleton's attorney argued that, by offering Singleton's co-defendant, Napoleon Davis, "something of value" (leniency), the government had violated the law and violated her right to a fair trial.

A three-judge panel of the 10th Circuit agreed, saying that a lighter sentence was something very valuable indeed, and that the government had violated the law by offering leniency to the co-conspirator: "If justice is perverted when a criminal defendant seeks to buy testimony from a witness, it is no less perverted when the government does so." Congress passed the law to prevent fraud and inherently unreliable testimony, the court said, and the bought testimony was no less unreliable if the government was doing the buying. Singleton's conviction was reversed, in a decision which everyone perceived was going to put a serious dent in the way law enforcement does business in the United States.

The matter was immediately accepted for *en banc* review by the entire 10th Circuit. This review resulted in a different finding. By a vote of 9-3, the court reversed the earlier decision. Once again, the question was whether section 201(c)(2) had been violated by the government's offer of leniency to Davis. Key to this discussion was the intent of Congress in passing the section.

The government argued that section 201(c)(2) was never intended by Congress to apply to the government nor to "the ingrained legal culture of our criminal justice system." Singleton argued the law applied equally to individuals and to the government attorneys. The court had little patience for this contention, saying that the U.S. Attorneys were acting on behalf of the government, which had unique "sovereign prosecutorial powers" in the enforcement of the law: "Extending that premise to its logical conclusion, the defendant implies Congress must have intended to subject the United States to the provisions of section 201(c)(2), and, consequently, like any other violator, to criminal prosecution. Reduced to this logical conclusion, the basic argument of the defendant is patently absurd."

The court also recognized that the practice of offering leniency in exchange for cooperation was an established practice with historical precedent. Accepting Singleton's argument would deprive the government of this "recognized or established prerogative, title, or interest:"

From the common law, we have drawn a longstanding practice sanctioning the testimony of accomplices against their confederates in exchange for leniency. See Hoffa v. United States *(385 U.S. 293, 1966);* Lisenba v. California *(314 U.S. 219, 1941);* Benson v. United States *(146 U.S. 325, 1892);* The Whiskey Cases *(99 U.S. 594, 1878). Indeed, no practice is more ingrained in our criminal justice system than the practice of the government calling a witness who is an accessory to the crime for which the defendant is charged and having that witness testify under a plea bargain that promises him a reduced sentence.*

United States v. Cervantes-Pacheco *(826 F.2d 310, 315, 5th Cir., 1987);* United States v. Juncal *(1998 U.S. Dist. LEXIS 13036, 1998 WL 525800, S.D.N.Y. Aug. 20, 1998; "The concept of affording cooperating accomplices with leniency dates back to the common law in England and has been recognized and approved by the United States Congress, the United States Courts and the United States Sentencing Commission.").*

This ingrained practice of granting lenience in exchange for testimony has created a vested sovereign prerogative in the government. It follows that if the practice can be traced to the common law, it has acquired stature akin to the special privilege of kings. However, in an American criminal prosecution, the granting of lenience is an authority that can only be exercised by the United States through its prosecutor; therefore, any reading of section 201(c)(2) that would restrict the exercise of this power is surely a diminution of sovereignty not countenanced in our jurisprudence.

The first Singleton *decision prompted dozens of appeals around the country and the prospect of congressional action if the decision were upheld. The issue is still pending in other circuits and may ultimately be resolved by the Supreme Court. In the meantime, it should be pointed out that* Singleton *never addressed the practice of offering an informant leniency in exchange for cooperation — only for testimony. Still, even this restriction would vastly change the face of law enforcement in America and undoubtedly deprive the government of valuable information about crime.*

Sentencing Guidelines and Substantial Assistance

Federal sentencing guidelines permit defendants who provide "substantial assistance to the government" in other criminal cases to receive consideration at time of sentencing. This consideration takes the form of a motion by the government for a downward departure from the sentencing guideline range. This provision, found at Title 18 U.S. Code, Appx. Sec. 5K1.1 (1998), "Substantial Assistance to Authorities (Policy Statement)," reads:

Upon motion of the government stating that the defendant has provided substantial assistance in the investigation or prosecution of another person who has committed an offense, the court may depart from the guidelines.

(a) The appropriate reduction shall be determined by the court for reasons stated that may include, but are not limited to, consideration of the following:

    (1) the court's evaluation of the significance and usefulness of the defendant's assistance, taking into consideration the government's evaluation of the assistance rendered;

    (2) the truthfulness, completeness, and reliability of any information or testimony provided by the defendant;

    (3) the nature and extent of the defendant's assistance;

    (4) any injury suffered, or any danger or risk of injury to the defendant or his family resulting from his assistance;

    (5) the timeliness of the defendant's assistance.

The sentencing guidelines have become almost as important as the question of guilt or innocence in this era of very heavy penalties, mandatory minimum sentences, and the abolishment of parole. Because the only means by which a court can depart downward from the guideline range is on a motion of the government, many more people are opting to attempt to provide substantial assistance in the investigation or prosecution of another person.

Officers who are working with informants who are going to be asking for this motion should keep close track of the five factors listed above. Because this will be an issue at sentencing, the officer will be required to articulate the informant's status with respect to each of the factors. The officer's comments may be included in the prosecutor's report or incorporated into the motion itself. Discrepancies between the officer's view of things and that of the informant may be challenged by the informant's attorney at sentencing, although the courts are instructed by the statute that, "Substantial weight should be given to the government's evaluation of the extent of the defendant's assistance, particularly where the extent and value of the assistance are difficult to ascertain."

Contingent Payments

The Attorney General's guidelines on the use of confidential informants expressly forbid contingent payments:

> Prohibition Against Contingent Payments. *Under no circumstances shall any payments to a Cooperating Individual or Confidential Informant be contingent upon the conviction or punishment of any individual.*

The reason for this rule is obvious; such payments provide an incentive for individuals to lie, entrap, or fabricate evidence in order to earn their money. Contingent payments make the courts very uneasy, as the three cases cited below indicate. The law in this area has changed over the 34 years between the first case, *Williamson v. United States,* and the last, *United States v. Cardenas Cuellar,* but note, too, that payments have changed as well. In *Williamson,* the informant received $300, plus gas expenses for his cooperation in cases against two individuals. In *Cardenas Cuellar,* the informant received $580,000. Making this sort of payment contingent on a conviction or forfeiture should give anyone pause for thought.

Jack "Big Boy" Williamson was convicted of tax violations in connection with his possession of 179 gallons of moonshine whiskey. In his appeal, Williamson claimed he had been entrapped by Robert Moye, an informant for the Alcohol and Tobacco Tax Division (ATTD) of the IRS. After serving 3 years on a charge relating to untaxed whiskey, Moye contacted agents of the ATTD and offered to help make some moonshining cases in exchange for money.

Moye testified that the agents accepted his offer and named three whiskey dealers they were interested in. They also proposed an arrangement whereby Moye would be paid $200 for a case on Williamson, $200 for James McBride, and $100 for "Hogie," whom Moye said was the brother of "Big Boy." The agents also agreed to pay $10 per day and Moye's gas expenses. There was no written agreement, but Moye said the agents did pay him $200 after Williamson's arrest and $100 for Hogie Lowrey's arrest.

The court reviewed the government's actions and found that under the law of entrapment which existed at the time, "no error would appear except for the evidence of employment of the informer Moye on a contingent fee basis." (See *Sorrells v. United States,* 287 U.S. 435, 1932; *Sherman v. United States,* 356 U.S. 369, 1958).

The contingent fee arrangement was sufficiently troubling that the court felt compelled to reverse Williamson's conviction:

Without some such justification or explanation, we cannot sanction a contingent fee agreement to produce evidence against particular named defendants as to crimes not yet committed. Such an arrangement might tend to a "frame up," or to cause an informer to induce or persuade innocent persons to commit crimes which they had no previous intent or purpose to commit. The opportunities for abuse are too obvious to require elaboration. No case has been cited by either of the parties involving a contingent fee agreement like that to which Moye testified, and we have found none. Under the principles settled in McNabb v. United States (318 U.S. 332, 340, 1943), and its progeny, however, it becomes the duty of the courts in federal criminal cases to require fair and lawful conduct from federal agents in the furnishing of evidence of crimes. Moye's testimony, standing alone and unexplained, discloses a form of employment of an informer which this Court cannot approve or sanction.

Concurring with the decision, Judge John R. Brown wrote an even more stinging denunciation of the contingent fee arrangement (see *Williamson v. United States,* 311 F. 2d 441, 5th Cir., 1962), saying:

I do not think however, that this is an aspect of entrapment. Its kinship to entrapment is not that the act of a Government representative induced the commission of a crime. Rather, it is that the means used to "make" the case are essentially revolting to an ordered society. …What we hold is that, recognized as is the role of informer in the enforcement of criminal laws, there comes a time when enough is more than enough — it is just too much. When that occurs, the law must condemn it as offensive whether the method used is refined or crude, subtle or spectacular.

It should be noted that *Williamson* has since been overturned by other decisions, notably *United States v. Cervantes-Pacheco* (826 F.2d 310, 5th Cir., 1987), in which the court held "that an informant who is promised a contingent fee by the government is not disqualified from testifying in a federal criminal trial. As in the case of the witness who has been promised a reduced sentence, it is up to the jury to evaluate the credibility of the compensated witness." *Williamson* is discussed here to illustrate some of the feelings that exist toward contingent fee arrangements and relationship to the informant.

The question of a contingent fee arrangement came up again in *United States v. Beard* (761 F. 2d 1477, 11th Cir., 1985), a narcotics case in which informant Selwyn Hall provided DEA with information and assistance in approximately 20 undercover drug transactions. Hall received regular payments ranging from $100 to $350, and he was told that at the end of the investigation he would receive an additional reward. Altogether, Hall received approximately $8000, including a $1000 relocation payment. The U.S. Attorney's Office also agreed to sponsor Hall as a participant in the Marshals' Witness Security Program.

Hall introduced an undercover agent to Charles Beard, who was later charged with two counts of drug trafficking. Hall's fee arrangement was duly reported to Beard's attorney, who filed a motion charging that these arrangements amounted to an improper contingency fee of the type barred by *Williamson v. United States* (311 F.2d 441, 5th Cir., 1962). The trial judge did not agree, nor did the appellate court.

The $8000 was not a contingent fee, the court believed, but subsistence payments made during the course of the investigation. Unlike the situation in *Williamson,* where the agents identified the targets and specified the price for each, Hall identified Beard, and the DEA was able to corroborate independently Beard's involvement in the drug trade. The question of entrapment which was raised in *Williamson* did not arise in *Beard* because the DEA's case was based on much more than the informant's word about Beard's predisposition to commit the offenses (see *United States v. Garcia*, 528 F. 2d 580, 586, 5th Cir., 1976):

> *Often, an oral agreement between the government and a confidential informant provides that an informant must furnish investigative field services and testify truthfully at trial. Following the informant's performance, he may be entitled to a reward based upon a review of all services rendered. We have refused to automatically condemn an agreement "where an informant is paid a subsistence allowance and given a reward," without considering the other contract provisions.*

In the Beard trial, the jury was instructed to exercise care in considering the credibility of a witness informant, who, like Hall, had been previously convicted of a felony or a crime involving dishonesty or false statements, and who used drugs during his government service.

United States v. Cardenas-Cuellar (96 F. 3d 1179, 9th Cir., 1996) is the latest word on contingent payments. In this California case, Sabulon Cardenas Cuellar was convicted on charges of distribution of 200 kilograms of cocaine and possession of 1 kilogram of cocaine with intent to distribute. Following his conviction, Cuellar appealed, saying that his due process rights were violated when the government contracted to pay the informant in the case a percentage of the money seized in an undercover operation. The question facing the court was whether this contract constituted outrageous government conduct.

The case stemmed from a complex money laundering investigation by the U.S. Customs Service. As part of their investigation, Customs entered into a Personal Assistance Agreement with Carlos Garavito, a confidential informant. As part of this agreement, Customs promised to "process purchase of information/purchase of evidence (POI/POE) payments for Garavito's participation in the investigation, predicated on the Source's participation in the investigation and the results of any subsequent criminal or civil proceedings." For his part, Garavito agreed not to apply for an award under Title 19 U.S. Code, Sec. 1619, which allows informants who provide information about violation of the customs laws that lead to a forfeiture of property to receive an award not to exceed 25% of the net amount recovered, up to $250,000 per case. Garavito was also entitled to a brokerage fee of 0.7% of the funds laundered during the investigation, up to $10,000 per month.

The undercover operation was a big success, ultimately resulting in currency seizures exceeding $7 million. Garavito did well, too, receiving $50,000 in brokerage fees and $130,000 for his time and risk. After the investigation was closed, he received an additional $400,000. Cuellar, who was implicated in the delivery of 200 kilograms of cocaine and found to be in possession of 1 kilogram, did not do nearly as well, being indicted and convicted on both counts.

He appealed, saying that the government's arrangement with Garavito was the sort of contingent fee deal which was barred by cases such as *Williamson*. Cuellar claimed that "when the government gives a confidential informant the authority to develop a crime and his monetary reward depends on getting people convicted and on the magnitude of the drug or money laundering transaction, the informant has too great an incentive to fabricate evidence and distort the truth."

The Ninth Circuit Court of Appeals rejected this claim, noting that *Williamson* had been overturned by *United States v. Cervantes-Pacheco* (826 F. 2d 310, 5th Cir., 1987; cert. denied, 484 U.S. 1026, 1988) and that nothing in Garavito or the government's conduct was "so grossly shocking and so outrageous as to violate the universal sense of justice" which would require dismissal of the indictment (see *United States v. Allen*, 955 F.2d 630, 631, 9th Cir., 1992).

There is a danger, the court said, in the use by the government of paid informants, especially, as in this case, where the "informant got paid a ton of money." The fact of payment alone is not enough to make the government's conduct improper (see *United States v. Bernal-Obeso*, 989 F. 2d 331, 9th Cir., 1993):

> *We have previously recognized that "few would engage in a dangerous enterprise of this nature without assurance of substantial remuneration."* United States v. Reynoso-Ulloa *(548 F. 2d 1329, 1338, 9th Cir. 1977; government's use of contingent fee arrangement whereby informant was paid a specific amount for each pound of heroin seized and for each "body" involved did not amount to entrapment per se; cert. denied, 436 U.S. 926, 1978). Congress has done the same thing, providing for compensation based on a percentage of successful forfeitures. 19 U.S.C. § 1619.*

The manner and means by which an informant is paid are only two of the factors which relate to the individual's credibility. Although some methods of payment, including a contingent fee arrangement, *could* induce informants to entrap others, the conclusion about whether such entrapment took place should be based upon all the evidence available in the case:

> *Accordingly, we hold that paying an informant based on a percentage of laundered funds and on results obtained in an extensive undercover operation did not constitute outrageous government conduct in violation of Cuellar's rights to due process.*

This arrangement causes judicial discomfort, however, as noted in the concurring opinion by Judge Charles Wiggins. Obviously disturbed by the large payment to Cuellar, and noting that this amount was more than the law enforcement officers were paid and more than the average person could accumulate in a lifetime, he wrote:

> *First, I am distressed to find that the U.S.C.S. is in fact authorized by Congress to pay informants in the amount and the manner employed in this case. Second, although I am forced to conclude under our prior cases that paying an informant $580,000, $400,000 of which is paid after the informant testifies against the defendant, is not "so excessive, flagrant, scandalous, intolerable and offensive as to violate due process,"* United States v. Garza-Juarez *(992 F. 2d 896, 904, 9th Cir., 1993; cert. denied, 114 S. Ct. 724, 126 L. Ed. 2d 688, 1994), I nevertheless am personally offended by the $580,000 payment.*

Contingent fee payments feel bad, look bad, and smell bad. Judges do not like them, juries do not trust them, and the prosecutor does not want to have to explain them to either group. For these reasons they should be avoided, as the Attorney General's guidelines prescribe.

Establishing Probable Cause

As stated in *Illinois v. Gates* (462 U.S. 213, 1983), "The standard for probable cause requires some showing of facts from which an inference may be drawn that the informant is credible and that his information was obtained in a reliable way."

Since the days of Jonathan Wild and Francois Vidocq, informants have not had the power to arrest violators whom they encounter. This is the duty of the law enforcement officer who, the law says, may arrest anyone whom he has reason to believe has committed a crime. The informant can provide the information leading to these arrests, however, and they frequently do. Information furnished by informants can be used to obtain court orders for wiretaps, to target specific locations for surveillance by the police, or introduce an undercover agent. Nowhere, however, is the informant more important than in the development of probable cause for search and arrest warrants.

According to the *National Law Journal,* the number of federal search warrants which relied exclusively on unidentified informants increased from 24% in 1980 to 71% in 1993. In some districts, informants were used in 90% of search warrant affidavits. In narcotics enforcement, this percentage might even be low.

This heavy reliance on informants for this purpose causes distress in some circles. Defense attorneys are highly suspicious of the claims made by officers and informants in affidavits, a suspicion heightened by the fact that the informant's identity does not have to be disclosed in the affidavit. Reviewing an affidavit that has references to "CI-1" or "CW-3" as the source of the information used against their client can make defense attorneys skeptical of the veracity or even the existence of this phantom informant. These questions can grow to criticism and even to accusations of police perjury.

The courts hear these questions and respond with decisions which try to reconcile the need to protect law enforcement's ability to protect its sources with the rights of defendants to confront their accusers. It is a tough job, made no easier by the cynicism present in both law enforcement and the defense bar.

The best place to start our discussion of probable cause and the informant is the Supreme Court decision in *Aguilar v. Texas* (379 U.S. 108, 1964). Together with a second decision, *Spinelli v. United States* (393 U.S. 410, 1969), this decision outlined a path for officers to follow in using informants to establish probable cause.

The problem, as the Supreme Court saw it, was that informants are often not very nice, nor very dependable people. If they have sufficient motivation, such a person might lie to an officer or fabricate evidence of a crime. Even more troublesome was the fact that in reviewing an officer's affidavit for a search or arrest warrant, the magistrate could not even identify this informant by name; an officer could simply say "an informant told me…" Given this limited information, how could a neutral and detached magistrate possibly do his Constitutional duty and decide whether probable cause *really* existed that would justify the issuance of the warrant? Looking at the facts in *Aguilar,* the Court said:

> *Although an affidavit may be based on hearsay information and need not reflect the direct personal observations of the affiant … the magistrate must be informed of some of the underlying circumstances from which the informant concluded that the narcotics were where he claimed they were, and some of the underlying circumstances from which the officer concluded that the informant, whose identity need not be disclosed … was "credible" or his information "reliable." Otherwise, "the inferences from the facts which lead to the complaint" will be drawn, not "by a neutral and detached magistrate," as the Constitution requires, but instead, by a police officer "engaged in the often competitive enterprise of ferreting out crime … or, as in this case, by an unidentified informant."*

The Court decided that a test was needed any time an undisclosed informant was to be used, and they devised what would become known as *Aguilar's* "two-pronged test." The first prong of the test relates to the "basis of belief" or "basis of knowledge" of the informant. The affidavit had to contain enough information to demonstrate to the magistrate that the informant had a basis for believing that the illegal activity was taking place, the evidence was at the location described, or the person was involved in the activity. This test is essentially a description of *how* the informant knows what he is saying.

The second part of the test is referred to as the "veracity prong." Can the magistrate have confidence in the veracity of the informant's information? Is it true and accurate on this occasion? The veracity prong can be met by showing either the informant's credibility or his reliability. Credibility can be shown by a recitation for the magistrate of the informant's track record. How many arrests, convictions, seizures, successful search warrants, or other actions have resulted from the informant's cooperation? How many tips have been borne out by independent investigation by the officer? A showing of past success can inspire sufficient confidence in the magistrate to have the warrant approved (if the first prong is met, as well).

What if the informant is new, with no established track record but a very good story? When this happens, the officer can present evidence of the reliability of the information in this specific instance. One of the means used to establish reliability might include a statement made by the informant which is against his penal interest — she is admitting to a crime: "I know he sells drugs because I bought from him." As stated in *United States v. Harris* (403 U.S. 573, 1971):

> *Common sense in the important daily affairs of life would induce a prudent and disinterested observer to credit these statements. People do not lightly admit a crime and place critical evidence in the hands of the police in the form of their own admissions. Admissions of crime, like admissions against proprietary interests, carry their own indicia of credibility — sufficient at least to support finding of probable cause to search. That the informant may be paid or promised a "break" does not eliminate the residual risk and opprobrium of having admitted criminal conduct.*

The decision in *Spinelli* further clarified how the first prong (basis of belief) could be satisfied:

> *If the affidavit rests on hearsay — an informant's report — what is necessary under Aguilar is one of two things: the informant must declare either (1) that he has himself seen or perceived the fact or facts asserted; or (2) that his information is hearsay, but there is good reason for believing it — perhaps one of the usual grounds for crediting hearsay information. ...In the absence of a statement detailing the manner in which the information was gathered, it is especially important that the tip describe the accused's criminal activity in sufficient detail that the magistrate may know that he is relying on something more substantial than a casual rumor circulating in the underworld or an accusation based merely on an individual's general reputation.*

Aguilar and *Spinelli* guided law enforcement officers, prosecutors, and judges until the 1983 decision in *Illinois v. Gates* (462 U.S. 213, 1983), which substituted a totality of the circumstances rule for determining probable cause. *Gates* involved an anonymous informant; the police received a tip by unsigned letter and were in no position to meet either prong of the *Aguilar-Spinelli* test. Never mind, the Supreme Court said in *Illinois v. Gates*:

> *In its place we reaffirm the totality of the circumstances analysis that traditionally has informed probable cause determinations. ...The task of the issuing magistrate is simply to make a practical, common-sense decision whether, given all the circumstances set forth in the affidavit before him, including the "veracity" and basis of knowledge of persons supplying hearsay information, there is a fair probability that contraband or evidence of a crime will be found in a particular place. And the duty of a reviewing court is simply to ensure that the magistrate had a "substantial basis for ... conclud[ing]" that probable cause existed.*

We do not need to get any more deeply into search and seizure law, but now is a good spot to take a look at the wisdom of the *Aguilar-Spinelli* structure, which is still useful even if it has been replaced in the courts with a new standard.

In our dealings with informants, we must constantly assess the individual's motivation and access. Even if *Aguilar-Spinelli* no longer governs a magistrate's decision about probable cause, the basis of belief and veracity tests should still be applied by the officer in every contact with an informant.

- Basis of belief/knowledge:
  - *How* does he know what he is saying is true?
- Veracity:
  - Is she reliable?
  - Is she motivated to lie?
  - Is she credible? What is her track record?

Each and every statement made by the informant should be subjected to this type of analysis. The fact that courts no longer apply this standard to search warrant affidavits does not mean that a cautious law enforcement officer should not test an informant on every prong available.

The totality of the circumstances rule works fine for warrants, but for our purposes there is no such thing as an anonymous informant; such a person would be missing at least one of the three elements (control) of an informant, and it would be difficult, if not impossible, for the officer to establish motivation. For these reasons *Aguilar-Spinelli* is still a useful tool in managing informants.

The Informant Privilege: Disclosure of Identity

J. Wigmore stated in his book, *Evidence* (McNaughton Publishing, 1961, p. 2374):

> *A genuine privilege must be recognized for the identity of persons supplying the govern-*
> *ment with information concerning the commission of crimes. Communications of this*
> *kind ought to receive encouragement. Whether an informer is motivated by good citizen-*
> *ship, promise of leniency or prospect of pecuniary reward, he will usually condition his*
> *cooperation on an assurance of anonymity — to protect himself and his family from*
> *harm, to preclude adverse social reactions and to avoid the risk of defamation or mali-*
> *cious prosecution actions against him. The government also has an interest in non-disclo-*
> *sure of the identity of its informers. Law enforcement officers often depend upon profes-*
> *sional informers to furnish them with a flow of information about criminal activities.*
> *Revelation of the dual role played by such persons ends their usefulness to the government*
> *and discourages others from entering into a like relationship. That the government has*
> *this privilege is well established, and its soundness cannot be questioned.*

Whenever possible, law enforcement would prefer to keep the "confidential" in "confidential informant." As Wigmore points out, there are a number of reasons why this is good for the informant and sound policy generally. The privilege of non-disclosure of the identity of the informant must be balanced against the rights of the defendant in a criminal prosecution, however. The Constitution guarantees that a defendant will have the right to confront his accuser. When will this right conflict with the privilege of the government to conceal the identity of its informant?

In *Rovario v. United States* (353 U.S. 53, 1957), the Supreme Court attempted to address this question. While the Court recognized the informant privilege and the need for protection of the informant's identity under some circumstances, they ultimately held that:

> *Where the disclosure of an informer's identity, or of the contents of his communication, is relevant and helpful to the defense of an accused, or is essential to a fair determination of a cause, the privilege must give way. In these situations the trial court may require disclosure and, if the Government withholds the information, dismiss the action.*

In *Rovario*, the informant purchased narcotics from the defendant while an agent concealed himself in the informant's car. The informant was searched before and after the transaction, and officers on surveillance saw the actual meeting between Rovario and the informant. The agent in the trunk overheard the conversation and even saw Rovario retrieve the evidence from a place of concealment. The Court noted that although the informant was not the only person who could describe the actual transaction, he was a material witness to it and could furnish evidence about issues of entrapment, if raised:

> *We believe that no fixed rule with respect to disclosure is justifiable. The problem is one that calls for balancing the public interest in protecting the flow of information against the individual's right to prepare his defense. Whether a proper balance renders nondisclosure erroneous must depend on the particular circumstances of each case, taking into consideration the crime charged, the possible defenses, the possible significance of the informer's testimony, and other relevant factors.*

On balance in this case, the Court felt that the defendant's rights outweighed the interest in protecting the informant's identity. The Court also ruled that reports or communications which did not tend to reveal the identity of the informant were not covered by the privilege, and once the identity of the informant had been disclosed to "those who would have cause to resent" him, the privilege would no longer apply.

Rovario dealt firmly with the informant privilege in cases where disclosure was needed to prepare a defense. This supposed that the case had already reached a trial stage, but some question remained about whether the privilege applied to the critical issue of probable cause. Because the information provided by informants is used so extensively in establishing probable cause for search or arrest warrants, this was a matter of no little import to law enforcement.

Affidavits for search warrants frequently contain references to informants who are identified only by a code name or number: "CI-1" or "CW-3." The law enforcement officers who prepare these affidavits know full well that they may someday be disclosed to the defendant and his lawyer. Every effort is made to conceal the identity of a source from this type of exposure. But, the defense attorney screams, how do we *know* this person *really* exists? If the source of the information is not named, might he not be a figment of the officer's imagination? Or worse, what if the "alleged informant" was a device to conceal wrongdoing or perjury by the officer?

Rovario v. United States addressed this question in passing, noting that:

> *Most of the federal cases involving this limitation on the scope of the informer's privilege have arisen where the legality of a search without a warrant is in issue and the communications of an informer are claimed to establish probable cause. In these cases the Government has been required to disclose the identity of the informant unless there was sufficient evidence apart from his confidential communication.*

Other decisions indirectly addressed the credibility question (see *Scher v. United States,* 305 U.S. 251, 1938), noting that "public policy forbids disclosure of an informer's identity unless essential to the defense, as, for example, where this turns upon an officer's good faith."

The issue was addressed more directly in *McCray v. Illinois* (386 U.S. 300, 1967). Another narcotics case, *McCray* involved the seizure of heroin from the defendant after he had been described by an informant. The officers testified that they had met the informant, who told them that McCray, an acquaintance, was dealing heroin at a specific location at a particular time. The informant accompanied the officers to the location, pointed McCray out to the officers, then left. The officers observed McCray doing some things that looked a lot like drug sales, then approached him, searched him, and found heroin on his person.

The officers testified that the informant had been reliable in their previous contacts with him, saying that he had given information that had led to at least 20 prior arrests and convictions. McCray wanted to know the name and address of the person who had provided the information, but the trial court refused to order the officers to identify their source. The Supreme Court agreed, saying:

> *When the issue is not guilt or innocence, but, as here, the question of probable cause for an arrest or search, the Illinois Supreme Court has held that police officers need not invariably be required to disclose an informant's identity if the trial judge is convinced, by evidence submitted in open court and subject to cross-examination, that the officers did rely in good faith upon credible information supplied by a reliable informant.*

The words "credible information," "reliable informant," and "good faith" would all figure in other Court decisions relating to probable cause. The *McCray* Court felt that the finding of probable cause was a "preliminary matter" which did not place guilt or innocence directly at stake. As such, the privilege could apply. In this case, the Court addressed *Rovario*, making a distinction between the two situations:

> *What* Rovario *makes clear is that this court was unwilling to impose any absolute rule requiring disclosure of an informer's identity even in formulating rules for federal criminal trial. Much less has the court ever approached the formulation of a federal evidentiary rule of compulsory disclosure where the issue is the preliminary one of probable cause and guilt or innocence is not at stake. Indeed, we have repeatedly made clear that federal officers need not disclose an informer's identity in applying for an arrest or search warrant.*

Rulings in both state and federal courts have followed the *McCray* and *Rovario* standards for decades. These decisions form a structure for the assurances which officers can give to informants about their anonymity. The Attorney General's guidelines cover this point:

> *The United States Government will strive to protect a Confidential Informant's identity, but cannot guarantee that it will not be divulged.*

Whether or not the informant is to be disclosed may dictate how the case is investigated. It may be possible to obtain evidence independent of the informant's statement. If the officer can conduct the investigation in such a way that the informant is not a material witness to any fact at issue, so much the better. The officer should explain these facts of life to the informant at the very outset of the relationship:

1. We will do everything in our power to keep your identity a secret.
2. The law permits us to do certain things to protect you, including not identifying you in affidavits for search or arrest warrants.
3. If the case goes to trial *and* if you are found to be a material witness whose testimony goes to the guilt or innocence of the defendant, the court may require us to identify you.
4. If that happens, we will either have to do so, *or* ask the court to dismiss the case against the defendant.

The officer needs to know which course of action the agency or the prosecutor will take in step 4 and make this very clear to the informant. Some rare informants may be worth dismissing cases for, but mostly we should try to keep the informant from becoming a material witness or being forced to call him or her.

Liability and Employment

Some non-criminal issues can occasionally arise in connection with law enforcement's use of informants. While these issues may not seem as urgent as the need to develop a successful prosecution, they can be very serious indeed, with ramifications for the informant, the officer, and the officer's department.

Liability for the Informant's Protection

Being an informant can be a hazardous occupation. The people being betrayed are criminals, often with access to weapons and a strong incentive to use them against someone who betrays their trust. To the extent that it is able, law enforcement has a responsibility to protect those who report crimes or act as informants. This obligation is not only practical (people who have no confidence in our ability to protect them will not come forward) and moral (we have an ethical responsibility to prevent harm to others), it is a legal one as well. Although the criminal code may have sanctions against those who threaten or injure an informant, the courts have found that civil remedies may be appropriate in some cases as well.

It is generally recognized that the police cannot protect everyone. Law enforcement does its best, but crimes are committed and bad things do happen to good people.

In February 1952, Arnold Schuster spied an individual whose face appeared on a wanted flier that was posted in his father's dry-goods store. The man was Willie "The Actor" Sutton, a bank robber and one of the most notorious fugitives in America. Schuster's information led to Sutton's capture and a brief moment in the spotlight for Schuster, by all accounts a reserved young man who was motivated by public spirit to aid the police. Three weeks later, Schuster was shot to death on the street near his home. Before his death Schuster had received threats and had been given police protection, which was withdrawn before the murder.

The slaying went unsolved. Sutton was not a member of organized crime; he was actually the epitome of the lone bank robber, as he did not have a gang which might have sought revenge for his arrest. The police were unable to identify a suspect, but it seemed clear that the gangland-style killing was connected to Schuster's role as an informant. The young man's family thought so, and filed a lawsuit against the City of New York for failing to protect their informant.

This case reached the New York Court of Appeals, which decided that Arnold Schuster's family had a point (see *Schuster v. City of New York*, 5 N.Y. 2d 75, 1958). The main question before the court was whether "a municipality is under any duty to exercise reasonable care for the protection of a person in Schuster's situation." They recognized that there is no liability for a general failure of police or fire protection; municipalities could not be "called upon to answer in damages for every loss caused by outlaws or by fire." Nevertheless, in this instance, the City of New York, which had sought the public's aid in apprehending a wanted criminal, did have a duty to protect the member of the public who answered the call:

> *Where persons actually have aided in the apprehension or prosecution of enemies of society under the criminal law, a reciprocal duty arises on the part of society to use reasonable care for their police protection, at least where reasonably demanded and sought. Such a duty would be performed by the regular organs of government, in this instance, by the City of New York. The duty of everyone to aid in the enforcement of the law, which is as old as history, begets an answering duty on the part of government, under the circumstances of contemporary life, reasonably to protect those who have come to its assistance in this manner.*

The court essentially held that by asking for and expecting the public's help, the government had created a special relationship with its informant, one which was effectively reinforced by a state law that made cities liable "for damages arising from the personal injury or death of persons injured or killed while aiding policemen at their discretion in making arrests." Another statute imposed a duty on the part of private citizens to assist law enforcement officers upon request, and made it a misdemeanor to fail to do so. The creation of this special relationship made it especially important "that the governmental policy behind the statute indicates care and solicitude for the private citizen who cooperates with the public authorities in the arrest and prosecution of criminals."

No one was ever arrested in Arnold Schuster's murder, but the case was eventually cleared by Mafia defector Joe Valachi. Ten years later, he reported that Albert Anastasia, the violent head of the mob's "Murder Incorporated," enraged at Schuster's television appearance, exclaimed, "I can't stand squealers. Hit that guy." Anastasia's orders were allegedly carried out by Frederick Tenuto, whom Anastasia then had killed to prevent Tenuto from talking to the police.

The clear-cut language of the *Schuster* court has been echoed in several other decisions, though ironically not with the results the injured informant might be seeking. In *Swanner v. United States* (275 F. Supp. 1007, M.D. AL, 1967) the court agreed that "under the circumstances existing, the United States Government was under a duty to provide Swanner and the members of his family with police protection."

The "circumstances" in Swanner's case are dreaded by those in law enforcement who work with informants. Swanner, a convicted felon and police character, was working for the Alcohol and Tobacco Tax Division of the Internal Revenue Service as a "special employee." Swanner furnished information that led to the arrest of a particularly violent moonshiner, and shortly after received threats against his life, both directly and indirectly from this person. These threats seemed to be borne out when a bomb exploded under Swanner's house, injuring several members of his family, including two children under the age of three. The survivors all sued for damages under the Federal Tort Claims Act, finding a somewhat sympathetic ear in federal court:

> *Whenever there is reasonable cause to believe that a government agent or employee, or any member of his family, is endangered as a result of his performance of his duty to the government, a duty on the part of the government to protect him and the members of his family arises. This duty arises without the necessity for formal request on the part of the [persons] endangered. It arises upon the communication to the government of facts which*

would create a reasonable belief that a government employee, or his family, is endangered as a result of his performance of duty, and it is immaterial whether the information is received directly from those endangered or from some other source.

Unfortunately for Swanner, the court also found that despite the fact that the government had "negligently breached its duty to provide protection" to him and his family, there was not sufficient proof that the bomb had been placed to retaliate for his actions as an informant. Swanner, the court noted, was a felon, ran a car repossession business, and lived in a heavily insured house on which the mortgage was in arrears. In short, Swanner could have been blown up for some reason other than his informant role.

Other, more recent decisions have taken a similar line. A "special relationship" is created when law enforcement officers and a confidential informant "anticipate that the informant's activities, if discovered, could result in a threat to the life of the informant (see *G-69 v. Degnan*, 745 F. Supp. 254, D.N.J., 1990). The scope of this relationship is such that the government takes on a responsibility for preventing harm to an individual as a result of their cooperation.

In *Summar v. Bennett* (157 F. 3d 1054, 6th Cir., 1998), the court acknowledged that special relationships are created in which the government takes on an obligation to protect an individual from harm, citing as an example a police officer who impounded a female motorist's car and left her alone on the side of the road in a high-crime area at night (see *Wood v. Ostrander*, 879 F. 2d 583, 9th Cir., 1989). The officer-informant relationship was special, the court felt, but was distinguished from cases like *Wood* because informants such as Summar entered into the relationship voluntarily, knowing the possibility of exposure and risk: "Summar's voluntary decision to become an informant with all the dangers it presented, not to mention his poor decision to fraternize with criminals in the first place, played a much greater role in his unfortunate demise."

The creation of a "special relationship" will effectively increase the responsibility which the government has for the protection of an individual member of society. The decision to use someone as an informant or to solicit information from that person creates this special relationship, one which is not only accompanied by increased obligations and liabilities, but is also acknowledged in statutes which seek to protect the informant or witness from harm.

Statutes Protecting the Informant

The U.S. Code and the criminal codes of the various states all have some provisions which make it a crime to threaten or injure a witness or informant. As we saw in *In re Quarles and Butler; In re McEntire and Goble*, retaliation against someone who provides information to law enforcement is hardly a novel concept. Congress and the legislatures, recognizing the need to discourage this sort of thing, have passed laws aimed at those who threaten not just a witness, but the entire criminal justices system. The system, after all, relies upon victims, witnesses, and informants to provide information testimony about crime. These people should be confident of the government's protection and support in coming forward.

In its findings relating to victim-witness protection legislation, Congress said in part:

The Congress finds and declares that without the cooperation of victims and witnesses, the criminal justice system would cease to function; yet with few exceptions these indi-viduals are either ignored by the criminal justice system or simply used as tools to identify and punish offenders. All too often the victim of a serious crime is forced to suffer physical, psychological, or financial hardship first as a result of the criminal act and then as a result of contact with a criminal justice system unresponsive to the real needs of such victim.

Under current law, law enforcement agencies must have cooperation from a victim of crime and yet neither the agencies nor the legal system can offer adequate protection or assistance when the victim, as a result of such cooperation, is threatened or intimidated.

The principle federal statute addressing this problem is Title 18 U.S. Code, Sec. 1512, "Tampering with a Witness, Victim, or an Informant," which reads,

(a)   (1)   *Whoever kills or attempts to kill another person, with intent to—*

      (A)   *prevent the attendance or testimony of any person in an official proceeding;*

      (B)   *prevent the production of a record, document, or other object, in an official proceeding; or*

      (C)   *prevent the communication by any person to a law enforcement officer or judge of the United States of information relating to the commission or possible commission of a Federal offense or a violation of conditions of probation, parole, or release pending judicial proceedings;*

    shall be punished as provided in paragraph (2).

   (2)   *The punishment for an offense under this subsection is—*

      (A)   *in the case of murder (as defined in section 1111), the death penalty or imprisonment for life, and in the case of any other killing, the punishment provided in section 1112; and*

      (B)   *in the case of an attempt, imprisonment for not more than twenty years.*

(b)   *Whoever knowingly uses intimidation or physical force, threatens or corruptly persuades another person, or attempts to do so, or engages in misleading conduct toward another person, with intent to—*

   (1)   *influence, delay or prevent the testimony of any person in an official proceeding;*

   (2)   *cause or induce any person to—*

      (A)   *withhold testimony, or withhold a record, document, or other object, from an official proceeding;*

      (B)   *alter, destroy, mutilate, or conceal an object with intent to impair the object's integrity or availability for use in an official proceeding;*

      (C)   *evade legal process summoning that person to appear as a witness, or to produce a record, document, or other object, in an official proceeding; or*

      (D)   *be absent from an official proceeding to which such person has been summoned by legal process; or*

   (3)   *hinder, delay, or prevent the communication to a law enforcement officer or judge of the United States of information relating to the commission or possible commission of a Federal offense or a violation of conditions of probation, parole, or release pending judicial proceedings;*

    shall be fined under this title or imprisoned not more than ten years, or both.

(c)   *Whoever intentionally harasses another person and thereby hinders, delays, prevents, or dissuades any person from—*

   (1)   *attending or testifying in an official proceeding;*

   (2)   *reporting to a law enforcement officer or judge of the United States the commission or possible commission of a Federal offense or a violation of conditions of probation, parole, or release pending judicial proceedings;*

(3) *arresting or seeking the arrest of another person in connection with a Federal offense; or*

(4) *causing a criminal prosecution, or a parole or probation revocation proceeding, to be sought or instituted, or assisting in such prosecution or proceeding;*

or attempts to do so, shall be fined under this title or imprisoned not more than one year, or both.

(d) *In a prosecution for an offense under this section, it is an affirmative defense, as to which the defendant has the burden of proof by a preponderance of the evidence, that the conduct consisted solely of lawful conduct and that the defendant's sole intention was to encourage, induce, or cause the other person to testify truthfully.*

(e) *For the purposes of this section—*

(1) *an official proceeding need not be pending or about to be instituted at the time of the offense; and*

(2) *the testimony, or the record, document, or other object need not be admissible in evidence or free of a claim of privilege.*

(f) *In a prosecution for an offense under this section, no state of mind need be proved with respect to the circumstance—*

(1) *that the official proceeding before a judge, court, magistrate, grand jury, or government agency is before a judge or court of the United States, a United States magistrate [United States magistrate judge], a bankruptcy judge, a Federal grand jury, or a Federal Government agency; or*

(2) *that the judge is a judge of the United States or that the law enforcement officer is an officer or employee of the Federal Government or a person authorized to act for or on behalf of the Federal Government or serving the Federal Government as an adviser or consultant.*

(g) *There is extraterritorial Federal jurisdiction over an offense under this section.*

(h) *A prosecution under this section or section 1503 may be brought in the district in which the official proceeding (whether or not pending or about to be instituted) was intended to be affected or in the district in which the conduct constituting the alleged offense occurred.*

(i) *If the offense under this section occurs in connection with a trial of a criminal case, the maximum term of imprisonment which may be imposed for the offense shall be the higher of that otherwise provided by law or the maximum term that could have been imposed for any offense charged in such case.*

Under Title 18 U.S. Code, Sec. 1512, even a potential witness falls within the scope of the statute, which expressly eliminated the requirement that an official proceeding be pending. The congressional intent was to broaden the scope of the obstruction of justice statute to include greater protection for those who have a knowledge of criminal activity, and to encourage those people to testify or provide information to law enforcement. As such, the protection is clearly extended to informants. There is no requirement that the person be a "witness." (See *United States v. Di Salvo*, 1986, ED Pa, 631 F Supp 1398, ED Pa, 1986, affd. without op. 826 F. 2d 1057, 3rd Cir., 1987.)

What types of conduct constitute tampering? Harassment, intimidation by physical force, killing or attempting to kill, misleading conduct, and other activity designed to forestall the cooperation of a witness. Some interesting decisions have emerged from prosecutions under this chapter, which, like the provisions against retaliation, are intended to protect not just the individual but the system which requires his or her cooperation and testimony.

In *United States v. Wilson* (796 F. 2d 55, 5th Cir., 1987, cert. denied, 1987, 479 U.S. 1039), the court addressed the harassment of witnesses waiting outside of a courtroom. The defendant approached three persons, two of whom had already testified and one who had just been excused as a witness, and, lowering his voice so that a nearby Deputy U.S. Marshal could not overhear, spoke in a low tone of voice with a sneer on his face. Judging from the "adverse reactions the witnesses suffered upon hearing the threats," it was concluded that some form of harassment had taken place, a conclusion supported by the witnesses.

Intimidation and attempted intimidation were found to be unlawful in *United States v. Capo* (791 F. 2d 1054, 2nd Cir., 1986). In this case the defendant attempted to prevent a witness from testifying in a grand jury proceeding by making a "gratuitous disclaimer that he was a member of a 'mob,'" dropping the name of a known organized crime figure and advising that if everyone kept silent nobody would have a problem. The defendant made these statements right after the informant indicated that he intended to testify before the grand jury.

Obviously, the killing or attempted killing of a witness or informant should be considered "tampering." In order to obtain a conviction pursuant to Title 18 U.S. Code, Sec. 1512(a)(1)(C), the government must prove: (1) the defendant killed or attempted to kill the person; (2) the defendant was motivated by a desire to prevent communication between any person and law enforcement authorities concerning commission or possible commission of offense; (3) the offense was actually a federal offense; and (4) the defendant believed that the person in (2) above might communicate with federal authorities. (See *United States v. Stansfield*, 101 F3d 909, 3rd Cir., 1996.)

Misleading conduct by the defendant which would convince someone else to lie falls squarely within the definition of "engaging in misleading conduct toward another person" under Title 18 U.S. Code, Sec. 1512, *United States v. Rodolitz* (786 F. 2d 77, 2nd Cir., 1986, cert. denied, 1986, 479 U.S. 826). In a case which has an eerie similarity to recent events, the former governor of Guam was found guilty of witness tampering when he engaged in misleading conduct by "urging and advising" a witness to lie to the grand jury by making false statements to that witness, intending the witness to believe them and testify to them. The issue was not denial of a consensual sexual relationship, but the governor's professed use of "campaign contributions" to help poor people. (See *United States v. Bordallo*, 857 F. 2d 519, 9th Cir., 1988, reh. denied, cert. denied, 493 U.S. 818, 1989.)

Threats against witnesses or informants are also considered witness tampering under the statute. Those in law enforcement who work with informants are aware that it is more common for people to threaten informants than it is for the threats to be acted upon. Nevertheless, threats have an unnerving effect on informants and discourage people from cooperating in criminal investigations. A fairly egregious example was *United States v. Murray* (751 F. 2d 1528, 9th Cir. 1985, cert. denied 474 U.S. 979, 1985), in which the defendant instructed a co-conspirator not to cooperate with an FBI investigation of a scheme to loot a bankrupt corporation. The defendant ultimately threatened his co-conspirator in the scheme with physical harm if he cooperated with the FBI.

Another unsubtle threat was reported in *United States v. Dunning* (929 F. 2d 579, 10th Cir., 1991, cert. denied 112 S Ct. 224, 1991). The defendant in this case told the female victim that if she caused the defendant's mother to go to jail, "She will not be on the face of this earth any longer. That goes for her or anyone else. ..." The court believed that "the jury could conclude that threat would make those who heard it think twice before going to law enforcement officers and giving information about defendant's mother."

Another statute that relates to witnesses and informants is Title 18 U.S. Code, Sec. 1513 (Retaliating Against a Witness, Victim, or an Informant), which considers such action as an obstruction of justice and reads as follows:

(a) (1) *Whoever kills or attempts to kill another person with intent to retaliate against any person for—*

(A) *the attendance of a witness or party at an official proceeding, or any testimony given or any record, document, or other object produced by a witness in an official proceeding; or*

(B) *providing to a law enforcement officer any information relating to the commission or possible commission of a Federal offense or a violation of conditions of probation, parole, or release pending judicial proceedings,*

shall be punished as provided in paragraph (2).

(2) *The punishment for an offense under this subsection is—*

(A) *in the case of a killing, the punishment provided in sections 1111 and 1112; and*

(B) *in the case of an attempt, imprisonment for not more than 20 years.*

(b) *Whoever knowingly engages in any conduct and thereby causes bodily injury to another person or damages the tangible property of another person, or threatens to do so, with intent to retaliate against any person for—*

(1) *the attendance of a witness or party at an official proceeding, or any testimony given or any record, document, or other object produced by a witness in an official proceeding; or*

(2) *any information relating to the commission or possible commission of a Federal offense or a violation of conditions of probation, parole, or release pending judicial proceedings given by a person to a law enforcement officer;*

or attempts to do so, shall be fined under this title or imprisoned not more than ten years, or both.

(c) *If the retaliation occurred because of attendance at or testimony in a criminal case, the maximum term of imprisonment which may be imposed for the offense under this section shall be the higher of that otherwise provided by law or the maximum term that could have been imposed for any offense charged in such case.*

(d) *There is extraterritorial Federal jurisdiction over an offense under this section.*

Victim and witness protection issues have been prominent on the political scene for years, with crime victims' "Bill of Rights" acts passing in many states. As collective consciousness of this issue grows, more attention will be paid to assaults against or intimidation of witnesses or informants in the media. The officer should be aware of the need for such crimes to be reported and prosecuted. Informants should be instructed to report any activity which might constitute a violation of the act to his or her case officer.

Several cases give us some idea of what Congress had in mind by passing this legislation. The purpose of the Victim and Witness Protection Act of 1982 was to strengthen existing legal protection for victims and witnesses of federal crimes. This protection specifically extended to victims, witnesses, or informants who cooperated with the government at his or her own risk. (See *United States v. Ferrugia*, 604 F Supp. 668, ED NY, 1985, affd. without op., 779 F. 2d 36, 2nd Cir., 1985.)

Proof is required that the defendant knowingly engaged in conduct that "either caused or threatened to cause bodily injury to another person with intent to retaliate" for attendance or testimony of a witness at an official proceeding. (See *United States v. Ferrugia*, 604 F Supp. 668, ED NY, 1985, affd. without op., 779 F. 2d 36, 2nd Cir., 1985.) The government is not required to prove an intent to carry out the threat, only to show that there was an intent to retaliate for the informant or witness' actions. (See *United States v. Maggitt,* 784 F. 2d 590, 5th Cir., 1985.)

In one case involving an informant, the jury heard evidence that "snitches" were disliked and the victim of the assault testified that the defendants yelled, "You are testifying against Billy Ryan" during the attack. The appellate court ruled that the evidence was sufficient to prove that the beating was in retaliation for providing information to the government about the defendants' friend, rather than to prevent the victim from testifying. (See *United States v. Tapia,* 59 F. 3d 1137, 11th Cir., 1995.)

Congress intended that those who are affected by these crimes be notified of the existence of these statutes and the protections they afford. This notification has been incorporated directly into the informant agreements which some federal agencies (notably, the DEA and IRS) require when informants are initially registered. Informants should be told to immediately report any conduct which might be considered a violation of these statutes, and the officer should not scoff at or laugh off perceived threats or attempts to intimidate the informant. Sometimes, as Arnold Schuster found out, the threats will be real.

Liability for Acts Committed by the Informant

What sort of trouble can the government get into by taking someone who may be a felon, putting him out on the street, then listening while he tells us of the crimes he has seen? One shudders to think of the possibilities. Informants can and do maneuver themselves into all sorts of scrapes. This is not surprising; no one should expect a person to switch off the mores and habits of a lifetime just because he or she made the (almost invariably self-centered) decision to cooperate with the police. Many of the people who become informants have been unsavory characters for whom crime is a vocation. As prosecutors often point out, we find few choirboys in these ranks.

The question of our liability for the actions of these non-choirboys can be subdivided into two categories, each of which can cause the officer major headaches: (1) things informants do on their own, and (2) things informants do for law enforcement.

Things Informants Do on Their Own

The officer-informant relationship is not a 24-hour-a-day babysitting service. In fact, one of the admonitions of this book is that the officer should spend as little time as possible with the informant — enough to get the job done and no more. Adherence to this policy leaves the informant lots of free time in which to get into trouble on his own. What kind of liability do we in law enforcement have for an informant who goes bad?

Not surprisingly, there have been quite a few lawsuits brought by people who have been injured in some way by criminals who also happened to be informants. The injury may be personal (death or maiming) or financial (perhaps the informant stole money while also cooperating in another investigation). Not only will these cases threaten the law enforcement agency and its officers, they are not much good for our public image, either. One headline reading, "Police sued in local man's death: informant held," will negate the effects of a hundred stories in which an informant was instrumental in *solving* a murder.

One of these situations involved Evertt John "Crazy Horse" O'Neil, an informant for the FBI. On the night he maimed Paul Ostera, O'Neil was not working with the FBI; he was drinking at the Foxy Lady Lounge in Savannah, GA. "Crazy Horse" was on the street because he had agreed to cooperate with the FBI in exchange for a reduction of his 1-year jail term to 90 days. In the altercation that night, O'Neil attacked Ostera, blinding him in one eye. Ostera sued the U.S. government, claiming that O'Neil's release "from the South Carolina jail system by the FBI was done with willful or negligent disregard by the FBI of O'Neil's vicious propensities."

There seems to be no doubt that O'Neil was an informant and Ostera was victimized. The question facing the court was whether Ostera had a valid claim under the Federal Tort Claims Act (FTCA). The Eleventh Circuit Court of appeals ruled in *Ostera v. United States* (769 F. 2d 716, 11th Cir., 1985) that he did not, saying that a "discretionary function exception" precluded any liability for claims "based upon the exercise or performance or the failure to exercise or perform a discretionary function or duty on the part of a federal agency or an employee of the Government, whether or not the discretion involved be abused."

There was no claim that O'Neil had been acting on behalf or even with the knowledge of the government when he assaulted Ostera, only that the FBI should not have been using him as an informant, given his "vicious propensities." Even Ostera's attorneys conceded that the decision to use informants is one of those discretionary functions, but claimed the decision to use a particular (and possibly a particularly nasty) informant is the officer's, made at an operational level. The court disagreed, saying:

> *The decision to seek the release of an informant from prison is inextricably intertwined in the decision to use him as an informant. The decision to use a particular person as an informant is inextricably intertwined in the policy decision to use informants for law enforcement purposes.* "Where there is room for policy judgment and decision there is discretion. It necessarily follows that acts of subordinates in carrying out the operations of government in accordance with official directions cannot be actionable." Dalehite *(346 U.S. at 36, 73 S. Ct. at 968) Neither the decision to use a particular person as an informant nor the decision to obtain release of that person from prison is subject to judicial scrutiny under the Federal Tort Claims Act, the Government being immune from suit based on those decisions under the discretionary function exception to the Act.*

Officials performing discretionary functions are generally shielded from liability for civil damages if their conduct does not violate clearly established statutory or constitutional rights which a reasonable person would have known. (See *Pleasant v. Lovell,* 854 F. Supp. 1082, Dist. CO, 1987; quoting *Anthony v. Baker,* 767 F. 2d 657, 664, 10th Cir., 1985).

The government enjoys sovereign immunity from many lawsuits, and in *Ostera* and other cases, courts have decided that the officer is afforded qualified immunity from liability for the actions of an informant who was developed and managed in the normal course of the agency's business. In *United States v. Muniz* (374 U.S. 150, 1963), a unanimous Supreme Court warned that "the Federal Tort Claims Act provides much-needed relief to those suffering injury from the negligence of government employees. We should not, at the same time that the state courts are striving to mitigate the hardships caused by sovereign immunity, narrow the remedies provided by Congress." This warning means that care must be taken and proper procedures followed in the use of informants, for people will be watching.

Things Informants Do for Law Enforcement

Decisions such as *Ostera* protect officers in situations where the informant is acting, not on the government's behalf, but on his own. This is not the only sort of hazard on the field, however. What if the informant commits crimes or other bad acts as part of his role as an informant? This can be a big problem, especially when a very highly motivated individual may be desperate to get the evidence needed to fulfill his or her end of a plea agreement. Entrapment is only one possible product of this predicament.

In furtherance of their work as informants, cooperating individuals have been known to lie, steal, burgle, illegally intercept conversations, and generally violate the Constitutional rights of the people under investigation. None of this can be tolerated by law enforcement. This is perhaps where control of the informant is most critical, because illegal acts by the informant can jeopardize not only the investigation, but also the officer, the agency, and the system which permits us to use informants in the first place.

The first question which must be resolved is whether the informant is acting as an agent of the government or as a private person. The general rule is that if the informant is operating on the government's behalf, its agent, as it were, the same rules for evidence gathering apply to the informant as they would to the officer. In other words, the officer cannot tell the informant to go do something the officer could not do. If you cannot break into the suspect's home and search his things, you cannot send the informant over there with instructions to do the same. This is a very bright line, but of course there are grayer areas.

What if an informant has legitimate access to a suspect's home or business? Can this person bring the officer's files or the contents of the trash? The answer will depend on the nature of the relationship between officer and informant. A case involving the IRS Criminal Investigation Division challenged the government's use of an informant who was employed in the defendants' office. The individual, a Ms. Pauline Adams, learning of what she believed were illegal activities, contacted the IRS, and volunteered to provide information about these to the government. For several months, she reported on conversations, gave the agents trash from the office, and wore a concealed recording device to some meetings with the subjects of the IRS criminal investigation.

In their civil claim against the IRS agents, the defendants objected to the informant's actions. Although the trial court found that "Ms. Adams was ... not an agent, as that term is defined by common law," and that the officers who worked with her had qualified immunity, the appellate court disagreed. (See *Pleasant v. Lovell*, 876 F. 2d 787, 10th Cir., 1989.)

In *Pleasant*, the court had to do what the officer should always do in evaluating the performance of the informant — ask the basic questions: What motivated her to act as she did? What was her access? How much control did the officers have over her and her actions?

Adams testified that she was a "volunteer, non-paid informant." Her motivation for volunteering is unclear, although she had previously worked as an informant for state officers who warned that she was difficult to control. Adams claimed to have come forward out of concern that the subjects of the investigation were law violators and possibly dangerous — a "good citizen" motivation.

Her access was good. She worked in the office, handled documents, and knew all of the principals. She was put in charge of taking the discarded documents home, where she was supposed to burn them in her fireplace. This access would ultimately cause problems for the government, as the court found that simply overhearing conversations and reporting activity back to the officers would have been acceptable, but taking documents constituted an improper search.

Control, however, was the most important question. The officers claimed that Adams operated independently and was not paid or rewarded for her work. Further, she was instructed on several occasions not to do anything illegal or remove anything from the subjects' office except the trash she had permission to take.

The court rejected the officers' claim of Adams' independence, noting that IRS agents met with her on ten occasions in a 7-week period and spoke with her by phone 19 times in 9 weeks. "Should it have been apparent to [the officers] that Adams would be perceived as an agent or instrument of the government, and thus subject to the requirements of the fourth amendment? Based upon the evidence ... a reasonable special agent could not believe all of the activity of Adams was private in nature."

This finding meant that Adams, the informant, was not a "private person" in her actions, but a government agent. This had a direct bearing on the legality of Adams actions in obtaining evidence from the subjects. By taking items from the office, including the trash, Adams was effectively conducting a search and seizure. The fourth amendment protects individuals from unreasonable searches and seizures by the government. The same acts, however unreasonable, are beyond the scope of the fourth amendment when performed by a private party who is not acting with government knowledge or participation. (See *United States v. Jacobsen*, 466 U.S. 109, 1984; *Burdeau v. McDowell*, 256 U.S. 465, 1921; *United States v. Walsh*, 791 F. 2d 811, 10th Cir., 1986.)

In this case, however, the searches and seizures were conducted, not by a private party acting independently of government knowledge and participation, but by an informant who was operating under government control and with the "encouragement or acquiescence" of the officers. Where the search and seizure is a "joint venture or product of collusion between the private party and the federal agents" the fourth amendment protections do apply. (See *United States v. Ford*, 525 F. 2d 1308, 1312, 10th Cir., 1975; *United States v. Harding*, 475 F. 2d 480, 483, 10th Cir., vacated on other grounds, 414 U.S. 964, 274, 1973; *United States v. Lamport*, 787 F. 2d 474, 476, 10th Cir., cert. denied, 479 U.S. 846, 1986.)

The court cited a couple of cases that also had informants in key roles. In one of them, *United States v. Walther* (652 F. 2d 788, 9th Cir., 1981), an airline employee opened an overnight case placed in a container for express delivery, discovered contraband, and reported it to the DEA. The employee was a confidential informant of the DEA and had been rewarded for providing drug-related information. The court of appeals upheld the district court's determination that a governmental search and seizure occurred because: (1) the DEA knew or should have known that the employee was searching express packages for illegal drugs because of its extensive contact with the employee, and (2) the employee's motivation probably was for financial reward. The court emphasized the narrowness of its holding: "We merely hold that the government cannot knowingly acquiesce in and encourage directly or indirectly a private citizen to engage in activity which it is prohibited from pursuing where that citizen has no motivation other than the expectation of reward for his or her efforts."

Did the government knowingly acquiesce in the conduct? Were the informant's actions intended to assist law enforcement or to further his own ends? The answers to these questions will determine whether the individual is acting as a private person or as an agent for the government. (See *United States v. Miller*, 688 F. 2d 652, 9th Cir., 1982; *United States v. Snowadski*, 723 F. 2d 1427, 1429, 9th Cir., cert. denied, 469 U.S. 839, 1984.) These are questions the cautious investigator should be asking *before* lawsuits are filed and appellate courts get involved.

Examining Adams' role in the investigation and taking into account her voluntary status and government participation, the court said

> *In this case, [the agents] knew of and acquiesced in the conduct of Adams. She informed them periodically of her activities and made numerous deliveries of items from the subjects' offices. The summary judgment evidence does not allow us to conclude that reasonable special agents could have believed that their receipt of documents from Adams was lawful because she was a private actor ... a government official who actually knows that he is violating the law is not entitled to qualified immunity even if actions objectively reasonable.*

Pay close attention. The court is saying that the officers are not entitled to immunity from lawsuit for the actions of the informant or for their actions in directing her. The fact that Adams was not receiving the sorts of compensation — cash or leniency — common to other confidential informants did not sway the court. Nor did the fact that the officers warned Adams several times about not committing crimes or entrapment.

It is highly likely that the average informant who conducts searches or otherwise attempts to gather evidence will be considered to be acting as an agent of the government. If so, their actions — legal or illegal — will not be those of a "private citizen," but those of a government agent. If, in the course of the relationship, the officer learns that these actions are illegal, the investigation may be jeopardized and the officer's liability increased.

Criminal Activity by Informants

The next question relates to the type of illegal activity in which the informant is alleged to have been involved, and whether that activity was authorized by the police. Although the Attorney General's guidelines allow informants to be authorized to participate in illegal activity under approved circumstances, the question of whether we should be allowing informants to break the law is bound to be controversial. Dan Thomasson, editor of the Scripps Howard News Service, wrote about these "authorized" crimes for the *Washington Times*, "prompted by all these disgusting revelations:"

> *Well, according to published speculation, the bureau will demand constant review whenever it sanctions informant participation in a crime. Bully for the bureau! Why, someone should ask, does the bureau go around sanctioning anyone to commit a crime, even under the historically disreputable policy of the end justifying the means?*

These are legitimate concerns, but it is sometimes necessary to allow an informant to continue in business with the people they are informing against. In one challenge to this policy, two Boise men convicted in a prostitution-related case alleged that, by permitting two informants to continue to work as prostitutes, the government was guilty of "conduct so outrageous that due process principles would absolutely bar" the federal government from invoking judicial processes to obtain a conviction. (See *United States v. Monaco*, 700 F. 2d 577, 10th Cir., 1983.) The court noted that "both women had worked for the defendants before, and both testified they would have continued to work as prostitutes regardless of their involvement in this case."

Courts have acknowledged that, to obtain evidence of certain crimes, informants or undercover agents frequently must participate in illegal activities. Some examples include *Hampton v. United States* (425 U.S. 484, 1976; government informant presumed for purposes of decision to have supplied drugs) and *United States v. Russell* (411 U.S. at 432, 93 S. Ct. at 1643; undercover policeman supplied necessary chemical for amphetamine production). In the *Monaco* case, the "defendants had been operating their prostitution enterprise for some time; the government informants in no way induced them to continue their activities against their will." (See *United States v. Russell*, 411 U.S. at 433-34, 93 S. Ct. at 1643–44; *United States v. Gentry*, 642 F. 2d at 387–88.)

Informant agreements such as the ones in the Appendices should clearly state that illegal acts by the informant will not be tolerated and may subject the informant to prosecution. The IRS-CID form reads:

> *Informant instructed not to engage in any unlawful acts, except as specifically authorized by the IRS. Informant further advised that he/she is subject to prosecution for any unauthorized unlawful acts and that engaging in such activity could terminate any arrangement the informant has with the service.*
>
> *Informant instructed not to engage in witness tampering; witness intimidation; entrapment; or the fabrication, alteration, or destruction of evidence.*
>
> *Informant instructed that in obtaining information, he/she shall not use unlawful techniques (i.e., breaking/entering; electronic surveillance; opening/tampering with the mail, etc.). Use of the informant will be terminated and the information will not be used.*

These admonitions follow the Attorney General's Guidelines on the Use of Cooperating Individuals and Confidential Informants. The officer who fails to follow these guidelines and who acts illegally or allows an informant to act illegally risks not only damage to career and reputation but a lawsuit, as well. For an example, check out *Bivens v. Six Unknown Named Agents of the Federal Bureau of Narcotics* (403 U.S. 388, 1971). In Bivens, the Court held that liability may attach when a federal official acting under color of authority engages in unconstitutional conduct and is then held to account for that conduct in his individual capacity. However, "government officials performing discretionary functions generally are shielded from liability for civil damages insofar as their conduct does not violate clearly established statutory or constitutional rights of which a reasonable person would have known." (See *Harlow v. Fitzgerald*, 457 U.S. 800, 1982.)

Employment Issues

Another provision in the standard informant agreement that informants sign reads, "I am not an employee of the United States Government and may not represent myself as such. Further, I may not enter into any contracts or incur any obligations on behalf of the United States Government, except as specifically instructed and approved." This is a point which must be made quite clear to the informant and any other interested party. As the Attorney General's guidelines specify, "The Cooperating Individual/Confidential Informant is not an employee of the United States Government and may not represent himself or herself as such."

In olden days — prior to 1965 or so — informants were referred to as "special employees." This undoubtedly sounded much better than "snitch" or even "informer," but the title also conveyed a status which could be misperceived; it is difficult for an outsider to know the difference between a "special employee" and a "special agent." This was only one reason why the term has been dropped.

Another reason involved attempts by "special employees" to claim civil service status or some of the benefits of employment with the federal government or a police department. A good example of this sort of attempt can be found in *Moncrief v. Moncrief*, a 1998 case in the Northern District of Texas. Billy Jarvis, who was employed as a consultant by Moncrief, was also furnishing information about Moncrief's business to the IRS. When this fact became known, Moncrief sued Jarvis in State court in Texas for breach of fiduciary duty, conspiracy, intentional infliction of emotional distress, and abuse of process/malicious prosecution. Jarvis sought the protection of the U.S. government by asking the federal courts to certify that his actions as an informant effectively made him a federal employee, a ruling which would have given Jarvis qualified immunity.

This the court declined to do. Instead, it found that "Jarvis was not a federal employee, but an independent contractor with the IRS." In reaching this decision, the court looked directly at the officer-informant relationship:

> It is undisputed that (Jarvis) was hired for a specific time, was to be paid based on a percentage of recovery flowing from the one task he was to do for the IRS, and necessarily worked independently to ensure that no one would detect he was an informant for the government. Any direction from the government to Jarvis was sporadic and not based on a "right to control" over Jarvis. ... The directions given to Jarvis supplied him information that he needed to complete his singular task for the government so that he might possibly get paid.

The court found some differences between Jarvis and the informant typically used by law enforcement, although there were some similarities, as well. Specifically, Jarvis had signed an Informant Reward Agreement, which read in part:

The informant is an independent contractor and is not an employee of the Internal Revenue Service. Accordingly, the United States Government is not responsible for any tortious conduct of the Informant otherwise compensable under the Federal Tort Claims Act (28 U.S.C. § 1346(b)) and is not liable to compensate for injuries, losses, or damages sustained which would otherwise be compensable under the Federal Employees Compensation Act (5 U.S.C. § 8101) or the Military Personnel and Civilian Employees Claims Act. (31 U.S.C. § 3721).

Signing this agreement, which is not standard in most law enforcement agencies, ultimately sank Jarvis' hopes. With most informants, however, the line is much hazier. In some cases, informants who are injured as a result of their cooperation may be eligible for compensation under the Federal Employees Compensation Act. In some cases, the informant's actions may make the government liable under the Federal Tort Claims Act. State and local officers should check with their department's counsel to determine which state statutes correspond to the federal laws, if any.

But You Promised...

Another wrinkle that occasionally arises in the officer-informant relationship is a dispute over whether the officer's promises have been fulfilled. Some informants have felt strongly enough about the matter to file suit against the government, usually seeking a percentage of forfeited funds or just additional payment.

Several of these disputes have made it to court, usually with results favorable to the government. In *Salles v. United States* (156 F. 3d 1383, Fed. Cir., 1998, confidential informant Rebecca Salles sued the government, claiming she had been orally promised a "twenty-five percent commission of the value of all the money and property seized as a result of her information." The appellate court agreed with the U.S. Court of Claims, ruling that none of the government officials with whom Salles dealt had either expressed or implied contracting authority which could bind the government. Salles claim was denied.

One judge dissented, though, saying the DEA had a written agreement with Salles, whose information produced "very large monetary returns to the United States." In an admonishment to officers who work with informants, he noted that, "The integrity of the United States as a promisor is not less stringent when dealing with informants."

A second case, *Rob Roy v. United States* (38 Fed. Cl. 184, 1997), had similar results for the same basic reason. Informant Roy was "flipped" by the FBI after being arrested for selling cocaine within 1000 feet of a school. He agreed to cooperate with the Bureau in investigations which eventually lasted for over 4 years and resulted in many arrests and seizures. In return for his assistance Roy received a sentence of 5 years' probation (he had faced a mandatory minimum 5-year prison term), $84,424.77 for his expenses during the investigations, and a $100,000 lump-sum payment.

Roy claimed "the F.B.I. agents told me that I would get up to 25% of money, property seized. They also said that they would give me the following ... a new identity, relocation, protection. They have not complied with any of the above. I want justice to be done."

The Court of Claims again looked at those who allegedly made the promises to Roy, once again determining that none of the FBI agents "had the requisite authority to bind the Government to a contract." The FBI also pointed out that it had paid a $100,000 award to the informant, plus another $84,000 for his expenses. Because Roy was claiming he had been promised an award "up to 25% of all forfeiture proceeds" and the FBI had paid $100,000, the contract's language had been complied with. Roy's claim, like Salles', was denied.

Still, getting sued is no fun, so officers should avoid this unpleasantness, if possible. To forestall problems like those described above, the officer:

- Should never promise a specific percentage of a forfeiture
- Should not promise any award in any amount
- Make it clear that the officer has no power to bind the government to a set award or percentage
- Make sure the informant signs off on the Informant Agreement or equivalent document

The officer can explain the statutory authority for awards to the informant but must make it clear that the decision to pay such an award rests with someone other than the officer.

Summing Up

Working with informants is like operating in a minefield. Some of the hazards are emotional, some physical, and some legal. All can have an explosive impact on the officers involved. It is important for the officer to understand how and when an informant can be used and some of the ramifications of that decision. The law enforcement officer makes the decision to use an informant. If we are doing things correctly, we also control how the informant will be used. Knowing our responsibilities, limitations, and abilities will allow us to maintain better control over the informant and the investigation.

Ethical Considerations and Integrity

12

"Integrity without knowledge is weak and useless, and knowledge without integrity is dangerous and dreadful." —Samuel Johnson, Rasselas

"If they'll snitch for you, they'll snitch on you." —anonymous narcotics agent

At this point in our study of informants, and if this book has done any good at all, we should have some more knowledge. Our comprehension of the law relating to informants and our understanding of the psychology of those who inform make it clear that we *can* develop and use informants in law enforcement. Another, and perhaps larger, question is whether we *should*.

One of the themes of this book is that betrayal always affects more than just the betrayer and the betrayed. Weighing these effects on *everyone* involved is not an easy task, but it is one which, if we are to continue to reap the value of the informant, must be performed. Law enforcement has the primary responsibility for conducting this analysis. We are, after all, the ones who make the decision to develop the informant and to use his information in various ways. Our decisions in managing the informant — what we or the informant will do — will determine whether others who sit in judgment will approve or disapprove. Ultimately, these judges, be they Supreme Court Justices, jurors, or ordinary citizens, will decide whether the knowledge which informants can provide is too "dangerous and dreadful" for law enforcement to possess.

Noted criminal defense attorney Tony Serra wrote in January 1999:

People in the American sub-culture experience paranoia because they never know who is a spy or an informant. There's paranoia in the court system because you never know whether your co-defendant is recording you. There's paranoia among the lawyers because you never know if your own defendant is rolling behind your back and recording you. In my opinion, the singularly unexpected and singularly worst aspect of our system of criminal jurisprudence is the use of the informant.

These are words we should expect to hear from defense counsel. A vigorous defense in any case involving an informant will always include attacks on that person's credibility or character. But Serra's criticism is not directed at a single individual or instance of alleged betrayal. Instead, he expresses a sincere concern that perhaps society pays too high a price for the benefits it receives from the use of informants in the enforcement of its laws.

Most of us would undoubtedly concede the existence of evil in some of our fellows. This has certainly been reaffirmed repeatedly in the criminal history of mankind. Our attempts over the centuries to seek justice have resulted in the development of a complex system to seek justice and punish wrongdoers. Nothing in criminal justice is immutable, however. The investigative techniques used to resolve crime have evolved over the centuries. Tools which were once integral parts of law enforcement's arsenal have been removed or replaced. Once upon a time, it was a standard law enforcement tactic to brand a suspect's hand with a hot iron, then bind the wound for three days. If, at the end of the "trial," the hand was not infected, the suspect was adjudged innocent. For hundreds of years, it was legally acceptable for police officers to beat a confession out of a suspect or to break into someone's home on mere suspicion.

"Efficient" though these procedures may have been, they are gone, lost in the recognition that neither the rule of law nor the ethics which underlie civilized society can tolerate the price of such efficiency. The excuse that "this is the way we've always done business" or the claim that no alternative exists must always be weighed against the possibility that the solution, as Serra alleges, is worse than the problem.

Ethics and the Informant System

Whether an informant is used for good or ill will depend solely upon the investigator or prosecutor in the case. The role of the informant in the criminal justice system depends upon the control of this resource by those employed by the government to investigate and prosecute criminal activity. This responsibility is a weighty one, because the fate of more than just one case or the work of one informant rests upon every officer who manages (or mismanages) an informant (*United States v. Bernal-Obeso*, 989 F. 2d 331, 9th Cir., 1993):

> *A prosecutor who does not appreciate the perils of using rewarded criminals as witnesses risks compromising the truth-seeking mission of our criminal justice system. Because the Government decides whether and when to use such witnesses and what, if anything, to give them for their service, the Government stands uniquely positioned to guard against perfidy. By its action, the Government can either contribute to or eliminate the problem. Accordingly, we expect prosecutors and investigators to take all reasonable measures to safeguard the system against such treachery.*

Is the use of informants ethical? In light of the heavy impact of betrayal, one might propose, as does Serra, that it is not. How could asking someone to do something so noxious to trust be morally correct? Our guide in the study of informants, Sun Tzu, had one utilitarian and very persuasive response. He said:

> *Raising a host of a hundred thousand men and marching them great distances entails heavy loss on the people and a drain on the resources of the State. The daily expenditure will amount to a thousand ounces of silver. There will be commotion at home and abroad, and men will drop down exhausted on the highways. As many as seven hundred thousand families will be impeded in their labor.*

Hostile armies may face each other for years, striving for the victory which is decided in a single day. This being so, to remain in ignorance of the enemy's condition simply because one grudges the outlay of a hundred ounces of silver in honors and emoluments, is the height of inhumanity.

One who acts thus is no leader of men, no present help to his sovereign, no master of victory. Thus, what enables the wise sovereign and the good general to strike and conquer, and achieve things beyond the reach of ordinary men, is foreknowledge.

Simply put, by far the greater good is achieved in the result of an informant's cooperation. In Sun Tzu's example, the negative effects of not winning the battle include starvation of the people, terrible disruption to the economy, and outcomes which go far beyond the battlefield. War is hell, he reminds us. So long as the war continues, everyone will suffer. In the face of this suffering, to "remain in ignorance of the enemy's condition simply because one grudges the outlay of a hundred ounces of silver in honors and emoluments, is the height of inhumanity."

In our war on drugs and crime, the consequences of *not* using informants may be equally inhumane. Rejecting David Kaczynski because he was betraying someone could well have cost additional lives. Ignoring Emad Salem because he was betraying his friends might have resulted in exactly the sort of suffering Sun Tzu sought to avoid. At minimum, turning away would-be informants means criminals would go uncaught and wrongdoers would go unpunished. This alone has a significant, unhappy effect on the people and their justice system.

Though Serra may beg to differ, many would argue that people — at least the criminal people — in America *should* know that an informant can turn them in. Everyone who violates the law should be aware that crime of any sort will not go unreported. Let those who trample on the rights of their fellow citizens by committing crimes "experience paranoia" that they might be detected.

The law and the Constitution certainly support the use of informants generally. As the Supreme Court said, "Neither this Court nor any member of it has ever expressed the view that the Fourth Amendment protects a wrongdoer's misplaced belief that a person to whom he voluntarily confides his wrongdoing will not reveal it." (See *Hoffa v. United States,* 385 U.S. 294, 1966.) But this still leaves the moral question, one only partly addressed by Sun Tzu's utilitarian example.

Justice Felix Frankfurter, in a dissent to a decision involving an informant wearing a body wire (*On Lee v. United States,* 343 U.S. 747), roundly condemns the eavesdropping, though not the presence of the informant:

The law of this Court ought not to be open to the just charge of having been dictated by the "odious doctrine," as Mr. Justice Brandeis called it, that the end justifies the reprehensible means. To approve legally what we disapprove morally, on the ground of practical convenience, is to yield to a short-sighted view of practicality. It derives from a preoccupation with what is episodic and a disregard of long-run consequences. The method by which the state chiefly exerts and influence upon the conduct of its citizens, it was wisely said by Archbishop William Temple, is "the moral qualities which it exhibits in its own conduct." Loose talk about war against crime too easily infuses the administration of justice with the psychology and morals of war. It is hardly conducive to the soundest employment of the judicial process.

Yet the officer has a duty to enforce the law and bring evil-doers to justice. Does the use of an informant constitute the "reprehensible means" to that end alluded to by Justice Frankfurter? Philosopher Benjamin Constant wrote of deception and duty (quoted in *Ethics and the Rule of Law,* by D. Lyons):

It is a duty to tell the truth. The notion of duty is inseparable from the notion of right. A duty is what in one being corresponds to the right of another. Where there are no rights, there are no duties. To tell the truth then is a duty, but only towards him who has a right to the truth. But no man has a right to a truth that injures others.

Given these utilitarian and moral parameters, is it ethically acceptable for law enforcement to encourage the informant's betrayal? Do the ends, which, despite the noble motive of seeking justice, also include the destruction of confidence, justify the means employed? I believe that so intrusive and divisive an instrument as the informant can *only* be justified if employed against an evil-intentioned person, and then only under limited legal and moral conditions.

The criminal and his defense attorney argue that an informant's betrayal is always bad. It directly harms the individual who is betrayed and, as Mr. Serra alleges, indirectly damages the society which relies upon mutual trust and confidence for harmony. But can the criminal have it both ways? On the one hand, he betrays that mutual trust and confidence by injuring his fellows and breaking the law. On the other hand, he argues that this mutual trust and confidence are inviolate; he should never have to worry about an informant's betrayal. What duty do we have to honor this rather dubious and mostly self-serving proposition? To paraphrase Constant, we may have a duty to discourage betrayal but only towards one who has a right not to be betrayed.

Compare this analysis to law enforcement's use of deadly force. We have been given the awesome power to use deadly force — but in very limited circumstances. We encounter bad or evil people every day, but we may not shoot a person just because he is certifiably bad or evil. We are only justified in taking this extreme step if he represents a clear and present danger to us or others. Does a gun-wielding criminal have a moral right not to be shot? Can he complain that "shooting people is always morally wrong" or "bad" and, therefore, the law enforcement officer, who professes to represent "good," must adhere to that rule even though the perpetrator need not? No, the criminal forfeits his right to that argument when he adopts an evil intention and injures or threatens his fellows. Our duty in such a situation is clear.

The majority in *On Lee v. United States* wrote of this obligation: "Society can ill afford to throw away the evidence produced by the falling out, jealousies, and quarrels of those who live by outwitting the law. Certainly no one would foreclose the turning of state's evidence by denizens of the underworld. No good reason of public policy occurs to us why the Government should be deprived of the benefit of On Lee's admissions because he made them to a confidante of shady character."

Even though the employment of informants in law enforcement may be ethically justified, this technique, like deadly force, is only acceptable under certain limited conditions. For example, non-criminal behavior should be none of the law's business; no officer should use an informant (or any other investigative technique) to explore that area of our lives. There is no evil intent on the part of the subject of that investigation. This use would be unethical by both Sun Tzu's utilitarian reasoning and by Constant's analysis of truth and duty.

The officer can, in his or her development and management of the informant also cross the ethical boundary. In fact, *only* the officer can breach the barrier. Responsibility for the informant's control rests solely with law enforcement and cannot be delegated to the informant. The informant has an inherent conflict of interest and, as a Los Angeles County Grand Jury observed in 1990, "Informants do not tend to follow mores. ...This disinclination to follow societal rules extends to their willingness to defile an oath." The officer, not the informant, must take care that societal rules *are* followed, the informant's interest or inclination notwithstanding. As Judge Stephen S. Trott wrote in the *Bernal-Obeso* decision, "By its action the Government can either contribute to or eliminate the problem. Accordingly, we expect prosecutors and investigators to take all reasonable measures to safeguard the system against such treachery." There is ample room for treachery in the informant system, and only the government "by its actions" can prevent the sorts of ethical breaches which can discredit not only the informant and the officer, but the entire system.

Having established that we have the legal and ethical right to use informants, the remainder of this book examines issues of ethics and integrity which relate to *how* the informant is employed. Informants are law enforcement's most valuable tool. By behaving unethically or without integrity in our relationship with these people, we risk losing access to this tool. While this may be something for the criminals to cheer, society and justice would suffer from this loss.

Ethics and Informant Development

In developing an informant it is possible to breach the ethical boundary and behave in a way which, though it may be legal, is immoral. We could do this by lying to a potential informant or by coercing the person into acting against his or her free will. These actions not only create bad informants, they also diminish the officer and the system in the process.

Free Choice and Coercion

J. Edgar Hoover wrote in the *FBI Law Enforcement Bulletin* (June, 1955, p. 10) that, "There can be no doubt that the use of informants in law enforcement is justified. The public interest and the personal safety of those helpful citizens demand the zealous protection of their confidence. Unlike the totalitarian practice, the informant in America serves of his own free will, fulfilling one of the citizenship obligations of our democratic form of government."

Many of those who critically examine the informant system today might dispute Hoover's "free will" claim. Some allege that the heavy penalties accompanying many federal crimes force people to become informants against their will. Others say that these same severe penalties induce people to testify falsely or invent evidence against others. We cannot deny that there are ethical dangers in this situation; in providing someone with the motivation to become an informant, we may also be laying the groundwork for some of that treachery that concerned Judge Trott. Nevertheless, the foundation for the ethical development of an informant is free choice.

Following the arrest of the Watergate burglars in 1972, the conspiracy of silence and stonewalling that surrounded President Richard Nixon began to unravel. As witnesses came forward, those on the trail of criminal activity moved steadily closer to the President's door. Two who were intimately involved in both the criminal activity and its cover-up were John Dean, an attorney in the White House Counsel's office, and G. Gordon Liddy, a former FBI agent who worked with the Special Investigation Unit, also known as the "Plumbers." As the evidence against these men mounted, both chose different roads toward the climax of the Watergate scandal. Like many of those implicated, Dean chose to cooperate with the investigators. His testimony exposed President Nixon's obstruction of justice and ultimately led to the resignation of the President after an impeachment vote by the House Judiciary committee.

Always known as a "stand-up guy," Liddy chose not to cooperate. He accepted a relatively severe penalty and went to prison without agreeing to "rat" on others. Dean did some time, too, and was housed for a while in the Marshals' Witness Security Program. Dean and Liddy each made different choices. Today, both appear to be happy with their respective decisions, though society was probably much better served by Dean's pick. After all, without Dean's cooperation and that of others, President Nixon might have gotten away with his actions, heralding a political morality which recent commentators believed threatened the republic.

Liddy's decision was essentially based upon his personal acceptance of responsibility for his actions. He did the crime and was prepared to do the time. Although his failure to assist in the investigation of others in the scandal may have impeded that case, his choice does illustrate that the decision was the product of his free will; he did not *have* to cooperate, so he did not.

Every potential informant has this same choice, regardless of the motivation which brings him or her to our door. Those who act out of a mercenary motive, for revenge, or from vanity or ego obviously make this choice voluntarily, many by walking in with their information. Those who inform from fear may find their choices more limited. The threat of a 20- or 30-year sentence or even a life term in prison introduces an element of urgency to the decision. Although some would argue that this urgency at least borders on compulsion, the element of free choice is still present.

In fact, the same person facing the prison sentence chose the path which led to that point. By his actions and evil intentions, he arrived at a crossroads he may have hoped to avoid but undoubtedly knew existed. Law enforcement cannot be faulted for offering the choice, even though the alternatives are not as attractive as one would like.

The ethical line is crossed in the coercion of the innocent, or by misleading an individual so that he cannot make a free choice. For an officer to threaten an unlawful punishment or to threaten the arrest of an innocent person in order to coerce his cooperation is particularly despicable.

Recall the biblical passage (Judges 1:24–25) in which an informant delivered the key to a city: "And the spies saw a man come forth out of the city, and they said unto him, Shew us, we pray thee, the entrance into the city, and we will shew thee mercy. And when he shewed them the entrance into the city, they smote the city with the edge of the sword; but they let go the man and all his family." Few of us would argue that coercion was not inherent in this situation. Even fewer could resist this sort of compulsion. Though the use of the informant to smite the city might be justifiable on Sun Tzu's utilitarian grounds, it cannot be considered morally valid.

Misleading someone to force them into cooperating is another form of compulsion because it deprives the individual of the opportunity to make a free and fully informed choice. Telling a person that he faces incarceration for 30 years when the penalty for that offense is really 5 years is a deception which crosses the line. Also over the line was an FBI agent's testimony that he placed a non-working explosive device under a mobster's car in the hope of persuading that individual of his associates' ill will. Fear of one's criminal associates can be a very potent motivation to inform, but manufacturing that fear — either in the creative way this agent did or by the more boorish threat to put a "snitch jacket" on the individual — goes beyond the moral pale.

Promises, Promises

Virtually all officer-informant relationships begin with a pair of promises. We have already commented on the irony inherent when two people make a contract to betray the trust of a third. Nevertheless, in order for someone to become an informant, they offer certain assurances to the officer, who in turn pledges certain actions on the informant's behalf. Typically, the informant agrees to some form of cooperation with an investigation (with all that cooperation entails), and the officer promises to pay the informant, make his cooperation known to the prosecuting attorney, or fulfill whichever need motivated the informant to come forward. Promises become an ethical issue in several situations:

1. The officer makes promises he or she has neither the power nor intention to keep.
2. The officer promises to deliver secret benefits which are not disclosed to the prosecutor or the defense.
3. The officer makes an illegal promise.

The Officer Makes Promises He or She Has Neither the Power nor Intention To Keep

In the recruitment process, the informant will be seeking the best deal he or she can possibly obtain. Often, prospective informants will ask for the moon and sometimes an officer will promise just that. "I'll cooperate for full immunity," is not a condition that is within an officer's power to grant. The authority to make this decision rests with the prosecuting attorney. Appearing to accede to this wish may secure the individual's cooperation, but at an unacceptable moral price. From a practical standpoint, the informant who finds out that he or she has been deceived in this fashion is not likely to have any further trust in or use for the officer.

The Officer Promises To Deliver Secret Benefits Which Are Not Disclosed to the Prosecutor or the Defense

Secret side deals are an absolute anathema to justice. The courts only allow law enforcement to use informants if *all* promises and benefits to the informant are fully disclosed. What promises have been made bear directly on the credibility of the informant and on the ability of jurors to assess that credibility. The consequences can be fatal, as the following editorial shows.

Sex for Testimony; Federal Foot Dragging

The Virginian-Pilot *(Norfolk, VA), Tuesday, August 12, 1997*

> *Again we ask, as we will continue to ask: Why has no disciplinary action been taken against two federal agents who in 1990 allowed a drug-case witness in custody to have sex with his wife and mistress in exchange for his testimony and then failed to inform defense attorneys of the deal, in violation of federal law? The trysts in federal offices might have been kept secret, except the witness's wife bore twins nine months later.*
>
> *Because information undermining the credibility of a key witness was kept secret, three of Portsmouth's most notorious drug dealers were freed from long prison sentences, and four other dealers got reduced sentences. They were members of a gang that distributed $20 million in heroin from 1984 to 1989. U.S. Attorney Helen Fahey said she was "outraged by the fact that major drug dealers had to be released back into the community and had to have their sentences substantially reduced because of the misconduct of law-enforcement officials." Both the FBI and DEA have completed their own investigations and cleared their own agents.*
>
> *Would the FBI and DEA have us believe that the agents, both still on the job, did no wrong? A justice system that secretly pays off witnesses is misnamed. Do the FBI and DEA think it matters that the witness was rewarded with sex instead of money? Either way, the witness was paid off. Admittedly deals are often made with witnesses who cooperate, but the details should be part of the public record so jurors can assess the veracity of testimony.*

The editor is quite correct in stating that, "Either way, the witness was paid off." Because the side benefit was not disclosed, cases were compromised. In *Giglio v. United States* (405 U.S. 150, 1971), the Supreme Court ruled that "Due process requires the reversal of a judgment of conviction ... where the government failed to disclose its promise to the accused's co-conspirator, upon whose testimony the government's case almost entirely depended, that he would not be prosecuted if he testified for the government." The promise need not be immunity or leniency at sentencing. The promise of a large reward or even the opportunity to have sex are benefits which must be disclosed. Courts detest this type of secret arrangement and tend to come down very hard on those officers or prosecutors caught in it.

The Officer Makes an Illegal Promise

Sometimes an officer will make a promise that he or she has every intention of keeping but which should never have been made in the first place. This sort of promise could be to allow the informant to continue with some illegal activity or to protect the informant from arrest by other officers while he is informing. This might be a very attractive benefit for some evil-intentioned people. Although it is not one likely to be disclosed by the officer to the prosecutor, they do tend to surface in embarrassing ways. Witness the recent hearings into alleged FBI misconduct with its informants James "Whitey" Bulger and Stephen "The Rifleman" Flemmi in Boston. Flemmi, an admitted FBI informant since the 1970s, but now charged in a rack-eteering case, claimed that he had been given immunity by the FBI for all crimes except murder. "I can see the value of using you people," Bulger the informant is alleged to have told the FBI when he was recruited. "It's good to have friends in law enforcement." Both Bulger and Flemmi remained active criminals for the duration of their careers as FBI informants — a remarkable 30 and 20 years, respectively. FBI agents have admitted tipping both men off to pending indictments, allowing them to flee before other officers could arrest them.

Flemmi and Bulger unquestionably furnished significant information on organized crime to the FBI. At least one Cosa Nostra family was seriously disrupted as a result of their cooperation, and other informants were developed with their assistance. Nevertheless, the FBI has suffered terrible publicity — with the case against Flemmi and other mob figures still hanging in the balance at this writing. If the two informants were promised FBI protection of their illegal operations as long as they continued to inform, an ethical line was crossed. Officers cannot promise to overlook criminal activity they have a legal and moral duty to stop.

Ethics and Informant Management

In the modern world of Management by Objectives and Quality Circles, the officer-informant relationship is certainly unique. There is no shared decision making or delegation of authority here, only the officer's control. Anything which interferes with that control can incur an immense cost to the informant, the officer, the department, and to the justice system itself.

Maintenance of that control is not a matter of harsh, unyielding, absolute discipline. Nothing but resentment flourishes in that environment. Control is maintained through mutual respect — the officer must respect the informant's position and the forces which led him to this point. The informant must respect the officer's authority and superior role. The officer's integrity provides the foundation for this mutual respect.

John Good, the FBI agent who managed ABSCAM informant Mel Weinberg, describes this relationship (in R.W. Greene's *The Sting Man*):

> *There is one basic secret to dealing with informants. You've got to give them respect. No matter what they might have done in the past, they are still human beings. These people have pride. To be called a stool pigeon, a canary, a fink is demeaning. They know what the words mean. They have to know that you are sincere, that you will keep your promises,*

that you value what they are doing. There's a chemistry to the relationship. It has to be based upon mutual trust. They have to know that you won't let them down as long as they follow the ground rules, and the ground rules have to be clear from the beginning of the relationship. There are times when you have to bend a little with them, be a little flexible. This doesn't mean that you condone anything improper, but you have to understand that they are going against their basic nature when they cooperate with law enforcement. It isn't easy for them and they don't approach situations with your moral and professional point of view. You have to understand that they come from a different world with different codes of behavior.

Some basic rules will cover most of the integrity issues that surface in the course of an officer-informant relationship. Remember that these rules function to protect everyone involved, and to maintain the control required in order for the relationship to be successful. They can also delineate the ethical use of an informant from the unethical.

1. Take nothing from an informant but information.
2. Give nothing to an informant except that which is officially promised.
3. Do not abuse your association with the informant.
4. Have no relationship but the official, professional one.
5. Honor your obligations where it is legally and ethically possible to do so.
6. Do not break the law to enforce the law, or allow the informant to do so.

Integrity

Listing the ways in which an officer can screw up with regard to an informant is a depressing enterprise which would take much more room than we have here. Make an inventory of every bad motivation you can think of, then add stupidity and carelessness, and you will have a very lengthy menu of bad choices, indeed. Although officers do fall into these miniature firestorms (many of which they started themselves), integrity problems with informants are not routine. What prevents these bad things from happening every day? To paraphrase Smokey Bear, only YOU can prevent these fires.

Management can make the rules that govern our conduct with informants. Most law enforcement agencies have several pages of regulations and procedures covering every aspect of the development and management process. Administrators know from long experience about the heat that can come from an officer-informant relationship gone astray. The legislature and the courts also have input into how the relationship is conducted. Laws may be passed restricting how and when an informant can be used. The courts put their own very emphatic stamp on our activity, throwing out cases in which officer or informant misconduct infringes on the defendant's rights.

Even citizens, in their roles as jurors in either criminal or civil cases, can have some say where integrity goes missing. All of these people look at law enforcement and its informants with a very critical eye. None has very high expectations for the informant. Jurors do expect more from us, however — not only that we will do our jobs capably and efficiently, but that we will also act with integrity. We must not only know the rules, we are ultimately the ones who will determine whether they will be enforced.

News clippings that follow illustrate some of the ethical lapses in informant management. Remember that the responsibility for preventing each of these little disasters resides primarily with the officer who allegedly committed the ethical breach.

Customs Accused of Being Lax on Corrupt Agents

Miami Herald, *February 14, 1999*

U.S. Senate and Treasury investigators have launched simultaneous nationwide probes of alleged mismanagement within the U.S. Customs Service, questioning systematic cronyism and undeserved leniency toward favored employees who break the law.

Both investigations were prompted in part by news reports that found dozens of examples of careers that flourished after misdeeds such as dating drug smugglers, tampering with evidence, skimming seized drug cash, having sex with a paid informant and other crimes and policy violations.

Integrity is doing the right thing even when nobody is looking, but in the officer-informant relationship someone is *always* looking. It is usually the informant, who invariably watches the officer's actions with the keenest interest, but, as the story above illustrates, lapses in integrity can come to others' attention as well.

Take Nothing from an Informant but Information

Robert Leuci, the NYPD Detective whose story formed the basis for *Prince of the City*, had admittedly improper relationships with a number of informants. One, a super-informant known as "The Baron," sold two cars to Leuci. The Baron later claimed that Leuci had given him heroin for the cars, which investigators found were titled in Leuci's wife's name:

"Those cars are mine," said Leuci, "but I never gave him narcotics for them. I paid for both of them. One was an old bomb, and the other was better. I probably paid in cash for them. I don't know."

"So you actually have those cars?" said Morvillo. "How the hell can you take cars from an informant?"

"This happened a long time ago," said Leuci. "The guy owned a taxi cab company. He owned a fleet of cars. I got cars from him for a couple of hundred dollars. I would have had to pay seven or eight hundred someplace else."

"He's an informant," said Morvillo. "You don't take things from informants."

No, you don't. And if you do, you may end up answering the same sort of unpleasant questions Leuci did. Informants are sources of information and nothing else. Taking anything from an informant raises a conflict of interest and diminishes the officer's control over that individual. This is a very dangerous situation for the officer. Informants have access to all sorts of attractive goods and services — stolen property, cash, illegal drugs, or even licit goods, such as The Baron's used cars.

Taking advantage of the informant's connections may be tempting; getting something for nothing or at deep discount is always attractive. The actual price can be quite high, however. In the FBI's Flemmi-Bulger informant fiasco in Boston, one agent admitted accepting small gifts from the informants, others exchanged Christmas gifts, and another received $1000 in cash so his girlfriend could fly to meet him at a conference. The damage to the reputations of these agents and the FBI is irreparable, and the fallout continues.

Officer Put on Restricted Duty

The Fort Worth Star-Telegram, *November 15, 1997*

A ... narcotics officer has been placed on restricted duty amid allegations that he coerced a drug informant to have sex on three occasions during the summer, officials said.

...If the case is presented to the grand jury, the panel would consider whether it consti-tutes sexual assault...

The officer can lose more than reputation. Behavior with an informant which is unethical can be illegal, as well. In the above case, criminal charges could result from the officer's alleged improper relationship with the informant. She claims that he took something from her by force, using his position and power to make her submit to what could amount to a sexual assault. There is nothing an informant has — including her information — which should compel an officer to abandon his ethical standards in taking it. By doing so, the officer risks paying an almost incalculable price.

Give Nothing to an Informant Except That Which Is Officially Promised

It sometimes seems that informants are almost always asking for something: Can you get me a few dollars? Can you get me out of jail? Can you make sure my family is safe? Whether these requests should be granted will depend upon the circumstances, and upon the "ground rules" of which FBI Agent Good spoke earlier. Some requests, such as Detective Leuci's informants' pleas for heroin, are obviously improper, while others may be part of the deal.

If it is part of the deal, it has to be official — and on the record. Major cases have been overturned on appeal because the officers cut side deals for continued cooperation by key witnesses. It is easy to rationalize these deals; a prosecution which may have taken years and millions of dollars to put together depends on the testimony of a few former accomplices. Granting a request for some small favor or trivial item may seem insignificant, but the courts feel otherwise.

One of the best examples of this sort of disaster is the federal prosecution of the notorious Chicago-based El Rukn street gang. Allegations against the 38 defendants included murder, extortion, robbery, fraud, drug trafficking, and weapons possession. Cases had to be retried after a judge found that "substantial evidence reflecting adversely on the reliability and biases of the El Rukn inmate witnesses was not disclosed to defense counsel before or during trial." Among the benefits provided to these inmate witnesses were "drug use while in custody as protected government witnesses; disciplinary actions and non-enforcement of disciplinary measures; failure to conduct routine drug testing; permissive and lax security measures, giving El Rukn inmate witnesses access to internal prosecution memoranda, drugs, sex, and unlim-ited free telephone calls; and various gifts, including cash, clothing, 'Walkman' radios, food, cigarettes, and beer." (See *United States v. Doyle*, 121 F. 3d 1078, 1997.)

Some of these items are perfectly legal and can easily be made part of a cooperation agree-ment. There is no question that they are all a form of payment, however, and must be completely disclosed. These were not, and the prosecution paid a stiff price for their concealment.

Some of the benefits enjoyed by the El Rukn inmate witnesses are completely improper and demean the provider. Certainly they will be the cause of intense criticism if revealed, as any such ethical breach should be. For additional information concerning the "favor currying between the government and the cooperating El Rukn witnesses," refer to *United States v. Burnside* (824 F. Supp. 1215, N.D. Ill., 1993); *United States v. Boyd* (833 F. Supp. 1277, N.D. Ill. 1993); and *United States v. Bates* (843 F. Supp. 179, 1994).

Do Not Abuse Your Association with the Informant

Working with informants puts law enforcement officers in intimate contact with criminals. This association creates several opportunities for the unethical to exploit the informant's access.

Overlooking Criminal Activity by Informants

Jerome Skolnick, who studied law enforcement in three California cities, observed that the police in those towns relied heavily on informants. He also noted that burglary detectives tended to tolerate narcotics offenses committed by their informants, while narcotics detectives tended to indulge burglaries committed by theirs. It appeared to Skolnick that as long as the informants were providing information relevant to the detectives' function, those other crimes were someone else's problem.

The officer cannot send the message that *any* crime is going to be tolerated. This is a key part of the informant agreement all should sign before agreeing to become informants. By overlooking criminal activity, the officer is ceding control to the informant. The moral or ethical justification for using informants is lost in such a situation.

A Gang's Unlikely Ally: The FBI.
Agent's Handling of Boston Mob Informant Roils Bureau

The Washington Post, *January 12, 1999*

"I can see the value of using you people," Whitey Bulger said when the agent first suggested he become an FBI informant. "It's good to have friends in law enforcement."

After a remarkable series of court hearings over the last year, it is clear Bulger was right. A barrage of evidence revealed that during the '70s and '80s, the FBI acted as a virtual protection racket for Bulger and his Winter Hill sidekick, Stephen "the Rifleman" Flemmi, turning a blind eye to their crimes in exchange for information that helped take down the New England Mafia.

As productive as the informant may be — and Whitey Bulger was a "once in a lifetime" informant, according to his handler — allowing him to continue to commit crimes for 20 years is undoubtedly something the FBI would not sanction today. In fact, the Justice Department is in the process of reviewing its guidelines for informant handling to prevent such a fiasco from reoccurring. In the meantime, the Bureau must bear the public's scorn for acting "as a virtual protection racket" for gangsters.

As John Good, an experienced FBI informant handler, said (in R.W. Greene's *The Sting Man*), "They have to know that you won't let them down as long as they follow the ground rules, and the ground rules have to be clear from the beginning of the relationship. There are times when you have to bend a little with them, be a little flexible. This doesn't mean that you condone anything improper." By condoning the improper, the officer allows himself or herself to become the informant's tool, rather than the other way around. Because the informant is acting with evil intent in continuing his criminal activity, the officer's ethical justification for using the informant is completely dissipated.

Using the Informant to Commit Crimes

In the days of Francois Vidocq and Jonathan Wild, officers conspired with informants to steal property which the officer could then recover and return for a price. This system was practically an institution for over 100 years. Officers no longer qualify for such rewards today, but some unethical officers may still find ways to exploit their association with someone who is willing to commit crimes.

FBI Agent Admits Taking Bribes; Man Gave Coke Dealer Inside Scoop

The Times-Picayune, *April 3, 1998*

A New Orleans FBI agent and former world-class sprinter pleaded guilty Thursday to taking $6000 in bribes from a cocaine dealer in exchange for information about drug *investigations. As part of a plea bargain, federal prosecutors dropped a charge accusing the agent of setting up a drug deal so he could confiscate and keep a second dealer's cash.*

The agent's arrest stemmed from a two-month investigation that began when an informant told FBI officials the agent had offered to help him in exchange for money. Through his attorney, the informant produced tape-recorded conversations he had had with the agent about a $1000 payment he had made to the agent, according to a sworn statement from an FBI official who interviewed the informant.

The narcotics business is a fertile field for corruption. There is a tremendous amount of money involved, and the landscape is peopled with informants. An officer who uses one of these informants to arrange drug deals, robberies, thefts, or other acts which benefit the officer has clearly crossed into unethical territory.

Benefiting from Confidential Information

Officers may have a number of opportunities to benefit from the confidential information provided by an informant. Consider this scenario. A reliable informant with ties to known gamblers reports that a syndicate has succeeded in fixing the outcome of a major sporting event. Would it be proper for the officer to get some of his own money down on the pre-determined outcome of this event?

Informants provide information, much of which can be used in prosecutions and some of which could be exploited for personal gain. Even the knowledge that an individual *is* an informant can be used for the benefit of the unscrupulous officer.

List of Police Informers "Leaked to Underworld"

Birmingham (England) Post, *October 12, 1998*

A major corruption inquiry is under way amid allegations that a secret list of police informants has been leaked to the criminal underworld ... It is feared that the informants ... could be in danger if the list fell into the hands of violent criminals.

Some officers have also taken advantage of their access to the funds used to support undercover programs and informants. The government entrusts some in law enforcement with the money used to pay informants or provide for their security or protection. This has led to some integrity problems in the past, one of which is illustrated below.

Federal Jury in San Francisco Convicts Former DEA Supervisor

Federal Times, *May 27, 1998*

A jury in the U.S. District Court yesterday convicted a former supervisor of the Drug Enforcement Administration, on all thirteen counts of an indictment charging him with mail fraud, theft from the government, and making false statements. The DEA kept an imprest fund in San Francisco to make undercover drug purchases and to pay informants. The jury found that the supervisor used his supervisory position to obtain money from the imprest fund, divert it to his own use, and then to cover up the crime with forged documents.

Have No Relationship but the Official, Professional One

Most agencies have regulations barring social or other contacts with informants by their officers. We are compelled by circumstances, they say, to deal with criminals, but we insist on a certain level of professional detachment. As we have seen, this detachment protects all concerned, but it also prevents the sort of moral hazards which accompany access, motivation, and lack of control.

A relationship between officer and informant can be extremely close. In the course of an investigation, an officer may spend hours every day with an informant, sometimes for weeks or months at a time. As they work toward a common goal, there may be shared danger or adversity. The mutual dependence of the relationship can easily be transformed into an unhealthy intimacy.

State Police Fire 18-Year Veteran for Improper Conduct

The Associated Press State and Local Wire, September 22, 1998

> *An 18-year veteran of the ... State Police accused of pressuring a drug informant into having sex has been fired. The undercover detective was dismissed for "violations of rules, regulations and department policies."*

In the ongoing Bulger-Flemmi informant scandal in Boston, FBI agents were compromised in a variety of ways, several because they had social relationships with the known criminals who also happened to be informants. One agent admitted that he had had one informant home for dinner. Another referred to one of the informants as his "friend." The officer-informant relationship endured for so long — decades in this case — that familiarity appears to have led to contempt.

The need to avoid this sort of compromise is the basis for the military's long-standing prohibition of fraternization between officers and enlisted personnel. Each person in that professional relationship has a clearly defined superior-subordinate role, one which is threatened by excessive familiarity or the formation of non-professional ties.

A Gang's Unlikely Ally: The FBI.
Agent's Handling of Boston Mob Informant Roils Bureau

The Washington Post, *January 12, 1999*

> *The fiasco has already had a national impact, prompting the Justice Department to revamp its guidelines for handling secret informants. The hearings spotlighted a series of FBI agents who socialized with the two snitches, exchanged Christmas gifts with them, ignored damning allegations about them, shielded them from investigations by other agencies and, in the case of one, accepted bribes from them.*

Honor Your Obligations Where It Is
Legally and Ethically Possible To Do So

Throughout the relationship, the officer's word will be tested. Informants are looking toward the resolution of their situation and the fulfillment of the promises made at the time of their recruitment. As they work with the officer, informants will attempt to determine through an examination process whether the officer can be trusted or not. It is important for the officer to pass the test, not only from a practical, but from an ethical perspective as well. The officer is duty bound to honor a legitimate obligation to an informant. For this reason alone, the officer's word should be given sparingly and with the greatest forethought.

Police Don't Keep Word, Informants' Lawyers Say

The Palm Beach Post, *July 21, 1997*

> *Like many criminals, she made a deal with police. For the informant, the deal turned sour. She was beaten senseless and sent to jail.*

We have a commitment, either spoken or unspoken, to protect those who agree to cooperate in our investigations. This is a moral obligation, with practical ramifications. People can be hurt or killed by way of their decision to aid law enforcement. No moral person would want this death or injury on his or her conscience. That person would take the necessary steps to prevent harm befalling someone who is effectively in their care.

There are wider ramifications, however. As noted previously, someone is always watching the officer's actions with the informant. If the officer fails to honor this commitment, not only the informant but others will notice. Some will decide that the risk is too great, and the value of their information will be lost. Others may take this opportunity to attack the officer or the informant system.

Slain Youth's Work as Informant Detailed

Los Angeles Times, *April 2, 1998*

> *Chad MacDonald, Jr., the Yorba Linda teenager who was tortured and killed last month, had worked as an informant for the Brea Police Department until 10 days before his body was found, according to documents released Wednesday.*

How far does the commitment to honor an obligation extend? Far enough that it can create a moral dilemma — the Hobson's choice between two unappealing ethical questions. Perhaps the best solution is not to create an obligation that you regret but are duty bound to defend later.

A Gang's Unlikely Ally: The FBI.
Agent's Handling of Boston Mob Informant Roils Bureau

The Washington Post, *January 12, 1999*

> *The agent said his superiors explicitly gave the two informants free rein to run gambling and loan-sharking operations. He said they could even extort "rent," as long as they didn't engage in "serious violence, you know, violence violence." And the way the agent sees it, a deal is a deal, even a deal with the devil.*
> *"You know," he said, "where I come from, a guy's word is all he's got."*

Don't Break the Law To Enforce the Law, or Allow the Informant To Do So

Another tempting trap for the unwary. We operate very close to the ethical line in our dealings with informant. The distinction between a solid case and illegal entrapment can be razor thin. Informants who know that an officer will cross the line will do so as well. If the officer perjures himself, the informant will view perjury as an approved method of investigation. If the officer knows about an informant's entrapment or perjury and does nothing about it, control of that informant is gone forever.

Judges, jurors, and ordinary citizens are *extremely* concerned about the possibility that an informant might, through a sense of misplaced zeal or plain evil intent, fabricate a case against an innocent person. The rules governing law enforcement's investigative techniques are put in place to avoid exactly this sort of injustice from occurring. By ignoring the rules or allowing the informant to do so, the officer's use of the informant becomes unethical, improper, and possibly illegal. The following example illustrates this point. In reviewing it, consider not only the ethical implications, but the impact this type of story will have on citizens called to serve as jurors on future cases in which an informant will testify.

Former Drug Agents Indicted.
They're Charged with Fabricating Evidence

The Providence Journal-Bulletin, *October 8, 1998*

Four men who once worked for the Attorney General's elite narcotics Strike Force were accused in federal court yesterday of violating the constitutional rights of seven Rhode Island citizens by arresting them on trumped-up drug charges.

Three former agents, along with their one-time star informant, allegedly filed false affidavits and witness statements to support the arrests of seven people during undercover drug operations in 1994 and 1995.

The purpose and object of the conspiracy was to falsely charge and criminally prosecute individuals without regard to their guilt or innocence," the indictment charges.

This case gives the court great concern about the integrity of the criminal-justice system and raised issues that go to the very core of our criminal justice system.

It is ironic, though perhaps fitting, that honor and integrity should play such a large role in the process of betrayal. I have no doubt that society would not tolerate the law enforcement use of confidential informants were it not for the integrity of the officers who control the informants. We will find no honor among the evil-intentioned thieves who are the targets of our investigations, and little enough in the informants we use in those cases. Only our ethical standards keep us from playing the dishonorable role Justice Frankfurter described in the *On Lee* (343 U.S. 747, 1952; quoting *Olmstead v. United States*, 277 U.S. 438) decision: "In all matters of social policy we have to choose, and it was the hardy philosophy of life that his years in the Army of the Potomac taught him that led Mr. Justice Holmes to deem it 'a less evil that some criminals should escape than that the government should play an ignoble part.'"

While the informant can make the free choice to inform, only the officer can choose a noble or ignoble role in the informant's action. As the examples in this chapter show, some have chosen poorly. Still, it is the basic integrity of the officer that enables the system to work and to be an ethical part of law enforcement.

Case Study: Judas and the Betrayal of Jesus

No discussion of informants would be complete without at least touching on the most infamous of the lot — Judas Iscariot. Still reviled after two millenia, Judas' name is synonymous with betrayal. His example is instructive; the practice of using informants in law enforcement has not changed much in all those centuries.

Those in law enforcement who still work with informants might like to disassociate themselves from this arch-traitor, but this will never be possible for two reasons. First, history has him pegged right; there is no escaping the fact that Judas was a police informant, complete with motivation, access, and control. Second, by his betrayal he became instrumental in the creation of a major religion with billions of adherents; he is, in short, rather widely known.

In the view of the authorities of 32 A.D. Jerusalem, Jesus was a troublemaker. Those in power, including the Romans, the high priests, and the Pharisees wanted him out of the way, preferably permanently. Having come to Jerusalem, the seat of the high priests' jurisdiction, undoubtedly (in their view) to stir up even more trouble among the people, Jesus made himself more vulnerable to arrest.

This was not to be an easy task, however. Jesus was always surrounded by twelve men, his disciples, at least some of whom were armed and prepared to defend their teacher. Indeed, on the night of his arrest, one disciple lopped the ear of one of the arresting officers. Of greater concern was Jesus' popularity among the masses. The people of Jerusalem flocked around him, and their reaction to his arrest was unpredictable. The possibility that there might be a riot or popular uprising was unsettling to the all-powerful.

Into their councils walked the solution to the problem. Judas Iscariot, one of the twelve, offered his services. Not only did he know the places where Jesus and his disciples could be found, he could also take officers there at a time when none of "the multitude" would be present. As an added bonus, Judas could identify the man he would betray, thereby preventing the embarrassing possibility that the priests and their police might grab the wrong messiah.

Judas came cheap. He sold out for 30 pieces of silver, probably Tyrian shekels. The religious police moved quickly. Judas led them to the garden where Jesus was resting with his disciples, identified him with a kiss, then watched as he was dragged off into martyrdom.

Judas' own fate was not pretty. After learning that Jesus was condemned to die, he tried to return the money, claiming it was tainted with innocent blood. Spurned and overcome with guilt over his betrayal, he hanged himself, thereby completing this notorious tale.

Analysis

Judas was a far more complex individual than the story lets on. Imagine for a moment the world in which Judas lived. He dwelt daily in the presence of a man whom he and all those around him believed to be the son of God. Those who lived and traveled with Judas were the true believers, forming a tight-knit group that uniformly adhered to the concept that this group, led by their teacher, would bring salvation to the world. What could have motivated such a person to betray all in whom he trusted and believed? How could this person "sell out" for mere money? These questions will be forever unanswered and we may never understand Judas, the man, but viewed in the context of this book we can understand a little of Judas, the informant.

Motivation

The obvious motivation is the one most cited — the 30 silver coins. This makes Judas a mercenary informant, which casts him in an even less sympathetic light in popular opinion. Money is a convenient, easily understood motivation, but not necessarily the correct one in this instance. As we have seen with other informants, the most obvious motivation is not always the most important to the informant.

Looking at this situation from our experience with other informants, it seems unlikely that money was the prime motivator in Judas' case. There was undoubtedly a reward on Jesus' head. Something that sounds very much like a wanted poster was signed by Pontius Pilate and quoted by the Jewish historian Josephus. Although money is not specifically mentioned, a reward for the capture of this "man of magical power ... whom certain Greeks call a son of God" could have been a tempting part of the package.

The scriptures offer a couple of clues to other motives which might have been at work. In the Gospel of Luke (22:3–6), Judas goes to the high priests first, who then agree to pay him:

Then entered Satan into Judas surnamed Iscariot, being of the number of the twelve.

And he went his way, and communed with the chief priests and captains, how he might betray him unto them.

And they were glad, and covenanted to give him money.

And he promised, and sought opportunity to betray him unto them in the absence of the multitudes.

While Satan's direct presence cannot be ruled out as a motivating force, it is more probable that Judas was driven by jealousy or some other emotional stimulus. As is the case with the desire for revenge, something common to other informants, this is a fleeting and short-lived, though intense emotion. Judas got over it quickly, returning in the Gospel of Matthew (27:3–5):

> Then Judas, which had betrayed him, when he saw that he was condemned, repented himself, and brought again the thirty pieces of silver to the chief priests and elders,
>   Saying, I have sinned in that I have betrayed the innocent blood. And they said, What is that to us? see thou to that.
>   And he cast down the pieces of silver in the temple, and departed, and went and hanged himself.

Whatever his motivation, the authorities acted quickly on the information, not giving their informant a chance to change his mind or flip back. In his defense, it does not appear that Judas knew Jesus would be condemned to death; when he found out that this was the case, he "repented" and tried to give back the money — too late.

Was there a perverse motivation for Judas' betrayal? It always behooves the officer to ask the *cui bono* question when dealing with a walk-in informant. In this instance, Judas could have been plotting to take over the group, eliminate competition, or discredit a rival. A perverse motivation cannot be eliminated in this case, and officers should always be alert for that possibility 2000 years later.

Access

As one of the twelve disciples, Judas was a member of Jesus' inner circle. He was perfectly placed to betray the trust of his teacher and the others in the group. When Jesus predicted that one of those at the Last Supper would betray him, he knew that only those who first belong can be in a position to betray. Those at the table were the ones who had the best access and the most information. Again, the Gospels (John 18:2) talk about this access:

> And Judas also, which betrayed him, knew the place: for Jesus oft times resorted thither with his disciples.

Judging from the mob's harsh feelings toward Jesus at his trial, there were a lot of people in Jerusalem who would have been prepared to turn him in for some reward money. These people lacked the access which those close to Jesus possessed. Among those who did have the access, only one had the motivation to actually provide the information to the police.

Control

As was the case in the apprehension of John Dillinger, the officers needed to locate a wanted person. They also wanted to take him in a non-public setting to avoid interference by supporters. According to the Gospels of John and Luke (John 18:3), Judas led the raid party to the garden, identified Jesus, then stepped aside (or fell to the ground) as he was arrested:

> Judas then, having received a band of men and officers from the chief priests and Pharisees, cometh thither with lanterns and torches and weapons.

Appendices

Appendix A.
Source Debriefing Guide

The following source debriefing guide was obtained from the *Financial Investigations Checklist* (U.S. Department of Justice, 1992):

A.   Who are the members of the group?
1.   How do you know?
2.   What evidence do you have?
a.   Phone books
b.   Toll records
c.   Photographs
3.   What role does each member have?
4.   What are the relationships among the members?
5.   Who are the key people?
6.   Who are their friends?
7.   Who are their girl/boyfriends?

B.   What are the criminal enterprises of the group?
1.   Critical to know for affidavit wording:
a.   Money launderers have certain records.
b.   Traffickers have different records.
2.   The affiant's experience identifies which types of records are maintained by which type of criminal enterprise.

C.   What are the receipts of the criminal enterprise?
1.   What volume of drugs are distributed per week/month/year?
2.   What are the expenses?
a.   Personnel
b.   Stash house
c.   Car rentals
d.   Cellular phones, etc.

3. Gross receipts (or cash on hand) = drugs sold per week − (cost of drugs + additional expenses)
    a. Use to show probable cause that cash will be on premises
4. What is the purity of the drugs received from the source?
5. What is the purity of the drugs when sold?
6. On what days are collections of drug proceeds made?
    a. Where are collections made?
    b. From whom are collections made?
    c. Who makes the collections?
    d. What denominations of currency are received?
    e. What does the organization do with the collections?
        i.   Is there a counting house?
        ii. Does the organization use a launderer?
        iii. Is the currency converted to larger bills?
        iv. Is the currency converted to money orders, checks, or other financial instruments?
        v.   Is the currency deposited into bank accounts or through other financial institutions?
             (1) Name and address of institution
             (2) Account numbers
             (3) Office or branch used
        vi. Is the currency negotiated through one or more businesses?

D. What front companies are used?
    1. Where do they bank?
    2. Who is their accountant?
    3. Who is their bookkeeper?
    4. Who is their stock broker?
    5. Who is their real estate broker?
    6. Where do they receive their mail from?
    7. Who is their attorney?
        a. Does the same attorney represent all the companies?
        b. Is the attorney compromised?
            i.   How is he/she compromised?
            ii. How is the attorney paid?

E. What records do the companies or principals maintain?
    1. What computers do they use?
    2. What computer software do they use?
    3. Where are the records kept?
        a. Where did the informant see the records?
        b. Who else was present?
    4. Who keeps the records?
    5. Who are the company's customers?
    6. Who are the company's suppliers?
    7. Who hauls the company's trash?

8. Do any of the subjects carry phone directories or computer data banks on their persons?

9. What is their beeper or cellular telephone number?

F. What assets do the subjects or their companies own?
1. Real estate
    a. Who owns it?
    b. Who is the registered owner?
       i. When was the property bought?
       ii. Who was it purchased from?
       iii. How was it paid for?
    c. What cars visit the property?
    d. Is there is evidence of the subjects' arrivals and departures?
    e. Where does the mail to the property come from?
    f. Who uses the property as a return address?
    g. Who pays for the phone and utilities?
2. Do any of the subjects own:
    a. Expensive jewelry?
    b. Furs?
    c. Cars?
    d. Boats?
    e. Airplanes?
    f. Gold or other precious metals?
    g. Art work?
    h. Antiques?
       i. What are the details of the purchase?
       ii. When did they buy it?
       iii. Where did they buy it?
       iv. From whom did they buy it?
       v. How did they pay for it?
       vi. Where is the property stored?
       vii. Who is the registered owner?
3. Do any of the subjects keep large amounts of cash...
    a. On their person?
    b. In their house?
    c. In their office?
    d. In their vehicle?
    e. In a bank safe deposit box?
    f. Elsewhere?
       i. Is the cash hidden?
       ii. Have they built hidden stash locations in their house, car, or office?

G. What are the favorite places of entertainment?
1. What credit cards do the subjects use?
2. What are their shopping habits?
3. What stores do they frequent?

4. Do they buy with cash, check, or credit card?
5. What trips have they taken?
6. Do they gamble?
    a. What types of gambling are they involved in?
        i.   Casinos
        ii.   Sports
        iii. Floating crap games
        iv.   Other bookmaking
    b. Do they have a favorite bookie?
    c. Do they have casino accounts?
7. Where do they go on vacation?
    a. What travel agent do they use?
    b. Where did they go?
    c. When did they go?
    d. What is their favorite vacation spot?
    e. What airlines do they use?
    f. What rental car companies do they use?

In addition to the above questions, we would suggest that informants or witnesses also be asked questions about other sources of funds, in anticipation of potential defenses raised by the subjects.

H. What legitimate income has the subject had over the past five years?
    1. Income from legitimate employment
    2. Income from trusts, gifts, insurance, or legal claims
    3. Income from foreign countries
    4. Proceeds of loans

Appendix B. Federal Sentencing Guidelines

Provisions Relating to Informants — Substantial Assistance

Chapter One. Introduction and General Application Principles

Part B. General Application Principles

Title 18 U.S.C. Appendix § 1B1.4 (1998)

§ 1B1.4. *Information To Be Used in Imposing Sentence (Selecting a Point Within the Guideline Range or Departing from the Guidelines)*

In determining the sentence to impose within the guideline range, or whether a departure from the guidelines is warranted, the court may consider, without limitation, any information concerning the background, character and conduct of the defendant, unless otherwise prohibited by law (see 18 U.S.C. § 3661).

Title 18 U.S.C. Appendix § 1B1.10 (1998)

§ 1B1.10. *Reduction in Term of Imprisonment as a Result of Amended Guideline Range (Policy Statement)*

    (a) Where a defendant is serving a term of imprisonment, and the guideline range applicable to that defendant has subsequently been lowered as a result of an amendment to the Guidelines Manual listed in subsection (c) below, a reduction in the defendant's term of imprisonment is authorized under 18 U.S.C. § 3582(c)(2). If none of the amendments listed in subsection (c) is applicable, a reduction in the defendant's term of imprisonment under 18 U.S.C. § 3582(c)(2) is not consistent with this policy statement and thus is not authorized.

    (b) In determining whether, and to what extent, a reduction in the term of imprisonment is warranted for a defendant eligible for consideration under 18 U.S.C. § 3582(c)(2), the court should consider the term of imprisonment that it would have imposed had the amendment(s) to the guidelines listed in subsection (c) been in effect at the time the defendant was sentenced, except that in no event may the reduced term of imprisonment be less than the term of imprisonment the defendant has already served.

Chapter Five. Determining the Sentence

Part K. Departures. 1. Substantial Assistance to Authorities

Title 18 U.S.C. Appendix § 5K1.1 (1998)
§ 5K1.1. *Substantial Assistance to Authorities (Policy Statement)*

Upon motion of the government stating that the defendant has provided substantial assistance in the investigation or prosecution of another person who has committed an offense, the court may depart from the guidelines.

  (a) The appropriate reduction shall be determined by the court for reasons stated that may include, but are not limited to, consideration of the following:

      (1) the court's evaluation of the significance and usefulness of the defendant's assistance, taking into consideration the government's evaluation of the assistance rendered;

      (2) the truthfulness, completeness, and reliability of any information or testimony provided by the defendant;

      (3) the nature and extent of the defendant's assistance;

      (4) any injury suffered, or any danger or risk of injury to the defendant or his family resulting from his assistance;

      (5) the timeliness of the defendant's assistance.

Commentary

Application Notes:

1. Under circumstances set forth in 18 U.S.C. § 3553(e) and 28 U.S.C. § 994(n), as amended, substantial assistance in the investigation or prosecution of another person who has committed an offense may justify a sentence below a statutorily required minimum sentence.

2. The sentencing reduction for assistance to authorities shall be considered independently of any reduction for acceptance of responsibility. Substantial assistance is directed to the investigation and prosecution of criminal activities by persons other than the defendant, while acceptance of responsibility is directed to the defendant's affirmative recognition of responsibility for his own conduct.

3. Substantial weight should be given to the government's evaluation of the extent of the defendant's assistance, particularly where the extent and value of the assistance are difficult to ascertain.

Background

A defendant's assistance to authorities in the investigation of criminal activities has been recognized in practice and by statute as a mitigating sentencing factor. The nature, extent, and significance of assistance can involve a broad spectrum of conduct that must be evaluated by the court on an individual basis. Latitude is, therefore, afforded the sentencing judge to reduce a sentence based upon variable relevant factors, including those listed above. The sentencing judge must, however, state the reasons for reducing a sentence under this section. 18 U.S.C. § 3553(c). The court may elect to provide its reasons to the defendant in camera and in writing under seal for the safety of the defendant or to avoid disclosure of an ongoing investigation.

Attorney General's Guidelines for FBI Use of Informants in Domestic Security, Organized Crime, and Other Criminal Investigations

December 15, 1976

To: Clarence M. Kelley
         Director, Federal Bureau of Investigation
From: Edward H. Levi
         Attorney General

Courts have recognized that the government's use of informants is lawful and may often be essential to the effectiveness of properly authorized law enforcement investigations. However, the technique of using informants to assist in the investigation of criminal activity, since it may involve an element of deception and intrusion into the privacy of individuals or may require government cooperation with persons whose reliability and motivation may be open to question, should be carefully limited. Thus, while it is proper for the FBI to use informants in appropriate investigations, it is imperative that special care be taken not only to minimize their use but also to ensure that individual rights are not infringed and that the government itself does not become a violator of the law. Informants as such are not employees of the FBI, but the relationship of an informant to the FBI imposes a special responsibility on the FBI when the informant engages in activity where he has received, or reasonably thinks he has received, encouragement or direction for that activity from the FBI.

To fulfill this responsibility, it is useful to formulate in a single document the limitations on the activities of informants and the duties of the FBI with respect to informants, even though many of these limitations and duties are set forth in individual instructions or recognized in existing practice.

As a fundamental principle, it must be recognized that an informant is merely one technique used in the course of authorized investigations. The FBI may not use informants where it is not authorized to conduct an investigation nor may informants be used for acts or encouraged to commit acts which the FBI could not authorize for its undercover Agents. When an FBI informant provides information concerning planned criminal activity which is not within the investigative jurisdiction of the FBI, the FBI shall advise the law enforcement agency having investigative jurisdiction. If the circumstances are such that it is inadvisable to have the informant report directly to the agency having investigative jurisdiction, the FBI, in cooperation with that agency, may continue to operate the informant.

A. Use of Informants: In considering the use of informants in an authorized investigation, the FBI should weigh the following factors:

1. the risk that use of an informant in a particular investigation or the conduct of a particular informant may, contrary to instructions, violate individual rights, intrude upon privileged communications, unlawfully inhibit the free association of individuals or the expression of ideas, or compromise in any way the investigation or the subsequent prosecution.

2. the nature and seriousness of the matter under investigation, and the likelihood that information which an informant could provide is not readily available through other sources or more direct means.

3. the character and motivation of the informant himself, his past or potential involvement in the matter under investigation or in related criminal activity; his

proven reliability and truthfulness or the availability of means to verify the information which he provides.

4. the measure of the ability of the FBI to control the informant's activities insofar as he is acting on behalf of the Bureau and ensure that his conduct will be consistent with applicable law and instructions.

5. the potential value of the information he may be able to furnish in relation to the consideration he may be seeking from the government for his cooperation.

B. Instructions to Informants: The FBI shall instruct all informants it uses in domestic security, organized crime, and other criminal investigations that in carrying out their assignments they shall not:

1. participate in acts of violence; or

2. use unlawful techniques (e.g., breaking and entering, electronic surveillance, opening or otherwise tampering with the mail) to obtain information for the FBI; or

3. initiate a plan to commit criminal acts; or

4. participate in criminal activities of persons under investigation, except insofar as the FBI determines that such participation is necessary to obtain information needed for purposes of federal prosecution.

5. Whenever the FBI learns that persons under investigation intend to commit a violent crime informants used in connection with the investigation shall be instructed to try to discourage the violence.

C. Violations of Instructions and Law

1. Under no circumstances shall the FBI take any action to conceal a crime by one of its informants.

2. Whenever the FBI *learns* that informant used in investigating any criminal activity has violated the instructions set for above *in furtherance of his assignment*, it shall ordinarily notify the appropriate law enforcement or prosecutive authorities promptly of any violation of law, and make a determination whether continued use of the informant is justified. In those exceptional circumstances in which notification to local authorities may be inadvisable, the FBI shall immediately notify the Department of Justice of the facts and circumstances concerning the investigation and the informant's law violation, and provide its recommendation on reporting the violation and on continued use of the informant. The Department shall determine:

a. when law enforcement or prosecutive authorities should be notified of the law violation;

b. what use, if any, should be made of the information gathered through the violation of law, as well as the disposition and retention of such information; and

c. whether continued use should be made of the informant by the FBI.

Note: Because the FBI has a special responsibility to control the activity of informants collecting information for the Bureau and is ordinarily familiar with these activities, a comparatively minimal degree of certainty on the part of the FBI (i.e., "learns") is required before the FBI must report informant misconduct to the appropriate law enforcement authorities.

3. Whenever the FBI has *knowledge of the actual commission* of a serious crime by one of its informants *unconnected with his FBI assignment*, it shall ordinarily notify the appropriate law enforcement or prosecutive authorities promptly and make a determination whether continued use of the informant is justified. In those exceptional circumstances in which notification to local authorities may be inadvisable, the FBI shall promptly advise the Department of Justice of the facts and circumstances concerning the investigation and the informant's law violation, and provide its recommendation on reporting the violation and on continued use of the informant. The Department of Justice shall determine:

    a. when law enforcement or prosecutive authorities should be notified of the law violation; and

    b. whether continued use should be made of the informant by the FBI

Note: Because of the criminal activity described in this provision of any government assignment, and because the FBI will have no special knowledge to determine such informant malfeasance, a substantial degree of certainty on the part of the Bureau is required before it must report to other authorities. The standard of certainty is derived from the federal misprision of felony statute, Title 18 U.S. Code, Sec. 4, "Whoever, having *knowledge of the actual commission* of a felony cognizable by a court of the United States, conceals and does not as soon as possible make known the same to some judge or other person in civil or military authority under the United States, shall be fined not more than $500 or imprisoned not more than three years, or both."

4. In determining the advisability of notifying appropriate law enforcement and prosecutive authorities of criminal activity by FBI informants, the FBI and Department of Justice shall consider the following factors:

    a. whether the crime is completed, imminent or inchoate;

    b. seriousness of the crime in terms of danger to life and property;

    c. whether the crime is a violation of federal or state law, and whether a felony, misdemeanor, or lesser offense;

    d. the degree of certainty of the information regarding the criminal activity;

    e. whether the appropriate authorities already know of the criminal activity and the informant's identity; and

    f. the significance of the information the informant is providing, or will provide, and the effect on the FBI investigative activity of notification to the other law enforcement agency.

Appendix C. Informant Management Guidelines and Procedures

These Guidelines and Procedures were adapted from those used by federal agencies to regulate the development and management of confidential sources of information. They are presented for informational purposes only.

I. Informants

General Policies

A. This section contains policies and procedures to be followed in the establishment, use, and handling of informants by the Law Enforcement Agency (LEA).

The title "Informants" covers the following:

1. *Informant:* A person who, under the direction of a specific LEA officer, and with or without expectation of compensation, furnishes information on criminal activity or performs a lawful service for the LEA in its investigation of criminal activity.

2. *Defendant/Informant:* As above, but subject to arrest and prosecution for a state or federal offense; or a defendant in a pending federal or state case who expects compensation for his assistance in either the form of judicial or prosecutive consideration, or compensation of another form.

3. *Restricted-Use Informant:* Any informant who meets any of the following criteria shall be considered a "restricted-use informant," subject to use as authorized below:

   a. Persons less than 18 years of age: only with written consent of parent or legal guardian.

   b. Persons on probation or parole (federal or state): management will establish procedures to obtain permission to use persons on probation (federal and state) and parole. For persons on federal parole, management will contact the Regional Parole Commissioner of the region in which the releasee is under supervision at least (except when emergency circumstances dictate otherwise) 30 days prior to the proposed use of the person (releasee). Management will furnish in writing an overview of the proposed utilization of the person's services to include:

    i.   Informant instructions

    ii.   Administrative controls

    iii. Potential risk to the person

    iv. Measures to be taken to ensure the person's safety

    v.   Why the potential benefit to the Government outweighs the risk of the person's reinvolvement

    vi. Length of time the person is needed (up to 90 days)

If the Commission approves the LEA's request, the conditions of the person's cooperation will be set forth in a memorandum from the Regional Commissioner to the Chief/Administrator.

Note: Where the person is currently a federal *prisoner*, and the intended utilization will require temporary furlough or transfer from his detention site, or the use of consensual monitoring devices, it is necessary to obtain prior Departmental approval. A request must be made by management to the Office of Enforcement Operations which contains the following information:

    i.   Name and identifying data of prisoner

    ii.   Present location of prisoner

    iii. Necessity of using the prisoner

    iv. Identity of target

    v.   Nature and circumstances of intended use

    vi. Security measures to be taken to ensure the prisoner's safety

    vii. Whether he is to remain in law enforcement custody or will be unguarded at any point

    viii. Length of time the prisoner is needed

    ix. Whether he will be needed as a witness

    x.   Whether it will be necessary to relocate the prisoner to another prison

Upon completion of the activity, submit a followup report setting forth the results of the utilization.

    c.   Persons formerly dependent on drugs, or currently participating in a drug-treatment program; with the approval of the office/division Commander.

    d.   Persons with two or more felony convictions; with the approval of the Commander

    e.   Persons who have been convicted of a drug felony; with the approval of the Commander

    f.   Persons who have been previously declared unreliable informants;

    g.   "Walk-in" informants, until subsequent investigation justifies a less stringent classification; with the approval of the Commander.

B. The title "informant" does not apply to "sources of information." A source of information is a person or organization, not under the direction of a specific agent, who provides information without becoming a party to the investigation itself (e.g., a business firm furnishing information from its records; an employee of an organization who, through the routine course of his activities, obtains information of value to the LEA; or a concerned citizen who witnesses an event of interest to the LEA).

Should a person who would otherwise be considered a source of information seek financial compensation, or become a continuing active part of the investigative process, his status should be shifted to that of an informant.

Generally, a person or organization fitting this definition can be identified by name in investigative reports. However, if there is cause to preserve anonymity, yet the circumstances do not warrant establishing the source as an informant, the term "source of information" may be used. Sources of information will be identified in an administrative memorandum attached to the report.

C. There are three criteria that must be met to establish a person as an LEA informant:

1. The person is in a position to measurably assist the LEA in a present or future investigation.

2. To the extent a prudent judgment can be made, the person will not compromise the LEA interests and activities.

3. The person will accept the measure of direction necessary to effectively utilize his services.

D. If there is reason to believe that an informant or defendant/informant has committed a serious criminal offense (i.e., a felony), the appropriate prosecuting attorney or U.S. Attorney's Office will be notified. The U.S. Attorney's Office. after consultation with DOJ, will determine whether the LEA may continue to use the individual as an informant.

E. In the situation described in (D) above, the law enforcement agency having jurisdiction over the crime will also be notified. If it is felt that immediate and full notification would jeopardize an ongoing investigation or endanger the life of an agent or other person, then this notification may be limited to just apprising the agency that the crime was committed. In this instance, all evidence of the crime will be preserved for subsequent transfer to the agency at a point in time when full disclosure is possible.

F. Informants under the control of another agency are not subject to the requirements of these guidelines. Frequently, however, situations occur in which control of the informant is shared between the LEA and the other agency, or the control by the other agency is nominal, or the LEA provides direction to the informant through the other agency. The nature of the relationship between the three parties will be continuously reviewed by the agent involved and his immediate supervisor. Should control shift to where more rests with the LEA than the other agency, the individual will be established as an informant for this LEA.

G. The following additional requirements shall apply to the LEA's development of defendant/informants:

1. The approval of the appropriate prosecutor (i.e., federal, state, or local) will be obtained *prior* to seeking the cooperation of a defendant.

2. A defendant may be advised that his cooperation will be brought to the attention of the appropriate prosecutor. No further representations or assurances may be given without approval by the Chief/Administrator. The prosecuting attorney shall have sole authority to decide whether or not to prosecute a case against a defendant/informant.

3. The appropriate prosecutor shall be advised of the nature and scope of the defendant's cooperation throughout the period of his use. The procedures and frequency of this reporting shall be set by the prosecutor.

4. Prior to formally seeking the *dismissal* of any criminal charge against a defendant/informant, the case officer must obtain the written approval of the Chief/Administrator.

Requests under this requirement will be made via memorandum. The memorandum will include the informant's code number, the specific charge, the informal views of the appropriate prosecutor, and a terse justification in terms of advantage to the LEA. Written approval or disapproval will be via return memorandum.

II. Establishing Informants

1. General

All persons who will be utilized as informants will be formally established as such. The specific procedures required in establishing a person as an informant vary somewhat, depending upon the characteristics of the person involved.

In instances of either extreme sensitivity or where a "source of information" is being established for payment purposes, certain establishment procedures may be waived by the Commander. Such exemptions from the norm will be used judiciously. Those procedures that may be exempted under this criteria are so indicated below. Any such exemption must be specifically documented in Establishment Report.

2. Informant Code Number

A. Each informant will be assigned a code number. This code will appear in all investigative reports in lieu of the informant's true name.

B. The code will have nine characters, each designated as follows:

(1) (2) (3) (4) (5) (6) (7) (8) (9)

(1): The first character will always be the letter "C".

(2) and (3): The next two characters will be the designator of the establishing office/division.

(4) and (5): The next two characters will be the last two digits of the fiscal year of establishment.

(6), (7), (8), and (9): The last four characters will be a sequential, four-digit number within the fiscal year and within the establishing office.

C. Once assigned, this code number will remain with the informant throughout his use, even if his services are temporarily used by another office/division. If a deactivated informant is subsequently reactivated, the same code will be reused. Exceptions to this are where an informant deactivated by one office/division is independently established by another office/division, or where his use by an office/division other than the establishing office/division is of a permanent nature. In the latter instances, he will be established by the second office/division, using a new code number.

D. Informants under the control of another agency will not usually be assigned a code numbers. This will be necessary, however, if the informant is to be paid with funds by the LEA.

3. Informant Code Book

Each office/division will maintain an informant code book. Informants will be logged in these books upon approval of their establishment report. Where written approval of the establishment report requires mailing it to and from the approving supervisor, then, in exigent circumstances, telephone approval will suffice pending receipt of the approval. Informant code books will have the following entries:

1. Informant's code number.
2. Type of informant (i.e., informant, defendant/informant, restricted-use informant).
3. Informant's true name (or "exempted by Commander")
4. Name of establishing agent.
5. Date the establishment is approved.
6. Date of deactivation

4. Informant Files

A. For each informant a separate the File Jacket will be established by the establishing office/division. These files will be kept in a separate and secure storage facility, segregated from any other files, and under the exclusive control of the office head or an employee designated by him. The facility will be locked at all times when unattended. Access to these files will be limited to those employees who have a necessary, legitimate need. An informant file may not leave the immediate area except for review by a management official or the handling officer, and will be returned prior to the close of business hours. Sign-out logs will be kept indicating the date, informant number, time in and out, and the signature of the person reviewing the file.

B. In certain instances of extreme sensitivity, files of those informants for whom a waiver of establishment procedures was granted may be stored separately from other informant files, accessible only to the Commander and those the LEA personnel designated by him to control the informant's utilization. Upon deactivating any such informant, the Commander will determine whether this file should be integrated into the regular informant file storage facility.

C. Non-employees, including those of other state or federal law enforcement agencies will not be permitted access to these files. An exception to this is the files of those informants under the control of a Task Force. Conditions of access to these files will be set by the LEA Task Force management. On an individual file basis, a prosecuting attorney may examine an informant file if such examination is necessary to the prosecution of a case. *Bona fide* and authorized evaluators may be permitted secondary access through review of the LEA prepared summaries of or extracts from these files. In no case will the identity of an informant be disclosed to an external evaluator.

D. Informant files will be maintained in code number sequence, under two headings: active informants and deactivated informants.

E. Informant files will contain the following documents:
   1. The Informant Payment Record, kept on top of the file
   2. The Informant Establishment Report, plus any other documents connected with the informant's establishment
   3. The Cooperating Individual Agreement
   4. The Voucher for Payment for Information and Purchase of Evidence, the signed copy being kept by the originating office
   5. Copies of all debriefing reports
   6. Copies of case initiation reports bearing on the utilization of the informant
   7. Copies of statements signed by the informant (unsigned copies will be placed in appropriate investigative files)

8. Any administrative correspondence pertaining to the informant, including documentation of any representations made on his behalf or any other non-monetary considerations furnished

9. Any deactivation report or declaration of an unsatisfactory informant.

F. For each informant in an active status, the controlling officer will review the informant file on a quarterly basis to assure it contains all relevant and current information. Where a *material* fact that was earlier reported on the Establishment Report is no longer correct (e.g., a change in criminal status, means of locating him, etc.), a supplemental Establishment Report/Personal History form should be submitted with the corrected entry. If the new information warrants a higher level of approval than was originally necessary, this approval will be sought. If the new information is routine, the approval of the immediate supervisor on the Establishment Report/Personal History will suffice, regardless of the original level of approval.

G. Where an informant is utilized and/or paid by an office/division other than the establishing office/division, its file on that informant need only consist of those documents pertinent to its utilization and/or payment.

5. Photographs

All informants will be photographed (unless a recent photograph is already available). One print will be attached to each copy of the Establishment Report. This requirement may be waived by the Commander. Informants controlled by another agency who are established for payment purposes only need not be photographed.

6. Fingerprinting and Criminal History

A. All informants being established will be checked in the LEA and FBI files. FBI files will be checked via NCIC, and Wanted Person and Criminal History Summary Files. If a verified FBI number is available, submit a Request for Criminal Records, to the FBI Identification Division for criminal record checks.

B. Where a verified FBI number is not available and the potential informant must be fingerprinted, submit a completed FD-249, Fingerprint Card, directly to the FBI. Do not enter the informant code number on the FD-249. On the FD-249, line through the space entitled "Your Number." Enter "Criminal Inquiry" in the space entitled "Charge."

C. A copy of the Request for Criminal Records will be attached to each copy of the Establishment Report.

D. The informant may be utilized on a provisional basis while awaiting a response from FBI. Information contained in the subsequent FBI response will be reviewed from the standpoint of whether it affects the current status and utilization of the informant. Adjustments to procedures, status, and/or use will be made as appropriate.

E. In instances of extreme sensitivity or where a source of information is being established for payment purposes, the fingerprinting requirement may be waived.

F. The foregoing criminal history/fingerprint requirements do not apply to informants controlled by another agency who are established for payment purposes only.

7. Informant Establishment Report

A. An Informant Establishment Report will be prepared for any person assigned an informant code.

B. The Establishment Report will be completed as fully as possible.

C. Enter a brief evaluation of the informant's potential and proposed utilization. If he is a defendant/informant or a restricted-use informant, enter the pertinent details. Also enter the details of approval for use, if applicable (name of approving party, date of approval, conditions of approval, the agent to whom the approval was given).

D. Enter the substance and circumstances of any non-monetary assurance given.

E. For informants other than defendant/informants and restricted-use informants, the approval of the immediate supervisor is sufficient. For defendant/informants and restricted-use informants, the additional approval of the Commander is required. This approval is also required where any establishment procedures were waived, or in the case of a re-establishment of an informant previously declared unreliable.

F. Attach a photograph and copies of written approvals, if any, to each copy of the Establishment Report

III. Utilization of Informants

1. General Policies

A. Informants are assets of the LEA, not a specific officer. At its discretion, LEA management may reassign an informant to the control of another officer or another office/division.

B. Officer/informant contacts will be of a strictly professional nature. Extrinsic social or business contacts are expressly prohibited.

C. Contacts with informants will be such that their knowledge of the LEA facilities, operations, activities, and personnel is kept to the minimum necessary to their successful utilization.

D. At least two officers must be capable of contacting an informant. Whenever practical, two officers (or an officer of another enforcement agency) will be present at all contacts with the informant.

E. All significant contacts with the informant, and all information obtained at these contacts, will be documented in writing.

F. Informants (and sources of information) shall be advised at the outset that

1. They shall not violate criminal law in furtherance of gathering information or providing services to the LEA, and that any evidence of such a violation will be reported to the appropriate law enforcement agency.

2. They have no official status, implied or otherwise, as agents or employees of the LEA.

3. The information they provide may be used in a criminal proceeding, and that, although the LEA will use all lawful means to protect their confidentiality, this cannot be guaranteed.

4. It is a federal offense to threaten, harass, or mislead anyone who provides information about a federal crime to a federal law enforcement agency. Should they experience anything of this nature, as a result of their cooperation with the LEA, they should contact their controlling officer immediately.

5. Cooperating Individuals will sign the (Cooperating Individual Agreement) acknowledging that he/she has read and agree to the above conditions. His/her signature and date will be witnessed by two officers. Should a cooperating individual refuse to sign

the agreement, the following statement will be entered on the form, and will be signed and dated by two officers: "On [date], [C.I. Number] was advised of and agreed to the conditions set forth on this form. [C.I. Number] refused to sign."

H. Where an informant is to participate in an undercover purchase in which he may come in contact with either official funds, controlled drugs, or anything else of potential evidentiary value, he will be thoroughly searched both before and after the undercover encounter, and where possible kept under continuous observation in between. The reason for this is to preclude questions as to the validity or integrity of the evidence.

I. All interactions with the informant including his development, establishment, debriefing, and utilization, will be carried out with the highest regard for confidentiality. When he is to be brought to the LEA office, it will be done in a manner so as to attract minimal attention, both upon entering and exiting, and while he is in the confines of the office itself. Unnecessary disclosure of his identity in discussions will be avoided. Documents and reports concerning his informant status will be kept secured. Meetings outside the office will be done insofar as possible in "neutral" locations. Where the disclosure of his informant status to a prosecutor is necessary, the prosecutor should be reminded to handle this fact with similar regard for security.

J. Informants who are injured or killed while engaged or as a result of their cooperation with the LEA are eligible for benefits under the Federal Employees Compensation Act.

2. Debriefing of Informants

A. As part of the establishment process, and prior to the supervisor granting approval to the establishment of the informant, a full debriefing will take place. The nature and extent of this debriefing will vary with the individual's background (e.g., whether he is a long-time associate of criminals, etc.). A line of inquiry will be developed such that all knowledge of criminals and criminal activity, will be covered.

B. The general order of priority to the criminal information sought will be as follows:

1. Actionable criminal information

2. General criminal information

The debriefing will not be limited to, nor overly focus upon, the first priority. It could well be that a broad coverage of the second priority will lead to a better choice of targets and objectives than an oversimplified discussion of actionable information.

In obtaining information on a criminal, the financial aspects of his activities will also be included (e.g., how money is transferred, assets, proceeds, etc.). The information sought will not be limited to the activity within the geographic or jurisdictional boundaries of the immediate office/division.

C. Information relating to criminal activity which falls within the jurisdiction of another agency will be disseminated to the appropriate agencies unless there is a valid reason not to do so. If the information is nonspecific or of low significance, the immediate supervisor will decide whether it should be disseminated.

D. Information which adversely reflects upon the integrity or conduct of an LEA employee will be handled in accordance with the LEA Standards of Conduct. Information which adversely reflects upon the integrity of an employee of another law enforcement agency or any information concerning public corruption will be handled in accordance with procedures established by the Chief/Administrator.

E. Informants will be debriefed subsequently on a periodic basis at least every 90 days.

F. All debriefings will be fully reported in an Informant Debriefing Report. These reports will be written to the appropriate case or general file, and a copy placed in the informant file. They will be crossfiled to other case or general files, as appropriate.

If the information contained in the report is of interest to another office/division or another agency, distribution will be indicated in the Distribution block. If only a portion of the information is of interest to another agency, it may be repeated in a letter to the agency. Such correspondence should be identified by the LEA investigative file number.

G. The format of an Informant Debriefing Report will be as follows:

1. No synopsis is necessary.

2. There will be three major headings: Current Criminal Activity, Historical Criminal Activity, and an Indexing Section. If no information is to be entered under any one of these headings, enter the word "negative."

3. Insofar as practical, the narrative sections should be formatted as follows:

    a. Information of interest to another agency should be paragraphed separately to facilitate extraction.

    b. Information that appears to exonerate a defendant or suspect should be paragraphed separately.

H. Notes taken by officers in the debriefing and used in the preparation of the debriefing report should be preserved.

Informant Statements

A. Where an informant has provided information or has participated in any activity at the direction of the LEA or otherwise to which he may be required to testify, a formal statement normally will be taken. However where taking a statement may adversely impact an investigative outcome, this procedure may be waived if all relevant information is reported in a Report of Investigation. The case officer and his or her supervisor, in consultation with the prosecuting attorney, will decide whether or not a formal statement is necessary.

B. The original copy of the statement will be signed and filed in his informant file. An additional copy, identified only by informant code number, will be filed in the case file (copies forwarded to the other appropriate offices maintaining this case file).

C. The statement normally will be typed. This is not a mandatory requirement, provided the handwriting is legible and in ink.

D. Any mistakes, cross-throughs, etc. will be initialed by the informant on the original copy. Each page of the original copy will be initialed immediately at the end of the narrative on that page.

E. At least two officers will take and witness the statement.

F. The format of the statement shall be as follows:

1. *Heading:* The heading will contain the informant's code number, the date, time, and place of the statement, the agents taking the statement, and a short explanation of the contents. For example:

    "Statement of CIC990017 at the offices of the Independent Counsel, Washington, D.C., at 10:00 a.m. on January 13, 1998, given to Investigators X and Y concerning perjury and obstruction of justice in case 12345."

2. *Body:* The body will be composed in the informant's words as long as the expressions are clear to the average person. The organization and sequence of material may be set

by the officers. Any factual gaps or statements which raise obvious questions will be explained.

3. *Conclusion:* The conclusion will state that the informant has read the foregoing statement consisting of ___ pages, that he/she has initialed each page and all corrections, that it is true and correct to the best of his/her knowledge and belief, and that he/she gave the statement freely and voluntarily, without threats, coercion, or promises.

4. *Signatures:* The officers will sign all copies, the informant will sign just the original.

4. Use of Polygraph Examinations

A. Information supplied by an informant is normally evaluated by a meld of proper debriefing techniques, prior knowledge of the facts being reported, and investigative follow-up. In certain situations, however, these approaches are not sufficient. Where this is the case, *and* where corroboration is essential to the furtherance of an important investigation or prosecution, the use of a polygraph examination should be considered.

B. Barring exigent circumstances, all polygraph examinations conducted in an LEA-controlled investigation will be done under the auspices the LEA, as opposed to using an outside examiner.

5. Disclosure of an Informant's Identity

A. As stated in the Cooperating Individual Agreement, informants shall be advised at the outset that the information they provide may be used in a criminal proceeding, and that although the LEA will use all lawful means to protect their confidentiality, this cannot be guaranteed. In extraordinary circumstances, Chief/Administrator may authorize that such a guarantee be given for any government initiated proceeding (provided the prosecutor is advised of this assurance). The LEA will honor any such guarantee, regardless of the outcome of any case. Therefore, such guarantees will be issued judiciously.

B. The disclosure of an informant's identity, even when no prior guarantee of confidentiality was made, will be avoided whenever possible. Informant confidentiality will be thoroughly discussed with the prosecutor prior to the trial or other proceedings; and any alternatives will be given full consideration.

C. In situations where the disclosure of an informant's identity might adversely affect the outcome of a more significant investigation, the LEA may conceivably recommend dismissal of the immediate case. A decision of this nature may only be made by the Chief/Administrator. Requests for such decisions will be via memorandum, and responses will be similarly documented.

D. If the issue of disclosure arises during an agent's testimony and he is uncertain of the legal requirement, he should request time to discuss the matter with the prosecutor.

6. Payments to Informants

A. Any person who is to receive payments charged against PE/PI funds must be established as an informant. This includes persons who may otherwise be categorized as sources of information or informants under the control of another agency.

B. The amount of payment must be commensurate with the value of services and/or information provided. It will be based on the following factors:

    1.   The level of the targeted individual, organization or operation

    2.   The amount of the actual or potential seizure

    3.   The significance of the contribution made by the informant to the desired objectives

C. All payments to informants will be witnessed by another officer. In unusual circumstances, an officer of another law enforcement agency, may serve as witness.

7. Types of Payment

There are three circumstances in which payments to informants may be made:

A. Payments for Information and/or Active Participation. When an informant assists in developing an investigation, either through supplying information or actively participating in it, he may be paid for his services either in a lump sum or in staggered payments. As well, the LEA can pay an informant a commission based upon some percentage of the value of cases he provides. However, because such payments are highly unusual, the following precautions are required:

    1.   Informants paid on a commission basis should be instructed in advance concerning the Law of Entrapment;

    2.   The fee arrangement should be discussed with the informant in detail, and there should be no gaps in understanding the terms of the arrangement;

    3.   The usual instructions to the informant, the details of the fee arrangement and the Entrapment instructions should be provided to the informant in writing at the beginning of the operation;

    4.   Every effort should be made to maximize the control and supervision of the informant;

    5.   Every effort should be made to corroborate the informant's statements concerning his activities;

    6.   Payments should be completed before the informant testifies; and

    7.   We should be prepared to give reasons why it is necessary to use informants in this unusual manner.

B. Payments for information leading to a seizure, with no defendants, should be held to a minimum.

C. Payment for informant protection: The Department of Justice has a formal witness protection program. Where circumstances are such that an informant needs protection, every effort should be made to have the U.S. Attorney enter the informant into this program.

    Where this cannot be done, or in the interim period until it can be done, the LEA may absorb the expenses of relocation. These expenses may include travel for the informant and his immediate family, movement and/or storage of household goods, and living expenses at the new location for a specific period of time (not to exceed 6 months). Payments for these expenses may be either lump sum or as they occur, and will not exceed the amounts authorized for the LEA employees for these activities.

    The Chief/Administrator can delegate the authority to approve payments of up to $5000 for informant security expenditures from his established PE/PI funds. Amounts exceeding $5000 must be pre-cleared and approved the Chief/Administrator.

D. Payments to informants of another agency: To use or pay another agency's informant in a the LEA-controlled investigation, he must be established as an informant by this LEA.

E.   The LEA will not normally pay another agency's informant in non-LEA controlled cases, and under no circumstance where the payment is a duplication of a payment from the other agency (sharing a payment, however, is acceptable). Such payments may not exceed $10,000 per informant per quarter, and may only be made with the approval of the Chief/Administrator.

The informant must be established and coded. The Establishment Report, must contain a statement identifying the individual as an informant of the other agency, the name and agency of the officer responsible for him, and a terse justification for the payment. Fingerprinting and photographing are not required. For record keeping purposes, such informants will be deactivated once payment has been made.

F.   Awards from the DOJ/DOT Assets Forfeiture Fund. In operations where seizures and forfeitures of money or other assets have been realized, a cooperating individual, established or otherwise, may qualify for an award from the DOJ/DOT Assets Forfeiture Fund. This award may not exceed "the lesser of $150,000 or one fourth of the amount realized by the United States from the property forfeited." Any payment from the Assets Forfeiture Fund may be in addition to payments from PI accounts. To qualify for an award from the fund, the following must be accomplished:

1.   The cooperating individual must make a written claim to the appropriate office/division.

2.   The office/division must evaluate the claim and the Commander must make a recommendation to the Chief/Administrator.

Awards of more than $10,000 will be forwarded, through the chain of command, to the Administrator for approval. The Chief/Administrator will forward approved claims for awards to the Department of Justice Assets Forfeiture Fund.

9. Documentation of Payments

A.   All payments to informants will be documented on the Voucher for Payment for Information and Purchase of Evidence. The informant will sign his true name on the green copy only. This copy will be detached from the completed form for filing in the payment office's informant file before distribution of the remaining copies.

B.   In addition to copies Voucher for Payment forms, each informant file will contain an Informant Payment Record. This record will be kept on top of all the other documents in the file, and will contain a continuous record of payments made. The employee responsible for maintenance of informant files is responsible for keeping this record current and complete.

IV. Deactivation of Informants

1. Criteria

A.   An informant will be deactivated when:

1.   He/she no longer has the potential to furnish information or services which could lead to a significant prosecution or otherwise contribute to a criminal investigation.

2.   He/she is no longer willing to cooperate.

3.   His/her cooperation has been determined to be unsatisfactory.

B.   An informant will be deactivated by the decision or with the approval of that level of supervision which approved his establishment.

2. Procedures

A.   A Report of Investigation, entitled "Deactivation of [code number]," will be written to the informant file, containing the reason for deactivation. No crossfiling to investigative files will be made. Upon appropriate approval of the report, it will be distributed to all offices maintaining a file on the informant.

B.   Should an informant be deactivated due to unsatisfactory cooperation or behavior, the officer will include information to that effect in a memorandum (with a photograph attached) to the attention of the Chief/Administrator Both documents will give supporting justification and request that he be designated unsatisfactory. Both documents must be approved by the office/division commander. Upon concurrence, the Chief/Administrator will identify the informant as unsatisfactory and so notify all offices/divisions that have utilized his/her services.

C.   A deactivated informant may be reactivated by submitting a Report of Investigation entitled "Reactivation of [code number]" as in (A) above. In addition to containing the reason for reactivation, this report will reflect any developments during the period of deactivation which would affect the informant's status as a restricted-use or defendant/informant. Approval for reactivating an informant must be at least at that level of management which approved his deactivation.

V. Management Review of Informants

1. Immediate Supervisor

A.   The immediate supervisor is responsible for assuring that all handling of informants by employees under his supervision is in compliance with the LEA's procedures and guidelines. Factors that will be routinely considered by the immediate supervisor in carrying out this responsibility include that:

1.   Any person whose cooperation with the LEA meets the criteria for informant establishment is, in fact, established as such.

2.   Any factors in an informant's background that would warrant his being established as a restricted-use informant or defendant/informant are properly brought to light, and that the informant is properly classified as such.

3.   Any required external approvals for utilization are properly and fully obtained.

4.   The cautions to be given to all informants at the outset are in fact given and noted per the Cooperating Individual Agreement.

5.   Each informant is fully and accurately debriefed on targets of immediate interest, knowledge of long-range or general interest, and knowledge of criminal activity. Further, that this information is fully and accurately reported.

6.   Each informant is being utilized in a manner so as to make best use of his potential.

7.   Monies paid to informants are properly documented and are not excessive.

8.   Informants warranting deactivation are deactivated.

9.   Any appropriate requirements pertaining to review by the commander, prosecutor, or the LEA administration are met insofar as it is his responsibility to do so.

There will be no separate reporting system by which the supervisor documents his adherence to the foregoing. His/her written approval of investigative reports signifies this adherence.

B.   The immediate supervisor and/or a member of the office/division establishing the informant will participate in a full debriefing of each active informant under his unit's control at least every 90 days. This debriefing will cover the full range of topics set forth in, and be properly reported as with any other debriefing.

2. Commander

A.   Where the nature of the informant is such as to require the Commander's approval for use, the Commander shall assume a responsibility paralleling that of the immediate supervisor for pertinent factors set forth in 1.A, above. This does not relieve the immediate supervisor of his responsibilities, but instead provides for a "double check."

B.   On a quarterly basis, the Commander shall conduct a review of all active informants with the supervisors under his command. This review will cover the following points:

1.   Whether these informants should remain in an active status

2.   Whether these informants are being appropriately targeted and utilized

3.   Whether the debriefings have been complete and fully reported

4.   Whether the appropriate initial or ongoing approval requirements are being met

C.   The results of the review in (B) above will be reported to the Chief/Administrator on a memorandum entitled "Quarterly Review of Informants." This memorandum will contain a listing of those informants (by code number) who will be kept in an active status, and those who have been deactivated since the last report. It will also list the total amount of funds paid to each informant in the quarter.

VI. Witness Security Program

(*Note:* Chapter 9-21.000 of the U.S. Attorney's manual contains more detailed instructions on this program.)

1. Criteria

A.   The Witness Security Program, operated by the Department of Justice, serves to ensure the appearance of significant government witnesses at trial. Admitting an individual into this program represents a major administrative and financial burden to the government. For this reason, candidates will be carefully screened. Factors that will be considered include the following:

1.   The individual must be a *witness.* Informants who are not witnesses are not eligible.

2.   Only those witnesses whose testimony is essential to the prosecution of the most significant violators will be recommended for admission. The Department of Justice uses the terminology of "(an individual having) a nexus to organized criminal activity." Generally, the LEA will limit its selection of candidates to those witnesses who are essential to the prosecution of more than one major violators and/or the immobilization of a major criminal network.

3.   There must be clear indication of a threat to the witness or a member of his immediate family. Evidence of a specific threat is not required if there is a documented pattern of violent behavior by the defendants and/or their associates.

4.   The individual must be willing to undergo a legal change of name and to permanently relocate to a place of the government's choosing.

5. The individual must not have any unresolved charges against him (federal, state, or local) involving any criminal violation.

B. Witnesses in the LEA cases, the LEA task force cases, and the LEA state and local cooperation cases are eligible for inclusion in this program. However, the total number of witnesses that can be assimilated is limited. Therefore, a non-federal witness will be considered only under the most extraordinary circumstances. Furthermore, the U.S. Marshals Service may make a non-federal witness's acceptance into the program conditional upon reimbursement by the state.

2. Protection Provided Outside the Witness Security Program

A. Individuals who warrant some measure of protection but do not meet the criteria for inclusion in this program may be provided financial assistance from the LEA PE/PI funds. The cost of relocation may be considered in determining the amount of reward paid to an informant/witness.

B. The cost of temporary relocation while awaiting formal admittance to the program may be provided from the LEA PE/PI funding.

3. Procedures

A. The Office of Enforcement Operations, Criminal Division, Department of Justice, controls the admittance to and operation of this program. The U.S. Marshals Service operates the program *per se.*

B. Formal requests for admittance must originate with a U.S. Attorney, not the LEA. Furthermore, these requests must be from the U.S. Attorney or the 1st Assistant U.S. Attorney, not an Assistant U.S. Attorney.

C. Requests will not be approved without the LEA concurrence. This concurrence, as well as all other dialogue with the Department, will be carried out by Administration in coordination with the appropriate office/division. The LEA offices/divisions will not make any direct requests of or inquiries to the Department.

D. It is important to avoid detailed discussion of the terms of the protection offered. If the witness is accepted into the program, the U.S. Marshals Service will establish all terms and provide all explanations of them to the witness. Agreements or commitments made by any other party may not be honored.

E. Where it is anticipated that a witness or potential witness will be a candidate for this program, it is important that the request for admittance be submitted as soon as possible (i.e., as soon as it is determined that the individual will be a witness and will likely need relocation). Although a provision for emergency admittance exists, its use severely taxes the resources of the U.S. Marshals Service. This procedure will only be used in the most extraordinary circumstance.

F. Prior to making a formal request to admit a witness into this program, he will be the subject of a background investigation and a thorough debriefing.

1. The background investigation will be oriented toward his criminal history; specifically, whether he is a fugitive, illegal alien, or in any other manner is the subject of unresolved criminal or civil matters.

2. The debriefing will be oriented towards *any* criminal information he may have that would be of investigative or intelligence value. In all probability, this will be the final opportunity for the LEA or any other agency to utilize this witness; it is therefore

incumbent upon the LEA as a law enforcement agency to take maximum advantage of a resource which will shortly become unavailable.

G.   The formal request shall be via memorandum from the U.S. Attorney to the Department, using the format set forth in USAM921.000. In practice, this report will likely be prepared by an Assistant U.S. Attorney and the LEA case officer. It is important that this report be prepared accurately and carefully. The LEA office/division should forward a copy of this report, with a concurring cover memorandum by the Commander. If the LEA office/division should have additional information, or a differing assessment from that contained in the report from the U.S. Attorney, this should be included in the cover memorandum. This is particularly important with regard to the significance of the informant and the assessment of the threat.

H.   Upon receipt of the report from the U.S. Attorney and written concurrence by the LEA, the Department of Justice will make the decision as to admission of the witness into the program.

I.   If the individual has not been previously assigned an informant code number, and is being proposed for inclusion in this program as a result of testimony in an LEA case, then a code number should be assigned to him/her. The Establishment Report should contain an appropriate explanation of the circumstances leading to the need for witness security. He/she may be deactivated upon the Justice Department's decision as to his inclusion in the program.

J.   Once admitted into this program, a witness will not be used as an informant again. This prohibition also extends to any family member who is relocated with the witness. This prohibition is permanent and will continue in effect even though the witness has ceased receiving any benefits under the program, or even if the individual wishes to disassociate or remove himself from protective status. In extremely rare instances, the Department of Justice may waive this prohibition and allow the re-use of a protected witness. The circumstances for such a waiver would have to be highly compelling. The witness may, of course, be called upon to testify in the immediate case or cases for which he is being provided protection. Requests for appearances at trial or pretrial should be made by the U.S. Attorney to the Department at least 10 days in advance of any required appearance.

General Guidelines — Sources, Informants, and Defendant Informants

A.   General

1.   A "source of information" is a person or organization furnishing information without compensation on an occasional basis (e.g., an observer of an event, or a company employee who obtains relevant information in the normal course of his employment), or a person or organization in the business of furnishing information for a fee and receiving only its regular compensation for doing so (e.g., a credit bureau).

2.   An "informant" is a person who, under the specific direction of a the LEA officer, with or without the expectation of payment or other valuable consideration, furnishes information regarding criminal activity or performs other lawful services.

3.   A "defendant-informant" is a person subject to arrest and prosecution for a federal offense, or a defendant in a pending federal or state case who, under the specific direction of a the LEA officer, with an expectation of payment or other valuable

consideration, provides information regarding criminal activity or performs other lawful services.

4. Any individual or organization may by a source of information. Restrictions placed on the use of informants and defendant-informants are not applicable to sources of information.

5. Informants, and defendant-informants are assets of the LEA, and are not to be considered personal resources of individual officers. At least two (2) LEA agents should be a position to contact an informant or defendant-informant, and whenever practicable two (2) the LEA officers shall be present at all contacts and interviews with informants and defendant-informants. Regular contacts shall be maintained with informants and defendant-informants. The first-level supervisor will be responsible for ensuring that contacts, and the information gained from them under this guideline are documented on a regular and timely basis.

6. Informants and defendant-informants shall be advised that they are cooperating with the LEA, but are not officers or employees of the LEA or the federal government. They shall be advised that information they provide may be used in a criminal proceeding. They may be told that the LEA will use all lawful means available to maintain the confidentiality of their identity. Except in extraordinary circumstances they should not be assured that they will *never* be required to testify or otherwise have their identity disclosed in a criminal proceeding. In extraordinary circumstances, they may be given this assurance after approval of the Chief/Administrator, provided the U.S. Attorney shall be notified of any such assurance given to any individual having information relevant to a pending investigation in advance of prosecution proceedings, including grand jury proceedings.

B. Informants

1. Only individuals who are believed able to furnish reliable enforcement information or other lawful services, and who are believed able to maintain the confidentiality of the LEA interests and activities, may be utilized as informants.

2. Except as provided in paragraph II.B.3, an officer must obtain the approval of his immediate supervisor prior to utilizing any informant. The approving supervisor should review the relevant data, including the criminal record, of any potential informant and ascertain whether he is the subject of a pending LEA investigation before deciding whether to approve him as an informant. Before an individual is asked to render services, in addition to supplying information, a more extensive investigation and evaluation of the individual shall be conducted. However, the LEA may use an informant temporarily without extensive investigation where a second line supervisor determines that lack of sufficient time precludes such investigation.

3. Individuals in the following categories represent particular risks as informants, and their use for an initial ninety (90) days may be utilized only as authorized below:

   a. individuals who are less than eighteen (18) years of age, with the written consent of a parent or a legal guardian, when authorized by the Commander;

   b. individuals on federal or state probation or parole, with the consent of the agency supervising them, and complete documentation by the LEA, when authorized by the Commander;

   c. former drug-dependent persons, or drug-dependent persons participating in an established drug treatment program, when authorized by the Commander;

   d. individuals with two (2) or more felony convictions, when authorized by the Commander;

    e.   individuals who have had a prior federal or state conviction for a drug felony offense, when authorized by the Commander;

    f.   individuals who have previously been declared unreliable by the LEA, when authorized by the Chief/Administrator.

4.   The use of an informant shall be reviewed at least every ninety (90) days by the appropriate second line supervisor, or the higher official indicated in paragraph B.3, above. Use of the informant may be continued if it is determined, upon review of his background and performance, that he is qualified to serve in this capacity as provided in paragraph B.1, above, and that he has the potential for furnishing information or services which it is believed will lead to the prosecution of one or more individuals who are or have been participating in criminal activity. The Commander shall be responsible for review of the utilization of each informant at least every 6 months, and continued use of an informant shall be authorized if it is determined that he meets these standards. The Commander shall be responsible for reporting all such decisions to the LEA administration.

5.   Informants may be paid money or afforded other lawful consideration. All funds paid to informants shall be accounted for, and specific records shall be maintained for any non-monetary consideration furnished to informants.

C. Defendant-informants

The purpose of this section of the guidelines is to ensure that defendant-informants provide information or render services in a manner that recognizes their status as individuals subject to legal sanctions for criminal violations. In addition to the requirements provided in paragraph B, use of defendant-informants is governed by the following guidelines.

1.   Only individuals who are believed to be able to furnish reliable enforcement information or lawful services, and who are believed able to maintain the confidentiality of the LEA interests and activities, may be used as defendant-informants.

2.   In addition to the steps necessary to utilize an informant which are set forth in paragraph, the approval of the appropriate U.S. Attorney or other prosecutor shall be obtained prior to seeking the cooperation of or utilizing a defendant-informant. The U.S. Attorney or other prosecutor shall be informed on a continuing basis of such cooperation or use of a defendant-informant.

3.   An individual approved as a defendant-informant may be advised that his cooperation will be brought to the attention of the appropriate U.S. Attorney, or other prosecutor, and the substance and circumstance of giving such advice shall be documented in writing. The U.S. Attorney has the sole authority to determine whether a defendant-informant will be prosecuted, and the LEA officers shall make no representations concerning such prosecution. Officers shall make no other representations or recommendations without the express written approval of the Commander.

4.   The Commander shall obtain the written approval of designated administration official prior to recommending dismissal of any criminal matter. The Commander shall inform the LEA administration of any other information concerning a defendant-informant's cooperation, or advice offered regarding disposition of a case, or imposition of a penalty.

5.   Use of defendant-informants shall be reviewed in the manner prescribed for other informants in paragraph II.B above, and their use may be continued only if they are found to meet the standards set forth therein.

D. Knowledge of criminal activity by informants and defendant-informants

  1. The case officer shall instruct all informants and defendant-informants that they shall not violate criminal law in furtherance of gathering information or providing other services for the LEA, and that any evidence of such violation will be reported to the concerned law enforcement authority.

  2. Whenever the LEA has reason to believe that a serious criminal offense outside its investigative jurisdiction is being or will be committed, it shall immediately disseminate all relevant information to the appropriate law enforcement agency.

  3. Whenever the LEA has reason to believe that an informant or defendant-informant has committed a serious criminal offense the appropriate law enforcement agency shall be advised by the LEA, and the appropriate U.S. Attorney shall be notified.

  4. In disseminating information in accordance with paragraphs D.2 and 3 above, all available information shall be promptly furnished to the appropriate law enforcement agency unless such action would jeopardize an ongoing major investigation or endanger the life of an officer, informant or defendant-informant. If full disclosure is not made for the reasons indicated, then limited disclosure shall be made by the LEA to the appropriate authorities, to an extent sufficient to apprise them of the specific crime or crimes that are believed to have been committed. Full disclosure shall be made as soon as the need for the restrictions on dissemination are no longer present. Where complete dissemination cannot immediately be made to the appropriate law enforcement agency, the LEA shall preserve all evidence of the violation for possible future use by the appropriate prosecuting authority. Nothing herein shall prevent full and immediate disclosure to the appropriate law enforcement agency if in the LEA's judgment such action is necessary even though an investigation might thereby be jeopardized.

  5. If the LEA desires to continue making use of an informant or defendant-informant after it has reason to believe that he has committed a serious criminal offense, the LEA shall advise the appropriate U.S. Attorney and a determination shall be made by him after consultation with the Criminal Division of the Department of Justice, whether continued use should be made of the individual by the LEA.

Appendix D.
Reward Provisions

Rewards Generally

18 U.S. Code, Sec. 3059 (1998): Rewards and appropriations therefor

(a) (1) There is authorized to be appropriated, out of any money in the Treasury not otherwise appropriated, the sum of $25,000 as a reward or rewards for the capture of anyone who is charged with violation of criminal laws of the United States or any State or of the District of Columbia, and an equal amount as a reward or rewards for information leading to the arrest of any such person, to be apportioned and expended in the discretion of, and upon such conditions as may be imposed by, the Attorney General of the United States. Not more than $25,000 shall be expended for information or capture of any one person.

   (2) If any of the said persons shall be killed in resisting lawful arrest, the Attorney General may pay any part of the reward money in his discretion to the person or persons whom he shall adjudge to be entitled thereto but no reward money shall be paid to any official or employee of the Department of Justice of the United States.

(b) The Attorney General each year may spend not more than $10,000 for services or information looking toward the apprehension of narcotic law violators who are fugitives from justice.

(c) (1) In special circumstances and in the Attorney General's sole discretion, the Attorney General may make a payment of up to $10,000 to a person who furnishes information unknown to the Government relating to a possible prosecution under section 2326 which results in a conviction.

   (2) A person is not eligible for a payment under paragraph (1) if—

      (A) the person is a current or former officer or employee of a Federal, State, or local government agency or instrumentality who furnishes information discovered or gathered in the course of government employment;

      (B) the person knowingly participated in the offense;

      (C) the information furnished by the person consists of an allegation or transaction that has been disclosed to the public—

        (i)   in a criminal, civil, or administrative proceeding;

        (ii)   in a congressional, administrative, or General Accounting Office report, hearing, audit, or investigation; or

        (iii)   by the news media, unless the person is the original source of the information; or

    (D) when, in the judgment of the Attorney General, it appears that a person whose illegal activities are being prosecuted or investigated could benefit from the award.

(3) For the purposes of paragraph (2)(C)(iii), the term "original source" means a person who has direct and independent knowledge of the information that is furnished and has voluntarily provided the information to the Government prior to disclosure by the news media.

(4) Neither the failure of the Attorney General to authorize a payment under paragraph (1) nor the amount authorized shall be subject to judicial review.

Rewards for Information Concerning Terrorist Acts and Espionage

18 U.S. Code, Sec. 3071 (1998): Information for which rewards are authorized

(a) With respect to acts of terrorism primarily within the territorial jurisdiction of the United States, the Attorney General may reward any individual who furnishes information—

(1) leading to the arrest or conviction, in any country, of any individual or individuals for the commission of an act of terrorism against a United States person or United States property; or

(2) leading to the arrest or conviction, in any country, of any individual or individuals for conspiring or attempting to commit an act of terrorism against a United States person or property; or

(3) leading to the prevention, frustration, or favorable resolution of an act of terrorism against a United States person or property.

(b) With respect to acts of espionage involving or directed at the United States, the Attorney General may reward any individual who furnishes information—

(1) leading to the arrest or conviction, in any country, of any individual or individuals for commission of an act of espionage against the United States;

(2) leading to the arrest or conviction, in any country, of any individual or individuals for conspiring or attempting to commit an act of espionage against the United States; or

(3) leading to the prevention or frustration of an act of espionage against the United States.

18 U.S. Code, Sec. 3072 (1998): Determination of entitlement; maximum amount; presidential approval; conclusiveness

The Attorney General shall determine whether an individual furnishing information described in § 3071 is entitled to a reward and the amount to be paid. A reward under this section may be in an amount not to exceed $500,000. A reward of $100,000 or more may not be made without the approval of the President or the Attorney General personally. A determination made by the Attorney General or the President under this chapter [18 U.S.C. §§ 3071 et seq.] shall be final and conclusive, and no court shall have power or jurisdiction to review it.

18 U.S. Code, Sec. 3073 (1998): Protection of identity

Any reward granted under this chapter [18 U.S.C. §§ 3071 et seq.] shall be certified for payment by the Attorney General. If it is determined that the identity of the recipient of a reward or of the members of the recipient's immediate family must be protected, the Attorney General may take such measures in connection with the payment of the reward as deemed necessary to effect such protection.

18 U.S. Code, Sec. 3074 (1998): Exception of governmental officials

No officer or employee of any governmental entity who, while in the performance of his or her official duties, furnishes the information described in section 3071 shall be eligible for any monetary reward under this chapter [18 U.S.C. §§ 3071 et seq.].

18 U.S. Code, Sec. 3075 (1998): Authorization for appropriations

There are authorized to be appropriated, without fiscal year limitation, $5,000,000 for the purpose of this chapter [18 U.S.C. §§ 3071 et seq.].

Customs Administration

19 U.S. Code, Sec. 507 (1998): Assistance for customs officers

(a) Every customs officer shall—

    (1) upon being questioned at the time of executing any of the powers conferred upon him, make known his character as an officer of the Federal Government; and

    (2) have the authority to demand the assistance of any person in making any arrest, search, or seizure authorized by any law enforced or administered by customs officers, if such assistance may be necessary.

    If a person, without reasonable excuse, neglects or refuses to assist a customs officer upon proper demand under paragraph (2), such person is guilty of a misdemeanor and subject to a fine of not more than $1000.

(b) Any person other than an officer or employee of the United States who renders assistance in good faith upon the request of a customs officer shall not be held liable for any civil damages as a result of the rendering of such assistance if the assisting person acts as an ordinary, reasonably prudent person would have acted under the same or similar circumstances.

Appendix E.
Informant Agreement

State of Arizona
Maricopa County
INFORMANT AGREEMENT AND WAIVER
("No-Deals Deal")

I, _____, acknowledge that I have been advised of and fully understand my Constitutional rights to remain silent and to an attorney, including, but not limited to, the following rights:

1. That I have a right to remain silent;
2. That anything I say can and will be used against me in a criminal prosecution, pursuant to and limited by the terms of this Agreement;
3. That I have a right to the presence of an attorney to assist me prior to questioning and to be with me during questioning if I so desire;
4. That if I cannot afford an attorney I have a right to have an attorney appointed for me prior to questioning at no cost to myself.

I further acknowledge that no one has used any sort of violence or threats or any promise of immunity or benefit whatsoever to encourage me to answer questions, and that no representations have been made to me other than the representations set forth in this Agreement.

My consent to cooperate with the investigation of _____ is limited to consent to derivative use of my statements, and to the direct use of my statements for impeachment and to the direct use of my statements in actions against myself for violations of any of the terms of this Agreement. I agree that the State may use any information, leads, evidence, or witnesses supplied by me (i.e., any "fruits" of my cooperation) in any way.

This interview is being conducted so that the State is made aware of all information I have in the matter of _____. At this point, I understand that the State makes no promises or benefits regarding any future plea negotiations or sentencing recommendations in [pending case].

I enter into this Agreement in the hope that my cooperation will be considered as a mitigating circumstance by the State in any future plea negotiations in [pending case]. However, I acknowledge that the State retains complete discretion in plea negotiations and sentencing recommendations and that the State has no power to assure that the Court will even consider any particular mitigating circumstances or sentencing recommendations. I agree that any favorable action by the State as a result of my cooperation is contingent on the State's evaluation of the truthfulness, completeness, and usefulness of my cooperation and that the State's judgment in all respects is final and binding upon me. In particular, I agree that any untruthfulness on my part will disqualify me from any benefit due to my cooperation whatsoever.

This Agreement and Waiver is to cover all statements made by me and/or actions taken by me at the request of the undersigned Interviewer(s) commencing at the time this Agreement and Waiver is signed by the Interviewer(s) and continuing until rescinded in writing by me or until superseded by another written Agreement or until the commencement of the trial in (pending case), whichever occurs first.

State of Arizona
Maricopa County
INFORMANT LETTER AGREEMENT

RE: Investigation of [ongoing] [nature of investigation]

Dear _____:

This letter is the written assurance and understanding of the State of Arizona through the Maricopa County Attorney regarding your cooperation with law enforcement in the investigation of the structure and potential or actual criminal activity being done on the part of [insert target].

The State is interesting in obtaining accurate and complete information about the above matters, and is willing to consider cooperation in these investigations as a factor in its future decisions regarding possible criminal charges against you. You are advised of your Constitutional rights to remain silent and to an attorney, including but not limited to, the following rights:

1. That you have a right to remain silent;
2. That anything you say can and will be used against you in a criminal prosecution, pursuant to and limited by the terms of this Agreement;
3. That you have a right to the presence of an attorney to assist you prior to questioning and to be with you during questioning if you so desire;
4. That if you cannot afford an attorney you have a right to have an attorney appointed for you prior to questioning at no cost to yourself.

You further acknowledge by signing this that no one has used any sort of violence or threats or promise of immunity or benefit whatsoever to encourage you to answer questions, and that no representations have been made to you other than the representations set forth in this Agreement.

You nevertheless agree that the State may use any information, leads, evidence or witnesses supplied by you, that is, any "fruits" of your cooperation in any way.

Within the limitations above, I assure you and agree with you that if your complete and truthful cooperation implicates you in past crimes, your statements themselves will not be used in evidence against you in any State criminal prosecution so long as the following conditions are met:

1. Your statements are complete and truthful to the best of your knowledge, and;
2. For your information to be useful, law enforcement will need time to follow up on it before possible defendants are aware you have given statements. So, as an additional condition of our Agreement, I will need your assurance that you will not disclose to anyone (except your attorney if you retain one and then only within attorney-client confidence) the fact that you have given statements or the contents of the statements or questions asked of you unless and until ordered to do so by a court. In consideration of this, and because of danger to yourself, any law enforcement people, including myself, involved in the follow-up will treat you as a "confidential" source, and will not disclose the fact of your statements or their contents unless and until ordered to do so.
3. You commit no criminal act except as specifically requested *in advance* by one of the Interviewers signing this Agreement, who will request such activity only to further the investigation and later prosecution of crime. If you commit any criminal act outside the condition set forth above, you are subject to prosecution for such act and this Agreement is null and void.
4. The State is opposed for reasons of principle to entering into Agreements with people who have directly caused a person's death or serious physical injury, so although we have no reason to believe you have done so, we specifically exclude liability for directly causing death or serious physical injury from this Agreement. Offenses within these two excluded areas, if any, will have to be dealt with on an individual basis on their individual facts.

I emphasize that the protection against State criminal prosecution granted to you under this Agreement is in no way dependent or conditioned upon the substance of the testimony or other information you may hereafter provide to the State, except for the requirements of complete honesty and truthfulness, nor is it in any way dependent or conditioned on the return of any indictment(s) or the obtaining of any criminal convictions against any individuals or entities. In short, your obligation hereunder is to tell the truth, the whole truth, and only the truth. If you fail to live up to or abide by any of the conditions, these assurances are no longer effective and the State will proceed accordingly, including, if it is determined that you have lied, in a prosecution for perjury or false swearing. Since your fulfillment of your part of this Agreement will constitute a waiver of your Fifth Amendment privilege against self-incrimination, if you violate any provisions of this Agreement, you will become subject to prosecution for having violated it, and any statements or information you provide to the State would be admissible in evidence against you, in addition to leads or witnesses gained pursuant to this Agreement.

In return for your cooperation, the State agrees that it [insert benefits].

To gain information on [insert target] it is agreed that your cooperation includes infiltration of that group by becoming a full fledged member and that you continue to give information for a minimum of six (6) months from the date you become a member. As stated previously in this Agreement, you are not to commit any crime during this investigation. Furthermore, if you become aware of activity that places another in jeopardy of death or serious physical injury, you are to report that immediately to one of the Interviewers signing this Agreement. It is also required under the terms of this Agreement that you shall have daily contact with one of the Interviewers signing this Agreement.

I fully understand and agree that the State will not file charges on the condition that the terms of this Agreement are fulfilled.

It is also understood that this Agreement binds the Maricopa County Attorney's Office but that other jurisdictions are not bound by this Agreement as they are not parties to the Agreement and the Maricopa County Attorney's Office has no authority to bind other jurisdictions.

Your signature in the space provided below will confirm that the foregoing accurately sets forth the terms of our understanding. Except as set forth above, there are no understandings or agreements of any kind between the State and you in this matter.

This Agreement and Waiver is to cover all statements made by you and/or actions taken by you at the request of the undersigned interviewers commencing at the time this Agreement is signed by the Interviewers and continuing until rescinded in writing by you or until superseded by another written agreement; or until the commencement of your trial on charges arising out of the above-mentioned investigation, whichever occurs first. Any modification of this Agreement must be in writing. No oral modification has any force or effect.

Maricopa County Attorney

by_____

Deputy County Attorney

ACCEPTED AND AGREED

_____   _____

Signature of Witness   *Date and Time*

INTERVIEWERS

_____   _____

Signature   *Date and Time*

_____   _____

Signature   *Date and Time*

U. S. Department of Justice

Office of Investigative Agency Policies

Washington, D.C. 20530

RESOLUTION 18

Pursuant to the Attorney General's Order Number 1814-93, dated November 18, 1993, and in my capacity as Director of Investigative Agency Policies, I hereby issue the following resolution concerning the utilization of Cooperating Individuals and Confidential Informants.

Background

The Attorney General requested the Office of Investigative Agency Policies ("OIAP") to develop a uniform policy regarding a vital law enforcement technique -- the use of Cooperating Individuals and Confidential Informants. The discussions that produced this policy demonstrated an unprecedented level of cooperation.[1]

This Resolution is the product of consensus recommendations of the OIAP Executive Advisory Board ("EAB").

Discussion

According to the terms of the Order creating the OIAP, I have been authorized, "in the areas of overlapping jurisdiction of the criminal investigative agencies," to:

> (1) Take all steps necessary to improve coordination among the criminal investigative agencies of the Department [of Justice], both within the United States and abroad; (2) Assure, to the extent appropriate, consistent operational guidelines for the criminal investigative agencies of the Department [of Justice]; ... (9) Provide advice to the Attorney General and the Deputy Attorney General on all investigative policies, procedures and activities that warrant uniform

---

[1]The Treasury Department's investigative agencies, as well as the office of the Assistant Secretary of the Treasury for Enforcement, fully participated in these discussions. Those agencies will seek any necessary approvals of this policy within the Treasury Department.

treatment or coordination among the criminal investigative agencies of the Department [of Justice]; [and] ... (11) Perform such other functions as may be necessary for the effective policy-level coordination of criminal investigations by the criminal investigative agencies of the Department [of Justice] ...

Order Number 1814-93, Section (b).

The uniform policy, set forth at Attachment A, provides an appropriate standard for the utilization of Cooperating Individuals and Confidential Informants.

Conclusion

As I noted above, this Resolution has been approved by the EAB. I am advised that no OIAP member agency will appeal this Resolution or the attached policy.

Dated: May 29, 1996
          Washington, D.C.

LOUIS J. FREEH
Director of Investigative
Agency Policies

General Guidelines on the Use of
Cooperating Individuals and Confidential Informants

1. **Purpose.** The purpose of these general guidelines is to set policy regarding Federal Law Enforcement Agencies' use of Cooperating Individuals and Confidential Informants.

2. **Scope.** This policy applies to the following Federal Law Enforcement Agencies:

 a. Federal Bureau of Investigation;
 b. Drug Enforcement Administration;
 c. United States Marshals Service;
 d. Immigration and Naturalization Service;
 e. Department of Justice Office of the Inspector General;
 f. United States Customs Service;
 g. Bureau of Alcohol, Tobacco, and Firearms;
 h. United States Secret Service;
 i. Internal Revenue Service; and,
 j. Department of Treasury Office of the Inspector General.

3. **Definitions.**

 a. "Federal Law Enforcement Agency" -- the agencies specified in ¶ 2.

 b. "Cooperating Individual" -- an individual who provides information concerning criminal or other unlawful activity to a designated representative of a Federal Law Enforcement Agency and (i) works under the direction and control of a designated representative of a Federal Law Enforcement Agency, or (ii) is paid more than $2,500 within a one-year period, as that period is defined by the Federal Law Enforcement Agency. United States military personnel and employees of law enforcement agencies who are working solely in their official capacity with a Federal Law Enforcement Agency do not qualify as Cooperating Individuals.

 c. "Confidential Informant" -- a Cooperating Individual who has a reasonable expectation of confidentiality or anonymity.

 d. "Source of Information" -- an individual who provides information concerning criminal or other unlawful activity to a designated representative of a Federal Law Enforcement Agency and who is not paid more than $2,500 within a one-year period, as that period is defined by the Federal Law Enforcement Agency. Sources of Information are not covered by this policy.

e. "Senior Field Manager" -- a Federal Law Enforcement Agency operational field manager of the GS-15 rank or higher.

4. **Use of Cooperating Individuals and Confidential Informants.**

a. **Suitability Determination.** Prior to utilizing a person as a Cooperating Individual or Confidential Informant, a supervisor of a Federal Law Enforcement Agency shall make a suitability determination. Thereafter, the Federal Law Enforcement Agency shall document in its files that the suitability determination has been made. Among the factors to be considered in assessing the person's suitability as a Cooperating Individual or Confidential Informant are the following:

(i) the person's age;

(ii) whether the person has a criminal history, is reasonably believed to be the subject or target of a pending criminal investigation, is reasonably believed to pose a danger to the public or other criminal threat, or is reasonably believed to pose a risk of flight;

(iii) the person's alien status, if applicable;

(iv) whether the person is a substance abuser or has a history of substance abuse;

(v) whether the person is related to an employee of any law enforcement agency;

(vi) whether the person is a public official, law enforcement officer, member of the military services, a representative of the news media, or a party to privileged communications (e.g. a member of the clergy, a physician, or a lawyer);

(vii) the person's reliability and truthfulness, including the person's motivation;

(viii) the extent to which the person's information is relevant to a present or potential investigation and can be corroborated;

(ix) the Federal Law Enforcement Agency's record, if any, of the person's past performance as a Cooperating Individual or Confidential Informant;

(x) whether there is reason to believe that the person is presently serving as a Cooperating Individual or Confidential Informant for another law enforcement agency;

2

(xi) when there is reason to believe that the person has previously served as a Cooperating Individual or Confidential Informant for another law enforcement agency, whether that law enforcement agency terminated that relationship for cause;

(xii) the nature and importance of the information to a present or potential investigation;

(xiii) the risk that the person may adversely affect an investigation or potential prosecution; and,

(xiv) the risk of physical harm that may occur to the person, his or her immediate family or close associates as a result of assisting the Federal Law Enforcement Agency.

b. **Registration.** After the supervisor has made a suitability determination, the person shall be registered with that Federal Law Enforcement Agency. At a minimum, the Federal Law Enforcement Agency shall:

(i) document the efforts to establish the person's true identity in the agency's files;

(ii) maintain the results of a criminal history check for that person in the agency's files; and,

(iii) maintain a photograph of the person in the agency's files.

c. **Instructions to Cooperating Individual/Confidential Informant.** After the Cooperating Individual or Confidential Informant has been registered, representatives of the Federal Law Enforcement Agency shall, at a minimum, review with the person written instructions regarding his or her responsibilities and relationship to the Federal Law Enforcement Agency, which review shall be documented in the agency's files. Additionally, at a minimum, the instructions shall state that:

(i) the Cooperating Individual/Confidential Informant must not engage in any unlawful acts, except as specifically authorized by representatives of the Federal Law Enforcement Agency, and is subject to prosecution for any unauthorized unlawful acts;

(ii) the Cooperating Individual/Confidential Informant must provide truthful information at all times;

(iii) the Cooperating Individual/Confidential Informant must abide by the instructions of the Federal Law Enforcement Agency and must not take or seek to take any independent action on behalf of the United States Government;

3

(iv) the Cooperating Individual/Confidential Informant is not an employee of the United States Government and may not represent himself or herself as such;

(v) the Cooperating Individual/Confidential Informant must not engage in witness tampering, witness intimidation, entrapment, or the fabrication, alteration, or destruction of evidence;

(vi) the Cooperating Individual/Confidential Informant is liable for any taxes that may be owed on monies the United States Government pays to him or her;

(vii) the Federal Law Enforcement Agency cannot guarantee any rewards, payments, or other compensation to the Cooperating Individual/Confidential Informant;

(viii) when a Cooperating Individual/Confidential Informant is cooperating with a Federal Law Enforcement Agency in exchange for consideration by a prosecuting office(s), and upon request of the Cooperating Individual/Confidential Informant, the Federal Law Enforcement Agency will advise the prosecuting office(s) of the nature and extent of the person's assistance to the Federal Law Enforcement Agency, but cannot make any prosecutive or sentencing promises;

(ix) in cases involving foreign nationals, no promises or representations can be made regarding alien status and/or their right to enter or remain in the United States;

(x) the United States Government will strive to protect a Confidential Informant's identity, but cannot guarantee that it will not be divulged; and,

(xi) the Cooperating Individual/Confidential Informant may not enter into any contracts or incur any obligations on behalf of the United States Government, except as specifically instructed and approved by the Federal Law Enforcement Agency.

d. **Debriefing.** After registration of the Cooperating Individual/Confidential Informant and documentation of instructions have occurred, representatives of the Federal Law Enforcement Agency shall fully debrief the person concerning his or her knowledge of criminal or other unlawful activities. When a Cooperating Individual/Confidential Informant is likely to provide information that is subject to a legal claim of privilege, the Federal Law Enforcement Agency will ensure that there is prior coordination with an appropriate prosecuting attorney.

5.   **Special Approval Requirements.**

    a.   **Office of Enforcement Operations ("OEO").**
Consistent with Department of Justice requirements, a Federal Law
Enforcement Agency must receive the approval of the OEO prior to
conducting any of the following activities:

    (i) utilizing a Cooperating Individual/Confidential
Informant, who is a federal prisoner, in an investigation;

    (ii) utilizing a Cooperating Individual/Confidential
Informant, who is a current or former participant in the Federal
Witness Security Program, in an investigation, provided further
that the OEO will coordinate such matters with the USMS; and,

    (iii) utilizing a Cooperating Individual/Confidential
Informant to engage in the warrantless interception of certain
sensitive categories of verbal communications as specified by the
Attorney General.

    b.   **Use of Federal or State Probationers, Parolees, and
Supervised Releasees as Cooperating Individuals/Confidential
Informants.** Prior to utilizing a Federal or State probationer,
parolee, or supervised releasee as a Cooperating
Individual/Confidential Informant, a supervisor of a Federal Law
Enforcement Agency shall determine if the use of that person in
such a capacity would violate the terms and conditions of the
person's probation, parole, or supervised release. The Federal
Law Enforcement Agencies are encouraged to consult with
appropriate prosecutors prior to making such a determination.
The determination shall be documented in the Federal Law
Enforcement Agency's files. If it is determined that there would
be a violation of probation, parole, or supervised release, prior
to using the person as a Cooperating Individual/Confidential
Informant, a representative of the Federal Law Enforcement Agency
must obtain the permission of the relevant probation, parole, or
supervised release official which, likewise, shall be documented
in the Federal Law Enforcement Agency's files. If permission is
denied or it is inappropriate to contact the appropriate
official, the Federal Law Enforcement Agency may, nevertheless,
obtain authorization for such use from the court or a supervisor
of a probation, parole or supervised release official.

    c.   **Use of State or Local Prisoners as Cooperating
Individuals/Confidential Informants.** Federal Law Enforcement
Agencies shall comply with any applicable state or local laws,
rules, and regulations pertaining to the use of state or local
prisoners as Cooperating Individuals/Confidential Informants.

    6.   **Monetary Payments to Cooperating Individuals and
Confidential Informants.** Monies that a Federal Law Enforcement
Agency pays to a Cooperating Individual/Confidential Informant in

5

the form of fees and rewards shall be commensurate with the value, as determined by the Federal Law Enforcement Agency, of the information he or she provided or the assistance he or she rendered to that Federal Law Enforcement Agency. A Federal Law Enforcement Agency's reimbursement of expenses incurred by a Cooperating Individual/Confidential Informant shall be based upon actual expenses incurred. All payments to Cooperating Individuals/Confidential Informants shall be made in a manner which avoids even the appearance of impropriety.

a. **Prohibition Against Contingent Payments.** Under no circumstances shall any payments to a Cooperating Individual or Confidential Informant be contingent upon the conviction or punishment of any individual.

b. **Approval for a Single Payment.** A single payment of between $2,500 and $25,000 per case to a Cooperating Individual or Confidential Informant must be authorized, at a minimum, by a Federal Law Enforcement Agency's senior field manager. A single payment in excess of $25,000 per case shall be made only with the authorization of the senior field manager and the express approval of a designated headquarters official.

c. **Approval for Aggregate Annual Payments.** Consistent with ¶ 6b, payments by a Federal Law Enforcement Agency to a Cooperating Individual or Confidential Informant that exceed an aggregate of $100,000 within a one-year period, as that period is defined by the Federal Law Enforcement Agency, shall be made only with the authorization of the senior field manager and the express approval of a designated headquarters official. The headquarters official may authorize additional aggregate annual payments in increments of $50,000 or less.

d. **Approval for Aggregate Payments.** Consistent with ¶¶ 6b and 6c and regardless of the time frame, any payments by a Federal Law Enforcement Agency to a Cooperating Individual or Confidential Informant that exceed an aggregate of $200,000 shall be made only with the authorization of the senior field manager and the express approval of a designated headquarters official. After the headquarters official has approved payments to a Cooperating Individual or Confidential Informant that exceed an aggregate of $200,000, the headquarters official may authorize, subject to ¶ 6(c), additional aggregate payments in increments of $100,000 or less.

e. **Documentation of Payment.** The payment of any monies to a Cooperating Individual/Confidential Informant shall be witnessed by at least two law enforcement representatives. At the time of the payment, the representatives shall advise the Cooperating Individual/Confidential Informant that the monies, except those representing payments for documented expenses, are taxable income and must be reported to appropriate tax

authorities. Thereafter, those representatives shall document
the payment and the advice of taxability in the Federal Law
Enforcement Agency's files. In the event of extraordinary
circumstances, the two representative requirement may be waived
by prior authorization of the relevant senior field manager,
which shall be documented in the agency's files.

    f. **Accounting and Reconciliation Procedures.** Each
Federal Law Enforcement Agency shall establish accounting and
reconciliation procedures to accomplish the policy objectives set
forth herein. Among other things, these procedures shall reflect
all monies paid to a Cooperating Individual/Confidential
Informant, subsequent to the issuance of these guidelines.

    g. **Coordination with Prosecutors.** In situations where
a prosecutor is either:

    (i) participating in the conduct of the underlying
investigation utilizing the Cooperating Individual or
Confidential Informant, or

    (ii) working with the Cooperating Individual or
Confidential Informant in connection with a prosecution,

payments to the Cooperating Individual/Confidential Informant
shall be coordinated with the prosecutor.

    7. **Continuing Suitability Reviews.** Each Federal Law
Enforcement Agency should conduct semi-annual reviews of each
active Cooperating Individual's or Confidential Informant's file
and provide a written determination that the person should be
continued, deactivated, or terminated for cause as a Cooperating
Individual or Confidential Informant.

    8. **Unauthorized Unlawful Conduct by a Cooperating
Individual/Confidential Informant.** If an active Cooperating
Individual/Confidential Informant is arrested or believed to have
engaged in unauthorized unlawful conduct other than a petty crime
or a minor traffic offense, continued use of the Cooperating
Individual/Confidential Informant must be reviewed, at a minimum,
by the agency's senior field manager. In addition:

    a. If more than one Federal Law Enforcement Agency is
involved in an investigation utilizing such a Cooperating
Individual/Confidential Informant, coordination among all of the
relevant agencies' senior field managers should occur; and,

    b. In situations where a prosecutor is either:

    (i) participating in the conduct of the underlying
investigation utilizing the Cooperating Individual or
Confidential Informant, or

(ii) working with the Cooperating Individual or Confidential
Informant in connection with a prosecution,

the Federal Law Enforcement Agency must immediately inform the
prosecutor of the arrest or nature and extent of the alleged
unauthorized unlawful conduct.

9. **Notification of Deactivation or Termination of
Relationship for Cause.** If a Federal Law Enforcement Agency
determines that a Cooperating Individual/Confidential Informant
should be deactivated or that his or her relationship with that
agency should be terminated for cause, appropriate notification
shall be made to the Cooperating Individual/Confidential
Informant if he or she reasonably can be located. Such
notification shall be documented in writing. A copy of this
documentation shall be maintained in the agency's headquarters
files. Notification of termination for cause shall be witnessed
by at least two law enforcement officials.

10. **Rights of Third Parties.** Nothing in these guidelines is
intended to create or does create an enforceable legal right or
private right of action.

11. **Compliance with Guidelines.** Within 180 days of the
issuance of these guidelines, each Federal Law Enforcement Agency
shall issue specific policies that comply with them. These
guidelines are not intended to limit the ability of a Federal Law
Enforcement Agency to impose more restrictive guidelines.[1]

---

[1]E.g. "Attorney General Guidelines on FBI Use of Informants
and Confidential Sources" (1978) and "Attorney General Guidelines
for the Development and Operation of FBI Criminal Informants and
Cooperative Witnesses in Extraterritorial Jurisdiction" (1993).

U.S. Department of Justice
Drug Enforcement Administration   **CONFIDENTIAL SOURCE AGREEMENT**

The undersigned confidential source agrees to the following:

1. I will provide truthful information at all times;

2. I am not an employee of the United States Government and may not represent myself as such. Further, I may not enter into any contracts or incur any obligations on behalf of the United States Government, except as specifically instructed and approved by the DEA;

3. I will abide by the instructions given to me, will not take any independent action, and I will not engage in any unlawful acts for which I may be subject to prosecution, except as specifically authorized by representatives of the DEA;

4. I will not engage in witness tampering, witness intimidation, entrapment, or the fabrication, alteration, or destruction of evidence;

5. I understand that if I am cooperating in exchange for consideration by a prosecuting office, the DEA will advise the prosecuting office of the nature and extent of my assistance to DEA, but cannot make any prosecutive or sentencing promises. Likewise, I understand that no promises or representations can be made to me regarding alien status and/or my right to enter or remain in the United States;

6. I understand that the United States Government will strive to protect my identity, but cannot guarantee that it will not be divulged;

7. I understand that I cannot be guaranteed any rewards, payments, or other compensation and I am liable for any taxes that may be owed on monies the United States Government pays me.

CONFIDENTIAL SOURCE: _____   _____
                                          Signature   Date

WITNESS: _____   _____
                                          Signature   Date

WITNESS: _____   _____
                                          Signature   Date

DEA Form
(Jun. 1998) – 473   Previous edition dated 1/86 is OBSOLETE.   *U.S. GPO: 1998-432-156/82205

APPROVED CONFIDENTIAL INFORMANT ADVICE

	Date Advised	
	Non-Paid	Paid
1. **PROVIDING TRUTHFUL INFORMATION/FOLLOWING INSTRUCTIONS/ETC.** Informant advised that he/she must provide truthful information; must abide by the instructions of the Internal Revenue Service; must not take any independent action on behalf of the US Government; and may not represent himself/herself as an employee of the Internal Revenue Service.		
2. **ENGAGING IN UNLAWFUL ACTIVITIES** Informant instructed not to engage in any unlawful acts, except as specifically authorized by the IRS. Informant further advised that he/she is subject to prosecution for any unauthorized unlawful acts and that engaging in such activity could terminate any arrangement the informant has with the Service.		
3. **TAMPERING WITH WITNESSES** Informant instructed not to engage in witness tampering; witness intimidation; entrapment; or the fabrication, alteration, or destruction of evidence.		
4. **USING UNLAWFUL TECHNIQUES TO OBTAIN EVIDENCE** Informant instructed that in obtaining information, he/she shall not use unlawful techniques (i.e., breaking/entering; electronic surveillance; opening/tampering with the mail, etc.). Use of the informant will be terminated and the information will not be used.		
5. **IRS REWARD PROCEDURES** Informant advised that the IRS cannot guarantee any rewards, payments, or other compensation to him/her. Informant advised of IRS reward policy and procedures, and the use of Form 211, Application and Public Voucher for Reward for Original Information.	▓▓▓	
6. **NON-EMPLOYER/EMPLOYEE RELATIONSHIP** Informant advised not to construe payments as establishing an employer/employee relationship between him/her and the Internal Revenue Service.	▓▓▓	
7. **TAXABILITY OF PAYMENTS** Informant advised that all monies paid for information are taxable and should be reported on his/her individual income tax return.	▓▓▓	
8. **NON-TAX VIOLATIONS** Informant advised that any information he/she submits concerning non-tax violations of federal, state, or local criminal laws will be furnished to the appropriate enforcement agency.		
9. **COOPERATION IN EXCHANGE FOR CONSIDERATION BY PROSECUTING OFFICE** If the informant requested assistance from the Internal Revenue Service to cooperate in exchange for consideration by a prosecuting office, the informant was advised that the Internal Revenue Service will advise the prosecuting office of the nature and extent of the informant's assistance, but cannot make any prosecutive or sentencing promises.		
10. **FOREIGN NATIONALS** If the informant is a foreign national, he/she was advised that the Internal Revenue Service makes no promises or representations regarding alien status and/or the right to enter or remain in the United States.		
11. **ENTERING INTO CONTRACTS** Informant advised he/she may not enter into any contracts or incur any obligations on behalf of the United States government, except as specifically instructed and approved by the Internal Revenue Service.		
12. **PROTECTING THE INFORMANT'S IDENTITY** Informant advised the United States government will strive to protect a confidential informant's identity, but cannot guarantee that it will not be divulged.		

By my signature below, I certify that the above information was discussed with CI   on the date(s) indicated.

Special Agent	Date
Backup Agent	Date

Form **9831** (Rev. 07-97)   Cat. No. 22253B   Department of the Treasury - Internal Revenue Service

APPROVED CONFIDENTIAL INFORMANT - IDENTITY RECORD

Place in Sealed Pink Envelope - CI # and Control Agents Names on outside

1.	INFORMANT NUMBER:	
2.	INFORMANT'S TRUE NAME:	
3.	ALIASES:	
4.	SSN:	5. DOB:
6.	INFORMANT'S LAST KNOWN ADDRESS:	
7.	TELEPHONE NUMBER:	
8.	OCCUPATION:	
9.	PLACE OF EMPLOYMENT: Address	
10.	PHYSICAL DESCRIPTION:	Height: ___ feet ___ inches Hair _____ Age ___ Weight ___ Sex : M ☐ F ☐ Race Distinguishing Physical Features:
11.	NAME OF SPOUSE	
12.	SPOUSE'S TELEPHONE NUMBER	

13. Criminal Record:

14. Is Informant subject of any Criminal Investigation? ☐ No   ☐ Yes   If yes, please provide details:

15. Tax Filing History and Payment:

16. Associates:

17. Other Identifying Information and Comments:

Special Agent	Date

REQUEST FOR APPROVAL TO USE CONFIDENTIAL INFORMANT

IMPORTANT: DO NOT USE AN INFORMANT'S TRUE NAME IN COMPLETING THIS FORM

Assigned informant number:

Does Approval Confidential Informant Expect to be Paid:		☐ Approved Confidential Informant will be gathering tax-related information under IRS direction.
☐ Yes	☐ No	

Contact Agents:	Primary:	Backup:

(DO NOT INCLUDE IDENTIFYING INFORMATION PERTAINING TO THE INFORMANT)

A. Age:

B. Criminal History:

C. Filing Status and Payment History:

D. Known Reliability Indicators (Information Provided to IRS & Other Agencies, etc.) Motivation:

E. Informant's Source and Means of Securing Information:

F. Extent to which information can be corroborated:

G. Presently serving as a cooperating individual/confidential informant for another agency:

H. Service or other agency record of past performance:

I. If informant previously served as a cooperating individual or confidential informant for another law enforcement agency, was relationship terminated for cause:

J. The nature and importance of the information to a present or future investigation:

K. Alien Status:

L. Substance Abuse/History of Substance Abuse:

M. Related to an Employee of a Law Enforcement Agency:

N. Risk of physical harm that may occur as a result of assisting law enforcement agency:

O. Risk of adversely affecting an investigation or potential prosecution:

P. Public Official, Law Enforcement Officer, Military, Representative of News Media, or Party to Privileged Documentation (e.g., clergy, physician. or attorney):

Q. Is it believed that the informant is the subject or target of a pending criminal investigation, poses a danger to the public or other criminal threat, or poses a risk of flight?:

APPROVED CONFIDENTIAL INFORMANT - MEMORANDUM of CONTACT
[Optional]

CI # :

Date :

Type of Contact		Payments Made	Attach CI - Part 6 (Receipt for Cash)
☐ Phone ☐ In Person		2506 Taxable	$

Information Received:

1. Taxpayer's Name

2. Narrative:

Disposition of Information

General Information	☐ No Action Taken							
Specific Information	☐ 3949 Prepared		☐ Primary		☐ Subject		☐ CI Referral	☐ Other Agency

SIGNATURES/APPROVALS:

Special Agent	Date
Group Manager	Date
Chief, CID	Date

RECEIPT for CASH

Imprest Authorization Number :   _____

Date: _____

Received in Cash from :   _____ ,   Special Agent

_____ ,   Special Agent

_____   and   _____ -- $ _____
(dollar total)   (100)

SOC 2506 Taxable (CI Form 5 for Details)	$ _____

This payment in no way should be construed as establishing an employer/employee relationship with the IRS.

All moneys paid for the information are taxable and should be reported on your income tax return..

_____
Acknowledgment of Receipt
(Signature and CI Number Required)

Fingerprint (if Required)

APPROVED CONFIDENTIAL INFORMANT - MONTHLY LOG   [Optional]

Assigned Informant Number:	Month

Original to be filed monthly for the duration of all open CI's. Chief's office will maintain the original. Monthly form is required even if no contact or activity. Any substantial contact will require the submission of a supporting document (CI-Part 5 and CI-Part 6).

Date of Contact	Purpose	Taxpayer Name	Payments Made / Taxable / 2506	Disposition (P#, S#, 3949, Referral to ... No Action.).

SIGNATURES/APPROVALS:

Special Agent	Date
Group Manager	Date
Chief, CID	Date

Form 9834 (Rev. 4-96)   Cat. No. 22256I   Department of the Treasury - Internal Revenue Service

SEMI-ANNUAL REVIEW OF CONFIDENTIAL INFORMANT ACTIVITY

Period of Review	☐ September 1 - February 28 ☐ March 1 - August 31

CI #

Number of Information Items Referred to Examination or Collection Divisions This Period:

Primary Investigations Generated This Period:

Primary Number	Name	Disposition		
		Closed	Open (Active)	Open (Subject)

Subject Investigations Generated This Period:

Subject Number	Name	Disposition			
		Open	Discontinued	Pros Rec	Pipeline

Other Information Provided: *(Information leading to search warrants, seizures, capture of a fugitive, etc.)*

Taxable Payments	This period:	Year to Date:

Payment Receipt(s) in File:

Taxable Advisement Made:

Date Tax Filing Verified *(if applicable)*:

Additional Comments:

Suitability Recommendation:	☐ Continue	☐ Deactivate	☐ Terminate for Cause

SIGNATURES/APPROVALS:

Special Agent	Date
Group Manager	Date
Chief, CID	Date

Internal Revenue Service

memorandum

date:

   to: Chief, Criminal Investigation Division CI

from:

---

subject: Deactivation of Informant #

(This memo may be suited to fit each individual reason, i.e., illegal activities, etc. or you may use the following)

There has been no significant contact with CI XXXX since 12/1/95; therefore, it is recommended that this informant be deactivated.

                                   Special Agent

Concur:

                                   Date

Group Manager

Approve:

                                   Date

Chief, Criminal Investigation Division

Bibliography

Bibliography

Books

Bandler, Richard and Grinder, John, *Frogs Into Princes: Neuro Linguistic Programming,* Moab, UT: Real People Press, 1979.

Bandler, Richard and Grinder, John, *Reframing: Neuro Linguistic Programming and the Transformation of Meaning.* Moab, UT: Real People Press, 1982.

Bergreen, Laurence, *Capone: The Man and the Era,* New York: Simon & Schuster, 1994.

Bloch, Peter B. and Weidman, Donald R., *Managing Criminal Investigations,* Washington, D.C.: U.S. Government Printing Office, 1975.

Blum, Richard, *Deceivers and Deceived: Observations on Confidence Men and Their Victims; Informants and Their Quarry; Political and Industrial Spies, and Ordinary Citizens,* Springfield, IL: Charles C Thomas, 1972.

Brooks, Michael, *Instant Rapport,* New York: Warner Books, 1989.

Buse, Renée, *The Deadly Silence,* Garden City, NJ: Doubleday, 1965.

Cantalupo, Joseph, *Body Mike,* New York: Villard Books, 1990.

Cialdini, Robert B., *Influence: How and Why People Agree To Things,* New York: William Morrow & Company, 1984.

Cialdini, Robert B., *Influence: Science and Practice,* New York: Harper Collins College Publishers, 1993.

Clarke, James W., *American Assassins: The Darker Side of Politics,* Princeton University Press, 1982, p. 162.

Copeland, Miles, *Without Cloak or Dagger: The Truth About the New Espionage,* New York: Simon & Schuster, 1974.

Cooper, H.H.A. and Redlinger, Lawrence J., *Making Spies: A Talent Spotter's Handbook,* Boulder, CO: Paladin Press, 1986.

Cundiff, Merlyn, *Kinesics: The Power of Silent Command,* West Nyack, NY: Parker Publishing, 1972.

Daley, Robert, *Prince of the City: The True Story of a Cop Who Knew Too Much,* Boston: Houghton Mifflin, 1978.

Delattre, Edwin J., *Character and Cops: Ethics in Policing,* Washington, D.C.: American Enterprise Institute for Public Policy, 1989.

DuBrin, Andrew J., *Human Relations: A Job Oriented Approach,* Englewood Cliffs, NJ: Prentice Hall, 1988.

Dwyer, Jim et al., *Two Seconds Under the World,* New York: Crown Publishers, 1994.

Ekman, Paul, *Telling Lies: Clues to Deceit in the Marketplace, Politics, and Marriage,* New York: W.W. Norton, 1985.

Frankel, Marvin E. and Naftalis, Gary, *The Grand Jury: An Institution on Trial,* New York: Hill and Wang, 1975.

Frasca, Don, *King of Crime: The Story of Vito Genovese, Mafia Czar,* New York: Crown Publishers, 1959.

Fried, Charles, *Right and Wrong,* Cambridge, MA: Harvard University Press, 1978.

Friedman, Lawrence M., *Crime and Punishment in American History,* New York: Basic Books, 1993.

Gage, Nicholas, *Mafia, U.S.A.,* Chicago: Playboy Press, 1972.

George, Claude S., *Supervision in Action: The Art of Managing Others,* Reston, VA: Reston Publishing, 1985.

Gerber, Samuel R. and Schroeder, Oliver, Jr., *Criminal Investigation and Interrogation,* Cincinnati, OH: W.H. Anderson Company, 1962.

Graysmith, Robert, *Unabomber: A Desire to Kill,* Washington, D.C.: Regnery Publishing, 1997.

Greene, Robert W., *The Sting Man: Inside ABSCAM,* New York: Dutton, 1981.

Halfon, Mark S., *Integrity: A Philosophical Inquiry,* Philadelphia: Temple University Press, 1989.

Harney, Malachi L. and Cross, John C., *The Informer in Law Enforcement,* Springfield, IL: Charles C Thomas, 1960.

Harney, Malachi L. and Cross, John C., *The Narcotic Officer's Notebook,* Springfield, IL: Charles C Thomas, 1973.

Harris, Don R., *Basic Elements of Intelligence,* Washington, D.C.: U.S. Government Printing Office, 1976.

Howe, Ronald Martin, Ed., *Criminal Investigation,* London: Sweet & Maxwell, 1950.

Howson, Gerald, *Thief-Taker General: The Rise and Fall of Jonathan Wild,* New York: St. Martin's Press, 1971.

Inbau, Fred E. and Reid, John E., *Criminal Interrogation and Confessions,* Baltimore, MD: Williams & Wilkins, 1967.

Jacobson, Ben, Informants and the public police, in *Criminal and Civil Investigation Handbook,* Joseph J. Grau, Ed., New York: McGraw-Hill, 1993.

Janzen, Sandra, *Informants and Undercover Investigations,* Washington, D.C.: U.S. Government Printing Office, 1992.

Johnson, David R., *Policing the Urban Underworld,* Philadelphia, PA: Temple University Press, 1979.

Johnson, David R., *American Law Enforcement: A History,* St. Louis: Forum Press, 1981.

Laborde, Genie Z., *Influencing With Integrity: Management Skills for Communication and Negotiation,* Palo Alto, CA: Syntony Publishing, 1997.

Lankton, Steve, *Practical Magic: A Translation of Basic Neuro-Linguistic Programming into Clinical Psychotherapy,* Cupertino, CA: Meta Publications, 1980.

Levine, Samuel M., *Narcotics and Drug Abuse,* Cincinnati, OH: W.H. Anderson, 1973.

Lyman, Michael D., *Practical Drug Enforcement: Procedures and Administration,* New York: Elsevier, 1989.

Lyons, David, *Ethics and the Rule of Law,* New York: Cambridge University Press, 1984.

Maas, Peter, *The Valachi Papers,* New York: G.P. Putnam's Sons, 1968.

Manning, Peter K., *The Narc's Game: Organizational and Informational Limits on Drug Law Enforcement,* London: MIT Press, 1980.

Marx, Gary T., *Undercover: Police Surveillance in America,* Berkeley: University of California Press, 1988.

Maslow, Abraham, *Motivation and Personality,* New York: Harper & Row, 1954.

Moore, Mark Harrison, *Buy and Bust,* Toronto: Lexington Books, 1977.

Nossen, Richard, *The Seventh Basic Investigative Technique: Analyzing Financial Transactions in the Investigation of Organized Crime and White Collar Crime Targets,* Washington, D.C.: U.S. Government Printing Office, 1975.

O'Flaherty, Liam, *The Informer,* New York: New American Library, 1961.

O'Hara, Charles E., *Fundamentals of Criminal Investigation,* 3rd ed., Springfield, IL: Charles C Thomas, 1973.

Ostrovsky, Victor and Hoy, Claire, *By Way of Deception: The Making and Unmaking of a Mossad Officer,* New York: St. Martin's Press, 1990.

Petacco, Arrigo (trans. by Charles Lane Markham), *Joe Petrosino,* New York: Macmillan Publishing, 1974.

Petrow, Stefan, *Policing Morals: Metropolitan Police and the Home Office, 1870–1914,* Oxford: Clarendon Press, 1994.

Pickens, James W., *The Art of Closing Any Deal: How To Be a Master Closer in Everything You Do,* New York: Warner Books, 1989.

Pincher, Chapman, *Traitors: The Anatomy of Treason,* New York: St. Martin's Press, 1987.

Pinkerton, Allan, *Thirty Years a Detective,* Montclair, NJ: Patterson Smith, 1975.

Ross, Nicholas, *The Policeman's Bible, or the Art of Taking a Bribe,* Chicago, IL: Henry Regnery, 1976.

Purvis, Melvin, *American Agent,* Garden City, NJ: Doubleday, Doran & Co., 1936.

Royal, Robert F. and Schutt, Steven R., *The Gentle Art of Interviewing and Interrogation,* Englewood Cliffs, NJ: Prentice-Hall, 1976.

Rusk, Tom and Miller, D. Patrick, *The Power of Ethical Persuasion,* New York: Viking Press, 1993.

Salerno, Ralph and Tompkins, John S., *The Crime Confederation: Cosa Nostra and Allied Operations in Organized Crime,* Garden City, NJ: Doubleday & Company, 1969.

Schoenberg, Robert J., *Mr. Capone: The Real — and Complete — Story of Al Capone,* New York: William Morrow, 1992.

Skolnick, Jerome H., *Justice Without Trial: Law Enforcement in Democratic Society,* New York: John Wiley & Sons, 1966.

Spiering, Frank, *The Man Who Got Capone,* Indianapolis: Bobbs-Merril Company, 1976.

Stead, Philip John, *Vidocq: A Biography,* New York: Roy Publishers, 1969.

Thompson, Mel, *Teach Yourself Ethics,* Chicago: NTC Publishing Group, 1999.

Tzu, Sun (Giles, L., trans.), *Sun Tzu on The Art of War: The Oldest Military Treatise in the World,* London: Department of Oriental Printed Books and Manuscripts, British Museum, 1910.

Vidocq, Francois (trans. by Edwin Giles Rich), *Vidocq: The Personal Memoirs of the First Great Detective,* Cambridge: Houghton Mifflin, 1935.

Waller, George, *Kidnap: The Shocking Story of the Lindbergh Case,* New York: Dial Press, 1961.

Warschaw, Tessa Albert, *Winning by Negotiation,* New York: McGraw Hill, 1980.

Williams, E.W. and Sader, Samuel J., *Modern Law Enforcement and Police Science,* Springfield, IL: Charles C Thomas, 1967.

Williams, Jay R., Redlinger, Lawrence J., and Manning, Peter K., *Police Narcotics Control: Patterns and Strategies,* Washington, D.C.: U.S. Government Printing Office, 1979.

Wilson, James Q., *The Investigators: Managing FBI and Narcotics Agents,* New York: Basic Books, 1978.

Government Publications

General Accounting Office, *Federal Drug Enforcement: Strong Guidance Needed,* GGD-76-32, 1975.

Office of the Independent Counsel, Communication from the Office of the Independent Counsel, Kenneth W. Starr, Transmitting Appendices to the Referral to the United States House of Representatives Pursuant to Title 28, United States Code, Section 595(c), September 21, 1998.

U.S. Department of Justice, Drug Enforcement Administration, *Drug Enforcement Manual.*

U.S. Department of the Treasury, *Informers,* Treasury Law Enforcement Officer Training School, July 21, 1961.

U.S. Department of the Treasury, *Informants,* Federal Law Enforcement Training Center, June 1980; January 1988.

U.S. House of Representatives, Legislation and National Security Subcommittee, Oversight Hearing on the Department of Justice Asset Forfeiture Program, 102nd Congress, 2nd Session, 1992.

U.S. Senate, Committee on Government Operations, Organized Crime and Illicit Traffic in Narcotics, Rep. No. 72, 89th Congress, 1st Session, 1965.

U.S. Senate, Committee on Government Operations, Federal Drug Enforcement Hearings, Part 4, 94th Congress, 2nd Session, 1976.

Periodicals

Haglund, Evan, Impeaching the underworld informant, *University of Southern California Law Review,* 63, 1405, 1990.

Higgins, George V., Whitey and the rifleman, *The American Lawyer,* July/Aug., 1998.

Lee, Gregory D., Drug informants: motives, methods, and management, *FBI Law Enforcement Bulletin*, Sept., p. 10, 1993.

Mauet, Thomas A., Informant disclosure and production: a second look at paid informants, *Arizona Law Review*, 37, 563, 1995.

Milgram, Stanley, Behavioral Study of Obedience, *Journal of Abnormal and Social Psychology*, 67(4), 371–378, 1963.

Mount, Harry A., Criminal informants: an administrator's dream or nightmare, *FBI Law Enforcement Bulletin*, Dec., p. 12, 1990.

Reese, James T., Motivations of criminal informants, *FBI Law Enforcement Bulletin*, May, p. 23, 1990.

Rhoads, S.A. and Solomon, Roger, Subconscious rapport building: another approach to interviewing, *The Police Chief*, April, p. 39, 1987.

Trott, Stephen S., The use of a criminal as a witness: a special problem, *Lecture Suppl.*, October, 1996.

Newspaper Articles

Anon., Investigator misused office for sex, *Federal Human Resources Week*, 5(19), 1998.

Furillo, Andy, Informant's false testimony sinks drug busts, *Sacramento Bee*, June 18, 1998, p. B-1.

Grunwald, Michael, A gang's unlikely ally: the FBI; agent's handling of Boston mob informant roils bureau, *The Washington Post*, January 12, 1999, p. A-1.

Grunwald, Michael, Informant fiasco prompts FBI review; new policies expected, *The Washington Post*, January 12, 1999, A-8

Malinowski, W. Zachary and Stanton, Mike, Former drug agents indicted. They're charged with fabricating evidence, *The Providence Journal-Bulletin*, October 8, 1998, p. 1.

Meersman, Nancy, "Snitch" may be key in Knapp murder, *The Union Leader (Manchester, NH)*, January 22, 1999, p. 2.

Moushey, Bill, German criminal finds a lucrative life as federal informant: Helmut Groebe's history of fraud ignored as he traps people for cash, *Pittsburgh Post-Gazette*, December 7, 1998, p. A-6.

Murphy, Shelley, Mob case hinges on depth of FBI ties; two views of immunity: rogues deal, agency way, *The Boston Globe*, October 18, 1998, p. B-1.

Prendergast, Alan, Liar, liar: a top DEA informant makes cases — and $200,000 a year — while breaking a few laws himself, *Denver Westword*, May 8, 1997, p. 1.

Ranalli, Ralph, Informant relations rarely go smoothly, *The Boston Herald*, June 21, 1998, p. 6.

Ranalli, Ralph, Agent hoped Bulger eluded feds; Connolly shocked FBI colleague with statement about "Whitey," *The Boston Herald*, August 11, 1998, p. 1.

Ranalli, Ralph, Secret stoolie system haunts FBI; former agents say FBI use of top informants was flawed, *The Boston Herald*, June 22, 1998, p. 1.

Serra, Tony, The KGB-ing of America, *Anderson Valley Advertiser (CA)*, January 13, 1999, p. 3.

Sex for testimony: federal foot dragging [editorial], *The Virginian-Pilot (Norfolk, VA)*, August 12, 1997, p. B-12.

Thomasson, Dan, The FBI's untamed informants, *The Washington Times*, January 18, 1999, p. A-16.

Index

Index